PRIVATE REGULATION OF LABOR STANDARDS IN GLOBAL SUPPLY CHAINS

PRIVATE REGULATION OF LABOR STANDARDS IN GLOBAL SUPPLY CHAINS

Problems, Progress, and Prospects

Sarosh Kuruvilla

ILR PRESS

AN IMPRINT OF CORNELL UNIVERSITY PRESS

CORNELL UNIVERSITY PRESS   ITHACA AND LONDON

Publication of this book was made possible, in part, by a grant from the Office of the Dean of the ILR School at Cornell University and through a gift from Elyse Nathanson.

Visit our website at cornellpress.cornell.edu.

First published 2021 by Cornell University Press

Library of Congress Cataloging-in-Publication Data

Names: Kuruvilla, Sarosh, author.
Title: Private regulation of labor standards in global supply chains :
    problems, progress, and prospects / Sarosh Kuruvilla.
Description: Ithaca [New York] : ILR Press, an imprint of Cornell
    University Press, 2021. | Includes bibliographical references and index.
Identifiers: LCCN 2020034859 (print) | LCCN 2020034860 (ebook) |
    ISBN 9781501754517 (hardcover) | ISBN 9781501754524 (paperback) |
    ISBN 9781501754531 (ebook) | ISBN 9781501754548 (pdf)
Subjects: LCSH: Industrial relations. | Industrial procurement—Moral and ethical
    aspects. | Industries—Self-regulation. | Employee rights. | Social responsibility of
    business.
Classification: LCC HD6971 .K858 2021 (print) | LCC HD6971 (ebook) |
    DDC 331.2—dc23
LC record available at https://lccn.loc.gov/2020034859
LC ebook record available at https://lccn.loc.gov/2020034860

For Rehana and Irit

Contents

Preface

In 2015, I watched an episode of John Oliver's *Last Week Tonight* on HBO in which he focuses on "Fashion." In it, Oliver pillories a number of companies—such as H&M, Forever 21, Gap Inc., Walmart, and The Children's Place—for continuing to source their production from suppliers with sweatshop conditions.

As I watched, I was struck by the fact that these companies have, for many years, had in place *private regulation programs* for their far-flung global supply chains designed to *solve* the sweatshop problem. These programs typically articulate standards for suppliers, state that the supplier will be audited or monitored to ensure their compliance, and include a pledge from the buyer companies to help suppliers remediate violations, rewarding those that do with continued business and axing those that do not.

Oliver lays bare several problems in private regulation, most notably the lack of progress. After nearly twenty-five years of these private regulation programs, we still have major disasters like Rana Plaza: in 2013, a structurally unsound eight-story garment factory in Bangladesh collapsed, killing 1,134 workers.

That realization sparked the idea of writing a book about private regulation. My first step was to create the New Conversations Project (NCP) at Cornell University's School of Industrial and Labor Relations (the ILR School), where I teach.[1] Its "tagline" is "sustainable labor practices in global supply chains." Bruce Raynor, a Cornell trustee, played a key role in obtaining funding, and we assembled an advisory board, headed by Anna Burger, to advise us regarding how to tackle the question of private regulation. The diverse board includes individuals from global brands, unions, nongovernmental organizations (NGOs) and multi-stakeholder institutions (MSIs) active in private regulation, and design and communications companies, as well as some Cornell students.

From the board's early discussions, we came to realize that what we needed was evidence and new research to understand the lack of progress. Doing research is easy for an academic, to be sure, but getting data from companies and other actors in the supply chain ecosystem proved to be a major challenge. It took us two years of consistent effort before we finally convinced companies, suppliers, auditing firms, and MSIs to share any data. But they did, and this book uses those data to provide the first comprehensive picture of private regulation in action.

I wrote this book not solely as a scholarly exercise. I want it to be *used* by all the actors in the private regulation ecosystem: global companies; suppliers; global and national trade unions; the many NGOs active in this space; the variety of MSIs, such as the Fair Labor Association, the Ethical Trading Initiative, and the Fair Wear Foundation; socially responsible investing companies; and, of course, my students. But most of all, I hope the publication of this book will stimulate improvements in private regulation in ways that will help the myriad workers in global supply chains.

Acknowledgments

Writing this book would not have been possible without the active assistance and engagement of a number of people. I first acknowledge the collaboration of the multi-stakeholder institutions, auditing companies, and global firms that have been willing to share data with me. Given that private regulation is essentially "private," it is not often that organizations in the private regulation ecosystem are willing to share data and provide access for researchers to undertake case studies (especially when the outcome is unknown). To the organizations that did so, I owe a major debt. I cannot name all the organizations involved because of non-disclosure agreements, but you know who you are—and I thank you.

Every project needs key catalysts. Besides John Oliver (see the preface), I had Harry Katz, Ian Spaulding, and Kevin Franklin. They provided encouragement, gave me the confidence that such a book needed to be written, and assured me it was possible.

This book also would not have been possible without support from the New Conversations Project (NCP) at Cornell, for which I serve as academic director, and especially the support and encouragement of Anna Burger, NCP's executive director. Anna strongly encouraged me to write the book and shielded me from my responsibilities to NCP getting in the way. I am also indebted to NCP's advisory board, and specifically to Bruce Raynor and David Hayer, who facilitated my access to several organizations.

I benefited from advice and the active interest of several people in the global supply chain and labor ecosystem. They include Arianna Rossi and Luisa Lupo from the International Labour Organization's Better Work program; Alexander Kohnstamm, Hector Chavez, and Martin Curley from the Fair Wear Foundation; and Victor Wong and Ashita Soni from Gap Inc.

Most of all, I have benefited from the work of many scholars. In addition to Mathew Amengual and Greg Distelhorst, whose ongoing research on sourcing and compliance has advanced both my own thinking and the New Conversation Project, this work stands on the shoulders of giants who have written extensively on labor issues in global supply chains. These include, in particular, Richard Locke, Tim Bartley, Niklas Egels-Zandén, and Michael Toffel (with their various colleagues), whose prior empirical work inspired me to persist in obtaining empirical data.

I wrote this book while on sabbatical leave from Cornell University and need to show my appreciation for my host institution, the department of management at the London School of Economics (LSE). I had a quiet corner office where I could write without interruption, and I benefited from the fellowship of colleagues at LSE, including David Marsden, Sarah Ashwin, Eddy Donnelly, Chunyun Li, Jonathan Booth, Jeff Thomas, Frido Wenten, Mariana Bogdanova, and especially Ruth Reaney, who edited some chapters and corrected my awful grammar.

I also thank workshop participants at Cardiff University, University of Warwick, LSE, Loughborough (London), and King's College (Chiara Benassi in particular) for helpful comments.

My gratitude goes to my postdoctoral associate Jinsun Bae, who spent inordinate amounts of time cleaning and organizing my data and doing the preliminary analyses that appear in the many tables of this book, and Chunyun Li, whose advice on data analysis was invaluable, as was the advice and assistance I received from Mingwei Liu and his student Yan Pan. Last, but not least, I thank my students who have assisted with writing some of the chapters: Matt Fischer-Daly, Chris Raymond, and Ning Li.

Fran Benson, the editorial director of ILR Press (an imprint of Cornell University Press), with whom I have interacted many times over the past three decades, deserves kudos for bringing this book out. And I thank Scott Cooper, whose professional editing expertise has turned an unreadable, imprecise, obfuscating, overly academic manuscript into a volume that is more accessible to all. He is an incredible editor.

Finally, to my colleagues at the ILR School: it has been a pleasure working with you all.

Ithaca, New York
August 2020

PRIVATE REGULATION OF LABOR STANDARDS IN GLOBAL SUPPLY CHAINS

PRIVATE REGULATION OF LABOR STANDARDS IN GLOBAL SUPPLY CHAINS SINCE THE 1990S

Writing about the global apparel industry, fashion journalist Tamsin Blanchard noted that 2018 may "be remembered as the year people finally took notice of the negative environmental and social effects of an industry that has been allowed to get out of control. It has been a year of reckoning for the fashion industry in which to take stock of a wasteful, polluting, exploitative business that has been responsible for the doubling of garment production in the past 15 years."[1] Earlier that year, Katharine Hamnett—fashion designer, early proponent of sustainability and organic fabrics, and owner of an eponymous brand—was quoted in the *Financial Times*: "The world has caught up with the sustainability aspect. People have changed their tune—it has just taken 30 years to happen."[2]

Are these observations accurate? We cannot yet say. As I write this, the world is reeling from the effects of Covid-19, which has had a major effect on supply chains generally—particularly in the apparel sector. The crisis has made it abundantly clear that concerns for workers in the supply chain take a back seat during a pandemic when it threatens markets. In fact, new research conducted early in the pandemic shows that many brands and retailers immediately halted payments to their supplier factories, using the *force majeure* clauses to abrogate their current contracts, with some not even paying for orders in process.[3] Consequently, supplier factories laid off their workers, many not even paying severance pay—a requirement in the Codes of Conduct for suppliers of most apparel brands.

Arguably, a global pandemic is an extreme test of the sustainability of corporate responsibility programs. Even before the crisis, however, we lacked sufficient generalizable empirical evidence that companies are focusing more on improving

1

sustainability in their global supply chains or that consumers care more about sustainability. But these observations do raise fundamental questions about the role of international regulation, both public and private, with respect to the labor and environmental impacts of far-flung supply chains in many industries, not just apparel and fashion. The globalization of supply chains and the absence of regulation at the global level generated demand for new forms of global governance.[4] The world's worst industrial disaster in the twentieth century, the Union Carbide accident in Bhopal in the 1980s, demonstrated the inadequacy of governance globally and the failure of national regulatory enforcement.

Over the past three decades, there has been a plethora of private, voluntary regulatory initiatives with regard to social (labor) and environmental issues. This proliferation has come about in part because of pressure from antiglobalizers calling for global governance, and consumer and activist movements calling for global corporations to be more socially and environmentally responsible. Naming and shaming campaigns by nongovernmental organizations (NGOs) tying Kathie Lee Gifford and Nike to sweatshops and the use of child labor in the early 1990s provided the impetus for the development of private regulatory efforts by global athletic shoe and apparel retailers. However, both governments and NGOs were involved in the development of private regulation, and its present form in the labor arena resulted from some debate and compromise between these groups.[5] For example, the Clinton administration provided both leadership and funding to start the Apparel Industry Partnership, which later became the Fair Labor Association; NGOs such as Social Accountability International, the International Labor Rights Forum, and American labor unions were also involved in that effort.

There are many different methods of private voluntary regulation for labor standards. Through certification schemes, organizations "certify" that a product has been made without child labor under nonsweatshop conditions; the Good-Weave NGO, for example, certifies that carpets from certain regions are made without child labor. "Reporting" methods such as the Global Reporting Initiative or United Nations (UN) Global Compact set particular standards of public disclosure of what member companies are doing to meet labor standards to which they agree.

What is known as the private regulation model is most common.[6] It has three elements: setting of standards regarding labor practices in global supply chains through a corporate code of conduct generally based on the conventions of the International Labour Organization (ILO); "auditing" or "social auditing" that involves monitoring whether supplier factories comply with the code of conduct; and incentives for suppliers to improve compliance by linking future sourcing decisions to their compliance records (penalizing or dropping noncompliant suppliers and rewarding more compliant ones).[7]

Some models vary these three elements. In "individual" private regulation, individual companies adopt a code of conduct and pay for audits from commercial auditors. In "business association" private regulation, business associations provide some guidance and standard-setting for their corporate members' private regulation programs, with a focus on ensuring members' supplier factories comply with the code. A "multi-stakeholder" version of this model involves other stakeholders, to some degree, in setting standards and the design of auditing. The Fair Labor Association (FLA), for instance, has corporations, NGOs, and universities working together to design and implement the different elements of private regulation. The Fair Wear Foundation (FWF) and the Ethical Trading Initiative (ETI) add labor unions to that mix. These multi-stakeholder initiatives, beyond requiring compliance with the code of conduct, also require that member companies examine their purchasing practices for how they affect factory labor standards.

We have seen explosive growth since the 1990s in the adoption of private regulation. From its beginnings in apparel and footwear (e.g., Nike, Gap Inc., and Adidas), it has diffused to many other industries over the past two decades—horticulture, home furnishings, furniture, fish, lumber, fair trade coffee, and others.[8] One study found that more than 40 percent of publicly listed companies in food, textiles, and wood products had adopted the private regulation model.[9] Meanwhile, both the business association model and the multi-stakeholder model have become more widespread.

This diffusion has created a large and growing ecosystem of actors and institutions. Multi-stakeholder initiatives have led to a "collective fora" for private regulation.[10] A large and growing number of auditing organizations—Verité, Intertek, and ELEVATE, for example—do social auditing for global companies and multi-stakeholder initiatives, claiming their services help improve private regulation and labor conditions in global supply chains. Social auditing is an $80 billion industry, and "hundreds of thousands of audits are conducted on behalf of individual firms and multi-stakeholder initiatives each year."[11] There are well over two hundred auditing programs (apart from those run by the brands themselves). A rough estimate suggests that the top ten auditing firms account for more than 10 percent of this total.[12]

The growing private regulation industry has given birth to critical NGOs that use investigative reporting to pressure brands to improve their performance on labor standards (e.g., Oxfam, Labour Behind the Label). Other organizations facilitate the exchange of audit information among global companies (e.g., Sedex) and provide myriad consulting services to global brands and supplier factories. There has also been growth in international organizations and institutions seeking to foster improvements in labor conditions in global supply chains, such as the ILO's Better Work program, a collaboration between the ILO and the International Finance Corporation, and the UN's Global Compact, business and human rights organizations. And a steadily increasing number of organizations, such as the Sustainable Apparel Coalition and the Better Buying Initiative, work to improve the efficacy of private regulation by layering new policies onto the basic model. A number of socially responsible investment companies are also actively engaged in evaluating private regulation programs. University centers have emerged that are devoted to private regulation and workers' rights, and the number of scholarly books, special issues of journals, and articles devoted to the subject continues to grow.

This book is about the current state and future trajectory of this form of private regulation. Part 1 relies on new developments in institutional theory to highlight, in a comprehensive way, the *problems* in private regulation. These chapters provide a new explanation and evidence for why private regulation has largely failed to meet the fundamental objective of sustainable improvements in labor standards in global supply chains. Part 1's key contribution is to elaborate a theory regarding the lack of improvement in the *general field* of private regulation with respect to labor issues.

Part 2 of this book is a comprehensive evaluation of progress to date. These chapters rely on several data sources, especially forty thousand audits conducted over a seven-year period in more than twelve countries and thirteen industries, as well as data from several global companies. These data show the effect of private regulation on a wide range of labor standards and represent the first comprehensive and generalizable evidence about whether private regulation actually improves the lives of workers in global supply chains. Given the relative lack of transparency among brands and multi-stakeholder institutions regarding how well their private regulation efforts are working, scholars have had to rely on selected case studies of a few companies[13] and NGO investigative reports[14] that do not allow for generalization because they focus largely on particular leading, reputation-conscious firms (e.g., Nike and Gap). But how is private regulation performing across multiple countries and industries?

Part 2's key contribution is a comprehensive picture of overall performance of private regulation across industries and countries generally. These chapters include a detailed evaluation of wages in global supply chains, drawn from disparate sources of data; the subject of wages generates more heat than light, and comprehensive data have been difficult to obtain. Part 2 also presents a detailed evaluation of progress on freedom of association, an enabling right that affects all other rights and worker outcomes and is a core labor standard.

Part 3 focuses on the future. These chapters evaluate current solutions, such as the innovations in corporate governance (benefit corporations) that hold the

promise of meeting stakeholder interests (including those of workers in the global supply chain), rather than attending to the interests of shareholders alone. There is also a detailed case study of how one global company managed to align its sourcing practices with compliance practices, laying the groundwork for real improvement in labor standards. This example offers valuable lessons for other companies that need to do the same. Part 3 concludes by employing institutional perspectives not only to evaluate contemporary developments but also to offer new directions and outline pathways by which private regulation could better meet the goal of improving the lives of workers in global supply chains.

All three parts involve analysis of new data and case evidence provided by global firms, auditing firms, and other actors. This comprehensive and hitherto unseen empirical evidence constitutes a contribution in its own right. Each part is introduced with an overview of the key problems and questions as well as some of the research in the field to date.

Part 1
OVERVIEW
Problems

Has private regulation brought about meaningful improvements in working conditions in the global supply chain over the past twenty-five years? The large and burgeoning body of research on the impact of private regulation with respect to labor standards suggests limited effect.[1] As one group of researchers has noted regarding the apparel and footwear industries, "Existing evidence suggests that they have had some meaningful but narrow effects on working conditions and the management of human resources, but the rights of workers have been less affected, and even on the issues where codes tend to be most meaningful, standards in many parts of the (apparel) industry remain criminally low in an absolute sense."[2]

Research shows unstable and limited improvements in working conditions (e.g., health and safety) and no improvement in freedom of association and collective bargaining rights, as well as a general absence of steady improvement in compliance over time.[3] Supplier factories "cycle in and out of compliance"; even Nike, a leading firm that pioneered adoption of the private regulation model, has shown no clear evidence of improvement.[4] This result suggests a discernible plateauing effect in compliance.

A case study of New Balance Athletics shows the remarkable variation in factory assessment scores on compliance over time.[5] One factory assessed thirteen times in three years had compliance scores that varied from as low as 5 to as high as 87 on a scale of 100. The researchers conclude that the code of conduct approach is "not producing the large and sustained improvements in workplace conditions that many have hoped it would."[6]

Factory disasters in Bangladesh and Pakistan are a continuing testament to the ineffectiveness of private regulation efforts. "Every one of the apparel factories where dozens or 100s of workers have died have been repeatedly inspected under the brands and retailers monitoring regimes. . . . All were covered by one or more of the multi-stakeholder organizations and all were producing for brands and retailers that claim to be operating robust inspection programs," write researchers.[7] And others suggest that "when it comes to rights and empowerment of workers, Codes of Conduct have scattered and short-lived impacts at best."[8]

What explains the lack of sustainable progress in improving working conditions? The answers can be found in conceptual problems with the design of the private regulation model and in a variety of problems in the model's implementation by global corporations. Getting to those answers requires posing several other questions.

First, is private regulation model "fit for its purpose"? Some argue it is the wrong solution, that companies developed a highly sophisticated corporate model when what was really needed was stronger government intervention and enforcement of legislation in supplier countries. The voluntary private model likely displaces government and trade union interventions and is designed *not* to protect labor rights but to limit legal liability and protect brand value.[9] This is a powerful criticism, to be sure, but clearly actors in the ecosystem have already adopted this "wrong solution," while governments have yet to actively enforce legislation in supplier countries.

Then there is the question of faulty assumptions underlying the model's design. There are suggestions that the assumption of asymmetric power relations between global buyers and first-tier suppliers—so that powerful global buyers have "leverage" to force suppliers to comply with buyers' codes of conduct or otherwise change suppliers' practices to improve labor conditions—may be unwarranted.[10] Some suppliers may have tremendous influence over buyers.[11] Further, each factory may produce for several brands, which allows them to spread their risk and insure themselves against an unforeseen change in consumer demand for any single brand's product. These possibilities reduce brand leverage over factories.

Another faulty assumption concerns aligning the interests of the different actors in the supply chain responsible for increased compliance through a system of incentives. Typically, though, relationships between buyers and suppliers are antagonistic rather than collaborative. Buyers and suppliers often have different interests that "provoke mixed and often contradictory behaviors."[12] Buyers want suppliers to invest to improve labor standards but consistently "squeeze" suppliers with lower prices for their products, thus prompting suppliers to hide or falsify compliance data.

Private regulation's audit methodology grew out of "quality control thinking"—the idea being that pointing out problems to suppliers will motivate them to fix these problems. But those differing interests militate against improvements that impose a significant cost on suppliers. It is not even clear that global buyers' sourcing departments, which are often evaluated on price, and compliance departments, evaluated on whether private regulation is driving improvements in supplier behavior, share similar interests. And then there is the question of whether it is even possible to get accurate and reliable information as a base for strategic decisions, given problems with the data auditors are provided and the process generally followed in auditing.

Empirical investigations suggest a second set of explanations for the lack of sustainable progress in improving working conditions. Empirical investigations have identified problems with each of the three components of the private regulation model presented in the introduction, consistent with some of these unwarranted assumptions.

- *Codes of conduct*: There is a multiplicity of codes across companies and multi-stakeholder initiatives. Codes vary in how they deal with different standards. The result is a multiplicity of auditing protocols that make it difficult for factories supplying multiple companies to meet differing standards.

To some extent, as more global companies join multi-stakeholder institutions and adopt the common MSI code, the problem of standards multiplicity has diminished. Standards in most codes are remarkably similar now, except when it comes to wages. As it turns out, the inability of private regulation to improve working conditions in supplier factories has more to do with implementation.

- *Auditing ("social auditing")*: This has attracted the most researcher attention to explain the failure of private regulation.[13] Well-worn criticisms include that audits are too short to uncover violations, so auditors "satisfice" through cursory document checks, quick walk-throughs, and "check the box" exercises without focusing on root causes of problems found. Findings suggest most auditors are not well trained and that auditing has become "commoditized" and outsourced to large third-party generalist firms that charge too little to do a good job. Worker interviews are also problematic: most of those conducted at the factory site are "staged," and workers are "coached" to provide "desirable" answers; workers are not interviewed at their homes, where they might provide more frank assessments of whether the factory engages in discrimination or union suppression. There is also considerable fraud and bribery, with auditors "willing to turn a blind eye when necessary to please factory managers,"[14] and increasing evidence that a large number of factory records are falsified to "pass"—which is easy to do because most audits are announced in advance. Suppliers also evade audits by subcontracting production to factories not subjected to brand auditing.

These problems also lend support to questioning the assumption that factory audits produce the high-quality, reliable information that global buyers are supposed to use to make sourcing decisions and that consumers need to make informed buying choices.[15] In sum, the myriad problems in auditing are an important part of explaining the failure of private regulation.

As with codes of conduct, there is also a multiplicity of auditing methodologies. There is a tendency among the actors in the private regulation ecosystem to fixate on standardizing audit tools and methodologies, rather than asking the bigger questions: Is standardization the right approach given the context-specificity of causes regarding compliance?[16] Is the model really producing improvements in working conditions?

- *Incentivizing suppliers to improve compliance*: When originally conceived, the model's intent was that global buyers would reward factories that showed steady improvement in compliance with more orders and perhaps longer-term relationships, while factories that did not remediate compliance violations adequately would be "punished" with fewer orders or would be completely axed from the buyer supply chains. Putting this element into practice requires that global buyers integrate their sourcing practices with their compliance practices. However, we know little about whether global buyers have done so, as empirical investigations of this third element of private regulation are rare; companies have not reported on their efforts to integrate sourcing and compliance, and the number of companies that have shared their data with researchers can be counted on the fingers of one hand.

The alignment of auditing and sourcing practices is necessary if auditing is to result in increased compliance with codes of conduct. But there are two problems. First, it is not at all clear that corporations have modified their business models to integrate rewarding more compliant factories.[17] Second, sourcing practices are often the root cause of noncompliance. A steady "squeezing" of the price paid induces suppliers to find noncompliant ways to cut labor costs, while orders sent late force suppliers to increase overtime beyond acceptable limits to meet the orders.[18] An ILO global survey of 1,454 suppliers reveals how purchasing practices of global buyers affect working conditions in their factories: low prices, in-sufficient lead times, and inaccurate technical specifications lead to lower wages and longer hours.[19] But sourcing practices are *not* an integral element of most types of private regulation.

Research suggests that a partial solution to these problems is better buyer-supplier relationships based on cooperation, trust, and commitment to better align the incentives of buyers and suppliers, but even today these are rare in the apparel industry.[20] Where long-term collaborative relationships hold, it is possible for brands to help suppliers through capacity-building programs, such as the design and adoption of lean manufacturing techniques.[21] The disconnect between sourcing and compliance within global firms has prompted the criticism that they have adopted the private regulation model largely as "window dressing," with little interest in actually implementing the model. "Symbolic" adoption is seen as necessary for preserving their reputation and legitimacy in the market.

Empirical investigations have identified many other correlates of compliance. It is generally better in host countries with stronger protective and effective labor law enforcement,[22] and in factories in countries where leading brands are involved in multi-stakeholder initiatives, such as the ILO's Better Work program—although this effect varies from country to country.[23] Further, *organizational characteristics* matter. Larger suppliers often exhibit better compliance, given their managerial capacity and resources to invest in better working conditions.[24] Suppliers owned by multinational corporations comply more than independently owned factories,[25] and corporate governance apparently matters, with privately owned companies likely to have better private regulation programs relative to publicly listed companies.[26]

There are no examples of sustained improvement in all labor standards in the global apparel supply chain, which likely accounts for the growing consensus that the private regulation model has failed to deliver, especially in the apparel industry where it began.[27] The case studies, limited as they are, show considerable variation in effectiveness. Some companies have more robust programs than others, and these have been more studied. Others, especially B-corporations, have strong reputations for sustainability, but their record of improving labor practices has been abysmal.[28] Large global firms are reputed to have more robust programs than others, but the empirical evidence is limited. As more and more firms join multi-stakeholder initiatives, their programs have become more similar.

Although there is variation, the general picture that emerges of the private regulation model is one of failure rather than success. What might explain this failure? Could there be problems with the entire organizational field of private regulation with respect to labor issues?

Institutional Theory: Toward a Field-Based Explanation

Institutional theorists have long paid attention to organizations' strategic responses to regulative and normative rules. Within this domain, the theme of organizational decoupling has received extensive attention, based on an explanation from the late 1970s for the observed gap between formal policies and actual practices.[29]

Much of the research on this *policy-practice gap* focuses on why organizations adopt policies but do not implement them. Institutionalists argue that policy-practice gaps typically occur when organizations respond to rationalizing pressures from the environment, such as by adopting an "externally induced" rule to gain "legitimacy" or avoiding legal sanction through "symbolic adoption," meaning policies are adopted but not implemented at all or implemented so weakly "that they do nothing to alter daily work routines."[30] Policy-practice decoupling is more evident early in the adoption process, when there is weak capacity to implement policies and internal constituents do not reinforce the external pressures for the policies.[31]

Many global firms, especially those not in the public eye, may have adopted policies "symbolically." However, over time, even symbolically adopted policies sometimes become integrated into the organization, particularly if they are monitored through hard- and soft-law channels. This is clearly the case with private regulation labor practices, as many firms that have adopted policies have gradually had to implement them, in some cases as a result of pressure from consumers or civil society.

A new strand of institutional theory hypothesizes the existence of a second decoupling form: means-ends decoupling, which occurs when formal structures are adopted, work activities are changed, and policies are implemented. But scant evidence exists to show these activities are linked to organizational effectiveness or outcomes,[32] resulting in *practice-outcome* gaps.[33] This type of decoupling could occur when private regulation structures are implemented within the organization without being clearly integrated with the core goals of the organization—that is, core goals such as profitability are internally "buffered" from more peripheral private regulation structures. The disconnect between sourcing and compliance noted earlier is an example of such buffering. It is argued that means-ends decoupling is more prevalent when external pressures are institutionalized via hard or soft law in *opaque* institutional fields, where "observers have difficulty identifying the characteristics of prevailing practices, establishing causal relationships between policies and outcomes and precisely measuring the results of policy implementation," as opposed to more transparent fields where these issues are clear.[34]

Therefore, field opacity contributes to "means-ends" decoupling so that even if the problem of symbolic adoption were resolved, there would still be inconsistencies between adopted practice and outcomes because of the opacity noted earlier. Such decoupling does not necessarily indicate organizational failure but "could well be the most functionally effective path in the face of constraints, and it may nonetheless confer legitimacy."[35] Field opacity and means-ends decoupling may explain why the private regulation model continues to be adopted, despite reports of its ineffectiveness.

Opaque fields, such as private socio-environmental governance, invariably have characteristics that impedes actors' compliance with sustainability standards on socio-environmental issues. Three factors drive this opacity.[36]

- *Behavioral invisibility*—the difficulty of observing and measuring the behavior of actors.

Behavioral invisibility enables suppliers with a low incentive to comply to disguise their noncompliance or "pretend to be substantively compliant."[37] This is what drives the prevalence of "multiple books" in factories. Poorer suppliers may agree to adopt standards spelled out in codes of conduct to reap the benefits of following the standard (signaling that they are responsible factories), but will resist implementation to avoid incurring the necessary costs). Thus suppliers, like many global buyers, engage in "symbolic" adoption.

Behavioral invisibility in the labor standards field occurs through multiple pathways, such as through the variety of problems with auditing well documented in the labor standards literature, and through the complexity involved in systematically *measuring* compliance of a variety of different labor standards in different national and regional contexts. Thus, even relatively easy-to-measure issues such as wages and hours can be complicated to assess in different locations, especially in the context of short audit time frames and the need for extensive auditor training.[38] Behavioral invisibility is also exacerbated considerably by the extensive incidence of audit falsification, or "cooking the books." In chapter 1, I use global audit data from a seven-year period in twelve countries and industries to show the extent to which data are falsified. And given that the rates of audit falsification appear to be exceptionally high in China, I also present an investigation into the "audit consulting industry" in Dongguan that helps suppliers "pass" audits by falsifying data.

- *Practice multiplicity*—the diversity of practices adopted by actors, spread across different geographic, institutional, economic, and cultural contexts, that makes it difficult to engage in compliant behavior.

Simply put, "the higher the number of divergent practices encountered, the more difficult it is for adopters to exhaustively understand and compare the merits and limitations of different practices, resulting in ambiguity."[39] In the labor practices field, there are more than two thousand different codes of conduct implemented differently in a variety of contexts (given cross-national differences in local labor markets, national laws and rules, and so forth).

In chapter 2, using data from a global supplier, I argue and demonstrate that the diverse practices of global brands sourcing from a *single* supplier contribute to opacity in four ways: the private regulation policies of brands differ; there are diverse auditing practices by the different brands (and auditing firms); brands use many different rating scales to assess supplier performance, resulting in conflicting "grades"; and brands vary in how they assign weights for different violations. Together, these result in inconsistent ratings that constitute confusing feedback for suppliers, making it difficult for them to engage in compliant behavior and link daily activities with the brands' programs. More important, this makes it impossible for brands to identify important causal factors in compliance data.

- *Causal complexity* resulting from the presence of heterogeneous actors and practices that are interconnected in different ways in different locations, which induces adopters to be unaware of critical drivers of compliant behavior.[40]

Causal complexity results in different types of uncertainty. Actors (such as global companies, auditing firms, suppliers) may find it difficult to understand what works and what does not, especially given the lack of transparency among companies that practice private regulation. The fact that compliance is a function of numerous heterogeneous actors, numerous different variables, and many direct and indirect effects in different institutional contexts leads to causal indeterminacy, which makes it difficult for actors to *disentangle* causes and consequences. Sometimes, outcomes feed back into their causes, blurring the distinction between causes and consequences.[41] Put together, this complexity makes organizational actors unaware of the most critical causes of compliance with codes and, consequently, unaware of best practices.

It is important to reiterate that labor standards cover a variety of matters, and companies often have to deal with different aspects in a context-dependent way. It makes no sense, for example, for codes of conduct to insist on freedom of association (FOA) in China, where it is not a right. Hence some codes focus on alternative arrangements known as "parallel means," such as worker committees, while others continue to insist on FOA. The key implication of causal complexity or indeterminacy is that it makes it difficult to identify best practices, highlighting the need for context-dependent approaches. But the private regulation model practiced today is "one size fits all." To demonstrate causal complexity, in chapter 3 I use data from a global home products retailer to show that variables that have been identified as causes of compliance in prior literature do not necessarily transfer across contexts.

Causal complexity poses problems for the current focus among ecosystem actors to search for a uniform code. While a uniform code could potentially reduce the problem of practice multiplicity, the drive for uniformity is at odds with the multiplicity of actors, practices, and different contexts that may call for different approaches. Thus, there are tradeoffs when trying to remedy policy-practice decoupling and practice-outcomes decoupling. Solving the first problem can be achieved through standardized rules, but standardized rules make it difficult to avoid practice-outcomes decoupling given that different contexts require different approaches.

Thus, the high degree of opacity brought about by practice multiplicity, behavioral invisibility, and causal complexity "renders the optimal design and implementation of sustainability standards impossible."[42] In essence, noncompliance with codes of conduct may be high in relatively opaque fields. While one option may be to standardize approaches to private regulation (such as the effect of the sustainable apparel coalition to create uniform standards and measurement), the drive for uniformity is at odds with the multiplicity of actors, practices, and contexts, which may call for different approaches in different contexts. Thus, tradeoffs exist when trying to remedy policy-practice decoupling and practice-outcomes decoupling. Solving the first problem can be achieved through standardized rules, but standardized rules imply that the second kind of decoupling cannot.

These new institutional arguments constitute a promising approach to examining private regulation with regard to labor standards, as this approach outlines *how* field opacity causes organizational decoupling and permits the articulation of an alternative organizational field-based explanation for the *general* practice-outcomes gap we observe in the labor standards arena. In part 1 of this book, I demonstrate with empirical data how field opacity causes practice-outcomes decoupling.

BEHAVIORAL INVISIBILITY

The Reliability of Supplier Data and
the Unique Role of Audit Consultants

with Ning Li

Institutional theory highlights that behavioral invisibility—the inability of actors to measure accurately the behavior of suppliers—is critical in driving opacity in the organizational field of private regulation of labor practices, causing the decoupling of global firms' organizational practices from the intended outcomes of those practices for workers. The ability to "readily observe and assess the behavior of actors" is crucial to the success of private regulation. Institutional perspectives suggest that behavioral invisibility is likely to be more prevalent when suppliers are shielded from external controls, such as when the supplier's practices with regard to workers "typically are not embodied in physical product characteristics . . . rendering them invisible to external stakeholders."[1]

Many other reasons, such as poor auditing practices, make it difficult to properly evaluate suppliers' labor practices. If the organizational field is characterized by a lot of behavioral invisibility, this could be one explanation for why we do not see as much progress for workers from private regulation efforts as we might expect.

Global firms have long had difficulties obtaining reliable information about supplier behavior.[2] There is a general consensus among critics that auditing, as currently practiced, does not capture the scale and severity of violations of labor standards.[3] Although thousands of audits occur each year, a relatively small number of studies have examined and analyzed audit data, identifying several problems: the short duration of audits; the practice of announcing audits in advance, thus enabling suppliers to "cheat"; generally inadequate training of auditors, who lack the diverse disciplinary skills to look for root causes underlying violations;

reliance on a "check the box" mentality rather than developmental approaches; and the prevalence of fraudulent behaviors such as bribing auditors.[4] The short duration has been shown to be a particular problem, making it hugely difficult even to measure wages and hours across suppliers.[5]

Beyond useful insights into these problems, these empirical investigations have not focused on whether the information auditors assess is reliable. It is crucial that auditors examine reliable data to do an effective job of monitoring compliance, since these data are the basis on which global firms act on their private regulation programs, especially if compliance results are to be linked to the firms' sourcing practices as the private regulation model requires. But while both anecdotal evidence and research suggest that suppliers often "cook the books" and falsify data, we know little about how widespread records falsification is and who does the falsifying.

This chapter focuses on assessing data reliability, using data provided by AUDCO (a large auditing company) from more than forty thousand audits spanning seven years across twelve countries and thirteen industries. The chapter also spotlights China, which reports very high levels of unreliable audit information, and examines the role played by a "gray" actor—the audit consulting company (ACC)—in helping suppliers "pass" audits. The chapter documents the variety of services provided by ACCs, including falsification of audit records. The discussion covers how ACCs "advertise" their services and how they work, through a detailed analysis of an audit consultant's work logs, as well as an assessment of why ACCs may be so successful.

The analysis here suggests that getting a clear picture of what is really happening in a factory requires a nuanced understanding of the nature of the data that auditors examine. The analysis points to the need for auditors to be better trained at spotting falsified data but also to triangulate with other data and information sources (perhaps from workers). The results suggest that the lack of reliable data provided to auditors is a major reason for the decoupling we see between private regulation practices and sustainable improvements in working conditions in global supply chains across multiple industries and countries.

The AUDCO Process and Data Credibility

AUDCO is distinguished from other social auditing firms by its focus on assessing the quality and reliability of audit information while undertaking an audit and the company's rigorous procedure for evaluating the credibility of the information auditors are given. AUDCO places great emphasis on hiring good auditors. The firm seeks people with college degrees and the ability to speak and write

English. The company chooses candidates from a number of basic disciplines, but the preference is for an engineering background, which helps auditors assess safety and health in factories, or some background in management or human resource management. AUDCO hires through a variety of sources; word of mouth and online platforms are particularly important. In a high-turnover industry, more than 50 percent of AUDCO's auditors have more than five years' tenure.

The AUDCO auditing process begins with auditors spending considerable time on building trust with factory management. In an open kickoff meeting with management, they highlight how the audit process can benefit the supplier and get a sense for how management views audits. This is important because while many view the process as adversarial, those who see it as constructive are typically less likely to falsify data.

Audits of small factories (fewer than one hundred workers) are typically completed in one day; others take two days. A significant amount of auditors' time is spent analyzing factory records. They pore through documentation provided by the factory, focusing on payroll records, working hours and overtime records, attendance records, leave requests, production records to examine the volume of production and things such as needle breakages, shipping records, health and safety issues, and legal permits. AUDCO provides its auditors with a very detailed governance document that shows them what to look for and how to analyze the information they obtain.

Some inconsistencies in the data auditors may find are easily explained, but others require more detailed investigations. So they conduct interviews with factory management, and specifically the person in charge of making or keeping the records, to probe further. Auditors may use other methods to triangulate. Often, comparisons are made with data from similar factories. If an auditor is satisfied with the explanations for observed inconsistencies, the data are deemed trustworthy, and the audit is considered *reliable*. If the auditor is unable to establish conclusively that the data are reliable or the factory is falsifying data, the audit is considered *difficult to determine*. If there are several inconsistencies that cannot be explained, or it becomes clear that some or all of the data are falsified, the audit is considered to have been *falsified*.

A host of clues may lead an auditor to suspect some falsification of records. These include large inconsistencies between the different sources of data, such as wage records and records of working hours. These are often checked against closed-circuit television (CCTV) records that show the times workers enter and leave the factory. Sometimes auditors, suspecting a factory is requiring workers to work excess overtime, try to triangulate with CCTV records, but factory managers say the CCTV was malfunctioning that day. This is a clue to some cover-up effort. Similarly, if all the workers interviewed by auditors say basically exactly the same thing, it is a clue that workers have been "coached" to follow a standard script. Auditors also pay attention to nonverbal communication by factory management. Nervousness on the part of factory managers is another clue, and further probing is warranted.

After completing the audit, auditors send in draft audit reports to AUDCO's audit review team along with a supplemental data sheet about the factory, the data from the audit, and auditing notes. In these detailed reports, auditors are required to provide extensive evidence to back their overall judgments regarding the final classification of the data from the factory. Auditors also document instances when "subjective" judgment has been exercised in coming to these "grades."

AUDCO's audit review team assesses these audit reports for quality, looking closely at the evidence provided and interviewing the auditors. Reviewers may ask an auditor to return to the factory for additional information. Once the review team signs off on an auditor's report, it is entered into the record.

AUDCO's process differs from other auditing firms in two respects: its focus on establishing whether the data are reliable; and the detailed and careful process by which auditor reports are reviewed by the audit review team. The rigor and extreme care taken by AUDCO before classifying audits was made clear in interviews with auditors and the firm's vice president for quality and integrity.

Our AUDCO Data and Results

AUDCO made available multiple datasets with varying numbers of audits reported, for a total of 40,458 audits conducted during 2011–2017 (the smaller datasets draw from this sample). These data encompass audit reports from twelve countries—China (which accounted for a large number of audits), India, Bangladesh, Vietnam, Cambodia, Ethiopia, Mexico, Turkey, Indonesia, Jordan, Italy, and the United States—and fourteen industries, including agriculture, apparel, apparel accessories, electronics, food, footwear, furniture, hard goods, soft goods, jewelry, kitchen and housewares, toys, and a catchall "other" category. The datasets contain a variety of information, such as the number of violations of different labor standards and actual hours and wages (analyzed in greater detail in chapters 4 and 5). The primary interest here is in AUDCO's evaluation of the reliability of the data provided to its auditors.

One problem in the AUDCO dataset given to us and used in this analysis (representing 40,458 audits in total) is that the company combined audits it considered to be *difficult to determine* or *falsified* into one general category it called *unreliable* (18,251 audits, or 45.2 percent), with others were categorized as *reliable* (22,207 audits, or 54.8 percent). Using a second and smaller dataset AUDCO provided in which the two categories were not combined, we were able to determine that the percentage of audits considered *difficult to determine* ranged from 13 to 17 percent, suggesting that *falsified* audits ranged from between 28 and 32 percent of all audits. (In the analysis that follows, we employ AUDCO's binary categorization of *reliable* and *unreliable*, since our interest is in whether the information provided for audits is fully credible.)

We first examined the percentage of audits based on reliable or unreliable information. We believe this to be the first systematic attempt to assess just how widespread the practice of audit falsification is across industries and countries. We then examined how reliable and unreliable audits differ in how they report on violations of key labor standards. Since the purpose of falsifying data is to pass the audit, one would expect that unreliable audits would generally report better performance and fewer violations.

Table 1.1 shows the credibility of the AUDCO data and suggests that the percentage of unreliable audits is far higher than was previously believed by observers of private regulation. The overall direction is positive, implying that suppliers in general are increasingly willing to provide "real" data that is reliable enough to inform global buyer decisions.

Table 1.2 shows how countries differ in terms of the proportion of audits classified as unreliable. The proportion of unreliable audits in China and India, the two largest countries, exceeds 50 percent. But Bangladesh and Cambodia, two significant exporters, also have high rates of audit unreliability. Ethiopia is relatively new as a garment-exporting country, and there are not enough data to get a good fix. In contrast, and as would be expected, the percentages of unreliable audits in the United States and Italy are very low; a more detailed investigation of the audit data revealed that both fell into the *inconclusive* category. Still, on the positive side, audit data are becoming more reliable, with Indonesia, Jordan, China, and Bangladesh showing steady improvement.

TABLE 1.1. Number and proportion of audits by credibility, 2011–2017

	2011	2012	2013	2014	2015	2016	2017	TOTAL
Reliable audits	1,522	1,845	2,233	2,741	3,431	4,240	6,195	22,207
Unreliable audits (including inconclusive)	1,635	1,353	2,246	2,934	3,460	3,424	3,199	18,251
Total	2,157	3,198	4,479	5,675	6,891	7,664	9,394	40,458
								Average
Unreliable and inconclusive	51.8%	42.3%	50.1%	51.7%	50.2%	44.7%	34.0%	45.11%

TABLE 1.2. Proportion of unreliable audits by country, 2011–2017

COUNTRY	AVERAGE PROPORTION BY YEAR							TOTAL NUMBER OF AUDITS	AVERAGE PROPORTION FOR ALL YEARS
	2011	2012	2013	2014	2015	2016	2017		
Bangladesh	24.0	26.6	24.8	26.3	22.1	15.6	14.4	2,042	20.76
Cambodia	20.0	40.0	17.2	33.3	29.7	30.6	8.22	250	23.20
China	60.3	51.1	58.3	62.0	58.0	53.2	44.5	27,903	54.44
Ethiopia	0.0	0.0	0.0	0.0	0.0	0.0	50.0	15	50.00
India	49.3	28.1	65.3	66	69.6	52.5	41.0	3,749	55.24
Indonesia	25.2	19.6	14.7	4.52	4.3	6.25	4.66	1,063	9.60
Italy	0.0	0.0	0.0	8.7	0.0	0.0	1.77	278	1.44
Jordan	26.3	33.3	20.0	22.2	25.0	26.6	5.0	119	22.69
Mexico	5.17	0.0	0.79	0.0	0.71	0.41	1.29	1,157	0.95
Turkey	0.0	0.0	19.2	13.7	25.9	16.1	9.93	506	12.25
United States	2.22	0.0	0.0	3.33	1.49	0.78	0.72	1,478	1.15
Vietnam	17.5	18.4	8.41	0.37	17.24	30.21	11.86	1,898	14.91

Prior research suggests that compliance with private regulation is generally better in so-called high-compliance environments—countries that score higher on indicators of the rule of law, labor laws, gross domestic product (GDP) per capita, and press freedom.[6] That explanation could account for the differences between countries. However, high-compliance environments do not seem to be related to the issue of audit credibility, as table 1.3 suggests. Audit credibility may be better explained by factory-level variables than by country-level variables.

Prior research is largely silent on whether the credibility of audits differs by industry. In general, one would expect that industries in which private regulation has been introduced earlier, such as footwear and apparel, would evidence more credibility. The ease of entry (and exit) may subvert that hypothesis, however; new factories come on line in different countries fairly regularly, and these newer entrants may be more prone to falsifying data to pass audits and gain business. In contrast, there is reason to believe that electronics factories may be more reliable about their data, because factory owners must make fairly large investments in plants and equipment; their factories tend to be larger than apparel factories; electronics factory owners generally have long-term established relationships with their buyers (e.g., Apple and Foxconn); and their products tend to have a more stable customer base relative to the apparel industry, with its rapidly changing fashions and tastes. Apparel factories allocate a relatively small proportion of their installed capacity to each global buyer (compared with electronics and footwear factories) precisely to avoid being held hostage to those changes. (There is no concrete basis to hypothesize regarding other industries.)

TABLE 1.3. Measures of a high-compliance environment

COUNTRY	PER CAPITA GDP (264 COUNTRIES)*	LABOR RIGHTS LAW[†] (199 COUNTRIES AND 45 RANKS, 2002)	COUNTRY RANKING BY RULE OF LAW (205 COUNTRIES, 2017)[‡]	COUNTRY RANKING BY PRESS FREEDOM (180 COUNTRIES, 2018)[§]	AVERAGE PERCENTAGE OF UNRELIABLE AUDITS IN AUDCO
		COUNTRY RANKINGS			
Mexico	86	18	135	147	0.95
USA	1	17	17	45	1.15
Italy	39	1	73	46	1.44
Indonesia	129	15	116	124	9.60
Turkey	64	37	108	157	12.25
Ethiopia	221	33	131	150	13.33
Vietnam	162	20	87	175	14.91
Bangladesh	188	16	142	146	20.76
Jordan	145	28	28	132	22.69
Cambodia	184	4	173	142	23.20
China	99	11	109	176	54.44
India	158	25	93	138	55.24

* From World Bank's World Development Indicators (2019).

[†] Toffel, Short, and Ouellet's 2015 article "Codes in Context: How States, Markets, and Civil Society Shape Adherence to Global Labor Standards" uses labor law information developed by Layna Mosley (2010) that quantifies the labor laws and practices of 199 countries from 1985 and 2002. Her database provides scores but *not* rankings. We computed rankings based on labor law scores in the database, which results in the ranking system ranging from 1 to 45. A number of countries share the same scores.

[‡] This ranking draws from the World Governance Indicator reporting on countries' rule of law (World Bank 2019). This dataset reports the rule of law in percentile rank terms, from 0 (lowest rank) to 100 (highest rank). We used the latest data from this dataset, measuring 2017, and computed the ranking by sorting the countries' percentile values in descending order.

[§] From the 2018 World Press Freedom Index (Reporters without Borders 2018).

Table 1.4 shows the substantial variation in reliability of audits across industries. The proportion of audits that are unreliable is generally quite high, except for agriculture, in which the number of audits, spread across different countries, is quite small. It appears that industries characterized by generally larger factories, such as footwear and electronics, are more likely to have more reliable audit information. There does appear to be general improvement since 2015.

In summary, the data in these tables show that globally, across multiple years, close to half the audit data have been essentially unreliable. China and India—which account for a significant percentage of all AUDCO audits—deserve attention for their high proportion of unreliable audits. Several industries—accessories, kitchenware and housewares, and toys—exceed the global average for unreliability. On a positive note, though, there has been a general decline in the proportion of unreliable audits in the past couple years across countries and industries.

TABLE 1.4. Proportion of unreliable audits by industry, 2011–2017

INDUSTRY	AVERAGE PROPORTION BY YEAR							TOTAL NUMBER OF AUDITS	AVERAGE PROPORTION FOR ALL YEARS
	2011	2012	2013	2014	2015	2016	2017		
Agriculture	100.00	0.00	80.00	50.00	7.14	0.98	2.38	351	4.56
Apparel	44.58	35.30	46.77	48.52	46.37	41.41	29.86	15,722	41.10
Accessories	58.69	40.65	55.99	54.90	56.86	54.42	37.44	2,628	49.47
Electronics	38.89	39.83	40.29	45.99	41.95	40.39	33.66	2,416	39.40
Food	54.84	14.29	29.55	26.00	24.81	21.74	12.92	669	24.07
Footwear	38.06	31.52	44.15	48.24	42.90	35.03	33.38	2,964	38.77
Furniture	50.00	40.94	35.03	44.20	57.14	50.00	34.48	941	43.78
Hard goods (other)	62.15	47.67	61.36	57.98	52.17	54.42	46.88	1,662	54.33
Jewelry	55.45	46.88	55.56	65.66	63.16	58.76	50.74	811	56.72
Kitchenware and housewares	58.33	37.55	54.79	56.86	60.74	63.04	50.17	1,652	54.54
Other	45.67	56.14	55.46	55.77	57.14	50.48	35.98	7,465	50.15
Soft goods (other)	48.00	67.31	72.92	69.54	65.83	60.77	42.34	1,024	58.59
Toys	72.04	72.83	66.42	70.81	78.66	66.85	51.42	1,246	64.45

Note: The "other" category included industries that do not fit in these standard classifications, and we have omitted 907 audits in which we could not find information that clearly identified an industry grouping.

What are the consequences of these findings? What does audit reliability tell us about a factory's labor conditions? It would seem unreliable audits will report "better" outcomes—that is, inflated positive results—given that the objective of falsifying audits is to present a good picture.

Table 1.5 summarizes the difference between reliable and unreliable audits on a variety of variables. Consistently, unreliable audits provide a much better picture of code compliance than more genuine audits.

Table 1.6, which compares countries by labor standards violations, makes clear that unreliable audits present a significantly positive picture of violations in these countries. Table 1.7 shows that unreliable audits typically report fewer working hours, as would be expected (the United States being the exception).

Table 1.8 provides a better picture of the differences between reliable and unreliable audits over time in each country, including all industries. That difference appears to be narrowing over time, most noticeably in China and India. while the pattern is more variable in other countries.

In terms of reporting actual working hours (table 1.9), there is a similar pattern of narrowing differences in most countries. Figure 1.1 provides a visual

TABLE 1.5. Reliable and unreliable audits on selected labor indicators

LABOR INDICATORS	MEASURES	WHAT RELIABLE AUDITS REPORTED	WHAT UNRELIABLE AUDITS REPORTED	WHICH AUDITS REPORT BETTER PERFORMANCE
Weekly working hours	Hours/week	60.87	53.75	Unreliable
Continuous working days	Days	10.41	7.10	Unreliable
Percentage of workers paid correctly	Percentage	78.72	95.67	Unreliable
Health and safety	Number of findings per audit	4.52	4.06	Unreliable
Labor standards		3.70	1.80	Unreliable
Business ethics		0.22	0.12	Unreliable
Environment		0.50	0.60	Unreliable
Management systems		1.23	1.85	Unreliable
Total number of audit findings		10.17	8.43	Unreliable

TABLE 1.6. Labor standards findings in selected countries, 2017

	AVERAGE NUMBER OF LABOR STANDARDS FINDINGS	
COUNTRY	RELIABLE AUDITS	UNRELIABLE AUDITS
Bangladesh	3.51	1.83
China	4.71	2.37
India	3.56	1.51
United States	0.51	0.33
Vietnam	2.56	1.80

TABLE 1.7. Average weekly working hours by audit credibility, 2017

	AVERAGE WEEKLY WORKING HOURS		
COUNTRY	RELIABLE AUDITS	UNRELIABLE AUDITS	PERCENTAGE DIFFERENCE*
Bangladesh	68.30	58.98	15.80
China	65.43	54.99	18.90
India	54.08	48.80	10.81
United States	43.59	49.12	12.60
Vietnam	56.72	53.22	5.54

*Percentage difference is calculated as the difference between the averages of reliable and unreliable audits expressed as a percentage from the average of unreliable audits.

TABLE 1.8. Average number of labor standards violations per audit by country and credibility, 2011–2017

COUNTRY	AUDIT CREDIBILITY	2011	2012	2013	2014	2015	2016	2017
Bangladesh	Reliable	3.70	3.74	3.31	3.56	3.74	3.36	3.51
	Unreliable	2.61	2.02	2.02	0.95	1.45	1.25	1.83
China	Reliable	4.42	4.73	4.55	4.44	4.64	4.99	4.71
	Unreliable	1.00	1.52	1.85	1.77	1.96	2.37	2.37
India	Reliable	3.41	3.59	3.36	3.46	3.71	3.71	3.56
	Unreliable	1.17	0.92	0.82	0.58	0.99	1.07	1.51
United States	Reliable	0.26	0.22	0.24	0.90	0.46	1.03	0.51
	Unreliable	2.50	N/A	N/A	0.14	0.00	0.00	0.33
Vietnam	Reliable	2.15	2.48	2.08	1.89	1.88	2.25	2.56
	Unreliable	1.67	1.00	1.47	1.36	0.97	1.45	1.80

TABLE 1.9. Average working hours by country and audit credibility, 2011–2017

COUNTRY	AUDIT CREDIBILITY	2011	2012	2013	2014	2015	2016	2017
Bangladesh	Reliable	69.44	69.79	71.03	72.79	71.84	71.23	68.30
	Unreliable	N/A	N/A	55.96	55.95	55.91	56.47	58.98
China	Reliable	64.28	63.50	63.98	64.35	64.42	64.77	65.43
	Unreliable	N/A	84.83	51.97	52.19	53.23	54.02	54.99
India	Reliable	62.85	62.07	60.16	57.50	56.16	55.81	54.08
	Unreliable	51.88	50.00	50.36	50.27	49.63	49.68	48.80
United States	Reliable	42.35	40.37	42.80	44.94	42.44	41.49	43.59
	Unreliable	39.00	N/A	N/A	39.85	20.77	87.01	49.12
Vietnam	Reliable	61.59	60.33	58.39	55.60	55.90	56.91	56.72
	Unreliable	53.07	54.77	54.22	N/A	53.02	53.64	53.22

representation. It appears AUDCO has been able, gradually, to convince suppliers it audits to provide more reliable data.

Is it possible to predict which suppliers are more likely to provide unreliable audits? It stands to reason that the decision by supplier factory management to falsify or present accurate data is influenced by a number of observable factory financial characteristics, the clients served, experience with auditing. and so forth, as well as by a number of unobservable management attitudes. Lacking data, an analysis of the factors affecting audit credibility is, at best, speculative.

Nevertheless, table 1.10 shows that country and industry matter, although *why* is unclear. Larger factories in which workers are paid better are more likely to have reliable audit information compared with smaller factories that pay less. Controlling for other factors, as the average monthly take-home pay increases by US$10, the odds of audits being more reliable increases by a factor of 1.043. Sim-

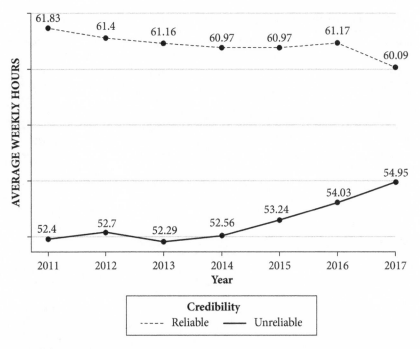

FIGURE 1.1. Weekly working hours, credibility of audits, all countries, average and yearly changes

Chart by author.

ilarly, while controlling for other predictors, the larger the factory, the more reliable are the audit data. For example, as a factory gains one thousand more workers, it is 1.428 times more likely to provide reliable data. (This result, it should be noted, is conditional on all the data in the dataset being reliable, which is not the case.) Reliability is likely to be higher in electronics, food, footwear, and toys than in the apparel industry; and most countries exhibit higher levels of audit reliability than China, controlling for other variables. Clearly the year of audit is significant as well. The data in table 1.10 suggest that the rate of change in the credibility of audits has declined since 2012. From 2015, the rate of decline in audit unreliability (compared with 2011) has become smaller, but, nevertheless, the odds of audit unreliability for 2017 are only 0.1036 times (that is, almost 90 percent of) those odds for 2011. In summary, country matters, industry matters, the year matters, and factory size and average take-home pay matter.

Replicating the analysis just completed within China and India reveals that states (in India) and provinces (in China) matter, although we do not know what characteristics of provinces and industries are driving those results.[7] The key implication of these analyses is that we do not have the right variables in our

TABLE 1.10. Factors affecting audit credibility

FACTORS	AUDIT CREDIBILITY	FACTORS	AUDIT CREDIBILITY
Worker number (by 1000)	0.428*** (0.031)	Agriculture	−0.093 (0.465)
Monthly take-home (by 10 USD)	0.042*** (0.002)	Apparel accessories	0.144** (0.063)
Bangladesh	2.259*** (0.117)	Electronics	0.458*** (0.07)
Cambodia	2.302*** (0.215)	Food	0.513*** (0.16)
Ethiopia	1.987** (0.829)	Footwear	0.434*** (0.059)
India	1.037*** (0.097)	Toys	0.327*** (0.105)
Indonesia	3.464*** (0.205)	Year 2012	0.752*** (0.271)
Italy	1.712* (1.037)	Year 2013	−2.576*** (0.178)
Jordan	2.390*** (0.410)	Year 2014	−3.203*** (0.176)
Mexico	6.169*** (0.728)	Year 2015	−3.162*** (0.177)
Turkey	1.879*** (0.206)	Year 2016	−2.909*** (0.177)
United States	0.489 (0.449)	Year 2017	−2.267*** (0.177)
Vietnam	2.287*** (0.109)	Constant	0.950*** (0.185)
Observations		19,007	
Log likelihood		−8,936.617	
Akaike inf. crit.		17,925.240	

$*p < 0.1$; $**p < 0.05$; $***p < 0.01$

Note: Values within parentheses are standard errors.

model; a number of variables related to factory characteristics are required to get at important determinants of why some factories choose to falsify audit data.

Overall, this analysis shows that we can trust only audits labeled reliable, or between 50 and 68 percent of all audits conducted over a seven-year period. Reliable and unreliable audits differ systematically: unreliable audits are liable to produce much more positive results on a variety of variables relating to working conditions as well as other aspects of codes of conduct.

Even though the percentage of unreliable audits appears to be steadily decreasing in most countries and industries, the high percentage of unreliable audits is a major cause for concern. The inability to measure the behavior of suppliers accurately calls into question the efficacy of private regulation programs of global firms. Behavioral invisibility, therefore, remains a key problem in private regulation with respect to labor standards.

The Role of the Audit Consulting Industry in Falsifying Data

Scant attention has been paid to how suppliers falsify their data to "pass" audits. To understand how suppliers are able to bamboozle the typical auditor, let's look at audit consulting companies, "gray" actors in private regulation that provide a range of services to help suppliers "pass" audits.

China is one of two countries with the highest percentage of unreliable audit data. The country is rife with both consultants and courses that help factories evade auditing.[8] ACCs help by falsifying records, coaching workers, and otherwise making the actual behavior of suppliers invisible to auditors. ACCs thus help suppliers reap the benefits of compliance without bearing the cost of improving labor conditions. The lack of reliable data that results from ACC activity is a major and hitherto unstudied cause of the decoupling between brands' practices and outcomes as a result of behavioral invisibility. ACC activities contribute to the opacity in the field of private regulation.

ACC Advertising

How do audit consulting companies obtain clients for their services? How do they work, and what do they do to help their supplier factory clients "pass" social audits? And why do these ACC services succeed? This is a secretive industry; fieldwork in these companies is impossible and potentially dangerous. To answer these questions requires more indirect methods.

We identified fifteen audit consulting companies (yan chang zi xun in Mandarin) in China's Guangdong Province (see table 1.11 for company names), clustered in and around the Pearl (Dongguan, Shenzhen, and Zhongshan) and Yangtze (Shanghai, Qingdao, and Ningbo) Rivers' delta regions—major production centers for a number of industries. On their websites, these companies typically describe themselves as business-management or corporate image-management consultants that provide training services aimed at helping their customers pass various types of social audits.

We also obtained data in the form of an audit consultant's work logs[9] posted publicly on Tianya, a popular online forum that bills itself as "an online home for global Chinese."[10] Tianya includes both advertisements and discussions about audit consulting. This consultant refers to himself as an "audit coach." We studied

TABLE 1.11. Audit consulting companies

NO.	COMPANY NAME	OFFICIAL WEBSITE	LOCATION OF HEADQUARTERS
1	Chuang Sheng	http://www.csr007.com/	Dongguan, Guangdong province
2	Bo Sheng	http://www.bsdgco.com/	Dongguan, Guangdong province
3	Chao Wang	http://www.sa8000cn.cn/	Shanghai province
4	Jiu Yu	http://www.bsci365.com/	Shenzhen, Guangdong province
5	Jin Ce	http://www.goldideaemc.com/	Shenzhen, Guangdong province
6	Zhong Bang	http://www.cocbang.cn/	Qingdao, Shandong province
7	Ai Er Li	http://www.allyservice.com/cn/	Guangzhou, Guangdong province
8	Wei Bo	http://www.vbcoc.com/	Shenzhen, Guangdong province
9	Jie Shun	http://www.ijetsun.com/	Shenzhen, Guangdong province
10	Feng Xin	http://www.chinacocservice.com/	Shenzhen, Guangdong province
11	Guo Han	http://www.nbguohan.com/	Ningbo, Zhejiang province
12	Yan Chang Bao	http://www.x-cotec.com/	Suzhou, Jiangsu province
13	Ken Da Xin	http://www.cts-com.com/default.aspx	Shenzhen, Guangdong province
14	Yuan Xin Da	http://www.yxd998.com/	Shenzhen, Guangdong province
15	Sheng Bang	http://www.sagd.cn/	Zhongshan, Guangdong province

the work logs dated June 19, 2016, to January 24, 2018, when the audit coach ceased making updates.

The analysis of what was gleaned from the fifteen ACC websites and the work log was conducted using grounded theory methodology, an inductive process to generate new theory by examining the concepts emerging from the data.[11] Table 1.12 summarizes the themes generated by analyzing the advertisements of the audit consulting companies. The audit news updates and tips typically reference the latest audit requirements and recent changes in codes of conduct and standards. One news update, for example, reported "Walmart's 2018 requirements for fire protection in the factory." Updates on audit developments are quite timely. Table 1.13 provides some other examples.

Examples of other common tips on ACC websites reveal how these companies aim to help suppliers "pass the audits." These are generally "teasers" to attract business. One ACC summarized its tip for documenting checks: "On the day of audit, all the old materials (workers' written requests for leave, record books, production orders, material labels, etc., all sets of documents that conflict with the set literally prepared for audit) must be packaged, sealed in cartons, and moved to areas that are not participating in this audit." This implication of this tip is that it is well-accepted that factories keep two sets of books with guidance from these consultants and that certain parts of the factories can be kept hidden from auditors.

Most ACCs also tout cases in which their customers successfully passed audits. Some list cases chronologically to advertise long-term high "pass" rates, whereas

TABLE 1.12. Main advertising points of fifteen companies

THEME	MAIN ADVERTISING POINT	FREQUENCY OF USAGE
Guarantee	100% pass if clients use the ACC's consulting services	15/15
	Pass audit in one training iteration	8/15
Information and advice	Provide auditing news and developments; share tips for success	15/15
Examples of success	Provide examples of successful cases in which suppliers have passed brand audits with help of the ACC	13/15
Guanxi	Emphasize the ACC's strong relationships and networks with auditing companies used by major brands	12/15
Expertise	Highlight expertise of team (especially prior work experience as auditors)	8/15
Software	High-quality management software that can generate falsified records quickly	8/15

TABLE 1.13. Audit news updates (translated from Chinese)

ARTICLE DATE	TITLE	KEY CONTENT
February 16, 2016	2016 Walmart audit: 24 problems that can be rectified on-site	In March 2016, Walmart clearly pointed out that the following problems are acceptable for on-site rectification: E.g., evacuation plan: emergency evacuation plan · Is not present; · Does not have "YOU ARE HERE" mark; · Does not match facility layout; · Is not in language spoken by majority of employees.
July 4, 2017	Walmart's latest announcement— officially accepted eight major programs from August 1, 2017	Walmart issued a notice that from August 1, 2017, they will officially accept the following eight audit programs for its factories. These include: ICTI, BSCI, SEDEX, EICC, WARP, SA8000, BAP, ILO.
November 22, 2018	Attention! Walmart's latest important official announcement	Beginning February 1, 2019, Walmart will require that audit reports used to satisfy Walmart's Responsible Sourcing audit requirements be conducted by an Association of Professional Social Compliance (APSCA)-registered auditor. And there is no change for eight audit programs.

others group cases by different brands' private regulation programs or different "certification" programs to show the wide range of their services. Figure 1.2 is an example; as shown, the list is explicit, showing the names of factories, type of audit, and brand or retailer whose audits the supplier factory has passed successfully. Each entry also includes a picture and a short story about how the ACC helped the factory.

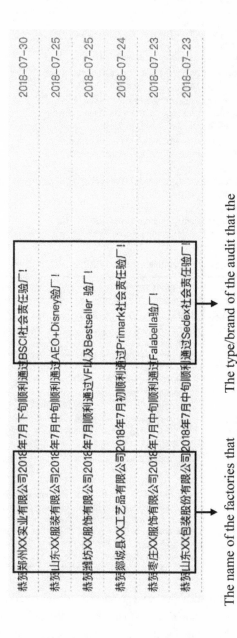

The name of the factories that have been trained

The type/brand of the audit that the factories passed successfully: e.g., BSCI, AEO+Disney, Bestseller, Primark, Sedex, and so on.

FIGURE 1.2. An example of a successful customer case list in an audit consulting advertisement: "Success Cases." Zhongbang Consulting, Zhongbang (accessed April 30, 2020, cocbang.com/cases).

ACCs also highlight *guanxi*—their strong social networks—in their website advertising, particularly their relationships with companies that do the auditing for various brands or with specific auditors that audit for brands. The implication is that this network can be leveraged when a factory is facing audit problems. In fact, some ACCs indicate these networks with auditing companies are so strong that the ACCs can even ensure that "that they can designate a specified auditor in advance."

With respect to team expertise of their personnel, ACCs often tout that their company includes many people who used to be auditors. For example, "Our core team is mainly composed of auditors from third-party notary banks and certification bodies (ITS, SGS, BV, UL, TUV, CQC, SAI, NSF, etc.). The team members have rich work experience and major industry connections. The network helps customers to successfully pass various audits and certifications." Figure 1.3, which highlights expertise with the SA8000 standard, is an example of such claims.

When it comes to "management software," ACCs generally claim they can generate falsified records quickly. For example, one ACC claims that "by using our management software, one month's audit data of a factory that has more than one thousand people can be generated in just thirty minutes." Figure 1.4 provides

我们的团队:
多名在中国最早参与企业推动COC/SA8000标准的专家及长期从事社会责任审核的资深审核员。
所有参与顾问人员都接受过正规的SA8000培训并在审核界具有丰富的实际经验及良好的人脉。

介绍及服务特点:
SAI认可之SA8000主任审核员
具有丰富的审核经验。服务于公证行及洋行期间，曾对数百家、各种不同类型的工作进行过SA8000、COC等方面的审核

"多名在中国最早参与企业推动COC/SA8000标准的专家及长期从事社会责任审核的资深审核员": "Many of them are experts who first to promote the COC/SA8000 standard in China and senior auditors who have long been engaged in social responsibility audits."

"SAI认可之SA8000主任审核员, 具有丰富的审核经验": "Our group leader used to work as a SAI-approved SA8000 senior auditor, with extensive experience in auditing..."

FIGURE 1.3. Claims regarding expertise of auditors: "About us." Shenzhen Fengxin Business Co. Ltd. (accessed April 30, 2020, chinacocservice.com /channel/type/1-1.html).

"工资考勤自动生成": "Payroll and attendance records can be automatically generated"

"百种验厂体系文件记录, 90 秒一键自动生成": "Hundreds of inspection system documentation, 90 seconds automatic one-click generation"

FIGURE 1.4. Advertising regarding "Software": "Jince Home." Goldidea; Jince Enterprise Management Consulting (accessed April 30, 2020, goldideaemc.com).

a further example; Figure 1.5 is a screenshot (with translation) of one ACC's website advertising most of the themes found.

Another ACC even designs an online questionnaire for factories to conduct self-assessments before training (see figure 1.6). These "self-assessment surveys for potential clients" are based on different audit programs of various companies (e.g., Disney) or various standards (such as BSCI and SA8000) and are designed to suggest to potential clients the ACC's deep expertise and familiarity with every criterion of the different standards and codes for different types of audits. The questionnaires also provide the ACC with a quick understanding of the potential client's situation and a baseline measurement that can be compared with outcomes after training. These before-and-after comparisons can be recycled as advertising.

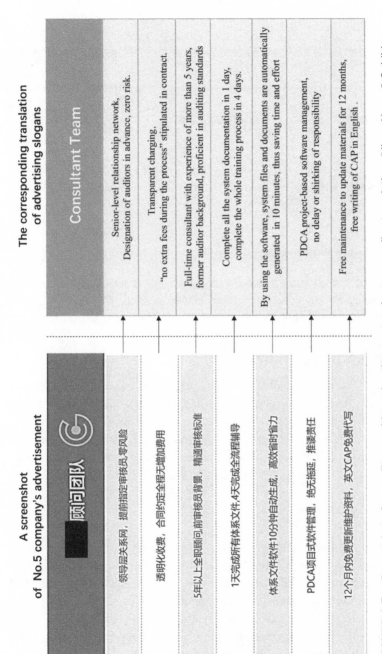

FIGURE 1.5. Screenshot of an audit consulting advertisement and corresponding translation: "Jince Home." Goldidea; Jince Enterprise Management Consulting (accessed April 30, 2020, goldideaemc.com).

"验厂项目自评": "Self-assessment of Different Audit Program"

FIGURE 1.6. Screenshot of online self-assessment of different audit programs from a company's advertisement: "Factory self-evaluation." CSR Home Factory Inspection (accessed April 30, 2020, csr007.com/selfcheck).

The Work of an Audit Coach

While the ACC website advertisements provide a look at how these audit consultants present themselves, the work logs of an actual audit consultant on the Tianya forum offer very different insights. The activities of the self-described audit "coach" can be classified into services provided immediately *before* an audit (apart from self-assessments), *during* the audit, and *after* the supplier has passed the audit. Figure 1.7 shows activities *before* and *during* an audit.

BEFORE THE AUDIT

The preparatory *before* stage focuses on preparing a set of "perfect" documents that present a positive picture of the factory. These include a complete set of documents recording falsified payroll (including wages, hours, overtime, and social security contributions), attendance, hours of work, and leave and holiday pay, as well as related documents. For instance, the work log states, "Around one hundred people's attendance data for twelve months was generated and summarized, as well as the salary calculation and payroll check, all finished within four hours. That was pretty fast!"[12] This note in the work log is consistent with claims

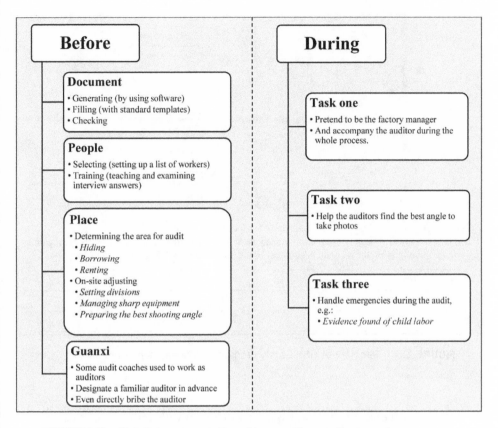

FIGURE 1.7. Pictorial representation of how audit consultants work

Chart by author.

regarding the sophisticated software ACCs advertise that they use; this particular audit coach uses a TP-HRMS, a specially designed software program that can generate professional-looking HR records.

The next step involves filling in standardized templates of management regulations, production manuals, and other documents relating to compliance with local regulations. By making only small changes to the templates, the audit coach can easily *manufacture* nonexisting management rules and pretend there is a well-organized management system. Figure 1.8, a template example, shows that other than the two factories' names and dates and document codes (circled), everything in these two "GSV Safety Production Management Manual" documents is exactly the same.

Moreover, the audit coach trains the factory managers to make freshly faked documents look more realistic—namely, not newly printed. The work log states,

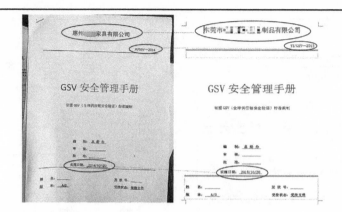

"GSV安全管理手册": "GSV Safety Production Management Manual"
Filled templates of GSV Safety Production Management Manual, while the only differences are regarding the two factories' names, the dates and document codes (in circles), also see in the table below.

"惠州**家具有限公司": Huizhou ** Furniture Co., Ltd.	"东莞市**制品有限公司": Dongguan ** Products Co., Ltd.
"实施日期" Implementation date: "2014/10/12"	"实施日期" Implementation date: "2015/10/20"
Code: "JF/GSV-2014"	Code: "YZ/GSV-2015"

FIGURE 1.8.   Template of GSV Safety Production Management Manual

Photo by Ning Li.

"And after the clerk printed it, I asked her to blow it with a fan to cool it down, and then wrinkle it several times before handing to the auditor."[13]

Checking involves a detailed examination of records for things such as employee dates of birth. For example, the audit coach wrote, "I began to organize the information of the workers for this audit. There were actually four underage workers, so then I just decisively deleted it."[14]

Figures 1.9 and 1.10 show further examples of falsification. The coach pays attention to attendance records on weekends and legal holidays, and figure 1.9 shows that, as he prepared for the QualSpec audit, when he noticed some attendance occurred on weekends and holidays, the dates were "fixed." Figure 1.10 shows the falsification of workers' birth dates. Under Chinese labor law, underage workers are those at least sixteen years of age and under eighteen, while work by those under sixteen constitutes child labor. China explicitly prohibits the use of child labor and imposes special labor protections for underage workers.[15] According to the work log, "when I printed attendance records, I discovered that there was actually an underage worker, so I immediately arranged for the assistant Xiaoqin to bring that worker's files and labor contract to the conference

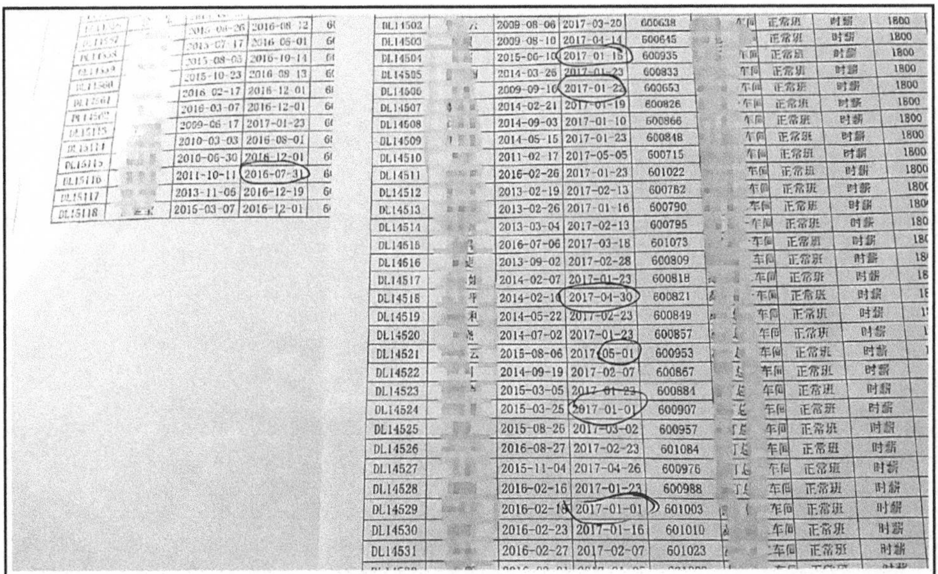

The dates circled, such as 2016-07-31, 2017-01-01, 2017-01-15, 2017-01-22, 2017-04-30, 2017-05-01, are either weekends or Chinese legal holidays.

FIGURE 1.9.   Checking details on attendance records on weekends/holidays

Photo by Ning Li.

room, and then asked Xiaolu to change the birth year from 1999 to 1998 on the worker's ID card by using photoshop."[16]

The second part of the *before* audit services concerns how the auditor will interact with real people. Most private regulation programs require that auditors interview workers to help determine whether the supplier is complying with the codes of the relevant companies. Typically, the auditors will select a sample of workers, but in many factories factory management provides the sample. The audit coach plays a key role in deciding which workers are selected. Audit consultants eliminate workers likely to cause trouble, and the workers selected are coached on how to respond to questions. Sometimes, these workers are tested through exams to determine how they might respond.

The work log provides several examples related to *selecting* and *training* workers: "The factory has nearly one hundred employees, and only eighty of them participated in this audit. The other twenty people do not have their ID card information or are underage, or usually are irresponsible and possibly will cause trouble, so they are excluded to avoid messing up the audit."[17] "Every time I go to the factory I have to provide a training lesson that lasts at least thirty minutes, and I also need to arrange a written examination to test."[18]

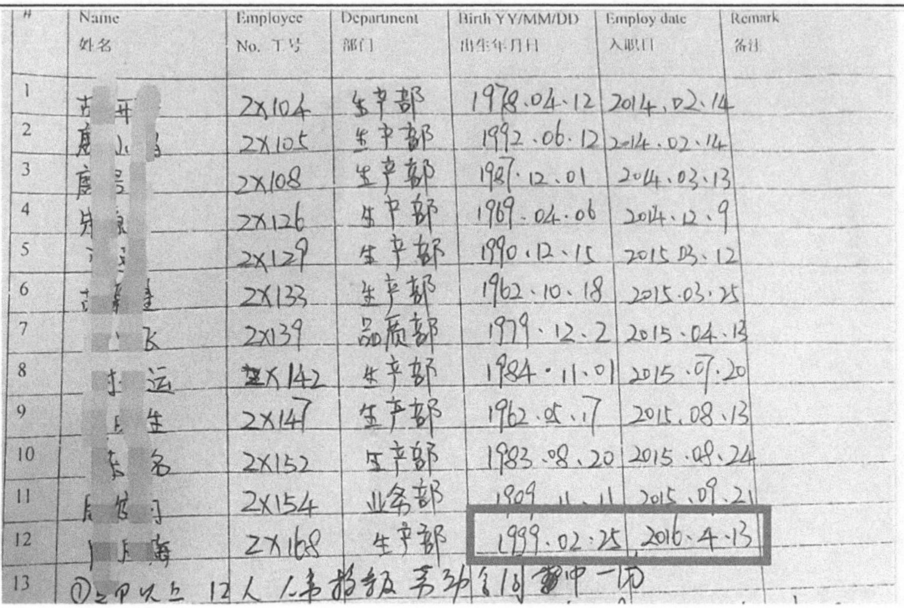

#	Name 姓名	Employee No. 工号	Department 部门	Birth YY/MM/DD 出生年月日	Employ date 入职日	Remark 备注
1	吉 平	2X104	生产部	1978.04.12	2014.02.14	
2	夏).)	2X10t	生产部	1992.06.12	2014.02.14	
3	虔 乇	2X108	生产部	1987.12.01	2014.03.13	
4	月 贫	2X126	生产部	1969.04.06	2014.12.9	
5	) 3	2X129	生产部	1990.12.15	2015.03.12	
6	? 耷 圭	2X133	生产部	1962.10.18	2015.03.25	
7	) K	2X139	品质部	1979.12.2	2015.04.13	
8	土 运	2X142	生产部	1984.11.01	2015.07.20	
9	王 生	2X147	生产部	1962.05.17	2015.08.13	
10	庄 名	2X152	生产部	1983.08.20	2015.08.24	
11	床 戊 了	2X154	业务部	1809.11.11	2015.09.21	
12	) 上海	2X168	生产部	1999.02.25	2016.4.13	
13	①z尸以上 12人 1.号指报 事3部门目事中一份					

On the original document, Employee No.2X168 (born on 02/25/1999) was only 17 years old on the employment date of 04/13/2016. To avoid problems regarding underage workers, the audit coach then falsified the birth year to 1998.

FIGURE 1.10.   Underage workers

Photo by Ning Li.

Table 1.14 shows how a typical audit consultant might coach workers to provide desirable answers to auditors, using a Disney audit as an example. The audit consultants summarize interview questions typically asked by auditors for Disney and provide a range of "correct" answers.

The third part of the *before* audit services involves preparing the factory workplace. Typically, the audit coach works with the owner or manager to determine which areas will be audited, often by *hiding* some areas from auditors—for example, by saying those areas are undergoing renovations or are not being used—as a way to narrow down the physical scope of the audit. The audit coach will then make several adjustments to the open areas so they will meet the requirements of the codes and standards. As the work log states, "On my suggestion, manager Z agreed to my plan: only the third floor will be audited, while the second floor will not be included in the BRC audit scope. In this way, the second floor can be vacated to store the messy materials, tools, equipment, etc. Meanwhile the third-floor workshop can be fully utilized. More important, this can save the cost of hardware renovation and facilitate construction."[19]

TABLE 1.14. Coaching examples for correct answers

STANDARD THEMES IN DISNEY'S CODE OF CONDUCT	EXAMPLE QUESTIONS	CORRECT ANSWERS ACCORDING TO COACHING
Compensation	How much was the salary last month?	Answer by the note provided; I can't remember; There was a payroll; I have signed it for confirmation; I sign it once a month (remember how much the base salary is per hour)
	When was it issued?	
	Was there a payroll?	
	Was there a signature confirmation?	
	How many times a month do you sign salary slips?	
	Is there any deduction for resignation?	Salary is paid without deduction. The salary will be settled by the last day of the resignation (or I am not very clear about it).
	Is salary paid immediately?	
Coercion and harassment	If employees make mistakes, does the managers of the company abuse employees?	No. The managers only criticize and educate employees who make mistakes.
Health and safety	Did you received training from the factory when you entered?	I have received training in factory discipline and regulations, labor insurance supplies usage, chemicals usage, machine operation safety, etc. Or I am not tired. I have no other opinions about the factory.
	What were the training contents? Were you tired?	
	What other opinions do you have about the factory?	
	How many fire drills a year?	Twice a year. The most recent one was in May (Exercise Content: Escape, Number Counting, Fire Extinguishing). The workshop has fire-fighting equipment/fire route map; if there is a fire, run away immediately from the scene.
	Does the workshop have fire-fighting equipment?	
	What if there is a fire?	
	Are there protective gloves, masks and earplugs on the production line?	Yes, there are. They are for free.
	Is there a charge?	
	Does the company buy insurance for you?	Yes, and no deduction. Unified purchases by the company. Just say you are not clear about it if being asked about details.
	No deduction?	
Association	Is there a trade union in the factory? Who are the employee representatives?	There is a trade union in the factory, and the employee representatives are XX, XX. They are elected by election meeting and employees voting. If we have any opinions about the factory, we can ask the employee representatives to reflect it, or write a letter of opinion, or directly go to the general manager.
	How did employee representatives come into being?	
	What if you have an opinion about the factory?	
Child labor	Have you ever seen children working or helping their parents work here?	No. No.
	Does the factory employ temporary workers or underage workers?	
Involuntary labor	Does the factory force employees to work or intentionally prolong their working hours (e.g. deducting money or voluntary rework if you do not work overtime, etc.)?	There is no forced or deliberate prolongation of working hours in the factory.

An alternative is to "borrow" certain areas from another factory in the same building or nearby. The work log explains how this works: "The factory's production workshop is connected to another factory of the same type, and every time, for audit needs, they have to borrow the workshop from the other factory . . . and they also need to temporarily fence up an area to hide their own paper cutting materials, raw materials, and finished products."[20] If borrowing is not possible, the audit coach will advise the factory to *rent* another workshop for a short period, especially if the real workshop is extremely old and does not meet certain basic standards, and the cost of hardware renovation is too high.

Once the physical space to be audited, the audit coach will lead the management team in making *on-site adjustments*, such as ensuring there are enough safety exits and that the width and opening direction of doors meet requirements. Creating or setting divisions involves demarcation of "messy" areas and providing a sense of order, with appropriate signage. The examples in figure 1.11 show signs for different areas, already prepared for use.

Finding the best shooting angle for photographs is an important task. The audit coach once taught a manager that "though we cannot completely meet all the standards, we must provide a perfect angle for the auditor to take photos, so it will be easier for them to write the report."[21] Figure 1.12 shows how messy and dirty workshops are transformed into acceptable ones; during this process, the best shooting angle is also determined.

Leveraging *guanxi*, the final part of the *before* audit services, is a key element of the preparation phase. Audit consultants use their networks to influence who the auditor might be, believing that auditors in their social networks can be swayed to ensure the factory will pass the audit. As the work log states: "This time it's

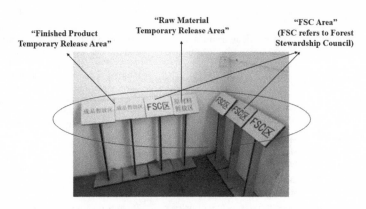

FIGURE 1.11.   Signs prepared for different areas

Photo by Ning Li.

FIGURE 1.12. "Before" and "after" photos

Photo by Ning Li.

auditor W. I met him at a factory in Zhongshan, and our relationship was quite good. At this point, the result of the audit was already known, and the rest was just going through the motions step by step."[22]

There is even evidence that the audit coach can, on occasion, use his network connections with auditing firms to designate a specific auditor to be sent out on that day to audit the factory:

> At 8:10 in the morning, I arrived at the factory on time . . . the IPS auditor came in.
> Auditor Z: It's you! This time it's still your order?
> Me: Yes, we meet again.
> Auditor Z: I didn't have this one. Did you designate on your side?[23]

DURING THE AUDIT

After preparation activities, the focus moves to services *during* the audit. This stage involves coaching management representatives to answer auditor questions.

The typical audit begins with a meeting between the auditors and the management of the company. It is imperative that management representatives have the confidence to respond to questions as well as handle on-the-spot situations as auditors inspect the factory. Preparation may involve auditors role-playing factory managers. The work log describes multiple instances of such role-playing.

Another *during* activity is to influence the auditor to take photos that show a positive image of the factory. One work log entry describes how, during an audit for Nestlé, an auditor took photos only from predetermined shooting angles and deliberately avoided unfavorable photos, such as views of moldy walls or a floor covered with water.[24]

Getting the right photographs is often a negotiated process between the audit consultant and the auditor. As the work log described it: "Back to the office, the auditor Z called me aside and warned me, 'I don't want to say anything. You should know that even though the materials are prepared so well, if I cannot take pictures for the report, the result still equals zero. Because we are acquaintances, this time I will still write the report according to the requirements of the C level, but if I come across a scene next time where I can't find the angle to take the photo again, I will not be so kind.'"[25]

The audit consultant also role-plays the manager to show how to handle emergencies during the audit. The work log provides an example. The coach knew through his network that auditor E would arrive on July 16 for an unannounced ALDO audit. Checking the employee roster that morning, the auditor found a man and a woman with birthdays and start dates that would classify them as engaged in child labor. Everyone was nervous, with no idea how to rectify the situation—the auditor had already seen the roster.

The consultant decided the best way to deal with the situation was to say that the roster entries were mistaken. He suggested the auditor should substantiate the information by examining the two workers' ID cards. While the auditor continued on his rounds, the consultant called an assistant to rush to the nearest advertising store and scan the two ID cards and then photoshop new birth dates. Twenty minutes later, the fake ID card copies were ready. In the intervening time, the coach trained the two employees to answer the auditors' questions about their "new" ages—including their signs on the Chinese zodiac. Both workers presented their newly photoshopped ID cards to the auditor and passed their age interviews.[26]

The benefits to the audit consultant if a factory successfully passes the audit are significant—generally referred to as a "double harvest." The factory management's satisfaction with the services ensures repeat business, which may turn into a longer-term contract rather than a per-audit contract. The work log provides an example: "We signed the contract for the whole year. Every month, I have to go to the factory for teaching, inspecting, and training for two days."[27]

The "success" can also be touted in advertisements and may result in the factory manager making referrals to other potential clients. In some cases, the close interactions between audit consultant and auditor can result in the auditor recommending the consultant. The work log offers an example: The coach met an auditor in 2015 while he was auditing a factory in Fuyong. The auditor realized that the outcome was due largely to the training the audit consultant had provided, and so the auditor introduced the consultant to another factory.[28]

The work log shows how audit consulting services are charged: "Consultation fee payment: All expenses involved in this contract are paid in RMB [renminbi] and in cash. If the factory declares the number of people within ninety-nine, the total amount in the contract is 43,000 yuan (excluding tax). If the factory declares the number of people more than one hundred, the total amount in the contract is 55,000 yuan (excluding tax). The price quoted in this contract includes consultant travel expenses, BSCI [Business Social Compliance Initiative] certification audit fee, red envelope fee for auditor, consultant accommodation fee, RSP [responsibility] fee (BSCI audit authorization), checking time fee. Lunch fee on the audit day is excluded."[29]

One training iteration typically costs around US$6,397 for factories employing less than one hundred workers and US$8,182 if there are more than one hundred workers. This includes the audit fee (the average fee per auditor in China is US$737) but is still relatively high. Why, then, do factories choose to spend that much? The training process saves time, and, for the factories, the more time saved, the less the impact on their normal production work. It typically takes less than three days for all the *before* work. Apart from the time savings, it may be that the cost to make genuine improvements may be higher than the cost of falsifying records.

AFTER THE AUDIT

Once a factory receives a "passing" grade from the auditors, it receives orders from the global buyer that commissioned the audit. The factory management is likely to hire the same audit coach or audit consulting firm to "pass" audits of other global buyers. The factory may well enter into a longer-term relationship with the audit consultant to coach its workers. Further, the factory management may recommend the audit consultant's services to other factories. The audit consulting company gets to advertise the success on its website, thus paving the way for more business. And finally, the audit consultant meets new auditors to add to his or her network. Clearly, it's a win-win situation—in the coach's words, a "double harvest."

All this indicates that, at least in the geographic regions of China analyzed, the audit consulting industry has become a mature industry and is thriving. The main product of this industry is the "symbolic" compliance of suppliers. The work log of the "third-level audit consultant" suggests that, in most cases, he had a roster of regular clients and substantial repeat business.

The audit consulting industry is thriving because it fills a need. The interests of brands and suppliers differ; brands want suppliers to introduce good labor practices but do not want to compensate suppliers for these labor practices through higher prices for their products.[30] From the suppliers' perspective, factories will truly adopt better labor practices only when they expect the associated benefits to outweigh the costs.[31]

The gap between buyer and supplier interests continues to grow, especially in the apparel industry, which has experienced relentless downward price pressure. A report from the Pennsylvania State University Center for Global Workers' Rights, for example, suggests that the price for trousers paid to Bangladeshi suppliers by US firms declined by 11.48 percent between 2013 and 2017. Such a "pricing squeeze" resulted in a decline in Bangladeshi exporter profits of about 13 percent and a decline in real wages paid to Bangladeshi workers of approximately 6 percent.[32]

For Bangladeshi factories that are expected to comply with global buyers' codes of conduct, engaging in "symbolic" compliance is a rational strategy. Research in 2020 among Chinese exporters shows that labor standard violators enjoy higher average labor productivity and profit margins than compliant firms, even after adjusting for key determinants of productivity and profitability.[33] This result implies that respect for worker rights is not necessarily associated with better performance, suggesting that there are real trade-offs to improving compliance for suppliers facing a pricing and sourcing squeeze from global buyers.

This rational strategy on the part of suppliers is facilitated by an audit consulting industry that helps supplier factories reap the benefits of adoption without bearing the costs.[34] As auditing has become more complex—the typical auditor has a list of two hundred issues that need to be checked in a very short time frame—the "professional" services and high-quality software developed by ACCs fill the void and ensure that supplier factories "pass" audits and continue to get business from brands. The growing complexity of auditing itself therefore has a direct impact on the growth of the audit consulting industry.

Conclusion

Viewed from the perspective of the institutional theory that anchors this book, the role of the audit consulting industry conforms to the notion of "ceremonial" management in the case of *suppliers*.[35] Institutional theory emphasizes that organizations are structured not only by the demands of technical production and exchange but also in response to rationalized institutional rules.[36] Technical production and exchange demand efficiency, while institutional demands require organizations to gain legitimacy. Given that maintaining legitimacy sometimes conflicts with efficiency, a decoupling of policy and practice occurs. Suppliers play the game by seeming to comply with the policies of global buyers, but this compliance is largely ceremonial and is designed for others to observe. Hence, audit consultants fill the role of "accrediting agencies" that proliferate in elaborate and complex institutional environments.[37]

More importantly, unreliable audits constitute a high percentage of all audits, and the unreliable data that audit consultants help to create make it impossible to measure the real behavior of suppliers, contributing to behavioral invisibility. Audit consultants' training services help factories disguise their noncompliance using perfectly faked evidence, which makes readily observing and accurately assessing the factories' behaviors impossible.[38] Global buyers have implemented a private regulation program, articulating codes of conduct and instituting elaborate auditing procedures, but without accurate measurement there will be a persistent gap between the practices of global buyers and concrete improvements in working conditions—the practice-outcome decoupling referenced earlier.[39]

It is surprising that the audit consulting industry is so open about offering these services. Chinese supplier factories appear well aware of ACC services and engage these consultants on a regular basis. It seems impossible that global buyers that use local auditors would not also be aware of these services and the sophistication these ACCs have when it comes to falsifying audit information and managing the audit process. Perhaps global buyers are complicit in this process of "myth and ceremony," and the technical procedures connected with auditing become ends in themselves for buyers who, because of behavioral invisibility, are unable to affect workers' outcomes meaningfully.[40]

PRACTICE MULTIPLICITY IN THE IMPLEMENTATION OF PRIVATE REGULATION PROGRAMS

Just as the behavioral invisibility discussed in chapter 1 creates opaqueness, so too does practice multiplicity—that is, the diversity of private regulation policies and practices adopted by the variety of actors in the private regulation ecosystem, spread across different geographic, institutional, economic, and cultural contexts. Simply put, "the higher the number of divergent practices encountered in a field, the more difficult it is for adopters to exhaustively understand and compare the merits and limitations of different practices. Ambiguity may be the result."[1]

As private regulation unfolded through the 1990s and early 2000s, the number of codes of conduct also proliferated—and there are now likely numerous different codes across different companies, each with some degree of variation. Where fire extinguishers should be placed in supplier factories is a notable example: One company's code specifies they should be mounted on the walls; another's specifies placement on the floor. Codes differ with respect to what is specified for safety and health, wages, and most labor standards.

Nongovernmental systems of private labor regulation is "more diverse" and "messier" than other regulatory approaches, since they "involve multiple actors in new roles and relationships, experimenting with new processes of standard setting, benchmarking and enforcement." As a result, we have "chains of standard setters, layers of monitoring and enforcement, and competing systems of incentives and action."[2]

While codes relating to labor standards were initially quite diverse,[3] individual company codes have gradually coalesced into multi-stakeholder institution (MSI) codes or industrywide codes, such as the Electronics Industry Code of

Conduct—eliminating some of the variation. Global companies agreed to abide by these MSI or industry-wide codes of conduct. By around 2003, there were at least seven different MSI codes in the apparel industry, several industry codes (such as those for electronics and toys), and many companies continued to have their own codes.

In the global apparel industry, the seven major MSIs include the Fair Labor Association (FLA), Worldwide Responsible Apparel Production (WRAP) certification, Social Accountability International (SAI), Ethical Trading Initiative (ETI), Fair Wear Foundation, Business Social Compliance Initiative (BSCI-Amfori), Workers Rights Consortium (WRC), and Sustainable Apparel Coalition (SAC). They compete for business participation and vary in how they approach private regulation in terms of the standards underlying their codes, how those codes are implemented and monitored, and how member companies are held accountable for progress.

While overall multiplicity was reduced through coalescence into these seven MSI codes, wide variations remain.

- *Scope*: Some codes focus on specific industries (e.g., FLA, FWF, and WRAP in the apparel and footwear sectors) and others on a broad range of industries (e.g., SAI).
- *Governance*: The issue of who controls the board of an association is quite crucial for membership; some are dominated by business representatives (e.g., WRAP), while others have multi-stakeholder representation on their boards.[4]
- *Monitoring processes*: Some, such as FLA and FWF, engage in internal monitoring, using their own auditors as well as selected external auditors, while others tend to outsource monitoring functions to global social auditing companies.
- *How factories are selected for auditing*: Some audit a sample of members factories (FLA and FWF), whereas others do no auditing at all (ETI).
- *What specifically is certified*: FLA and ETI, for example, certify a company's private regulation program, whereas SAI certifies specific factories.
- *Member requirements and reporting*: Audit reports are provided either to the multi-stakeholder organization (e.g., FLA), directly to factories (SAI), or both (WRAP); one commonality across most MSIs is that none requires public disclosure of audit reports (FLA does disclose a few audit reports on its website; SAI discloses the names of certified factories but not the associated audit reports).
- *Underlying standards*: All MSI codes rely on the International Labour Organization's core labor standards of freedom from forced labor,

freedom from child labor, freedom from discrimination at work, and freedom of association and the right to collective bargaining. Regarding noncore standards such as wages, MSI codes show variation. Most require a minimum wage, and several (e.g., ETI, WRC, SAI, and FWF) require a wage above the minimum that provides some amount of discretionary income for the worker—in other words, some form of a "living wage." WRAP's code, for example, refers to wages paid in accordance with national and local laws. FLA's code requires the minimum wage but generally encourages its members to ensure a wage that provides discretionary income.

The factory auditing research project at the University of California, Santa Barbara, has developed a more fine-grained comparison of the *wording* of codes of conduct of several MSIs.[5] However, evaluating differences in the wording of codes of conduct can be misleading, since some MSIs may keep their code of conduct documents brief while relying on additional documents to elaborate members' obligations.

Within MSIs themselves, members may vary in how they implement private regulation because of how they interpret code provisions. For instance, after years of intense internal discussion, the FLA agreed to a fair compensation principle but did not add to the code an *unambiguous* statement of measurable standards that could guide action and evaluation. Rather, regarding compensation, the code states:

> Every worker has a right to compensation for a regular work week that is sufficient to meet the worker's basic needs and provide some discretionary income. Employers shall pay at least the minimum wage or the appropriate prevailing wage, whichever is higher, comply with all legal requirements on wages, and provide any fringe benefits required by law or contract. Where compensation does not meet workers' basic needs and provide some discretionary income, each employer shall work with the FLA to take appropriate actions that seek to progressively realize a level of compensation that does.[6]

Clearly, this allows FLA member companies to meet the FLA code by ensuring that their suppliers pay "minimum wages," not necessarily "living wages."

Why do these variations persist, despite overwhelming agreement on the need for some degree of policy convergence to prevent a regulatory race to the bottom? Some research suggests a "political difference" explanation—that the different private governance organizations are "tailored to a fragmented market in terms of sectors and geography, with complex power relationships between firms" that lead to a lack of convergence. Further, differences in the governance of these organizations, especially between organizations controlled by business versus organizations with more widely shared governance, prevented convergence. The history of the evolution of these organizations, especially when they had conflicting views regarding standards and implementation, has some "repertoires of contention" created between the organizations that prevented convergence. These political differences account for the persistent divergences we see in private governance.[7]

Such differences are evident in other industries as well. The "ongoing co-existence of multiple standards" in the coffee industry, for example, is partly the result of the 'countervailing mechanisms' of 'convergence' (increasingly, the standards focus on the same basic rules) and 'differentiation' (driven by the interests of the firms and standards organizations in preserving their identity and autonomy)."[8] In apparel, rather like with Fair Trade Coffee, persistent divergences are driven by the diverse interests of firms, NGOs, and standards organizations in preserving their identities and autonomy and control over the private regulation implementation process.

All this variation is a problem: it "complicates the work that industry players have to do to implement policies" and "contributes to a sense of confusion among an external audience of consumers, governments, and activists groups." Even more significantly, variation "increases the risk of a regulatory race to the bottom."[9] The diversity of approaches has led to "confusion and debate" about the costs and benefits of private regulation, since "the substance, scope, implementation, participation, accountability, and transparency of inspection results can vary considerably," while their underlying models are also quite different.[10]

This confusion and debate is the result of practice multiplicity and is a fundamental cause of the decoupling between private regulation policies and positive outcomes for workers. For a more detailed view of practice multiplicity in action, I now turn to an empirical investigation regarding multiplicity in the *implementation* of private regulation approaches by different companies sourcing from the same supplier.

Practice Multiplicity in Action

To examine the consequences of divergence within the private regulation initiatives in the global apparel industry, let's examine more directly the different ways in which global firms *enact* private governance. I've chosen a global supplier to many global brands in both the United States and Europe that belong to different multi-stakeholder organizations. If, rather than the brands, we study the supplier, and how the supplier *experiences* the approaches to private regulation of different brands, we can see better how brands differ in their implementation of private regulation approaches.

My argument is that the differences in how brands enact private regulation reflects a multiplicity of practices that causes opacity in the labor practices field, resulting in considerable supplier confusion about how to couple their labor practices to the needs of differing brands. This opacity also creates confusion among the brands themselves, hampering the identification of best practices that could create what in the theoretical literature is referred to as *isomorphic pressure* for convergence in the implementation of private regulation—that is, pressure on companies to imitate leading companies thought to be doing a good job, in a process that causes convergence to "best practice."

AAA is a vertically integrated manufacturer of woven and knit shirts, with annual revenues in excess of US$1.2 billion. It supplies more than seventy global brands. AAA is reputed to be a technological leader in shirt manufacturing, with a proven managerial capacity and a well-developed sustainability strategy.[11] As such, AAA is a very different entity from the stereotypical depiction of a low-cost garment supplier.

I collected general data regarding audits at AAA by its customer brands from all of its nine factories and specific data from two of its most advanced factories. Factory A, in Guangdong, China, was established in 1992 and has 4,038 employees (81 percent female); its workers are mainly local (73 percent), not migrants. The factory employs relatively advanced equipment (radio-frequency identification tags, pattern sewing machines, button machines, auto-run collar and cuff machines) and several processes are automated (folding, cutting, and spreading). Factory A had also met ISO9000 and ISO14001 quality standards. Factory B, also in Guangdong, is similar, except that it was founded in 1998 and has 6,400 employees. At the time of my visit, each of these two factories supplied approximately sixteen brands. As such, they constitute appropriate locations to see how the private regulation approaches of global brands differ.

My numerous interviews at the factories, which were largely unstructured, focused on understanding how AAA experiences the audits of the brands.[12] Table 2.1 lists the general variation in AAA customers' general private regulation approach.

In general, there is considerable variation in how AAA's customers—all well-known brands—have instituted their private regulation programs, and even more variation in how they evaluate supplier performance. Eight of the brands are members of the FLA, and seventeen are members of the Sustainable Apparel Coalition and thus are leading adopters of the private regulation model. I was surprised to find that twenty-four of the seventy-four global customers did not have a regulation

TABLE 2.1.   Overview of audits experienced by supplier AAA, 2014–2015

ITEM	ALL CUSTOMERS OF SUPPLIER AAA	FACTORY A	FACTORY B
Number of global customers with no known private regulation program (percentage of total customers)	24 (32%)		
Customers that provide AAA with code of conduct but do not audit	9 (12%)		
Customers that provide code of conduct and conduct audits regularly	11 (15%)		
Customers that provide code of conduct and accept generic audits or audits of other brands	20 (27%)		
Customers that provide code of conduct, audit regularly, and request other programs and initiatives	10 (14%)		
Total	74 (100%)		
Number of customers		14	18
Number of audits 2014–2015		24	32
Brand-conducted audits		7	11
Third-party audits		15	18
Number of third-party audit firms		9	9
Announced audits		19	20
Surprise audits		5	11
Audit fee paid by customer		15	13
Audit fee paid by factory		9	18
Person-days per audit		Range: 1–5 Mean: 2.2	Range: 1–9 Mean: 2.6
Mean cost per audit		$1,782	$1,398
Mean cost per auditor		$737	$632

program with respect to AAA, while the others varied in the extent to which private regulation was implemented. As for auditing, some brands do less than others.

The two factories experienced roughly one or more audits every month, with more than four audits in some months.[13] Some brands audited the factories themselves, but most subcontracted to third-party auditing firms. The majority of the audits were announced in advance, although a surprisingly large number were unannounced. In nearly half the cases, the brand required the factory to pay the auditors—a serious design flaw that can result in collusion between factory management and auditing firms. The cost per audit varied from as little as US$645 to as much as US$3,700.

AAA's chief sustainability officer described for me a key way in which auditing varies across customers: the extent to which auditors function as "coaches who are interested in removing root causes of violations" versus auditors who simply "check the box."[14]

Practice multiplicity became even more apparent when I examined specifics regarding how different brands conduct audits. Auditors must provide an overall rating of the factory; brands require this rating so that they can choose to factor it into their sourcing decisions. Factory managers, in my interviews, expressed their frustration with the problems caused by the *different rating scales* used by different brands and auditors, and the apparent lack of a clear connection between audit violations and the final rating.

Table 2.2 lists the rating scales used by brands. Given the differences between these rating scales, it is quite possible that the factory might receive an "acceptable"

TABLE 2.2.   Rating scales used by different brands when auditing supplier AAA

RANK OF CUSTOMER BY VOLUME	NUMBER OF POINTS ON RATING SCALE	SCALES
1	2	Acceptable, Needs improvement
2	6	Gold, Green, Yellow, Orange1, Orange2, Red
3	5	Good, Satisfactory, Improvements needed, Risky, Insufficient
4	5	Gold, Silver, Bronze, Yellow, Red
5	4	Accepted, Developmental, Pending rejection, Rejected
6	–	No scale
7	4	0–15, 16–49, 50–99, 100 + (not acceptable)
8	–	No scale
9	3	Green (86–100), Yellow (65–85), Red (0–64)
16	5	SAT (Satisfactory), NI (Needs improvement), NMI (Needs major improvement), DIA (Demands immediate action), ZT (Zero tolerance)
< 20	4	Excellent, Good, Fair, Poor
< 20	6	CAT1 (Excellent), CAT2 (Good), CAT3 (Fair), CAT4 (Needs improvement, CAT5 (unacceptable), CAT6 (Absolutely unacceptable)
< 20	4	Green (Satisfactory), Yellow (Needs improvement), Orange (Temporary), Red (Unacceptable)
< 20	4	Green (Low risk), Yellow (Medium risk), Orange (High risk), Red (Zero tolerance)
< 20	5	Green (Satisfactory), Yellow (Moderate violations), Orange (Needs significant improvement), Dark orange (Substantial remediation required), Red (Immediate remediation required)
< 20	5	A (Green, meeting compliance), B (Yellow, approaching compliance), C (Orange, substantial improvement required), D (Red, immediate remediation required), F (Gray, zero tolerance)

Note: The brands that rank below 20 change in the relative standing of volumes, year by year.

rating from one brand and an "unacceptable" rating from another brand in audits conducted during the same time frame. Factory corporate social responsibility (CSR) representatives suggested there was little effort by brands or auditors to link their rating scales to the findings found in the audit. In fact, the representatives suggested that the *rationale* for the ratings was shared in only 57 percent of the audits.

Using different rating scales leads to variation in the practices of auditors, resulting in different findings. Consider two scenarios. Table 2.3 shows audits done by different brands and auditing firms at Factory A only two days or a couple of weeks apart. The numbers and types of findings vary significantly, as do the ratings. This variation suggests that auditors of different brands and audit companies are looking for very different things in an audit, despite the commonality of most brands' codes of conduct.[15]

Table 2.4 shows audits in Factory B by one auditing firm representing three different brands within a two-week period. Although the individual auditors may have been different, it is curious that the same auditing *firm* found quite different violations, even one day apart. More significantly, the variations led to quite different ratings. While two of the ratings were in the "major deficiencies" class, one was much higher.

What is missing is any indication of the weight attached to each individual item (of more than two hundred items in most audits) used to arrive at the overall rating given by the auditors. It is possible that brands give their auditors generalized guidance in arriving at overall ratings and the leeway to exercise their own judgment. What these findings suggest is considerable variation in what auditors look for and actually find during their audits and how much weight auditors assign to each violation.

My interviews with AAA's sustainability staff suggest that the focus of auditing efforts—what auditors look for—is often influenced by brand experiences at other factories or in other countries. For instance, following the April 2013 fire at the Rana Plaza factory in Bangladesh, which killed more than 1,100 workers, most brands focused more on fire safety issues relative to other issues, and fire safety violations tended to have a greater weight in overall ratings in Factories A and B during the period of my data. Similarly, a brand experienced a chemical safety issue in one of its supplier factories elsewhere, and that experience was reflected immediately in a heightened focus on chemical issues in the auditing of these factories.

I found no relationship between the number of instances of noncompliance and the overall ratings provided by the auditors in fifty-six audits of AAA.[16] It is reasonable to hypothesize that audit reports that find a higher number of instances of noncompliance would result in a lower final rating. This hypothesis, however, does not appear to be confirmed by the data, as tables 2.5a and 2.5b show.

TABLE 2.3. Findings by different audit organizations when auditing Factory A, 2015

DATE	AUDIT ORGANIZATION	PERSON DAYS*	CODE CATEGORY	VIOLATION	RATING
3/16	Third-party A	2	W&B	One-week delay in payment to resigned employee	Major deficiencies
			Hours of work	Exceeded overtime extension permits	
3/18	Third-party B	2	Hours of work	Monthly overtime hours exceed legal maximum	Acceptable rating (No corrective action required)
			W&B	Wage to terminated employee not paid in 7 days	
			Hours	Buffer time exceeded 15 minutes	
			EHS	Rolling door not working properly	
7/7	Brand A	2	EHS	No eye protection on grinding machine	Brand has rating system, but no rating given by auditor
				No sandbag in chemical storage room	
				Door to dyeing room broken	
				Poor housekeeping issues	
			ER	Code of conduct not posted in location	
7/21	Brand B	1	W&B	Commercial accident insurance not yet paid for new workers	Developmental
			EHS	Smoke detector not working in dormitory	
				Third-party water testers not from approved list	
			ER	Joint fire safety program for two subunits not established, only individual fire safety program	

* Number of days auditors spent on auditing.
Note: W&B = wages and benefits; EHS = environmental health and safety; ER = employment regulations.

These tables suggest considerable heterogeneity in the way brands practice private regulation. While there is variation in what auditors look for and find during the same period, the different findings are not always systematically linked to the rating scales; the rating scales differ from company to company; and, again, auditors do not communicate to the factory the rationale for the rating given. Communicating the rationale for auditors' ratings to factories is necessary to educate factory management on how to improve. As AAA's chief sustainability officer told me, "My customers fall variously into two camps. One wants to do good

TABLE 2.4. Findings by the same audit organization when auditing Factory B, 2014

DATE	AUDIT ORGANIZATION	CODE CATEGORY	VIOLATION	RATING
9/22	Third-party auditor C, auditing for Brand A	EHS	Fire extinguishers blocked by table on floor 2	Major deficiencies, must improve
			Electricity switch boxes in major bulkhead were missing covers	
		HRS	50% of workers had worked 7–13 consecutive days in January, February, and March 2014	
			Weekly work of some employees was more than 60 hours	
9/23	Third-party auditor C, auditing for Brand B	HRS	Monthly OT exceeded 36 hours for employees in June–August 2014, with maximum 92 hours in July and 79.5 hours in August	Zero tolerance, may result in immediate termination
		EHS	Lower pulley guard missing for at least 10 viewed sewing machines	
			Need rolling doors or sliding doors for safety exits on work floors—for 90% of cases	
		W&B	Too much delay in severance payment	
10/6	Third-party auditor C auditing for Brand H	EHS	Smoke detector missing	Good (Yellow rating), one step below highest rating, Green
			Warning sign not standard	
			Not using protective equipment	
			Health certificate of canteen staff had expired	
			Electrical switches not explosive proofed	
			Sewing machines without needle guards	
		HRS	12/15 sample were working in excess of statutory OT limits in August 2014—some worked for 70.5 hours	
			Working continuously without rest	

Note: W&B = wages and benefits; EHS = environmental health and safety; HRS = working hours.

and is often willing to work with us, while others just follow rigid rules, with a 'check-off mentality' that does not address the root causes of problems." She added that the "brands differ in terms of priorities and how much compliance is important to them."[17]

Despite efforts by this supplier to "regulate" this multiplicity of practices by suggesting to its long-term clients that they accept an audit done by one auditor, only two global brands took the advice. This multiplicity of practices among heterogeneous brands provides diverse or conflicting signals to the supplier, making

TABLE 2.5A. Numbers of audit violations and audit ratings in Factory A, 2015

DATE	AUDIT ORGANIZATION	PERSON DAYS	TYPE OF VIOLATIONS	TOTAL VIOLATIONS	RATING
1/7	Brand A	2	2 HRS	2	CAT3
3/16	Brand B	2	1 HRS, 1W&B	2	Major deficiencies
3/18	Third-party A	2	2 HRS, 1 EHS, 1 W&B	4	Acceptable
4/14	Third-party B	2	2 EHS	2	Rating system exists but not communicated
6/18	Third-party C	3	4, EHS, 2 HRS, 1 W&B	7	Rating system exists but not communicated
6/23	Brand C	2	14 EHS, 7 ER, 5 W&B, 5HRS	32	Good
7/7	Brand D	2	7 EHS, 1 ER	8	Rating system exists but not communicated
7/21	Brand E	1	1W&B, 2 EHS, 1 ER	4	Developmental
9/23	Third-party D	2	2 EHS, 1 HRS, 1 harassment	4	Orange
11/4	Third-party A	4	1 EHS, 1 HRS, 1 W&B	3	No rating
12/17	Brand F	–	10 EHS, 2 W&B, 2 HRS	14	Labor: Bronze; EHS: Yellow
12/23	Third-party E	2	4 EHS, 1 W&B, 1 HRS	5	Green

Note: W&B = wages and benefits; EHS = environmental health and safety; HRS = working hours.

it difficult for a supplier—even a leading multibrand supplier like AAA—to effectively align its work conditions with different company requirements.

These differences in auditing are complemented by differences in how brands use the audit results to determine future relationships with suppliers. Recall that a key element of private regulation is the third component: brands reward suppliers that are generally compliant in terms of regular orders, resulting in the long-term relationships that bolster compliance (at least in theory). Research has shown the importance of long-term relationships, such as the benefits of "relational contracting" rather than "arms-length" contracting.[18] Collaborative partnerships have been developed between big suppliers and buyers in the global electronics industry and the global automotive industry, which also makes extensive use of subcontracting.[19] The garment industry is not characterized by these collaborative relationships, in part because most garment suppliers supply to multiple brands, reserving only a small portion of their capacity for each individual brand.[20] And there is typically no guarantee of repeat business, as there is a strong tendency toward a short-term transaction rather than a long-term collaborative

TABLE 2.5B. Numbers of audit violations and audit ratings in Factory B, 2015

DATE	AUDIT ORGANIZATION	PERSON DAYS	TYPE OF VIOLATIONS	TOTAL VIOLATIONS	RATING
1/27	Third-party D	1	2 EHS, 1 W&B, 1 HRS	4	Zero tolerance
2/4	Third-party D	2	3 EHS, 1 HRS	4	Yellow
3/16	Third-party A	2	2 EHS, 1 HRS	3	Needs improvement
5/19	Third-party B	2	2 EHS, 2 W&B	4	Acceptable
5/26	Brand E	2	3 W&B, 2 EHS	5	Developmental
6/3	Third-party F	2	7 EHS, 3 HRS, 2 W&B, 2 other	14	Needs improvement
6/24	Brand C	2	40 EHS, 5 HRS, 3 W&B 2 ER, 1 other	51	Needs improvement
10/15	Third-party G	4	5 EHS	5	Good condition
10/26	Third-party H	2	6 EHS, 2 W&B, 2 HRS	10	Needs improvement
11/17	Brand D	2	9 EHS	9	Rating not communicated
12/1	Brand E	2	3 EHS	3	Developmental
12/17	Third-party 4	2	2 EHS, 3 HRS, 1 W&B, 2 other	8	Needs improvement
12/29	Brand F	9	7 EHS, 3 W&B, 2 ER 1 HRS	13	Labor: Yellow; EHS: Bronze

Note: W&B = wages and benefits; EHS = environmental health and safety; ER = employment regulations; HRS = working hours.

relationship. Easy substitutability of garment suppliers and intense competitive price pressure in the garment industry encourage this form of transactional contracting. Global buyers will defect to different suppliers even for a small price differential. As one supplier of garments in Cambodia told me in January 2020, "Walmart will defect for a one-cent price differential."

The AAA case is quite different. It is one of the largest suppliers of shirts in the world, serving more than seventy global brands, many for more than fifteen years. One would expect a buyer-supplier relationship of such duration to result in a stable long-term relationship in which the global buyer knows the supplier well. With fifteen-plus years' experience auditing and sourcing from that particular supplier, it stands to reason that buyers would have acquired a good understanding of the supplier's capabilities. Hence, buyers would not need to audit as frequently or would be willing to use audits other companies had already done. This approach would be optimal and would reduce the buyer's auditing costs.

One would expect a long-term relationship to lead as well to longer-term orders. Given that AAA is a very high-quality supplier with a vast product range, enviable reputation for quality, and its own very well-developed CSR capabilities, guaranteeing orders for multiple years would seem a worthwhile step, at least for products consistently in demand. Several of the products sourced from these two factories are name-brand business shirts and high-end sportswear for which there is a steady demand. Some of these brands have been around for more than thirty or forty years.

Nevertheless, the data suggest considerable "practice multiplicity" in terms of how global brands deal with this supplier. Table 2.6 provides data on the top fifteen customers of supplier AAA. The customers are ranked by volume for the years 2015 and 2016. The table indicates variation. Some top-ranked customers audit regularly. Other top-ranked customers evidently have developed relationships of trust and do not audit, or accept the supplier's own audit, or accept the audits of other companies that source from the same supplier. The table does not exhibit any consistent relationship between the length of the relationship and auditing. Some buyers with short business relationships of less than three years tend to not audit (trusting the supplier) while others with long established relationships audit frequently.

It is also not clear that sustained relationships result in guaranteed orders for multiple years. AAA marketing managers told me in interviews that 90 percent of the brands they supply did not make orders based on audit results, supporting my contention that there is little or no coupling between brands' auditing and sourcing practices. These managers also told me that only a few of the supplier's seventy-four brands threatened to withhold orders if AAA did not improve

TABLE 2.6.   Supplier AAA's relationship with buyers and their audit practices

RANK OF CUSTOMER BY VOLUME	YEARS OF BUSINESS RELATIONSHIP	NUMBER OF AUDITS IN FACTORIES A AND B, OR ALTERNATIVE TO CONDUCTING AUDITS
1	15	6
3	15	5
4	10	5
5	10	10
7	10	7
8	10	3
9	10	10
11	10	9
2	10	Accepts supplier's own audit
6	10	Accepts a WRAP audit
10	10	No audit required
12	10	No audit required
13	3	No audit required
14	10	Accepts any brand audit
15	< 10	No audit required

compliance—although those brands have not acted on their threat. Thus, it is clear that brands differ in the extent that they reward compliant suppliers with more orders, a key element of the private regulation model.

One marketing manager told me that the "idea that long-term relationships will result in repeated/advance orders is ludicrous" and that customers "see themselves as free to make changes anytime." Another noted that even long-term customers "will often defect" after placing their orders. Since a linkage between auditing and sourcing is crucial to incentivizing compliance, the absence of this linkage in long-term relationships is problematic.

Thus, my results show considerable practice multiplicity in a global supplier's experiences of the private regulation practices of many global brands. This multiplicity is a particular problem for the supplier, which is left with no idea of what it is doing wrong and how best to improve given the vast differences in how these brands implement private regulation. Brands' different overall approaches to private regulation, auditing practices, and rating scales result in the supplier receiving conflicting "grades" for the same performance from one audit to another. Moreover, different brands to tend to assign varying weights to different violations.

Such inconsistency enhances the decoupling between brands' practices and intended improvement in labor standards. Even more important, this practice makes it difficult for the global buyers themselves to get a sense of what is best practice, especially given the lack of transparency that results in buyers' inability to see the audit results of other brands sourcing from the same factory.

Convergence Initiatives

Practice multiplicity could be reduced by greater collaboration among the brands sourcing from AAA's factories, promoting convergence of private regulation in this particular case. This is an implicit recognition that to bring about sustainable change, individual global buyers *must* collaborate.

The Social and Labor Convergence Project (SLCP) is an initiative that commenced in 2016, under the sponsorship of the Sustainable Apparel Coalition (SAC), to promote a convergence of standards in the apparel industry. The initial impetus came from a collaboration between Walmart and Patagonia, whose CEOs came together to develop an index that could be used to measure the environmental impact of their products. This initiative prompted other brands to join, and the Higg Index was developed as a measure of *environmental* sustainability. More than ten thousand manufacturers used the index in 2017. SAC membership includes 104 global brands and retailers, about eighty manufacturers, and seventy diverse nongovernmental organizations.[21]

The SLCP aims to develop a framework that creates convergence in private regulation approaches with regard to labor standards in global supply chains. The program is designed to improve working conditions in global supply chains through collaboration between global buyers and retailers. The goal is to develop a "converged assessment framework" that will eliminate practice multiplicity in assessing suppliers. This effort is to create *one* standard for the apparel and footwear industries, with a unified measurement instrument complemented by a verification methodology that will allow for greater comparability of factory social and labor data. The underlying idea is that such a convergence will not only reduce the number of audits and eliminate "audit fatigue" but also reduce practice multiplicity and thereby promote the coupling of practice and outcomes that will result in improved labor conditions at supplier factories.

The SLCP has witnessed impressive membership growth. By the end of 2018, the total membership stood at 190, including six industry associations, six global intermediary firms such as agents (e.g., the supply chain management company Li & Fung), thirty-five manufacturers (suppliers), sixty global buyers and retailers, two national governments, and thirty-seven service providers in the global supply chain ecosystem. As of this writing, however, several established MSIs, such as the Fair Labor Association and ETI, have not yet joined the SLCP.

The model being developed requires that suppliers do a self-assessment using the SLCP measurement instrument. Once completed, the data will be verified by selected verifier bodies. SLCP members have overwhelmingly approved the "converged assessment framework," and the assessment tool has been tested in 170 facilities across twenty-three countries where apparel and footwear are produced.[22] The verification protocol was also tested and refined with community input, and actual verification is expected to begin in 2020. The overall goal is twenty-five thousand verified assessments by 2023. Once the verification results have been scrutinized by the suppler, they will be uploaded to accredited host platforms, and the information will then be available to the larger ecosystem of SLCP members. As of January 2020, three organizations—Fair Factories Clearinghouse, SAC Higg, and Sedex—were serving as accredited hosts.

The SLCP's model differs from other approaches in several ways. Unlike current multi-stakeholder approaches, it does not set minimum requirements and is not intended to be a ranking, scoring, or certification system. The model does not replace a code of conduct. The model is nonjudgmental and, as an SLCP director told me, "agnostic." It simply provides a systematic basis for collecting compliance information, with a verification process. Consistent with efforts by other multi-stakeholder organizations, there will be no public disclosure, but information will be shared among members.

Some aspects of the SLCP's approach are debatable in terms of whether they will help achieve desired improvements in labor standards. The lack of specified minimum standards and the unwillingness to define a threshold for acceptable practice may be a significant problem. It is only because minimum standards were set by the International Labour Organization (ILO) and a variety of codes of conduct that we have seen some progress in curtailing child labor in apparel supply chains (see chapter 4). The verification methodology being contemplated must also collect actual outcomes data that are extensive enough to help assess whether private regulation is having an impact on workers' lives. It is not clear at present that those extensive outcomes data are being collected.[23]

Sharing factory data on a website accessible to SLCP members may help by reducing some degree of practice multiplicity among the global brands that are part of SLCP. The total number of global buyers, however, is considerably larger than the SLCP membership. The lack of public disclosure presents a problem, as this approach does little to assist other actors not part of SLCP in identifying best practices. Public disclosure is a crucial issue because the public and consumers have been some of the most important engines driving global buyers and brands to invest in sustainability.

One key concern is that only suppliers that have already met most minimum standards of the ILO and codes will participate in the SLCP system. In fact, the thirty-five manufacturers (suppliers) listed on its website are the "superstars" among suppliers, and many are professionally managed global companies in their own right. But most apparel manufacturing facilities are small, independently owned, and family managed. Their owners are the ones who use the audit consulting firms discussed in chapter 1. So as laudable as the SLCP effort may be, it will not affect the vast majority of garment producers—making the initiative quite limited in its ability to improve labor standards in global supply chains.

Conclusion

More broadly, it is unclear whether universal convergence in terms of a standardized code of conduct and verification methodology is the correct approach. Institutional theory would suggest that a one-size-fits-all approach might solve the problem of policy-practice decoupling, since such an approach would make clear to all actors what is required in terms of the specific practices that need to be adopted for implementing private regulation programs. However, the adoption of a standardized approach would result in practice-outcomes decoupling.[24] This result would come about because there is a need to tailor approaches to specific contexts.

As is clear from the experiences of supplier AAA, brands that source from the same supplier in a country could collaborate to develop common approaches in that country. It might also be necessary for brands and buyers to collaborate to establish regional or provincial consortia to devise effective frameworks for auditing regionally and locally, given the vast differences across contexts, local laws, and local customs and norms that affect important code provisions.[25] Assessing even easy-to-measure variables such as wages and hours are fraught with difficulty across different parts of China.

The notion of brand collaboration in different regions and locales is more consistent with the notion of the need for "niche institutions" to enable coupling of practices with outcomes.[26] This topic is discussed in detail in the concluding chapter. Contemporary examples of such niche institutions include the Accord and Alliance in Bangladesh, which is focused on one region and has accomplished much with regard to fire safety. Similarly, the Indonesian Freedom of Association Protocol is a niche institution that has some brand collaboration to further freedom of association in one context.

Only context-sensitive approaches will promote the coupling of practices with outcomes. Until that happens, practice multiplicity will continue to create opacity in private regulation of labor in global supply chains.

CAUSAL COMPLEXITY

The Varied Determinants of Compliance and Workplace-Level Improvements

with Chunyun Li

Practice multiplicity and behavioral invisibility are key drivers of the opacity that contributes to practice-outcomes decoupling, as shown in chapters 1 and 2. Here the focus is on the third key driver, *causal complexity*.

The determinants of improvement in working conditions in supplier factories in global supply chains are complex. The complexity arises from the interaction between heterogeneous actors (companies, auditing firms, suppliers) following a multiplicity of practices, combined with the effect of local institutional conditions and industry and workplace context. Together, these make it difficult to identify determinants of improvements in working conditions. And along with the general lack of transparency in private regulation, this combination of causal factors leads to uncertainty with respect to cause-effect relationships.

Given this uncertainty, global companies, suppliers, auditing firms, and nongovernmental organizations critical of the process may find it difficult to understand the crucial variables in improving workplace conditions in different locales, the direct and indirect effects of different causal variables, and how to disentangle determinants from consequences of specific actions. In more transparent fields, there is little difficulty in identifying and generalizing the influence of different variables, but in an opaque field, where there is little disclosure, this lack becomes serious inhibitor to identifying and adopting best-practice approaches.

The central assumption of the private regulation model is that if standards are set by codes of conduct (whether based on international conventions or local laws), and if supplier factories comply with the codes, sweatshop conditions will be avoided and improvements will be made in the lives of workers in global supply chains. But this assumption, again, may not be warranted; buyers and brands may not have the power to force suppliers to compel compliance.[1] And within the businesses of most global buyers and retailers, sourcing may not be sufficiently well integrated with compliance, so the incentive effects of rewarding good factories that are making improvements in compliance are not realized in practice—even though such incentives are the very basis for the model of private regulation of first-tier supplier factories.

What Are the Determinants of Compliance?

Because global companies do not release their private regulation data into the public domain, only a limited number of studies have analyzed the determinants of compliance and compliance improvements. These studies have largely been of two types. The first has relied on quantitative analyses of compliance data drawn from certain multi-stakeholder organizations—such as the Fair Labor Association (FLA) or Fair Wear Foundation (FWF)—or from global auditing firms; the second type includes empirical examinations of supply chain data from select companies and qualitative case studies of brands' private regulation programs. Compliance data drawn from multi-stakeholder organizations or auditing firms provide longitudinal and cross-sectional data on audit violations that can be analyzed across countries and industries to find generalized determinants, whereas data and case studies from individual companies can potentially identify determinants of compliance in a particular context. Several other potential determinants of compliance identified in labor relations research have not been analyzed by scholars focusing on private regulation. Appendix A presents results from all prior studies on the determinants of compliance.

The salient point here is that generalizing these determinants is inhibited by the fact that they have been found in different studies using differing methods and in different contexts. In addition, a number of important determinants have not been studied, such as local laws and rules, and the quality of management in supplier factories. Further, the absence of unions in most sourcing countries means there is insufficient evidence that workers can exercise their independent voice to improve their working conditions (an important determinant of compliance *improvement*).

The fundamental assumption of private regulation researchers—that an improvement in audit score or compliance score implies an improvement in working conditions—is suspect, especially given the problems of behavioral invisibility and practice multiplicity. It is important to note that improvements in working conditions are often highly dependent on the context: country, province, industry, and supplier management. It is reasonable to assume that specific policies and practices that lead to compliance in one context will not necessarily work in another.

In general, studies do not control for all factors that affect compliance improvement, and the variables included in studies of compliance or compliance improvement appear to be determined in part by the availability of analyzable data. Qualitative case studies provide context-specific information regarding compliance but cannot be generalized to other contexts. The bottom line, therefore, is that despite more than twenty-five years of regulation there is no clear sense of the key determinants of compliance improvement, and the effects of some variables is often uncertain. And we have very little information about the direct and indirect effects of the various determinants.

This is a classic case of a field characterized by opaqueness resulting from causal complexity. There is little clarity about which predictors of compliance are the most important or what will lead to actual improvements in working conditions in global supply chains. Consequently, there is no evidence to determine best practices or whether what works in one place might work elsewhere.

Causal Complexity: An Empirical Investigation

Do variables emanating from private regulation affect compliance? Specifically, what about three key private regulation variables at the core of the private regulation model: *audit score, leverage,* and *long-term buyer-supplier relationships*? Once we control for supplier and worker characteristics, how do they affect compliance?

The *audit score* (or *compliance score*)—the score auditors give to suppliers after assessing their compliance—has been the most important metric by which global brands evaluate the progress of their private regulation efforts and by which outsiders evaluate progress. The score is typically calculated in terms of the number of violations found. Most researchers who have studied compliance using company data use those companies' audit scores.[2]

Leverage is important to a key assumption underlying private regulation: that buyers are capable of forcing their suppliers to comply with their codes through the specifics of their private regulation programs. A global buyer's *leverage* relates to the percentage of a factory's production that is accounted for by that buyer. High leverage means significant buyer influence over that supplier.[3]

The argument concerning *long-term buyer-supplier relationships* is that these indicate that the parties have arrived at an understanding and that suppliers have been improving in compliance terms (otherwise, they would have been dropped). Thus, long-term buyer-supplier relationships are predicted to be associated with compliance improvement. (Several of the studies in appendix A have shown support for this idea.)

It is not clear whether these are significant determinants of compliance and compliance improvement when examined in conjunction with other variables identified in industrial relations research, such as supplier and workplace characteristics. And it is important to examine whether these "causal influences" found in given contexts translate to other contexts. A finding that causal influences do not "work" in different contexts would provide some evidence of the causal complexity or causal indeterminacy to which institutional theorists allude.

To examine the causal influence of these and other private regulation variables on compliance, we conducted a quantitative study of compliance in one hundred China-based suppliers of a large global retailer, HomeRetailer (not the company's real name), which has an extensive global supply chain spread over many countries, producing a range of products for the home. This supply chain is very diverse, encompassing a large range of industries, including apparel, lighting, metalworking, furniture, and other miscellaneous industries. HomeRetailer was an early adopter of the private regulation model; the retailer has been much admired for its progressive practices and has been the subject of several case studies used in business schools. HomeRetailer even trains its own employees to do audits, avoiding the practice of subcontracting the auditing function to third-party audit firms and thus minimizing the potential for audit fraud.

Our investigation concerns thirty of HomeRetailer's suppliers in China. One of HomeRetailer's in-house auditors provided extensive details about the audit protocol and how auditors measure supplier compliance. HomeRetailer monitors supplier performance with two auditors once every twelve months over a two-day period. HomeRetailer provided its audit data so we could understand how the audits affect outcomes for workers at the company's suppliers; these data contain a number of contextual attributes, or characteristics (see table 3.1).

Several of these characteristics are particularly noteworthy. The suppliers, mostly with small factories, produce a variety of products; most have been in business for a long time (fourteen years on average); and they have been supplying HomeRetailer for nearly seven years on average. Importantly, HomeRetailer's share of their production is quite high—60 percent on average—indicating a high degree of leverage.

Measuring leverage and buyer-supplier relationships was relatively easy. The problem was to examine whether the audit score was a reliable indicator of compliance. Doing so required getting an alternative source of information to compare with the audit score. So HomeRetailer provided us with payroll data for 1,549

TABLE 3.1. Characteristics of HomeRetailer suppliers

ID	CITY AND PROVINCE	INDUSTRY	OWNERSHIP	FIRM AGE IN YEARS	TOTAL WORKERS	HOMERETAILER SHARE	YEARS SUPPLYING HOMERETAILER
1	Suzhou, Jiangsu	Lighting	HMT	6	228	90	6
2	Jiangyin, Jiangsu	Textile	DPE	8	1,700	100	11
3	Shanghai	Textile	FIE	22	485	35	6
4	Kunshan, Jiangsu	Misc.	FIE	8	65	60	15
5	Shanghai	Metal	FIE	13	1,560	50	7
6	Yuyao, Zhejiang	Misc.	FIE	8	122	20	4
7	Wuxi, Jiangsu	Furniture	DPE	7	99	90	2
8	Changshu, Jiangsu	Metal	DPE	21	330	40	7
9	Shaoxing, Zhejiang	Misc.	FIE	5	120	40	5
10	Jiangyin, Jiangsu	Textile	DPE	12	470	10	4
11	Yichang, Hubei	Metal	FIE	6	175	40	6
12	Xiaoshan, Zhejiang	Textile	DPE	10	200	100	14
13	Liyang, Jiangsu	Misc.	DPE	24	260	30	1
14	Yuyao, Zhejiang	Furniture	FIE	7	500	100	8
15	Ningbo, Zhejiang	Furniture	FIE	28	300	40	6
16	Anji, Zhejiang	Furniture	DPE	2	106	100	4
17	Ningbo, Zhejiang	Misc.	DPE	45	242	80	4
18	Yuyao, Zhejiang	Textile	FIE	8	500	30	15
19	Jiangyin, Jiangsu	Misc.	DPE	20	350	80	4
20	Yuyao, Zhejiang	Metal	FIE	14	550	100	6
21	Xiamen, Fujian	Lighting	HMT	13	200	80	9
22	Ningbo, Zhejiang	Lighting	DPE	20	1,050	20	1
23	Tonglu, Zhejiang	Furniture	DPE	8	300	30	8
24	Hangzhou, Zhejiang	Metal	DPE	24	95	80	10
25	Ningbo, Zhejiang	Metal	DPE	13	150	65	6
26	Ningbo, Zhejiang	Metal	DPE	18	132	60	8
27	Jiaxing, Zhejiang	Furniture	DPE	10	360	80	8
28	Yangzhou, Jiangsu	Metal	DPE	11	350	80	3
29	Jinjiang, Fujian	Furniture	HMT	14	570	70	6
30	Jiaxing, Zhejiang	Misc.	DPE	14	324	15	3
Average				14	400	60	7

Note: HMT = Hong-Kong, Macao, or Taiwan-invested; DPE = domestic private enterprise; FIE = foreign-invested enterprise; Misc. = miscellaneous.

workers from these thirty suppliers, in the form of copies of their pay stubs. Using information from the pay stubs, along with a detailed analysis of regional and industry laws, rules, and practices, we calculated the extent of compliance on four "outcome standards" in HomeRetailer's code of conduct: (1) suppliers shall pay wages according to local laws, and average hourly wage shall not be lower than the local minimum; (2) suppliers shall pay overtime compensation according to local laws; (3) weekly working hours shall not exceed sixty hours; and (4) payment of benefits such as social security shall comply with local laws.

HomeRetailer also provided us with its audit scores on these four outcome standards, which allowed for a comparison between the audit scores and compliance based on workers' payroll data.[4] We calculated a compliance index for each worker based on payroll records (e.g., a worker who experienced only one violation out of four items on wages and hours would receive a compliance index score of 0.75).[5]

Table 3.2 compares our compliance findings and those of HomeRetailer. It appears that HomeRetailer's audit scores underreport violations for nine of thirty suppliers (or 30 percent). For instance, HomeRetailer gave Supplier 1 an audit score of 83.3 percent, with only one violation, but our calculation shows Supplier 1 had two violations, concerning weekly hours and social security contributions.[6]

It is interesting that while there were no hourly wage violations found across all thirty suppliers, the number of social security contribution violations was quite large. And the severity of violations involving social security (i.e., the share of workers affected by this violation) ranged all the way up to 100 percent for some suppliers. Payroll information showed that all nine of the suppliers whose violations were underreported violated standards for social security contributions.

Model 1 of table 3.3 tests the effects of variables related to private regulation on the compliance index we computed for each worker—the audit score derived from HomeRetailer's audit reports; HomeRetailer leverage (the company's share of the supplier's production, ranging from 15 to 100 percent); and years supplying HomeRetailer (between three and fifteen years)—controlled for the effect of several variables, including supplier and worker characteristics.

It turns out that *none of the three private regulation variables is a significant predictor of compliance*. However, as Model 2 in table 3.3 shows, *several supplier characteristics and worker attributes are significantly associated with better compliance*: supplier ownership, location, and size. Among worker attributes, *hukou* (household registration), gender (male), tenure, and age also relate positively and significantly with better compliance. Compliance was generally better for workers who had an urban *hukou* than for those who had a rural *hukou*.

The results in table 3.3 suggest that the effect of private regulation variables found to be major predictors of compliance in other studies in different contexts

TABLE 3.2. Violations reported in audits and identified from pay stubs

SUPPLIER ID	NUMBER OF VIOLATIONS REPORTED BY AUDIT (OUT OF SIX ITEMS)	NUMBER OF VIOLATIONS REVEALED FROM PAY STUBS (OUT OF FOUR ITEMS)	PERCENTAGE OF HOURLY WAGE VIOLATIONS	PERCENTAGE OF MONTHLY HOURS VIOLATIONS*	PERCENTAGE OF OVERTIME PAY VIOLATIONS	PERCENTAGE OF SOCIAL SECURITY CONTRIBUTION VIOLATIONS
1	*1*	*2*	*0*	*63.3*	*0*	*100*
2	1	0	0	0	0	0
3	*1*	*2*	*0*	0	18	62.2
4	1	0	0	0	0	0
5	3	0	0	0	0	0
6	2	1	0	0	0	8.2
7	2	1	0	0	0	2.0
8	*1*	*2*	*0*	*10*	*0*	*2*
9	*1*	*2*	*0*	*0*	*2*	*6*
10	2	0	0	0	0	0
11	1	1	0	12.7	0.0	0
12	1	0	0	0	0	0
13	1	1	0	0	0	42.4
14	1	0	0	0	0	0
15	1	0	0	0	0	0
16	1	1	0	1.9	0	0
17	*1*	*2*	*0*	*2*	*0*	*4.26*
18	1	0	0	0	0	0
19	1	0	0	0	0	0
20	1	0	0	0	0	0
21	*1*	*2*	*0*	*74*	*0*	*100*
22	4	0	0	0	0	0
23	4	2	0	10	0	100
24	2	1	0	0	98	0
25	1	1	0	0	0	21.4
26	2	2	0	18.3	0	1.8
27	1	1	0	0	0	88.1
28	*1*	*2*	*0*	*0*	*2*	*10.2*
29	*1*	*2*	*0*	*14*	*0*	*71.4*
30	*1*	*2*	*0*	*88*	*0*	*100*
Average	1.4	1.00	0	8.8	3.9	23

*HomeRetailer's code of conduct limits maximum weekly work hours to 60, which translates into approximate 257 hours monthly.

Note: Numbers in **bold italics** represent HomeRetailer's underreporting of violations in its audit scores.

TABLE 3.3.   Effects of private regulation variables on compliance

INDEPENDENT VARIABLES	DEPENDENT VARIABLE: INDIVIDUAL COMPLIANCE INDEX	
PRIVATE REGULATION VARIABLES	MODEL 1	MODEL 2
Six-item audit score on wages & hours	−0.014	−0.026
Retailer A's share	0.000	0.001
Years supplying HomeRetailer	−0.007	−0.004
OWNERSHIP (BASE GROUP IS TAIWAN OR MACAO-INVESTED ENTERPRISE)		
Joint venture		**.382*****
Foreign-invested enterprise		**.362*****
Domestic private enterprise		0.209*
LOCATION (BASE GROUP IS SHANGHAI)		
Jiangsu province		**.321*****
Zhejiang province		**0.205***
Non–Yangtze River (Fujian & Hubei)		0.217
INDUSTRY (BASE GROUP IS TEXTILE)		
Metal		0.01
Lighting		−0.046
Furniture		−0.015
Miscellaneous		−0.057
Total workers		0.000
Firm age		0.001
WORKER INDIVIDUAL ATTRIBUTES		
Male		.011**
Education (years)		0.002
URBAN *HUKOU*		.025**
Age (years)		.001*
Tenure (months)		.0003***
Constant	.987***	.435**
N	1,491	1,489
Log likelihood	1,485	1,520

Note: Results based on multilevel linear regression; * $p < 0.1$, ** $p < 0.05$, *** $p < 0.01$.

do not generalize to our sample. Rather, Models 1 and 2, taken together, show that compliance is a function of supplier and worker heterogeneity, while the effects of variables related to private regulation are not significant. This result clearly highlights the importance of context in compliance.

Of course, these results could have been influenced by the specific nature of our compliance variable. Therefore, we examined the effects of *leverage* and the *length of buyer-supplier relationships* on the six outcome-standard compliance scores for a much larger sample of one hundred suppliers of HomeRetailer. This analysis was not complicated by our alternative measure of individual worker compliance but relied instead on the audit scores of HomeRetailer as the criterion variable. Admittedly, we did not have data on other firm-level variables (such as worker variables), like the data we obtained from payroll stubs for thirty of these one hundred suppliers discussed earlier. Thus, the analysis is more limited. The results of this more limited analysis are provided in table 3.4.[7]

As table 3.4 suggests, the variables do a poor job of explaining compliance. The only significant variables appear to be ownership, with foreign-invested firms showing lower compliance scores, and firms in the Yangtze River delta showing higher compliance scores. Most important is that both leverage and the length of relationships appear to have no effect on compliance. This finding substantiates the results in table 3.3 and is consistent with the ideas from prior research that compliance scores are *influenced* by a number of other variables not measured here, but the associated variables are not significant *predictors* of compliance. Clearly, these data do not include key variables that influence compliance, such as measures concerning supplier management and a variety of factory variables. In other words, this is an underspecified model. But the results support the

TABLE 3.4. Effect of leverage and length of relationship on the compliance score of wage and hours for one hundred suppliers

INDEPENDENT VARIABLE	COEFFICIENT
PRIVATE REGULATION VARIABLES	
Leverage (lead firm share)	0.000
Length of buyer-supplier relationship (months)	0.000
OWNERSHIP VARIABLES	
Foreign-invested firms (vs. domestic)	−0.019**
INDUSTRY VARIABLES	
Furniture (vs. miscellaneous)	−0.001
Lighting (vs. miscellaneous)	−0.004
Textile (vs. miscellaneous)	−0.016
Steel (vs. miscellaneous)	−0.014
REGION VARIABLES	
Yangtze River delta	0.027**
Pearl River delta	0.009
Constant	1.495***
N	100
Log likelihood	−174.68.59
Pseudo R-square	0.01

Note: Results based on multilevel linear regression; * $p < 0.1$, ** $p < 0.05$, *** $p < 0.01$.

argument that private regulation variables that other researchers have found to explain compliance will not necessarily explain compliance in other, varied contexts.

Conclusion

Confusion and debate persist regarding the *true* determinants of compliance and the variables that make private regulation successful. Variables found to have a causal influence in one study are not found to be significant predictors in another that uses different data and is conducted in a different context. This causal indeterminacy is manifested in our own investigation as well. Given how central the audit or compliance score, leverage, and length of buyer-supplier relationships are to private regulation, we would expect these variables to matter in any context. But it turns out that they do not.

These results are consistent with the arguments made by institutional theorists that the complex configuration of actors in private regulation contributes to causal complexity so that it is difficult to attribute worker outcomes to private regulation practices in some contexts.[8] This uncertainty about cause-effect relations as a result of contextual differences inhibits identifying practices that work (best practices) in all situations, and explains the persistent practice-outcomes gaps in private regulation.

Causal complexity contributes to making the private regulation field opaque with respect to labor standards. Combined with the opacity generated by behavioral invisibility and practice multiplicity discussed in the two preceding chapters, it is not surprising that we see the prevalence of decoupling between private regulation policies of global firms and outcomes for workers in the supply chain.

Part 2
OVERVIEW
Progress

The debate over the effects of private regulation continues. There have been some positive effects, to be sure, but the extent to which these effects are generalizable is not known. What we lack is a clear sense of progress over the past twenty-five years.

Where and under what conditions does private regulation in labor standards work? That is a question not yet fully answered. While there is some consensus among researchers that there have been clear improvements in workplace safety and health, it is not clear that these are sustainable improvements, generalized to all locations.[1] We continue to see evidence of industrial accidents in the garment industry, and some recent factory disasters occurred *after* inspections by auditors.[2] Established after the Rana Plaza factory fire that killed more than 1,100 workers, the Accord on Fire and Safety in Bangladesh, and its sibling organization the Alliance for Bangladesh Worker Safety, have led to substantial improvements in fire safety and some improvements in general labor standards. The former has been extended until December 2021, while the latter ceased operations in December 2018.

Several analyses of the ILO's Better Work program report fairly consistent improvements in compliance with codes overall—especially with respect to safety and health and overtime hours and payments.[3] These studies also suggest that private regulation has reduced but not entirely eliminated the incidence of harsh and abusive treatment of workers.[4] And the analyses of Better Work data also suggest that when it comes to working conditions such as verbal abuse and sexual harassment, positive effects appear to decay after three or four rounds of assessments.

Many studies suggest clear, marked decreases in the incidence of child labor and forced labor in first-tier suppliers, although we do not have generalizable evidence. In addition, private regulation has been found to make factory managers more sensitive to "worker welfare," but again, we don't know whether such sensitivity translates into improved employment policies in the supply chain.[5]

Some studies have suggested that there is increased compliance with regard to minimum wages, which most codes require, but we do not have systematic generalizable evidence. Chinese workers are paid, on average, considerably more than the minimum wage, but that is a function of general labor market trends in China. Many other codes require suppliers to pay an "adequate wage" that takes into account employees' basic needs and that also provide some small amount of disposable income. Since 2010, there has been increased debate about whether companies should include in their codes a commitment to paying living wages, and several, such as H&M and Marks and Spencer, have made explicit living wage commitments in their codes. However, there is no evidence that these commitments have been met. Overall, there are considerable gaps in our knowledge regarding wages; most companies are unwilling to share wage compliance data from their supply chains publicly.

There is clear evidence that freedom of association has *not* improved. While Bartley and colleagues cite some studies indicating a decline in discrimination, the evidence on discrimination is rather thin, as it is not clear that the auditing process uncovers instances of discrimination adequately.

The three chapters in part 2 aim to show what overall progress can be shown *despite* these limitations. The chapters draw on data from a seven-year period, between 2011 and 2017, provided by a large auditing firm. The data offer an *initial* comparative picture of progress, across time, and across industries and countries. These data cover the number of violations per audit for several labor standards, as well as actual hours worked and wages paid. Because these data come from thirteen industries and ten countries, the data also make it possible to see variations. Further, an extract of the data allows for examining the progress of the same factories over time to determine whether those factories improve after repeated audits.

Using a different dataset, part 2 also examines whether compliance by factories in the ILO's Better Work program varies based on the number of assessments they have undergone. And using a new dataset from a global home products company, part 2 also examines the conditions under which sustainable improvements in compliance and worker outcomes are possible. Chapter 4 is, therefore, a comprehensive evaluation of progress on labor conditions in global supply chains.

Chapters 5 and 6 examine progress on what may well be the two most important issues: freedom of association and wages. Chapter 5 systematically evaluates progress on wages. The topic of wages in the global supply chain generates a lot of heat, but relatively little light has been shed on the subject given the absence of good data. Chapter 5 draws on longitudinal data from multiple countries and industries, provided by a global auditing company, and cross-sectional data from nearly a dozen countries in a large global retailer's supply chain. These data allow for examining average wages in multiple industries and countries, the extent to which average wages are above a specified minimum wage, and the gap between average wages and the living wage.

Chapter 6 examines progress on freedom of association, the one core labor right for which earlier research has indicated relatively little progress. Data from a global retailer, a global auditing firm, two multi-stakeholder organizations (the FLA and FWF), and Better Work show that freedom of association is not a major focus of leading firms, and that the quality of data on the topic is worse than that for any other core labor standard.

These data also show clear and measurable improvements in compliance where freedom of association exists. Thus we have a puzzling question here. If there is strong evidence that freedom of association improves compliance and working conditions, why is it the one core labor right private regulation doesn't emphasize? We outline pathways to how freedom of association can be improved.

In sum, part 2 provides a picture of overall progress of private regulation in improving labor standards generally, and specifically with regard to freedom of association and wages. As the pressure for increased transparency grows, we expect companies will disclose more data, and so we may come to know even more.

HAS PRIVATE REGULATION IMPROVED LABOR PRACTICES IN GLOBAL SUPPLY CHAINS?

An Empirical Examination

with Jinsun Bae

The prevailing view is that private regulation has not brought about expected improvements in labor conditions in global supply chains. "Since virtually all major firms today profess socially responsible business practices, have adopted codes of conduct, and employ auditing firms to monitor compliance," writes one researcher, "it should be possible to see beneficial results of CSR in terms of working conditions. Yet, this has not been the case."[1]

Another, more nuanced position is that "existing evidence suggests that [private regulation programs] have had some meaningful but narrow effects on working conditions and the management of human resources, but the rights of workers has been less affected, and even on issues where codes tend to be most meaningful, standards in many parts of the [apparel industry] remain criminally low in an absolute sense."[2]

While researchers have lamented the lack of sufficient progress, their conclusions have been based on a limited number of studies and, of course, events such as the Rana Plaza factory fire in Bangladesh and critical NGO investigations of selected factories that supply global companies. However, we lack a picture of the incidence of violations of labor standards and how those violations change over time in different countries and industries. There has not been a comprehensive empirical answer to the question whether private regulation has brought about meaningful and sustainable improvements in labor standards and the lives of workers.

This chapter aims to answer that question, first by examining overall progress in terms of the number of violations recorded through more than twenty thousand reliable audits in multiple industries and countries over a seven-year period and then by examining progress in specific factories that have been audited multiple times in India to see whether the improvement is being sustained. It appears reasonable to assume that a factory that is audited multiple times over a three-year period will register improvements (in terms of having fewer violations) after each audit. The data for these two examinations were provided by AUDCO, the same global auditing company introduced in chapter 1. In addition, this chapter explores progress in specific factories, with data from the Better Work program. Finally, the chapter examines the specific case of the supply chain of a global home products retailer, in which the factories have demonstrated remarkable progress in compliance over a short time frame. The objective here is to understand how such dramatic progress was achieved in this case.

Study 1: A Snapshot of Overall Progress

By examining the number of violations with respect to different labor standards, as well as key outcome variables, it is possible to get a snapshot of overall progress over time. Study 1 focuses on the number of violations found per audit and hence measures progress, in terms of both core labor rights and outcomes standards, including the following:

- Child labor
- Forced labor
- Discrimination
- Freedom of association
- Sexual harassment
- Health and safety
- Hours of work
- Wages and benefits

In addition to the number of violations for each standard, the chapter looks at specific progress in terms of three specific outcomes:

- Average weekly hours of work
- Continuous days of work (average)
- Percentage of workers paid correctly

Box 4.1 explains the data used for this first snapshot.

Tables 4.1 and 4.2 show the number of reliable audits (as explained in chapter 1) upon which the Snapshot 1 findings are based.

The figures that follow explore various findings by country and industry.

Box 4.1. Data for Snapshot 1

Snapshot 1 uses AUDCO data from 21,041 reliable audits in multiple countries during 2011–2017, aggregated at the levels of country (ten countries) and industry (thirteen industries). The key
variable is the *number of violations per audit*, which controls for the
number of audits in each country and industry and thus allows for
comparing changes over time. A second AUDCO dataset aggregates
the violations into categories—business ethics, environment, labor
standards, management systems, and safety and health—and allows
the examination of violations in each category over time, across
countries and industries.

There are important caveats regarding these data. First, they
give no indication of the *severity* of any violation, which is arguably
a more important outcome variable. Nevertheless, it is possible
that a child labor violation in these data may indicate a documentation violation rather than an actual incidence of child labor being used in a factory. Second, the number of factories in each
country and industry continually changed during the seven-year
period—a common feature of low-cost supply chains. Thus, the
inclusion of data for violations per audit does not mean that the
same factories were audited every year.

Because the data relate to auditing protocols of multiple clients of
a particular auditing company, the specific nature of the various
points in their codes with regard to individual labor standards are
not available.

Finally, nothing about these data overcomes the common criticism that audits are not of a sufficient duration to identify violations
of key rights, such as freedom from discrimination and freedom of
association, because auditors do not take time to talk with workers
outside the factory premises. However, because the auditors are
from AUDCO, it is reasonable to assume they are experienced and
well trained (as highlighted in chapter 1). The key here is that these
data are from audits *not* determined to have been falsified.

TABLE 4.1. Number of reliable audits by country, 2011–2017

COUNTRY	2011	2012	2013	2014	2015	2016	2017	TOTAL
Bangladesh	117	141	134	238	272	319	365	1,586
Cambodia	N/A	12	23	17	29	26	50	157
China	914	1,115	1,303	1,507	2,011	2,480	3,355	12,685
India	138	136	155	152	193	313	439	1,526
Indonesia	63	73	94	135	155	162	153	835
Jordan	13	14	N/A	14	12	11	15	79
Mexico	28	56	97	92	114	221	358	966
Turkey	N/A	N/A	14	39	10	72	238	373
United States	68	69	87	160	176	233	540	1,333
Vietnam	55	100	181	253	279	223	410	1,501
Total								21,041

TABLE 4.2. Number of reliable audits by industry, 2011–2017

INDUSTRY	2011	2012	2013	2014	2015	2016	2017	TOTAL
Agriculture	N/A	N/A	N/A	N/A	15	95	200	310
Apparel	562	767	872	1,189	1,492	1,829	2,411	9,122
Accessories	71	147	111	132	136	217	396	1,210
Electronics	74	134	159	144	209	302	401	1,423
Food	24	N/A	13	58	93	90	141	419
Footwear	83	107	131	186	317	407	410	1,641
Furniture	70	68	94	68	36	52	78	466
Hard goods (other)	73	78	105	61	53	79	209	658
Jewelry	73	22	24	19	27	26	53	244
Kitchenware/ housewares	61	129	82	77	80	98	140	667
Other	93	208	387	547	626	655	1,088	3,604
Soft goods (other)	23	17	12	43	75	73	148	391
Toys	26	24	43	42	29	51	195	410
Unknown	163	15	55	41	63	86	53	476
Total								21,041

Overall violations per country have remained stable over time; Vietnam is the only country that shows a trend toward increasing violations. The picture across industries is quite similar, except in the footwear and furniture industries, which show an increasing number of overall violations.

Special Findings on Violations

Figure 4.1 addresses *child labor*, which is quite consistent across both countries and industries, and show a very small number of violations per audit. Two explanations are equally plausible to explain the low numbers: audits do not do well finding violations of this core labor standard, or private regulation has been largely successful in eliminating such violations in global supply chains. It is important to note that these violations may be related to documentation, record-keeping, and reporting and may not indicate actual use of child labor.

As with child labor, the number of findings per audit of *discrimination*—at hiring, during employment, and also with respect to pregnancy and HIV testing (which codes do not typically allow)—is also low, and the trend line is fairly steady over time (figure 4.2). It is possible, however, that the low number reflects that audits conducted over only one or two days are ineffective at uncovering some instances of discrimination because auditors do not have time for detailed discussions with workers.

The picture is similar for *forced labor*, although the variation across countries and industries is greater than in the case of discrimination or child labor (figure 4.3). The measures here include whether workers' travel documents (passports) are withheld from workers or whether there are policies that restrict workers' movement during working hours (such as systems that require workers to obtain a card to go to the toilet).[3] Overall, while there is some variability, the average number of violations per audit is less than 0.10 and has been declining since 2016. Here, too, the ability of a two-day audit to uncover violations of forced labor is limited.

Figure 4.4 reports the incidence of *freedom of association* (FOA) violations per audit. These data are relatively sparse, with more than half the audits not reporting FOA violations, and hence these results do not instill a high level of confidence.[4] But where audits do report these violations, the number of violations on average is significantly higher than for child and forced labor and discrimination. While the trend line shows a steady state, the variations across countries are quite large.[5] The variation across industries is also similarly larger than for other core labor standards, with sharp increases in the food, apparel accessories, and agriculture industries. As noted for other measures, the contemporary audit regime does *not* do a good job of detecting FOA violations, and so these figures should be taken with a grain of salt.[6] (See chapter 6 for a more detailed investigation of FOA.)

Although not a core labor standard, *harassment and abuse* (figure 4.5) are increasingly parts of corporate codes of conduct. The measures include physical, sexual, and verbal harassment by supervisors, typically assessed based on complaints

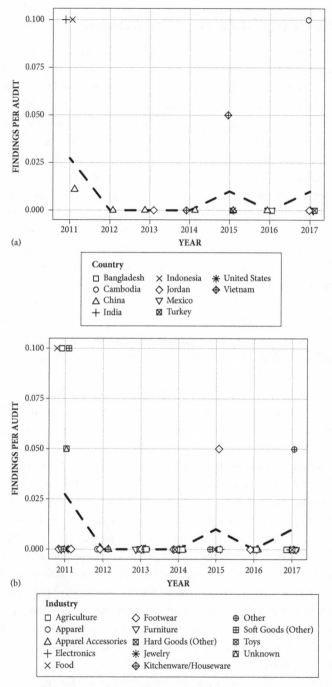

FIGURE 4.1.   Child labor findings by country (a) and industry (b)

Chart by author.

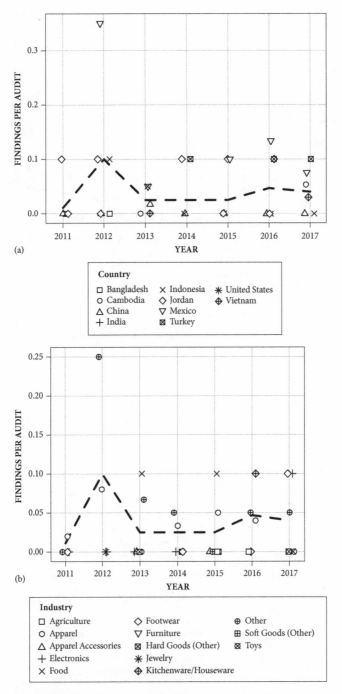

FIGURE 4.2. Discrimination findings by country (a) and industry (b)

Chart by author.

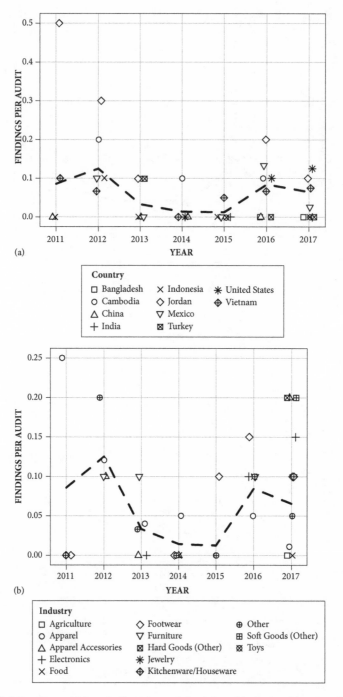

FIGURE 4.3. Forced labor findings by country (a) and industry (b)

Chart by author.

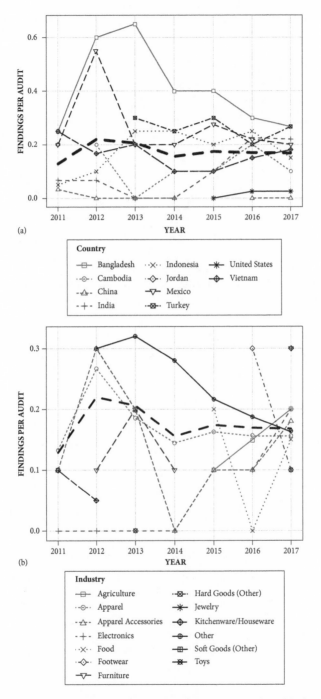

FIGURE 4.4. Freedom of association findings by country (a) and industry (b)

Chart by author.

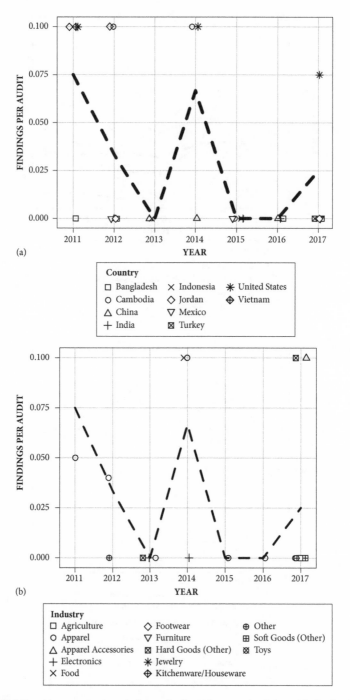

FIGURE 4.5.   Harassment and abuse findings by country (a) and industry (b)

Chart by author.

made by workers to auditors. That basis, of course, is the source of the measurement problem: workers, fearing management reprisals, may not complain. The difficulties in uncovering workplace sexual harassment, even in advanced industrial countries, are well known, and there is little reason to believe these difficulties are any less of a problem in these countries. There are lots of missing data here—we cannot get consistent trends for each country and industry—and so the trend lines are not a reliable guide.

Ever since the series of tragic factory fires in Bangladesh, most companies have increased their attention on *health and safety* (H&S), and thus AUDCO has as well. Most codes have extensive H&S provisions that take a significant amount of time in each audit. H&S accounts for a high percentage of total violations. The metrics include building safety and access issues, blocked aisles, insufficiently wide aisles, usable exits, whether evacuation drills are conducted and a detailed evacuation plan exists, the number of fire extinguishers and hydrants, the use of smoke detectors, and whether public address systems are in working order. H&S also includes chemical safety (storage, eye-washing facilities) and machine safety (safety guards, gloves, etc.). For its customers, AUDCO aggregates only data that are broadly similar across the many different company codes. Figure 4.6 shows high numbers of H&S violations.

Figure 4.7 reports violations associated with *hours of work* (actual hours worked are covered later). Typical violations include longer hours than mandated, inadequate rest, and whether overtime is within prescribed limits. The typical audit finds at least two violations of the hours of work standard, but the variation across countries is quite large, as it is across industries. Higher production volumes during certain seasons explain some of the variations.

The number of violations with respect to *wages and benefits* is also high, with one or two violations found per audit. Typically, these involve not paying the correct regular or overtime wage, delayed payments, and inaccurate calculation of benefits (particularly social insurance in China). Figure 4.8 shows a fairly steady downward trend in these violations over time both in countries (except India) and across industries.

AUDCO also reports on the percentage of workers who receive correct basic and overtime wage payments. Figure 4.9 (a) suggests that the overall percentage of workers paid correctly has increased over time, on average, and now exceeds 90 percent—despite significant variation across countries. Figure 4.9 (b) shows the figures for industries.

It is heartening to note a steady decline in the *average weekly hours of work* by country, across the board (figure 4.10 (a)). Clearly, this is an area in which private regulation is having a definite impact in overall terms. The Fair Labor Association (FLA) code suggests that "the regular work week shall not exceed 48 hours" and

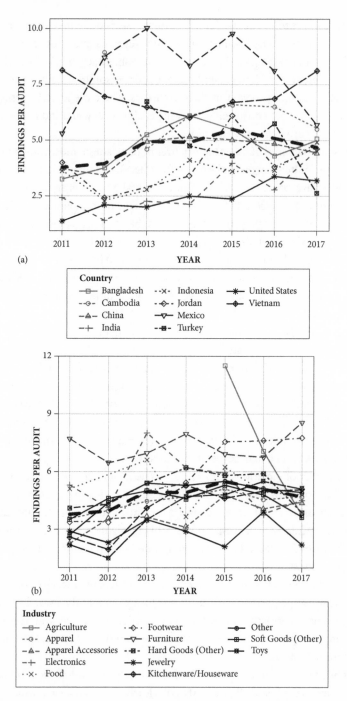

FIGURE 4.6. Health and safety findings by country (a) and industry (b)

Chart by author.

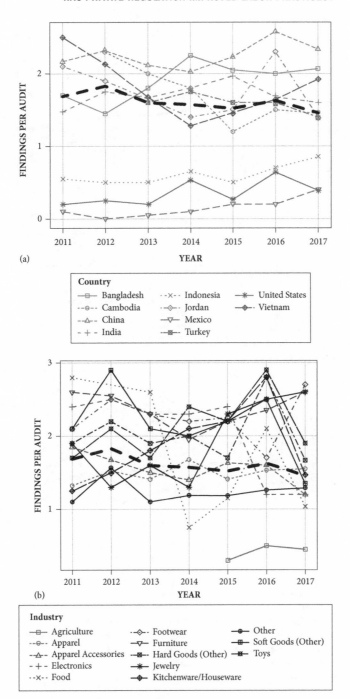

FIGURE 4.7. Hours of work findings by country (a) and industry (b)

Chart by author.

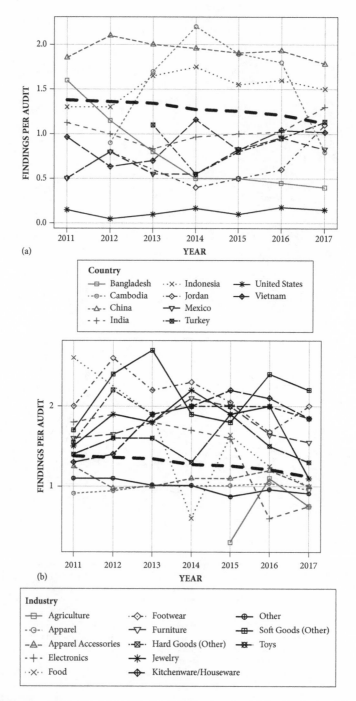

FIGURE 4.8. Wages and benefits findings by country (a) and industry (b)

Chart by author.

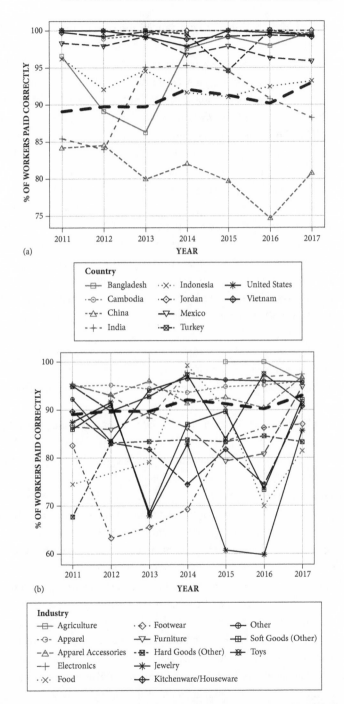

FIGURE 4.9. Percentage of workers paid correctly by country (a) and industry (b)

Chart by author.

that "other than in exceptional circumstances, the sum of regular and overtime hours shall not exceed 60 hours." AUDCO's data accounts for both regular and overtime hours, and if its auditors are correct, the FLA standard is largely being met—despite some anomalies, such as workers in Bangladesh working well above the FLA working-hours standard. The pattern across industries is much more variable, however. It is important to point out that AUDCO's data do not report normal and overtime hours separately. And significantly, a key dimension of overtime is that it should be voluntary, not forced—a variable that AUDCO's data do not report. Figure 4.10 (b) shows the figures by industry.

Linked to average hours per week is the standard that all workers must have at least twenty-four consecutive hours of rest in every seven-day period. This is generally the same across all MSI and company codes. The overall country trend for *continuous days of work* is positive, but the range is still disturbing (figure 4.11 (a)). As for industries (figure 4.11 (b)), footwear is the only one that has shown an increase in working hours after 2016. The consistent decline over time noted for other industries could be attributed to better education of factory management by auditors about code of conduct provisions or to better enforcement by national governments.

Figure 4.12 provides an indication of gross progress on *hourly wages* (chapter 5 discusses actual wages in much greater detail). The trend for both countries and industries is a steady (if slow) increase, just as hours are steadily (though also slowly) decreasing.

AUDCO also made available a second dataset that incorporates data from twelve countries and seven industries. Drawing on this dataset, table 4.3 shows the percentage of total violations accounted for in aggregate in each of five categories over time.

In the table, the *health and safety* category includes violations involving building safety, chemical safety, emergency evacuation, fire safety, machine safety, occupational safety, injuries, and general dormitory and kitchen conditions. *Labor standards* include child labor, forced labor, freedom of association, foreign migrant workers, wages, working hours, harassment, abuse, and disciplinary practices. *Management systems* relate to code awareness, factory size, the use of unauthorized subcontracting, and documentation of wages and working hours and worker contracts. *Business ethics* includes issues connected with factory transparency, business licenses, bribery, and the presence of clear policies regarding the core labor standards articulated by the ILO. And the *environment* category includes air emissions, environmental management, environmental permits, waste management, and waste water management. While in my view the specific violations that make up each category are not always internally consistent (particularly

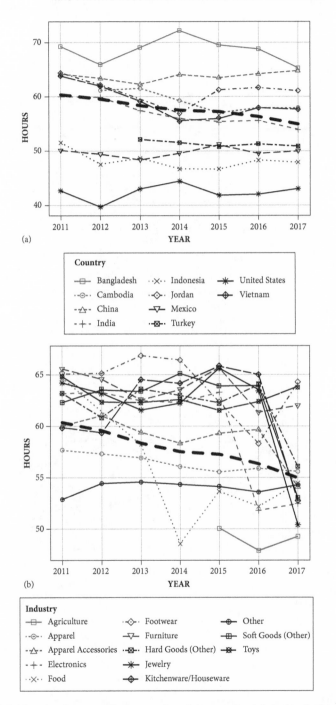

FIGURE 4.10. Average weekly hours of work by country (a) and industry (b)

Chart by author.

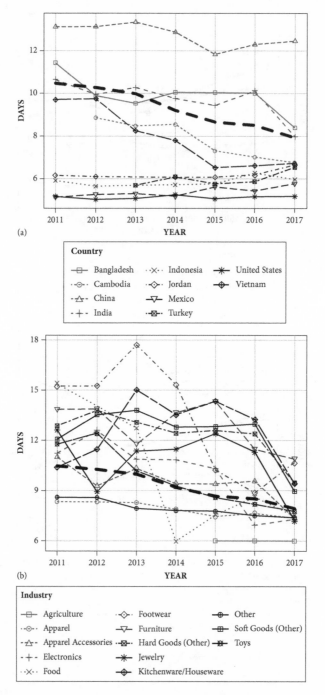

FIGURE 4.11. Continuous days of work by country (a) and industry (b)

Chart by author.

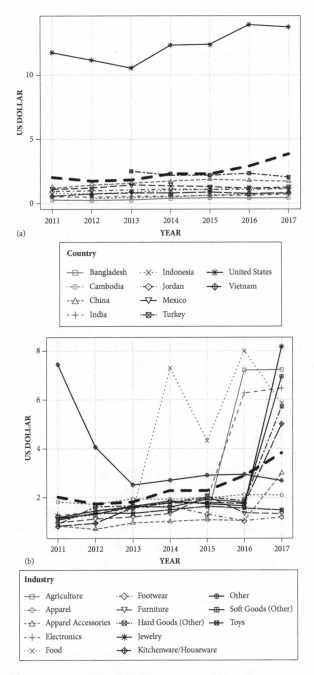

FIGURE 4.12. Average hourly wage by country (a) and industry (b)

Chart by author.
Note: Wages were reported in local currencies and converted into US dollars for this analysis, using the prevailing exchange rates on May 1 of each year.

TABLE 4.3. Violations per audit by category

YEAR	HEALTH AND SAFETY	LABOR STANDARDS	MANAGEMENT SYSTEMS	ENVIRONMENT	BUSINESS ETHICS
2011	39.69	33.39	20.62	3.59	2.71
2012	37.40	36.56	19.33	4.54	2.17
2013	44.28	29.03	17.78	7.40	1.52
2014	48.27	26.86	16.81	6.17	1.89
2015	48.90	27.60	15.73	6.11	1.66
2016	45.19	31.95	15.17	6.20	1.48
2017	47.17	32.23	13.42	4.95	2.22

in the *management systems* category), they do represent AUDCO's internal classification, and presumably their client companies may have requested it.

Most crucial in the context of this book is the overall trend for labor standards violations, which shows a slight increase. The considerable variation over time may be linked to factories' entry into and exit from the database (tracking the same factories over time is not possible). The results are consistent with the notion that factories "cycle in and out of compliance."[7] The data also reveal an overall increase in labor standards violations across industries. These gross measures of violations per audit suggest that private regulation has resulted in only limited improvement in adherence to labor standards over time.[8]

Overall, the picture of progress that emerges from this gross *macro* analysis in Study 1 is mixed. The number of child labor, forced labor, discrimination, and freedom of association violations has been remarkably low, with no specific trend—but it may be that auditing is not doing a good job of uncovering violations. Wages have increased and hours worked have decreased, and workers are increasingly paid correctly—results we see even with factories dropping in and out of the dataset. These quantifiable results suggest that private regulation is indeed having an effect, although there are several countries and industries where hours worked remain unacceptably high and where wages remain low.

When it comes to other kinds of violations, we see health and safety violations are high and increasing—perhaps because of a greater focus by auditors, or because new factories are added to the dataset every year. Overall, the effect of private regulation in terms of labor standards is uncertain: during the seven-year period studied, the number of violations per audit has remained mostly stable, and increases or decreases other than for H&S violations have not been remarkable. There is no basis, therefore, to conclude that private regulation is working well overall; a more focused examination of progress is necessary, one that focuses on the *same* factories over multiple years and audits. Such a longitudinal examination—as in Study 2, which follows—allows for observing whether there has been sustained progress.

Study 2: Progress in Specific Factories

Again, factories "cycle in and out of compliance."[9] Factories audited regularly should, in theory, show evidence of sustainable improvement in terms of the number of violations. For the second study, we use two different datasets to test this hypothesis. The first dataset is from AUDCO; the second dataset is from Better Work.

AUDCO Data

AUDCO provided a unique subset of data from its audits in India that allows for examining audit violations for the factories that have been audited multiple times. We identified a total of 340 factories that had been audited more than once during the 2014–2018 period, ranging from twice to as many as a dozen times. These data not only allow for examining audits between two time periods but also across multiple time periods.

Figures 4.13 through 4.17 show the results of the analysis for selected variables, based on looking at average improvement after each audit (the bolded black line in each figure). Each circle represents a factory, making it possible to see the distribution of factories at each audit.

There is no clear improvement in continuous working days, and working hours appear to decrease only after the fifth audit (and are generally lower by the tenth). Hourly wages show yearly variation but are roughly the same at the beginning and end of the period—and this variation (especially decreases in the same factory) may well be caused by the practice of employing casual and temporary workers or by changes in the labor force pool, given high turnover rates in this industry in India. Monthly take-home pay shows a slight increase over multiple audits, likely reflecting higher rates of overtime hours, because hourly pay has not increased. Finally, there is no definite trend with respect to paying workers correctly, although it is encouraging to note that the percentage of workers paid correctly is high at 90 percent.

The overall finding—*nonsignificant* improvements over time, despite multiple audits—points to fundamental problems with how private regulation works. Clearly these data show that multiple audits do *not* result in sustained improvement over time.[10] They are a damning indictment of private regulation, as

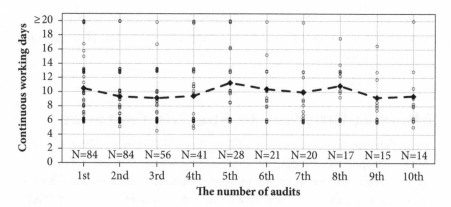

FIGURE 4.13. Continuous working days in Indian factories audited multiple times, 2014–2018

Chart by author.

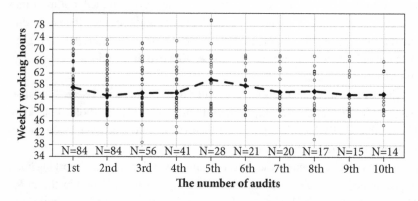

FIGURE 4.14. Weekly working hours in Indian factories audited multiple times, 2014–2018

Chart by author.

repeated "treatments" (audits) do not result in "cures for the illness" (outcomes for workers).

What explains the lack of progress? AUDCO's auditors are generally well trained, so it is unlikely that these data are just poor or inconsistent. There may be something systemic concerning Indian factories that accounts for the absence of significant progress. What if we could examine progress in factories that have been audited multiple times across *several* countries? That is the focus with the Better Work data.

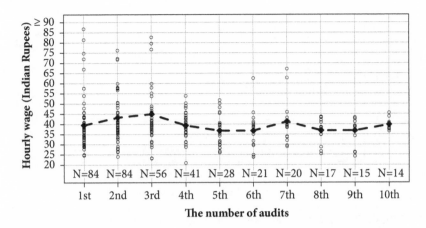

FIGURE 4.15. Hourly wages in Indian factories audited multiple times, 2014–2018

Chart by author.

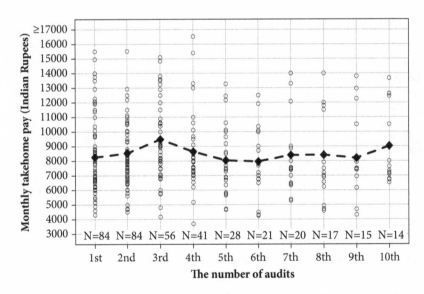

FIGURE 4.16. Monthly take-home pay in Indian factories audited multiple times, 2014–2018

Chart by author.

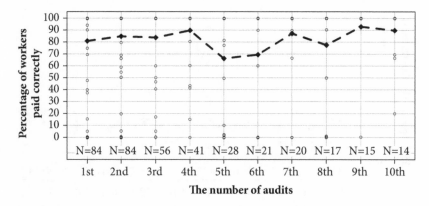

FIGURE 4.17. Workers paid correctly in Indian factories audited multiple times, 2014–2018

Chart by author.

Better Work Data

The Better Work program, a collaboration between the ILO and the International Finance Corporation (IFC), focuses on assessing compliance in what the program calls "clusters": four *core labor standards* clusters, including child labor, forced labor, discrimination, and freedom of association; and four *outcomes standards* clusters, including compensation, human resource policies and contracts, working time, and occupational safety and health.[11] Better Work operates in seven countries and made data available from 1,968 factories operating in six of them: Cambodia, Nicaragua, Haiti, Vietnam, Indonesia and Jordan.[12] (Box 4.2 describes incentives for factories' participation in the program.)

Our dataset from Better Work includes compliance data for the years 2015 through 2017 and includes factories at different stages (cycles) of Better Work assessments. Some factories have been assessed only once (one cycle) while others have been assessed multiple times. We report data for factories that have been assessed eight times (eight cycles). In essence, the analysis of the Better Work data asks the same question asked with AUDCO's India data: Do factories exposed to repeated audits or assessments show a sustained pattern of improvement?

The "process of improvement at the core of the Better Work model is built upon factory-level social dialogue" through "a Performance Improvement Consultative Committee (PICC) comprised of equal numbers of factory management and worker representatives." In general, factories participating in Better Work tend to show substantial improvements in compliance. As one researcher writes regarding Cambodia, "By the fourth assessment visit, average compliance rates

---

Box 4.2. Incentives for Participating in the Better Work Program

In most of the seven Better Work countries, a "market-based" incentive gets factories to participate.[1] These factories pay a fee to participate, and they primarily supply reputation-sensitive buyers whose orders depend substantially on a factory showing improvements in compliance. The Better Work program works cooperatively with several global brands, requiring that those brands continue to source from these factories provided they show those improvements.

While the brands are, therefore, driving the decision of factories to participate, the chances are high that participating factories are better managed and more compliant, having already successfully garnered orders from buyers concerned about their reputations. It is, of course, also possible that factories with a genuine desire to improve would participate in Better Work.

In Haiti and Cambodia, the incentive is related to trade agreements, and participation is not an option. Haiti's free trade agreement with the United States requires all exporting factories to join Better Work. In Cambodia, the program began under a bilateral trade agreement with the United States that covers all textile-exporting factories.

1. Rossi 2015.

---

range from a low of 52% to a high of 95% with the mass of the distribution lying between 75% and 95%."[13] Here's what our results showed.

We calculated the overall compliance for each of the eight clusters by adding up the total number of violations found for each cluster, divided by the total number of questions on which the factories were assessed, and multiplied by one hundred. As would be expected of Better Work factories, the compliance rate is extremely high in our data (table 4.4).

Was there, however, improvement with each successive cycle? Table 4.5 answers that question (it should be noted that table 4.5 does *not* follow the same factories

TABLE 4.4. Overall compliance rates by country, 2017–2018

	CAMBODIA	VIETNAM	INDONESIA	JORDAN	HAITI	NICARAGUA
Number of factories	814	560	351	149	47	47
COMPLIANCE						
Overall	84.50	91.57	87.60	89.17	87.09	94.86
Without FOA	82.66	91.12	85.99	89.54	85.57	94.25
Forced labor	99.79	99.95	99.96	99.63	100.00	100.00
Discrimination	99.65	99.71	96.26	96.48	99.91	100.00
Child labor	98.87	96.55	99.57	98.99	99.39	100.00
FOA	97.97	95.51	98.21	86.85	99.26	99.52
Compensation	84.54	93.52	85.72	91.50	83.71	97.79
Contracts and HR	80.24	89.10	81.64	89.83	93.35	94.56
Working time	81.21	82.27	83.86	98.32	91.75	94.83
OSH	65.60	85.14	79.37	82.60	71.67	85.46

over time, but compares average compliance of all factories in a particular cycle and reports data for eight cycles). Factories in their second cycle of Better Work assessment have higher compliance rates, on average, than factories in their first cycle. Factories in their eighth cycle report higher compliance, on average, than most factories in their sixth or seventh cycles. Compliance improves particularly when it comes to forced labor and child labor, whereas compliance with freedom of association and discrimination standards remains stable over multiple assessments. Broadly speaking, these results suggest higher factory compliance in later cycles than in earlier cycles.[14]

The Better Work data suggest that repeated assessments *do* result in improvements. But can the Better Work results be generalized? Participation in the Better Work program is compulsory in countries such as Haiti, Jordan, and Cambodia under the free trade agreements they have with the United States. Participation is voluntary in other countries. Among garment factories around the world, the Better Work factories are likely the better ones in terms of labor standards. As a result of their participation in Better Work, these factories have top management commitment to improving compliance as a condition of participation, and the factories gain from the assessments and the advice of Better Work assessors. Factories' compliance is monitored by the active participation of workers through PICCs, and most of these factories (in countries where participation is voluntary) are encouraged to participate by reputation-conscious global buyers. Even if PICCs do not work well in some contexts,[15] worker involvement in plant-level compliance issues is still a unique feature of the Better Work program. Hence, the positive results here are not generalizable—the data come from the best of the

TABLE 4.5. Compliance across assessment cycles in Better Work factories

CYCLE	NO. OF FACTORIES	FORCED LABOR	DISCRIMINATION	CHILD LABOR	FOA	COMPENSATION	CONTRACTS AND HR	WORKING TIME	OCCUPATIONAL SAFETY AND HEALTH
1	311	99.80	98.40	97.49	95.41	85.99	79.21	80.39	71.23
2	476	99.81	99.11	98.16	97.12	85.65	81.50	81.15	69.29
3	522	99.86	99.24	98.44	97.15	86.79	83.60	82.50	73.88
4	232	99.96	98.98	98.42	97.36	90.45	87.01	85.19	80.95
5	103	99.86	97.77	99.03	96.57	90.96	88.36	88.39	84.04
6	103	100.00	98.27	98.71	95.53	92.96	89.77	90.09	86.02
7	98	100.00	98.83	99.66	95.99	94.11	91.55	89.40	85.87
8	63	99.86	97.82	99.47	95.34	96.02	93.44	91.64	87.38

bunch among factories, and the assessment program is not quite the same as the typical private regulation approach.

The Better Work results stand in contrast to those in AUDCO's India data. An academic analogy helps explain why. One would think that a student taking the same test repeatedly would show improvement over time. The India data, though, show that repetition does not necessarily result in improvement. The Better Work data suggest that improvement depends on the type of student, classroom environment, and teacher.

If studying Better Work tells us nothing about the average factory in private regulation, is the program an inappropriate test of the effect of repeated assessments? An even more stringent test of whether the private regulation program is working at improving compliance must look at average factories *without* the variety of Better Work institutional aspects described here. That is the focus of the section that follows.

Study 3: Progress in a Single Retailer's Supply Chain in One Country

Examining improvements in a single retailer's supply chain in one country is a way to explore whether a specific private regulation program is capable of inducing sustained improvements in compliance among its supplier factories. Here, we find a case of success in which there was a clear and definite improvement in a sample of factories supplying a global home products retailer—and we can inquire why such a sustained improvement occurred.[16]

We obtained data from the audit results of one hundred supplier factories located in China that comprise part of the supply chain of HomeRetailer (not the company's real name), a global home products retailer that sources from suppliers around the world. We introduced this retailer in chapter 3. HomeRetailer is a leader in the home products industry and an early adopter of private regulation, and the company enjoys a reputation for effective private regulation honed over a period of twenty years.

The one hundred suppliers (table 4.5), located primarily in the Yangtze River and Pearl River deltas, are distributed across a range of industries, including furniture, lighting, textiles, metalworking, and others. Most of the suppliers are domestically owned; less than 20 percent are subsidiaries of mostly Taiwanese corporations. The suppliers employ from seventeen to seventeen thousand workers and at the time of data collection had been in business for three to twenty-eight years. HomeRetailer enjoys a high degree of leverage over these suppliers, generally accounting for a significant share of the suppliers' production.

HomeRetailer's private regulation program is quite similar to those of most companies, except that it uses its own auditors rather than subcontracting auditing companies. HomeRetailer's internal auditors audit its suppliers in China approximately every twelve months. Its code of conduct consists of seventy-five different assessment items, incorporating all the content typically found in most corporate codes. Each audit reports the factory's overall compliance, as well as compliance for employment practices (a sixteen-item subset of overall compliance) and for wages and hours (a six-item subset of employment practices).[17] An audit score (compliance score) is calculated for each of the three sections as a percentage of complied-with items out of all items in that section. For instance, a supplier that complies with seventy-four items and violates only one item on wages and hours would receive an overall audit score of 98.6 (100*74/75) percent, 93.8 (100*15/16) percent for employment practices, and 83.3 (100*5/6) percent for wages and hours. (Because these factories are located in China, there is no effort to assess freedom of association, which is not allowed by the government.)

HomeRetailer's private regulation program in China was introduced in 2001. After the annual audits during the first several years, HomeRetailer's auditors would share the results with each of its suppliers and discuss remediation plans for violations. As long as a supplier could demonstrate it was remediating, it could be reasonably confident it would continue to be part of HomeRetailer's supply chain. In 2008, however, in part in response to criticism from NGOs and others that private regulation was not working, HomeRetailer changed its compliance requirement. It mandated that all its supplier factories in China reach a minimum compliance score of 90 percent by August 2010 and 98.6 percent by August 2012. Suppliers were allowed to be noncompliant on only one issue—overtime hours (which accounted for 1.4 points on a 100-point scale). Thus, 98.6 percent became the "new normal" for compliance.

Failure to reach the new normal within the specified time frame means being axed from the supplier list. In terms of the private regulation model, HomeRetailer buttressed the "carrot" of incentivizing suppliers to improve compliance by making more orders from these suppliers with a stronger "stick"—the threat of discontinuation of the relationship. However, factories were given five years (from 2008 to 2012) to reach the "new normal," and were given an extra year if they faltered for one year during the five-year period.

To check compliance improvement and the impact of this strict policy, we obtained audit scores of each of the one hundred suppliers at *four* times: two *before* the policy changes introduced in 2010 and two *after* the private regulation program was changed. Most *before* audit reports were for the years 2006 and 2007; all the *after* reports were for 2012 and 2013. This provides four waves of audit data that allow for a before-after comparison.

Figure 4.18 shows that compliance improved across the four waves. There was a particularly sharp increase in average compliance on human resource standards and wage and hours standards between the second audit in 2007–2008 and the audit in 2012, understandable given HomeRetailer's mandated 90 percent compliance minimum by 2010—a strong incentive for suppliers to improve their historically weak compliance on wages and hours. The improvements on these issues between the 2012 audits and 2013 audits were much more moderate because there was less room to improve once the minimum threshold had been reached.

Pooling the audits across the years shows that compliance was uneven before the 2010 change (figure 4.19). After the strict requirement of 90 percent compliance was imposed, there was stable improvement. In 2014, while overall compliance decreased about 3 percent, the average compliance with human resources standards and wage and hours standards was maintained at the level required by HomeRetailer.

We examined differences between overall compliance, compliance in terms of human resources items, and compliance for wages and hours. Given the increasingly small room for overall improvement after reaching 86.2 percent compliance during the second round of audits and 97 percent in the 2012 audits, the *rate* of improvement in *overall* compliance did not increase across the waves. There were, though, cases of deterioration (improvement falling below zero) between the second audit and the 2012 audit for some suppliers and between the 2012 and 2013 audits for others. This finding suggests that maintaining high compliance at a steady state is not easy.

For compliance on human resources standards and wages and hours, improvement was much greater between the second audit and the 2012 audit than between the first and second audits. This improvement might be attributable to HomeRetailer's stricter requirement since 2010. Moreover, for compliance on human resources, the number of audits with lower compliance decreased across the waves of audits. For compliance on wages and hours, there was greater variation in the rate of improvement. In fact, for three suppliers, compliance on wages and hours decreased from 83.3 percent (complied with five items) to 66.7 percent (complied with four items), again suggesting the difficulty of maintaining such a high level of compliance.

The results of Study 3 here are potentially important for private regulation. The study clearly shows that adopting a very strict policy on compliance does pay dividends (assuming audits are done correctly), as long as suppliers are given a *reasonable time to improve and orders are guaranteed* through the improvement process.

Most global companies with private regulation programs have been hesitant to adopt such strict compliance requirements. While they use audit data to

TABLE 4.6. Summary statistics on one hundred suppliers in China

	NUMBER OF SUPPLIERS (MAX = 100)	MEAN	STD/DEV	MIN	MAX
Domestically owned	83				
Foreign owned	17				
Yangtze Delta	58				
Pearl River Delta	30				
Other regions	12				
Furniture	13				
Lighting	26				
Textiles	28				
Metal	19				
Others	14				
Number of workers		649	1,708	17	17,000
Firm history (years)		12.5	4.9	3	28
Retailer share of supplier production		63.4	32	1	100

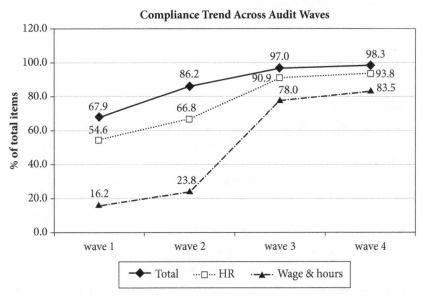

FIGURE 4.18. Changes in audit scores of one hundred suppliers (before and after)

Chart by author.

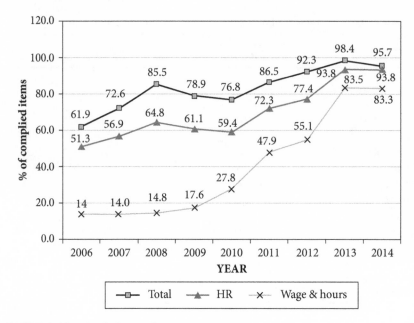

FIGURE 4.19. Pooled compliance across years

Chart by author.

direct suppliers to remediate violations, very few buyers threaten outright to drop suppliers from the supply chain or provide the positive incentives Home-Retailer adopted.

The key implication here is that global buyers can use their buying power to enforce stricter compliance norms if they so wish—particularly when they have a high degree of leverage. To be sure, not every firm can do that. Smaller retailers often depend on large vendors to organize their sourcing, affording these small retailers very little leverage over their suppliers.

One could argue that the private regulation model as designed allows companies to have a strict compliance model, at least in theory. In this case, HomeRetailer provided its suppliers with advance notice, provided interim and final targets, and allowed its suppliers enough time to reach those targets. Perhaps such a staggered approach has promise. There is some evidence that stricter approaches have worked in the toy industry.[18] The case of an apparel company in chapter 8 stands out as an example of the potential to use HomeRetailer's approach. In the apparel industry, where buyer-supplier relationships are more transactional and buyers rarely give suppliers firm guarantees of future orders, copying HomeRetailer's approach may not be possible without radical changes in sourcing practices.

Conclusion

So what do we learn from the multiple sources of evidence in this chapter regarding the overall progress of private regulation efforts? AUDCO's data on violations from more than 20,000 reliable audits over time show that the violations on core labor rights tend to be few in number, with some variations across countries and industries. Whether the low number of violations is a function of the inability of current auditing practices to uncover the violations is an open question. Because the audits deal with potentially different factories over time in each country and industry, we can report only cross-sectional averages across factories by year, and so it is difficult to find a clear trend toward improvement.

A more stringent investigation of the progress of private regulation in Indian factories audited multiple times during a four-year period does not augur well for private regulation efforts. There were no significant improvements in several outcome variables and only very slight improvements in working hours. Looking beyond Indian factories to a sample of 1,968 Better Work factories in multiple countries, there were improvements in core labor rights after multiple factory assessments. Factories exposed to multiple cycles of auditing generally reported higher compliance. This study shows that the Better Work model, which has worker involvement at the core of improving compliance, does have relevance for contemporary private regulation efforts that lack such worker involvement. Even though Better Work factories differ from the average garment supplier, there are implications for transferability.

The best evidence of compliance progress can be seen in the HomeRetailer study. This global retailer provided its long-term suppliers sufficient advance notice of a new zero-tolerance policy and four or five years to reach the desired compliance level—and all suppliers did so. HomeRetailer promised to continue to source from the suppliers during the period of improvement, giving them some degree of financial security. But it is a strict model, possible only when there are long-term relationships and a commitment by the buyer to longer-term purchases; it is not generalizable to the apparel industry, which is characterized by more short-term contracting.

WAGES IN GLOBAL SUPPLY CHAINS
Where They Stand and Where We Need to Go

with Jinsun Bae

Of the many labor standards embodied in corporate codes of conduct, the gap between what is stated and actual practice is perhaps greatest for wages—and has been ever since these codes were established in the early 1990s in the global apparel industry. As many studies have shown, workers in global garment supply chains are paid well below a living wage and are often paid less than their country's legal minimum wage. As the Joint Ethical Trading Initiatives (representing multi-stakeholder initiatives in Norway, Denmark, and the United Kingdom) wrote in 2015, "How can we talk meaningfully about 'doing ethical trade' where wages are firmly stuck below the level at which people can live decent lives, and companies feel that it is beyond their power to change this."[1] Even studies of companies such as H&M and Marks and Spencer that have made specific living wage commitments have found significant gaps between the promise and the reality.

This chapter examines progress on wages in global supply chains, using AUDCO data. This examination allows for generating light, rather than the heat created by occasional investigative reports on supply chain worker wages. The data include hourly wage rates, the gap between actual wages and minimum wages, the gap between actual wages and take-home pay, and finally the gap between these paid wages and a number of different living wage estimates drawn from 14,315 reliable audits done during the period 2011–2017 in ten countries and seven industries. To triangulate the effort, this examination also includes *cross-sectional* data on wages from the supply chain of a global apparel company for the year 2016. Together, these data provide a baseline against which future developments can be compared.

These data show that wages in all countries have increased and are above the minimum wage (with a few exceptions in a small number of audits). Of course, it is difficult to credit private regulation programs with these increases, given the numerous other influences on wage levels—not the least being local labor market conditions as well as prices paid to suppliers for their product. But the fact that wages paid are above the minimum in most countries is at least *consistent* with code of conduct commitments. The evidence also shows that wages have been increasing every year—some codes require annual year-on-year increases. And it demonstrates that wage levels are nowhere near the living wage required by many codes of conduct. The gaps are large, and wages would need to increase considerably to reach the living wage commitments made by global firms in different countries and industries.

Wage Provisions in Codes of Conduct, and How Those Standards Are Determined

The starting point for examining progress on wages is the standard against which to assess that progress. The standards are laid down in the codes of conduct of individual companies and the codes of multi-stakeholder associations.

It is important to highlight that these standards draw inspiration from several international "soft-law" initiatives: the Universal Declaration of Human Rights, which highlights a living wage as a human right; the United Nations Guiding Principles for Human Rights and Business (the "Ruggie Principles"), which highlight the need to pay living wages; and the Organisation for Economic Co-operation and Development (OECD) guidelines for multinational enterprises, revised in 2011, which suggest companies have a responsibility to pay living wages in their operations and supply chains and imposes due diligence in terms of reporting how companies are acting responsibly with regard to living wages, while incorporating a grievance mechanism. Living wages are also mentioned in the ILO's 2008 Declaration on Social Justice for a Fair Globalization, and the ILO's 2006 Tripartite Declaration of Principles concerning Multinational Enterprises and Social Policy encourages multinationals to observe the principle that wages, benefits, and working conditions should be no less favorable to the workers than those offered by comparable employers in the countries concerned.

Codes of conduct draw on these soft-law instruments in many different ways. Box 5.1 is a representative sample of what the codes of multi-stakeholder institutions and individual companies *say* about wages. These codes all provide for paying wages according to local law, and most require that the wage be based on standard working hours. Beyond these requirements, the codes vary, with

Box 5.1. Sample Code of Conduct Provisions Regarding Wages

The *Fair Labor Association* establishes the right of every worker to weekly compensation that meets "basic needs" and provides "some discretionary income," and stipulates that employers "pay at least the minimum wage or the appropriate prevailing wage, whichever is higher, comply with all legal requirements on wages, and provide any fringe benefits required by law or contract." Employers not in compliance must "work with the FLA to take appropriate actions that seek to progressively realize a level of compensation that does."[1]

The *Fair Wear Foundation* stipulates that wages and benefits for a standard working week "meet at least legal or industry minimum standards" and always be sufficient to meet basic needs of workers and their families and provide some discretionary income. FWF has developed a tool to help calculate increases necessary for compliance.[2]

The *Ethical Trading Initiative* code states that a standard week's wages and benefits "must meet, at a minimum, national legal standards or industry benchmark standards, whichever is higher" and also meet basic needs and provide some discretionary income.[3]

The code of the *Worldwide Responsible Apparel Production* requires payment of "at least the minimum total compensation required by local law including all mandated wages, allowance and benefits."[4]

Social Accountability International (SAI) declares a living wage to be a "right" and that a normal week's wages, not including overtime, must always meet "meet at least legal or industry minimum standards, or collective bargaining agreements (where applicable)."[5] SAI works with the Global Living Wage Coalition to develop country-specific living wage estimates. SA 8000, SAI's social standard, defines a living wage as "the remuneration received for a standard work week by a worker in a particular place to afford a decent standard of living for the worker and his or her family."

Box 5.1. (continued)

The *Business Social Compliance Initiative* requires partners to pay at least "wages mandated by governments' minimum wage legislation, or industry standards approved on the basis of collective bargaining, whichever is higher."[6]

Action, Collaboration, Transformation defines living wages as "the minimum income necessary for a worker to meet the basic needs of himself/herself and his/her family, including some discretionary income. This should be earned during legal working hour limits (i.e. without overtime)."[7]

H&M requires that employers pay "at least the statutory minimum wage, the prevailing industry wage or the wage negotiated in a collective agreement, whichever is higher," along with any other "legally mandated benefits and compensations." The company forbids "unfair deductions" and ensures a worker's "right to a written specification of how the wage has been calculated."[8] In 2013, H&M announced that "strategic suppliers should have their pay structures in place to pay a fair living wage by 2018," and its 2014 Sustainability Report stipulates the implementation, by 2018, of "improved pay structures at all strategic supplier factories, impacting 850,000 workers."[9]

Gap Inc. facilities must "pay wages and overtime premiums in compliance with all applicable laws" and "at least the minimum legal wage or a wage that meets local industry standards, whichever is greater." The company recommends that these be "sufficient to cover workers' basic needs and some discretionary income."[10]

Finally, *Marks and Spencer* requires that compensation of workers by its suppliers "include wages, overtime pay, all legally required benefits and paid leave which respectively meet or exceed the national legal minimum wage, and all applicable laws and regulations," and

Box 5.1. (continued)

that there also be "a transparent process to ensure that workers fully understand the wages that they receive." If industry benchmark standards, collective agreements, or both are in place and require a wage that is higher than the minimum wage, they must be followed.[11]

1. Fair Labor Association n.d.
2. Fair Wear Foundation n.d.
3. Ethical Trading Initiative 2006.
4. Worldwide Accredited Responsible Production 2019.
5. Social Accountability International 2016, 82.
6. Amfori 2017, 5.
7. ACT n.d., 4.
8. H&M 2010.
9. McMullen and Majumder 2016; Turn Around H&M 2018; H&M 2014, 29.
10. Gap Inc. 2016.
11. Marks and Spencer 2018, 9.

references to "industry standards" and "minimum wages" and "living wage." Some mention collective bargaining. Others require that the wage meet "basic needs" and provide some "discretionary" income.

As box 5.1 shows, the provisions regarding wages in private regulation can be considered to be on a continuum. But how are the actual wages determined?

Most national governments in supplier countries have a process by which minimum wages are determined (e.g., wage boards), which often reflects the different parties' interests. Governments may wish to keep minimum wages low enough to attract foreign investment, while ensuring they are high enough to satisfy workers' demands; employers generally will lobby for a lower threshold; and workers and unions (where they exist) will attempt to get a higher minimum wage. Whatever the process, the evidence suggests that in many countries the minimum wage is not significantly higher than poverty wages, is rarely adjusted to keep pace with the rising cost of living, and often does not provide enough to meet basic needs.

Some codes require that wages be set according to prevailing industry standards if these standards require a wage higher than the minimum wage or require that wages be set by collective bargaining (a rare occurrence given the very limited collective bargaining in the global apparel industry, detailed in chapter 6). It is reasonable to assume that employers will benchmark with other employers in the same industry and region (employers would need to do so to retain workers in a typically high-turnover industry). Hence, it is possible that wages reflect industry, regional, and local labor market norms, even if the wages are low.

There is considerable variation in how a living wage is conceptualized, measured, and implemented, as the following examples show:[2]

- The *Asia Floor Wage Alliance* (AFWA), an international alliance of trade unions and labor activists, launched a regional effort (most garments are produced in Asia) in 2008 to develop a wage that would be sufficient for workers to live on in dignity and safety. The AFWA calculates a wage measured in Purchasing Power Parity dollars (PPP$) that no wage in Asia should drop below. The calculation assumes that workers in Asia generally spend more than 50 percent of their income on food, that an adult needs to take in three thousand calories per day, and that workers need to support themselves and at least two "consumption units" (one unit equals one adult or two children). AFWA researches a "food basket" in select Asian countries to estimate costs of food, clothing, medical, education, health care, and savings and to determine a PPS$ for those countries—which allows for comparing living standards and creating a regional average.[3]
- The *Global Living Wage Coalition* (GLWC) is an alliance of sustainability standard organizations working together with the ISEAL Alliance, a global membership association for sustainability standards and accreditation bodies.[4] According to GLWC, a living wage is the "remuneration received for a standard workweek by a worker in a particular place sufficient to afford a decent standard of living for the worker and her or his family. Elements of a decent standard of living include food, water, housing, education, health care, transportation, clothing, and other essential needs including provision for unexpected events."[5] The calculation methodology involves estimating expenditures on food (accounting for World Health Organization nutrition recommendations and local food prices), housing (using international and national standards for decent housing), other essential needs, and a small margin for unforeseen events. These are added up to arrive at a net living wage that represents the cost of a basic but decent life for a family, divided by the number of workers per family. This particular wage specifically excludes overtime pay, productivity bonuses, and allowances and considers both mandatory taxes and the fair and reasonable value of in-kind benefits (with rules to decide on what is fair and reasonable). Local stakeholders (workers and

local experts such as government officials and academics) provide input to the process. As of September 2019, GLWC had created benchmark wages in sixteen countries, with a total of twenty-six regions covered, and was working on more. It should be noted that GLWC benchmarks in Asia are *consistently* lower than AFWA estimates.[6]

- *WageIndicator Foundation* (WIF) estimates living wages based on the calculation of "monthly expenses necessary to cover the cost of food, housing and transportation, with a 10 percent margin for [a family's] other expenses (including expenditure for education, health, clothing, etc.)."[7] WIF also accounts for tax liabilities and social welfare entitlements and assumes that two adults paid these wages can support a decent quality of life for their family. The calculation methodology is different from others: WIF surveys more than one hundred goods and services to obtain timely, accurate, and comparable estimates of costs of food, housing, and transportation and updates the living wage estimates quarterly.[8] WIF living wages are calculated for a "typical" family (two adults plus the number of children defined by the country's current fertility rate), a "standard" family (two adults with two children), and an individual. WIF wages are published in ranges, with a lower-bound estimate based on prices at the twenty-fifth percentile of the distribution and an upper-bound estimate based on prices at the fiftieth percentile. WIF has completed living wage benchmarks for sixty-eight countries.

- *Action, Collaboration, Transformation* (ACT) is a new, joint initiative between the IndustrALL Global Union federation and global apparel brands that aims to pay living wages in the textile and garment sector.[9] ACT defines a living wage as "the minimum income necessary for a worker to meet the basic needs of himself/herself and his/her family, including some discretionary income. This should be earned during legal working hour limits without overtime." ACT believes that winning these wages in global supply chains must come through negotiations between national representatives of manufacturers (such as employer organizations) and trade unions to reach legally binding collective bargaining agreements that cover *every* worker in the industry in each country. While at the time of writing the new ACT had not yet completed a pilot in any country, the organization states that where necessary its members will provide capacity-building to support negotiations and work with the ILO to promote technical assistance, while ensuring that their purchasing practices will facilitate the payment of living wages. ACT members will also work with suppliers to develop and implement improvements in manufacturing standards and efficient human resource and wage payment systems with the assumption that productivity growth and industrial upgrading will help manufacturers secure business contracts and make paying living wages possible.

- The objective of the *Fair Wage Network* (FWN), created by Daniel Vaughan-Whitehead and Auret Van Heerden in 2009, is to ensure wage progression in global supply chains through the articulation and implementation of a set of fair wage dimensions (see box 5.2) that FWN believes will lead to fair living wages if coherently addressed. FWN's focus is to create "holistic pay structures" that "enable and sustain fair living wages and facilitate improved dialogue between employers and employees."[10] FWN provides tools and assessment systems to help companies assess and monitor their total payment systems.[11]

There are a number of other approaches not described here, as well as estimates of living wages that have been proposed by a range of organizations in different countries. There are also tools aimed at helping companies attain their living wage goals. For instance, the Fair Wear Foundation (FWF), which requires its members to commit to increase wages in the supply chain and pay a living wage, has created a Labour Minute Costing tool[12] to help its member companies calculate realistic wage increase estimates and incorporate those increases into normal product costing systems in a transparent and verifiable manner, with guidance regarding how those increased costs can be shared among all of a factory's customers. In addition, FWF provides an online "Wage Ladder" that "allows the wages paid at any factory to be compared against a range of wage benchmarks."[13] Meanwhile, the FLA is attempting to provide guidance to its members regarding fair compensation, and its fair compensation reports are a first step in that direction.[14]

Thus, we see variation in how different actors in the private regulation ecosystem approach the issue of living wages, as well as variations in living wage estimates (see box 5.3) and how they are calculated. Empirical studies of progress tell us more.

Much has been written about wages in global supply chains, particularly regarding the apparel industry. Overwhelmingly, investigative case studies—many by the critical NGO community—lament that wages are low and that code of conduct provisions are frequently unmet. These reports suggest that wages in their specific investigations are lower than specified minimums or below World Bank poverty lines. Scholarly research, too, which has been limited to case studies in specific countries or regions from which it is difficult to compare or generalize, generally reports negative results of private regulation's efforts to improve supply chain wages.[15] In fact, barring the well-known case of the Alta Gracia factory

Box 5.2. Fair Wage Dimensions and How They Are Defined (adapted from Fair Wage Network)

- *Payment of wages*: A wage that is regularly and formally paid to workers.
- *Living wage*: A wage that ensures acceptable living standards.
- *Minimum wage*: A wage that respects minimum wage regulations
- *Payment of working hours*: A wage that does not generate excessive working hours and properly rewards normal work hours and overtime.
- *Pay systems*: A wage structure balanced between basic wages and additional bonuses and benefits, which reflects different levels of skill, education, and experience; rewards both individual and collective performance; is not dominated by disciplinary wage sanctions; and complies with regulations regarding holidays and social insurance payments.
- *Communication and social dialogue*: A wage about which workers receive information in advance, in the course of the production process, and at the time of the wage payment (detailed pay stub). A wage that is negotiated individually or collectively between employer and freely elected accepted workers' representatives.
- *Wage discrimination and disparity*: A system for equal wages for equal work that does not generate wage differentials within the company that grow too rapidly.
- *Real wages*: A wage that progresses in relations to price increases.
- *Wage share*: A wage that progresses proportionately with enterprise sales and profits and that does not lead to a fall in the wage share in enterprise performance growth.
- *Wage costs*: A wage whose progression does not lead to a dramatic reduction in wage costs within total production costs and as a percentage of employment.
- *Work intensity, upskilling, technology*: A wage that progresses along changes in intensity, technological content, and evolving skills and tasks of the labor force.

Box 5.3. Significant Variation in Living Wage Estimates

Estimates of what constitutes a living wage can differ significantly from one organization to another and from one calculation methodology to another. India provides a good example; what follows is only a partial picture.

The Global Living Wage Coalition living wage for India in 2018 for a typical family—2 parents and 2.5 children, with 1.6 people working—ranged between 13,500 and 19,400 rupees, and the estimate for a standard family—2 parents and 2 children, with 1.8 people working—was between 11,500 and 16,700 rupees. The estimate for an individual was between 6,450 and 10,300 rupees.

Comparing Wageindicator Foundation estimates with those of GLWC and AFWA is problematic because the year the data were collected differs, as do assumptions about family size. Also, GLWC calculates a wage for a region, whereas AFWA and WIF calculate a wage for an entire country, although WIF's calculation is provided in a range. Nevertheless, WIF estimates for India fall well below AFWA estimates (23,588 rupees) but are within the ballpark of GLWC's estimate for Tiruppur in Tamil Nadu (14,670 rupees).

in the Dominican Republic, which pays three times that country's minimum wage, it is difficult to find any wages paid to workers in global supply chains being described as at least *adequate*.[16]

The combination of unrepresentative investigations, journalistic reports, disparate scholarly case studies in which wages were not the sole focus, numerous interviews with workers in the supply chains, and a few cross-country analyses make it impossible to present a coherent picture of wages in global supply chains.[17] Nevertheless, let us take a quick look at *two strands* of these studies: the extent to which companies have fulfilled the requirements of their corporate codes of conduct for wages in the global supply chain; and the approach to defining and measuring living wages.

- Marks and Spencer made a public commitment to have its suppliers in Bangladesh, India, and Sri Lanka pay a living wage to their workers by 2015, while H&M committed to its strategic suppliers pay a living wage by 2018. A joint effort by four NGOs (Labour Behind the Label, Cividep, Stand Up Movement, and the Center for Alliance of Labor and Human Rights) studied eight garment factories and surveyed 150 workers in Marks and Spencer's supply chain in those three countries, along with H&M's supply chain in Cambodia. The report highlights the gap between private regulation commitments of leading brands and actual wages paid to workers.[18] The Marks and Spencer commitment was difficult to gauge because no specific target wage was stipulated. There was considerable falsification of overtime records in the Sri Lankan factories, and the basic pay was, on average, less than one-third of the living wage estimate. Workers in India reported unspecified wage deductions, and their take-home pay was more than 60 percent below the AFWA wage. Bangladeshi workers were taking home well below one-third of the living wage estimate. In Cambodia, the average monthly take-home pay was also considerably less than the living wage estimate. All these workers provided estimates of what they could live on with dignity.

- A Clean Clothes Campaign (CCC) study focused on everyday European shoe brands, rather than leading brands, and investigated footwear factories in Hungary, Ukraine, and Serbia in 2017, building on prior studies.[19] The study's findings suggest that the majority of workers did not even receive the legal minimum wage, which was only between 10 and 40 percent of the living wage estimates for these countries.

- In a survey of twenty leading brands (also a CCC study)—85 percent of which had made living wage commitments in their codes of conduct—grades were given for compliance: A if 100 percent of workers in the supply chain earned a living wage; B if 50 percent did; C if 25 percent did; D for having begun to contribute toward the payment of a living wage, including incorporating a higher labor cost into the prices paid to suppliers; and E for an inability to show evidence of a living wage paid to any worker. Nineteen of the twenty brands earned an E, and only one, Gucci, earned a C—mostly because 25 percent of its workers in Italy were paid at that level.[20]

- The Fair Labor Association in 2016 issued a detailed report on worker compensation in apparel and footwear factories—124 in twenty-one countries—produced for its members that were obligated to comply with local labor laws and FLA's Workplace Code of Conduct.[21] Making a *systematic* effort to identify barriers to fair compensation in particular, FLA found a persistent hurdle in violations of legal pay provisions at about one-third of the suppliers—in direct contravention of FLA's code stipulation that pay systems be accurate, transparent, and clearly communicated to the workers. Wage levels generally were not high enough to meet basic needs and provide discretionary income, as specified in the code. Median compensation in all countries was above the applicable minimum wage, but both legal minimum wages and the purchasing power of that compensation fell below the World Bank poverty line to varying degrees in many of the countries.[22]

- One scholar set out to understand the process by which global companies try to implement living wages in the supply chain using Nudie Jeans—a relatively small brand rather than a multinational corporation—as a case study.[23] Nudie Jeans's Indian supplier, Armstrong, calculated the living wage based on a food basket survey and interviews with workers and their families as well as relevant community members, such as doctors, school system representatives, and other stakeholders, and what emerged was lower than the AFWA wage for the country. The wages were paid as bonuses to employees, but it was difficult to figure out which employees should get the bonus: only those who worked in cut, make, and trim; those who worked on the specific Nudie product; or all employees, which would then reduce the payout per employee substantially. The case highlights the difficulty brands face in trying to create a sustainable living wage through increases in basic wages (which is the overall goal of private regulation) when the brand operates individually and accounts for only a portion of a supplier's production.

- Finally, there is the issue of how pricing strategies and purchasing practices affect wage payment in global supply chains. One study focuses on the steadily decreasing prices paid for garments, raising the question whether commitments to paying a living wage are meaningful, and found that the price paid to suppliers for trousers exported to the United States declined by 13 percent between 2013 and 2017—a "pricing squeeze" that reduced supplier profits and workers' real wages. An accompanying "sourcing squeeze" (shorter lead times and last-minute changes in orders) intensified work hours and forced overtime. A key implication of the research is that the hypercompetitive nature of the global apparel industry can render commitments to living wages to be essentially "false promises."[24] Another complementary study by the ILO surveyed 1,454 suppliers in eighty-seven countries and found that wages can be affected by purchasing practices and other factors. Further, the study identified a host of factors that tend to depress wages: inadequate technical specifications provided to the suppliers by global buyers (which in this study tended to reduce wages by nearly 22 percent); global buyers' expectations of a high degree of flexibility from suppliers, changing orders at the last minute and providing short lead times (6 percent); buyers' bullying of suppliers to sell below cost (11 percent); and a high degree of buyer leverage (up to 20 percent). In contrast, when buyers agree to pay at least the full production cost of their orders, the possibility is that wages increase by 10 percent.[25]

All in all, these studies show that the commitments made regarding living wages by leading brands are "hollow" and that these brands have made relatively little progress in achieving their wage objectives. Workers' wages in apparel supply chains are higher than the minimum wages, to be sure, but fall far short of the living wage ideal or even the notion that workers must be paid a wage that assures them some degree of disposable income. And sourcing and pricing "squeezes" create little room for, or actually undermine, suppliers' efforts to increase wages beyond legal minimums and toward living wages. It is clear that individual buyers cannot ensure that suppliers pay living wages, given the structural problems that one supplier services multiple buyers and that buyers do not act in concert.

Wages and How They Have Been Changing

There is little in the way of *systematic* evidence across countries and industries regarding actual wages, as noted in earlier chapters. The following presents a systematic, cross-national picture of the current state of actual wages in global supply chains as well as changes over time. This examination fills a severe gap in the research. The varying commitments in codes of conduct presented earlier are the standards against which the empirical examination in this chapter is based. Box 5.4 presents an overview of the data used and the method employed for analysis.

To begin the analysis, we first show the wage amount and progression of wages in different countries and industries over time using AUDCO data. We exclude the data from the United States and Italy that were in the dataset; the significantly higher wage levels in those two countries compared with the others would inflate the average wages across industries.

Out of ten countries remaining, six—Bangladesh, China, India, Indonesia, Mexico, and Vietnam—account for 95.9 percent of the AUDCO audits, and China alone accounts for 57 percent of the number of audits.

Average Hourly Wages Over Time

For the purposes of comparative analysis, tables 5.1 and 5.2 show average basic hourly wages by country and industry, converted into US dollars using the exchange

Box 5.4. Data and Method for Studying Wages
and How They Have Been Changing

Two sources of data were used to examine progress on wages in
global supply chains. The first source is the global auditing firm
AUDCO, whose data is presented in previous chapters. This chapter
draws on wage data collected from 14,315 "reliable" audits conducted over a six- year period (2011–2017) in ten countries and seven
industries, including apparel. The analysis unfolded in five steps:

1. Examine the progress of average basic hourly wages (not including overtime or any allowance), highlighting annual percentage increases.
2. Examine the gap between the basic hourly wage and the legal
   minimum wage for that locality (AUDCO annually updates
   legal minimum wages in its data), using the basic hourly wage
   data for the latest available full year, 2017. The data are aggregated across countries and industries, making it possible to examine the difference between legal minimum hourly wages and
   average basic hourly wages.
3. Calculate average monthly basic wages by multiplying the basic
   hourly wage by legal working hours per week and by 4.33, the
   average number of weeks in a month,[1] and then compare this
   basic monthly wage with AUDCO's data on average monthly
   take-home pay (a gross figure, inclusive of overtime and allowances, that takes into consideration wage deductions for a variety of issues that vary across country, province, and industry).
   The AUDCO dataset did not have specific numbers for allowances and deductions. (It is instructive to examine the gap between basic *monthly wages* and *monthly take-home pay*, which
   suggests the importance of overtime payments in workers' earnings, although the aggregate data provided by AUDCO does *not*
   allow for a more precise measure of overtime.)

Box 5.4. (continued)

4. Estimate the gap between the two wage measures, monthly basic wages and monthly take-home pay, with a variety of living wage estimates as well as World Bank poverty lines. Identifying these gaps allows for examining, comprehensively, just how much further global buyers must go to meet the living wage commitments expressed in codes of conduct.

5. Present the percentage by which basic monthly wages would have to increase to meet differing living wage benchmarks.

1. Following the methodology of FLA (2016) and Anker and Anker (2017a).

TABLE 5.1.   Average basic hourly wages in USD by country, 2011–2017

COUNTRY	2011	2012	2013	2014	2015	2016	2017
Bangladesh	0.26	0.24	0.27	0.38	0.39	0.40	0.40
Cambodia	0.51	0.39	0.47	0.51	0.63	0.71	0.79
China	1.20	1.42	1.58	1.71	1.82	1.77	1.67
Ethiopia	0.28	0.26	N/A	0.14	0.17	0.25	0.31
India	0.50	0.46	0.51	0.52	0.56	0.60	0.64
Indonesia	0.77	0.74	0.79	0.94	0.93	1.07	1.00
Jordan	0.94	0.98	1.23	1.11	1.07	1.09	1.14
Mexico	1.08	1.09	1.38	1.30	1.25	1.11	1.19
Turkey	2.39	2.33	2.46	2.10	2.24	2.17	1.91
Vietnam	0.55	0.75	0.84	0.79	0.84	0.75	0.80

TABLE 5.2.   Average basic hourly wages in USD by industry, 2011–2017

INDUSTRY	2011	2012	2013	2014	2015	2016	2017
Agriculture	N/A	N/A	1.75	1.83	1.26	1.32	1.25
Apparel	0.82	0.94	1.03	1.11	1.14	1.20	1.18
Apparel accessories	1.00	1.10	1.22	1.37	1.39	1.54	1.51
Electronics	1.25	1.44	1.59	1.78	1.92	1.86	1.74
Food	1.09	1.16	1.24	1.21	1.49	1.41	1.48
Footwear	1.09	1.24	1.51	1.56	1.66	1.53	1.48
Toys	1.10	1.37	1.33	1.44	1.50	1.49	1.49

rate for May 1 of the given year (which may not have been the exact exchange rate on the date of the audit; the annual variations in wages in these countries could thus be an artifact of the exchange rate variations).[26] These are the basic hourly wages found in the audit data, aggregated by country and industry; the average basic hourly wage for each year was calculated taking into account the number of audits in each country in that year.

The average basic hourly wage shown by country varies considerably. As for industry wages, the data are heavily influenced by both the number of audits and the exchange rate, but the apparel industry appears to pay the least—even less than the toy industry, which is surprising.

Average hourly basic wages in table 5.3 represent how much these wages would have been worth in terms of 2017 USD, accounting for inflation. In the vast majority of countries, basic hourly wages appear to increase moderately in real wage terms. In Turkey, average basic hourly wages were declining in nominal terms but slightly increasing in real terms. Table 5.4 shows industry averages of basic hourly

TABLE 5.3. Average basic hourly wages in 2017 USD by country, 2011–2017

COUNTRY	2011	2012	2013	2014	2015	2016	2017
Bangladesh	0.33	0.32	0.32	0.42	0.41	0.40	0.40
Cambodia	0.60	0.45	0.52	0.55	0.67	0.73	0.79
China	1.27	1.43	1.52	1.60	1.67	1.68	1.67
Ethiopia	0.39	0.30	N/A	0.16	0.18	0.26	0.31
India	0.52	0.52	0.51	0.56	0.59	0.63	0.64
Indonesia	0.61	0.61	0.67	0.84	0.87	0.97	1.00
Jordan	1.08	1.08	1.28	1.13	1.09	1.12	1.14
Mexico	0.83	0.91	1.04	1.01	1.10	1.07	1.19
Turkey	1.68	1.74	1.74	1.61	2.01	1.90	1.91
Vietnam	0.57	0.72	0.76	0.68	0.72	0.77	0.80

TABLE 5.4. Average basic hourly wages in 2017 USD by industry, 2011–2017

INDUSTRY	2011	2012	2013	2014	2015	2016	2017
Agriculture	N/A	N/A	1.69	1.72	1.12	1.27	1.25
Apparel	0.84	0.93	0.97	1.03	1.06	1.15	1.18
Apparel accessories	1.05	1.1	1.17	1.28	1.28	1.48	1.51
Electronics	1.32	1.44	1.52	1.67	1.76	1.77	1.74
Food	1.15	1.18	1.12	1.05	1.34	1.36	1.48
Footwear	1.15	1.24	1.46	1.47	1.53	1.46	1.48
Toys	1.17	1.37	1.28	1.34	1.38	1.42	1.49

wages by year, and, while the degree of yearly fluctuation is little less than what is shown in table 5.2, wage trends over time remain identical.

To look at wage progression over time, we examined the average annual percentage change in wages (nominal) across the time period. Given the problems of exchange rate variations, we used national currencies for the country estimates (except in Cambodia, with its heavily dollarized economy; its wages are reported in USD). We took into consideration the number of audits in each country when calculating each country's average hourly wage figures. These are reported in table 5.5; figure 5.1 is a visual representation.

As table 5.5 suggests, there have been steady increases in the average hourly wage in most countries. But note that the factories audited each year keep changing, as do the number of factories. Since these are aggregate figures provided by AUDCO, it is not possible to examine the progression of wages in the same factory over the five-year period.

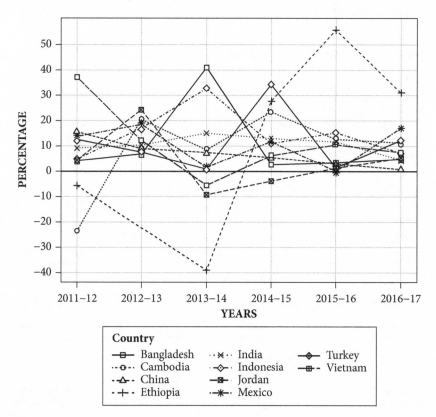

FIGURE 5.1. Annual percentage increases in actual average hourly wages, by country (in national currencies)

Chart by author.

Examining the wage progression per industry (aggregate figures across all the countries in the dataset) reveals that wages, in general, have steadily increased year by year, but the rate of wage increases declines over time, with exceptional declines in agriculture and the apparel, apparel accessories, electronics, and footwear industries during the 2016–2017 period. Table 5.6 shows this progression by industry expressed in percentages.

The overall evidence suggests that average basic hourly wages have been increasing, consistent with the codes of some MSIs that require a year-to-year improvement in basic hourly wages. But is the basic hourly wage significantly higher than the legal minimum wage?

TABLE 5.5. Annual percentage increase in the average basic hourly wage in national currencies by country

COUNTRY	PERCENTAGE INCREASE IN AVERAGE BASIC HOURLY WAGE FROM THE PREVIOUS YEAR					
	2012	2013	2014	2015	2016	2017
Bangladesh	4.2	6.9	41.0	2.7	3.4	4.8
Cambodia	−23.5	20.5	8.5	23.5	12.7	11.3
China	15.6	9.0	7.5	5.5	3.0	0.8
Ethiopia	−5.6	N/A	−39.0	27.7	55.8	31.1
India	9.2	10.4	15.1	13.0	11.7	4.6
Indonesia	4.8	17.1	32.7	11.0	15.3	7.3
Jordan	4.5	24.3	−9.2	−3.8	1.3	5.2
Mexico	13.8	18.5	1.6	11.8	0.1	17.1
Turkey	12.6	7.6	0.9	34.4	1.5	12.2
Vietnam	37.2	12.2	−5.5	6.2	10.5	7.5

TABLE 5.6. Annual percentage increase in average basic hourly wage by industry

INDUSTRY	PERCENTAGE INCREASE IN AVERAGE BASIC HOURLY WAGE FROM THE PREVIOUS YEAR					
	2012	2013	2014	2015	2016	2017
Agriculture	N/A	N/A	4.6	−31.1	4.8	−5.3
Apparel	14.6	9.6	7.8	2.7	5.3	−1.7
Apparel accessories	10.0	10.9	12.3	1.5	10.8	−1.9
Electronics	15.2	10.4	11.9	7.9	−3.1	−6.5
Food	6.4	6.9	−2.4	23.1	−5.4	5.0
Footwear	13.8	21.8	3.3	6.4	−7.8	−3.3
Toys	24.5	−2.9	8.3	4.2	−0.7	0.0

Average Hourly Wages and Legal Minimum Wages

Because AUDCO's auditors report the prevailing legal minimum wages in each location at the time of their audits, it is possible to compare average the basic hourly wage to the legal minimum wage in each country. Here, we focus on the 2017 data (using exchange rates prevailing on May 1, 2017) to make it easy to compare across countries. Ethiopia is excluded from this analysis because of the absence of minimum wage data. Table 5.7 reports the results.

Most audit results indicate that the average wage paid is higher than the minimum wage in countries. There are a few instances where it is lower. In these instances, although countries vary in terms of just how much the average basic hourly wage is lower than the legal minimum wage, the gaps are significant, amounting to more than 10 percent of hourly wages in India, Turkey, Bangladesh, and Indonesia. These results lend some credence to investigative reports that suggested workers in global supply chains have been getting paid less than the minimum wage. However, the incidence of such cases is relatively small in these data.

The gap between average basic hourly wages and legal minimum hourly wages is not as pronounced when data are examined at the industry level (aggregated across all countries). Table 5.8 reports these results.

TABLE 5.7. Average basic hourly wages and legal minimum hourly wages by country, 2017

COUNTRY	ALL AUDITS (WAGES IN USD)			AUDITS IN WHICH BASIC HOURLY WAGE FALLS BELOW LEGAL MINIMUM WAGE	
	NUMBER OF AUDITS IN 2017	AVERAGE BASIC HOURLY WAGE	AVERAGE LEGAL MINIMUM HOURLY WAGE	PERCENTAGE OF AUDICTS	GAP BETWEEN BASIC AND MINIMUM WAGES AS PERCENTAGE OF BASIC WAGE
Bangladesh	331	0.40	0.30	0.30	17.5
Cambodia	53	0.79	0.73	0.00	N/A
China	2,241	1.67	1.35	1.12	7.8
India	341	0.64	0.57	5.57	21.9
Indonesia*	146	1.00	0.99	8.90	13.0
Jordan	15	1.14	0.95	0.00	N/A
Mexico	299	1.19	0.54	0.67	1.7
Turkey	187	1.91	1.58	1.60	18.3
Vietnam	340	0.80	0.64	0.59	3.8

* Indonesia's outlier status in our wage calculations regarding minimum wage has to do with the fact that minimum wages are determined regionally in the country and there is substantial variation across regions. AUDCO's data are drawn from audits that are in higher minimum-wage regions.

TABLE 5.8. Average basic hourly wages and legal minimum hourly wages by industry, 2017

INDUSTRY	ALL AUDITS (WAGES IN USD)			AUDITS IN WHICH BASIC HOURLY WAGE FALLS BELOW LEGAL MINIMUM WAGE	
	NUMBER OF AUDITS IN 2017	AVERAGE BASIC HOURLY WAGE	AVERAGE LEGAL MINIMUM HOURLY WAGE	PERCENTAGE OF AUDITS	GAP BETWEEN BASIC AND MINIMUM WAGES AS PERCENTAGE OF BASIC WAGE
Agriculture	185	1.25	0.55	0.54	< 0.001
Apparel	2,314	1.18	0.98	1.90	11.9
Apparel accessories	393	1.51	1.22	2.80	9.3
Electronics	391	1.74	1.39	1.28	2.9
Food	69	1.48	0.98	1.45	23.0
Footwear	443	1.48	1.17	0.68	3.4
Toys	160	1.49	1.29	0.00	N/A

Because codes of conduct typically require suppliers to pay at least the minimum wage, these results suggest that most suppliers around the world *do* pay minimum wages. Only in roughly 10 percent of the cases across countries are basic hourly wages paid below the legal minimum. Thus, these results broadly suggest that most suppliers are meeting the standards laid down by the code of conduct provisions of both WRAP and Amfori BSCI regarding wages. However, it is important to remember that most codes of conduct go beyond paying the minimum wage to require a wage sufficient to meet basic needs and provide some discretionary income.

Average Basic Monthly Wages and Take-Home Pay

Just how much of monthly take-home pay is accounted for by the basic monthly wage? If monthly take-home pay is significantly higher, it might suggest that much of the balance is accounted for by overtime pay (assuming that allowances and deductions are a very small part of monthly take-home pay). While the gap between basic monthly wage and monthly take-home pay is a poor estimate of the magnitude of overtime in monthly take-home pay (absent accounting for those allowances and deductions), this gap may still be indicative. Table 5.9 presents the analysis.[27]

The difference between basic monthly wage and monthly take-home pay is generally large, hinting at the central role of overtime in worker earnings. Assuming

TABLE 5.9. Average monthly basic wages and monthly take-home pay by country, 2017

COUNTRY	BASIC MONTHLY WAGE (USD)	MONTHLY TAKE-HOME (USD)	GAP BETWEEN MONTHLY TAKE-HOME AND BASIC WAGES (USD)	GAP (%)
Bangladesh	82.22	113.61	31.39	38.2
Cambodia	163.84	227.14	63.30	38.6
China	318.49	527.79	209.30	65.7
India	134.01	130.59	−3.42	−2.6
Indonesia	173.96	190.80	16.84	9.7
Jordan	237.95	293.40	55.45	23.3
Mexico	246.86	293.99	47.13	19.1
Turkey	373.28	456.47	83.19	22.3
Vietnam	166.63	234.40	67.77	40.7

TABLE 5.10. Average monthly basic wages and monthly take-home pay by industry, 2017

INDUSTRY	BASIC MONTHLY WAGE (USD)	MONTHLY TAKE-HOME (USD)	GAP BETWEEN MONTHLY TAKE-HOME AND BASIC WAGES (USD)	GAP (%)
Agriculture	259.60	303.58	43.98	16.9
Apparel	229.86	340.23	110.37	48.0
Apparel accessories	289.73	451.77	162.04	55.9
Electronics	332.24	546.09	213.85	64.4
Food	291.12	398.87	107.75	37.0
Footwear	284.33	469.96	185.63	65.3
Toys	284.71	465.03	180.32	63.3

that allowances and deductions are relatively small components of take-home pay, it is reasonable to assume that overtime pay accounts for the bulk of the differences we see.

The difference between monthly average wages and monthly take-home pay is just as pronounced when we examine the data aggregated across industries for the year 2017 (table 5.10). Consistent with what we find for countries, in most industries, monthly take-home pay is significantly higher than monthly average wage. Clearly, workers in most industries and countries must work some overtime to earn the wages they do.

These results hint at the potentially large role played by overtime in take-home pay, consistent across countries and industries. However, we do not know the precise figure regarding overtime's contribution to take-home pay, which is not part of the AUDCO data.

Monthly Minimum and Average Wages, Take-Home Pay, and Living Wages

How do monthly minimum wages (legally determined), average monthly basic wages (which in most countries are more than the minimum wage), and monthly take-home pay relate to different measures of living wages? This relationship is important to understand because most codes of conduct require workers to be paid a decent wage that assures a minimum standard of living and provides some discretionary income; although these concepts are not well defined, they do approach what is generally meant by "living wages." Estimating the gap between monthly wages, monthly take-home pay, and living wage estimates provides some evidence of the extent to which private regulation provisions are met.

Using AUDCO's data for 2018, arriving at the monthly minimum wage is relatively easy: the dataset includes hourly legal minimum wages, which can be multiplied by the hours in a legally defined standard workweek. That calculation provides the legal weekly minimum wage, which we then multiply by 4.33, the average number of weeks in a month (52 weeks per year divided by 12 months), to arrive at a monthly legal minimum wage. We calculate average monthly basic wages in the same way, using basic hourly wage reported in AUDCO data. AUDCO data directly report the average monthly take-home pay. Thus, there are three estimates from that data to compare with living wage estimates.

For the living wage estimates themselves, we use the three estimates described in box 5.5 and organized our data to allow for comparison. Using 2018 data enabled comparison with WIF living wage benchmarks for the same year. The results are separated into those for lower-middle-income countries (Bangladesh, Cambodia, India, Indonesia, and Vietnam) and those for upper-middle-income countries (China, Jordan, Mexico, and Turkey), according to the World Bank classification.[28]

LOWER-MIDDLE-INCOME COUNTRIES

Figure 5.2 plots average basic monthly wages and monthly take-home pay side by side, overlaid with lines that represent different living wage benchmarks. The figure shows that monthly basic wages in all these countries are higher than the monthly minimum wage mandated by national law, except in the case of Indonesia. The figure also shows that the basic monthly wage is higher than the monthly estimate of the World Bank Poverty line in almost all countries, with Cambodia

Box 5.5. Estimates of Living Wage

We use three estimates to determine the "living wage." The first is the World Bank's estimates of poverty lines, because most code of conduct provisions require that wages meet the basic needs of workers. The World Bank has calculated *daily wages* for countries at different income levels to indicate a poverty line: $1.90 (international poverty line); $3.20 (lower middle-income countries); and $5.50 (upper middle-income countries).[1] These figures are in 2011 purchasing power parity (PPP) dollars, a currency figure that matches AFWA's. We converted these poverty line estimates into monthly terms and multiplied these estimates by two, assuming that each worker's salary must support two dependents.[2]

The Wageindicator Foundation's (WIF) living wage estimates for 2018 are our second estimate. Specifically, we use WIF's estimates for a typical family: two adults and a number of children consistent with country's national fertility rate. These estimates are provided in ranges; a lower one considers prices of food, housing, and so forth at the twenty-fifth percentile of their distributions, and a higher one at the fiftieth percentile.[3] We have WIF benchmarks for most countries in our analysis, except China and Jordan.

Finally, we use the latest (2017) AFWA estimate of 1,181, which is calculated in PPP dollars and that thus enables comparison across countries. It is typically the highest living wage estimate available but is applicable only to Asian countries.

While the Global Living Wage Coalition also calculates living wage estimates, its figures are for different regions *within* a given country, and so we do not use them here.

1. Ferreira and Sánchez-Páramo 2017.
2. This adjustment was done to compare with the wages in our data and to be consistent with the FLA's cross-country study of fair compensation (Fair Labor Association 2016, 2018, 2019).
3. As Guzi and Kahanec (2018, 10) note, the former is "a rather conservative scenario implying a cost-optimizing household seeking cheaper-than-average housing, food and other expenses compared to the national average (median)."

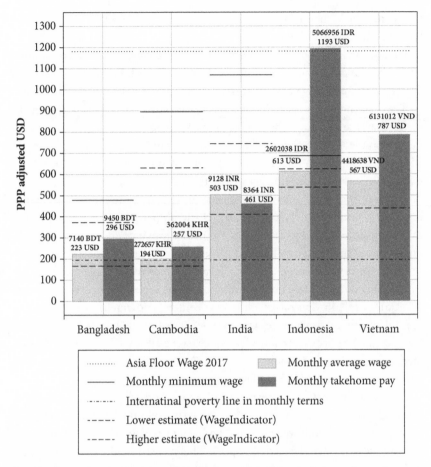

FIGURE 5.2. Comparison of different wages with different living wage estimates, 2018, for lower-middle-income countries

Chart by author.

falling short slightly. Notably, monthly take-home pay is less than basic monthly wage in India (perhaps reflecting larger deductions), whereas monthly take-home pay is much greater than basic monthly wage in Indonesia.

Comparing our wage figures with living wage estimates reveals that in all countries except Indonesia, the basic monthly wage (although higher than the monthly minimum wage) falls significantly *below* the lower bound of WIF's living wage estimates. Thus, the data suggest that legal minimum wages in these countries for a standard workweek are insufficient to cover the lowest estimates we have for living wages. The gap between monthly minimum and basic wages and living wage estimates is particularly large in Bangladesh, Cambodia, and India, and even monthly take-home pay in these countries (which includes overtime pay) is well below the lower bound of WIF estimates.

Finally, in all but one of the countries there is a large gap between monthly basic wages and take-home pay and the AFWA standard. Indonesia is a curious exception and presents a puzzling case.

The basic monthly wage in Indonesia is below the legal monthly minimum but higher than the WIF lower-bound benchmark, while monthly take-home pay is as much as the AFWA estimate. There are two possible explanations. We have 142 audits from Indonesia for the year 2018. While, on average, legally mandated hourly minimum wages are higher than actual hourly average wages for these audits, the range of legally mandated minimum wages is quite pronounced, ranging from as little as 8,098.26 to 35,391.19 rupiah per hour. The reason is that minimum wages in Indonesia are determined at province, district, and occupational levels.[29] In USD terms, the monthly minimum wage in Indonesia varies substantially across provinces. In West Java and Banten, the older centers for garment production, the monthly minimum wage varies between 128 USD and 302 USD, while in Central Java, the new center for garment production, the monthly minimum wage varies from 119 USD to 149 USD. In fact, a 2017 ILO study shows the wage dispersion by province has been growing steadily in the garment industry.[30] It is possible that AUDCO-audited factories in Indonesia in 2018 were concentrated in West Java or Banten.

A second explanation concerns AUDCO's method of recording legal wages. If AUDCO's auditors used the wage determined by collective bargaining as the applicable legal minimum wage, this method would explain why we see more audits in Indonesia in which actual wages fall below legal minimum wages, hence making the average basic monthly wage fall below the average of legal minimum wages. Explaining why Indonesian wages are higher than the lower bound of the WIF benchmark is more difficult, because we do not have enough information to verify whether WIF's calculation of the survey of the cost of living in Indonesia produced realistic estimates that informed the calculation of the lower-bound living wage estimate.

A second problem concerns why Indonesia's monthly take-home pay exceeds AFWA's 2017 benchmark. Again, two potential explanations exist. The first is that AUDCO's audited factories might be located in West Java or Banten, which have higher minimum wages than other regions and therefore may have higher take-home pay than the national average. Unfortunately, the subnational location of audited factories is often missing in the Indonesia data, and, therefore, we cannot precisely calculate how many AUDCO-audited factories in Indonesia were located in places with higher regional minimum wages. The second explanation rests on PPP calculation differences.[31]

UPPER-MIDDLE-INCOME COUNTRIES

In all four countries, as figure 5.3 suggests, average basic monthly wages are higher than legally mandated minimum monthly wages and also higher than the monthly estimates of the international poverty line (based on 5.5 USD per day for two dependents). However, in no country does the basic monthly wage or monthly take-home pay reach the WIF lower-bound estimates. Basic monthly wages in China are significantly below the living wage estimate of AFW, although the monthly take-home pay comes quite close.

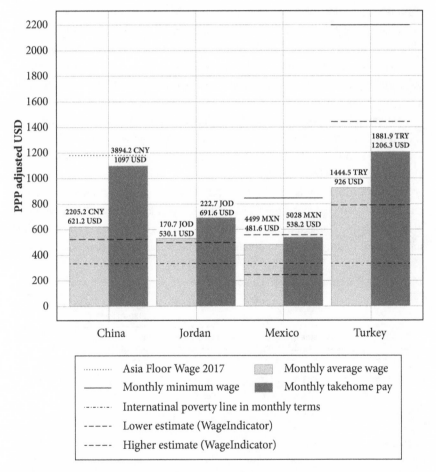

FIGURE 5.3. Comparison of different wages with different living wage estimates, 2018, for upper-middle-income countries

Chart by author.

In sum, these diverse analyses paint a picture of wages in global supply chains not quite meeting the goal of paying workers a decent wage that covers their needs and also leaves a little left over for discretionary purposes. In no country does the basic monthly earning *without overtime* reach close to the lowest estimate of living wages, and in only one country, Indonesia, does the monthly take-home pay come close. The commitment made by global companies and MSIs through their codes of conduct is not being realized in these countries.

Wage Increases Required to Meet Code Commitments

If global companies want to follow through on their code commitments to pay living wages in the global supply chain, companies need to ensure that wages in supplier factories are increased substantially. Table 5.11 shows what these increases need to be—and readers may be shocked when they look at the table's rightmost column. To put it mildly, this is an uphill task—reaching the AFWA estimates for a living wage would require an increase of 90 to 500 percent in different countries.

Motivated by curiosity, we estimated the percentage by which *take-home pay* should increase to meet living wage standards, although we reiterate that living wages are supposed to be achieved by working regular hours without overtime. Table 5.12 presents these results.

The extensive analysis of AUDCO's data permits several general conclusions regarding wages. First, basic hourly wages have been increasing in all countries and in all industries, although the annual rate of increase is decreasing. Thus, the minimum commitment in codes of conduct that there must be year-to-year increases

TABLE 5.11.   Basic monthly wages and gaps with living-wage benchmarks, 2018

		PERCENTAGE INCREASE FROM BASIC MONTHLY WAGE NEEDED TO MEET:		
COUNTRY	AVERAGE BASIC MONTHLY WAGE ($PPP)	WAGEINDICATOR LOWER ESTIMATE	WAGEINDICATOR HIGHER ESTIMATE	ASIA FLOOR WAGE 2017
Bangladesh	223.4	66.7	114.3	428.6
Cambodia	193.8	225.0	361.9	509.4
China	621.2	N/A	N/A	90.1
India	502.9	47.9	112.5	134.8
Indonesia	612.9	−12.3	11.9	92.7
Jordan	530.1	N/A	N/A	N/A
Mexico	481.6	15.8	75.6	N/A
Turkey	926.0	55.8	137.4	N/A
Vietnam	567.0	21.0	74.9	108.3

TABLE 5.12. Monthly take-home pay and gaps with living-wage benchmarks, 2018

COUNTRY	MONTHLY TAKE-HOME PAY ($PPP)	PERCENTAGE INCREASE FROM MONTHLY TAKE-HOME NEEDED TO MEET:		
		WAGEINDICATOR LOWER ESTIMATE	WAGEINDICATOR HIGHER ESTIMATE	ASIA FLOOR WAGE 2017
Bangladesh	295.7	25.9	61.9	299.4
Cambodia	257.3	144.8	247.9	359.0
China	1,097.0	N/A	N/A	7.7
India	460.8	61.4	132.0	156.3
Indonesia	1,193.5	−55.0	−42.5	−1.0
Jordan	691.6	N/A	N/A	N/A
Mexico	538.2	3.6	57.1	N/A
Turkey	1,206.3	19.6	82.3	N/A
Vietnam	786.8	−12.8	26.1	50.1

in wages appears to be met. Second, average hourly basic wages are higher than the minimum wages in most countries and industries (with a few exceptions). Less than 2 percent of audits report an average hourly wage lower than the minimum wage in *most* countries. Thus, the conditions for wages in codes at the lower end of the code spectrum (WRAP, Amfori BSCI codes) has been largely met.

The majority of codes, however, require that wages be high enough to assure a decent standard of living and provide some discretionary income. Using that standard, wages workers receive from regular working hours without overtime must be higher than the basic needs wage (which we measured by the World Bank's poverty line) *and* must approximate some measure of living wages. We found that average monthly basic wages in most countries are higher than the corresponding World Bank monthly poverty lines, so it is safe to assume that basic needs are likely met (although whether the World Bank's poverty line is a good proxy for estimating basic needs is debatable). The data analyzed here, however, suggest that basic monthly wages (i.e., without overtime pay or allowance) are considerably below the lowest available estimate for living wages (the lower bound of WIF's living wage benchmarks) for most countries and industries.

There are large gaps between basic monthly wages (based on legally allowed working hours per week before overtime) and monthly take-home pay in all countries and industries. This large gap can be explained in part by the prevalence of overtime earnings, but since the data do not reveal individual components of monthly take-home pay (such as pay for allowances, pay for overtime work, as well as a variety of standard deductions), we cannot lay the entire blame for this gap on overtime pay.

In summary, these results show that there is still a long way to go before wages in global supply chains reach the lowest estimate of living wages. Hence, they do not yet live up to commitments global companies have made through their codes of conduct.

Triangulation through a Cross-Sectional Analysis

The second data source mentioned earlier allows for triangulation. ApparelCo (not the company's real name), a large global retail brand, provided wage data across its supply chain for 2016. ApparelCo is considered a leader in terms of its corporate social responsibility initiatives. Its labor and environmental practices have drawn NGO and media attention, and in response the company has developed strong and widely recognized social and environmental sustainability programs and has a robust compliance program.

ApparelCo's commitment to wages in its code requires that they be similar to minimum wage or industry standards (whichever is higher), and its membership in several multi-stakeholder initiatives requires payment of wages to meet basic needs and allow for some discretionary income.

Box 5.6 provides an overview of the ApparelCo data and the method of analysis.

Monthly Basic Wage and Components of Take-Home Pay

Table 5.13 reports average basic wages per month and the specific components of monthly take-home pay. The table shows substantial variation in the monthly basic wage across the different countries and also shows that monthly take-home pay varies considerably.

It is far more instructive to examine the composition of monthly take-home pay in terms of percentage and compare how the composition varies across countries (table 5.14).

On average, allowances account for 13.6 percent of take-home pay, while the average deductions from pay constitute 5 percent of take-home pay. Deductions generally include workers' contribution to national and private social security systems, taxes, union membership fees, and in some cases dormitory fees—although rules regarding deductions vary substantially across countries. What is most interesting is the high percentage of overtime pay as a percentage of take-home pay, which, on average, is significantly smaller than what was indicated in the AUDCO data.

Box 5.6. Data for Triangulation

ApparelCo data are aggregated at the country level and are cross-sectional. Because the data identify wages, overtime (OT) payments, allowances, and deductions, it is possible to examine the significance of OT payments in workers' earnings. The methodology is similar to that described for AUDCO data (see Box 5.4: estimate the gap between basic monthly wages, take-home pay, and a variety of living wage estimates.

The ApparelCo data are drawn from 283 factories located in nineteen countries. The data are comprehensive, reporting each factory's basic monthly wage, overtime, allowances, and total deductions as well as monthly take-home pay. Thus, it is possible to look at the percentage contribution of each of these components in making up take-home pay. ApparelCo reports these wages in nominal USD, using exchange rates prevailing at the time when the data was collected. ApparelCo collected these data by surveying its factories and marrying the survey data with audit reports, but the data cannot be said to be completely representative of its supply chain, because not all factories in each country responded to the survey. We eliminated from our analysis those countries in which the number of factories was small, and we eliminated factories in countries with very high wages (e.g., the United States and South Korea), ultimately focusing on nine countries. Thus, our analysis draws from a dataset of 256 factories. We report wage figures aggregated at the country level only.

Some caveats are in order. First, because the data are cross-sectional data for only one year, wage progression cannot be measured. Also, because the data are for 2016, they cannot be compared directly with the AUDCO data of 2017–2018.

TABLE 5.13. Composition of monthly take-home pay in nominal USD, 2016

COUNTRY	BASE WAGE	OVERTIME	PRODUCTION BONUS	SKILL BONUS	OTHER ALLOWANCE	TOTAL DEDUCTIONS	MONTHLY TAKE-HOME PAY
Bangladesh	81.2	24.9	5.2	0.3	16.7	0.9	127.4
Cambodia	130.9	41.9	11.6	4.1	43.9	0.2	232.2
China	296.5	150.4	33.4	9.9	27.0	32.1	485.1
India	103.9	51.3	0.9	0.1	10.9	13.2	154.0
Indonesia	152.9	84.7	0.3	0.2	5.8	4.7	239.2
Pakistan	121.5	61.2	10.4	1.3	10.2	1.1	203.5
Philippines	193.1	52.2	0.0	0.5	20.6	11.4	255.0
Sri Lanka	104.2	40.7	14.4	8.5	17.4	15.0	170.1
Vietnam	155.5	51.8	11.2	3.2	29.0	17.1	233.6

TABLE 5.14. Different wage components as proportions of monthly take-home pay

COUNTRY	BASE WAGE (%)	OVERTIME (%)	TOTAL ALLOWANCES (%)	TOTAL DEDUCTIONS (%)
Bangladesh	64.9	19.7	16.0	0.7
Cambodia	56.9	18.1	25.2	0.1
China	61.6	32.1	13.6	7.2
India	67.5	33.3	7.7	8.5
Indonesia	64.1	35.0	2.8	2.0
Pakistan	59.8	30.1	10.6	0.5
Philippines	75.8	20.5	8.2	4.5
Sri Lanka	62.0	24.2	23.0	9.1
Vietnam	66.7	22.1	18.6	7.4

Paid Wages and Minimum Wages

Were the wages paid above the minimum in each country? ApparelCo obtained the legal minimums for the year in which it collected the data. Table 5.15 reports basic wages (excluding overtime pay, allowances, and deductions) in the company's supply chain in nominal USD in 2016, compared with the legal minimums.

Compared with AUDCO's results, in which some audits revealed wages below the legal minimum, average basic wages in ApparelCo's supply chain exceed the legal minimum in most countries and are equal to the legal minimum in one. But although ApparelCo's suppliers paid workers a little more than or on par with legal minimum wages, did these basic wages satisfy the company's wage commitment of meeting basic needs and leaving some discretionary income?

TABLE 5.15. Average base wages and legal minimum wages in USD

COUNTRY	BASE WAGE	LEGAL MINIMUM WAGE	DOLLARS BY WHICH BASE WAGE EXCEEDS MINIMUM WAGE
Bangladesh	81.2	68.3	12.9
Cambodia	130.9	128.0	2.9
China	296.5	228.6	67.9
India	103.9	85.2	18.7
Indonesia	152.9	152.3	0.6
Pakistan	121.5	114.6	6.9
Philippines	193.1	193.1	0.0
Sri Lanka	104.2	69.7	34.5
Vietnam	155.5	118.3	37.2

Basic Wages and Living Wage Benchmarks

To answer the question, we used as the benchmark the World Bank international poverty line for 2016: $1.9 per day, using PPP based on 2011 prices.[32] In line with the FLA's cross-country compensation studies (2016, 2018, 2019), we used the monthly estimates of international poverty lines multiplied by two (based on the assumption that a wage earner is likely to support at least two dependents).

The living wage estimates provided by WageIndicator Foundation we used earlier for the AUDCO analyses, as well as the AFWA wage for Asian countries, comprise the second benchmarks. Because the World Bank poverty lines and AFW living wage estimates are reported in PPP$, we converted all wages in the ApparelCo dataset to PPP$, using the conversion factor provided by the World Bank for 2016.[33] Table 5.16 shows the gap between average basic wages and living wage estimates.

There is some good news in table 5.16. ApparelCo's supplier factories clearly paid well above the World Bank poverty line estimates in 2016 in all countries—which is quite consistent with the AUDCO analysis. Average basic wages paid by ApparelCo's suppliers are significantly lower than WIF's lower-bound estimates in Bangladesh, India, Pakistan, and Vietnam. And consistent with our findings from the AUDCO analysis, wages in all countries are substantially lower than the AFWA wage in all countries.

Take-Home Pay and Living Wage Benchmarks

While there is no particularly sanctity to looking at the gap between take-home pay and living wage benchmarks—since most code of conduct commitments

TABLE 5.16. Basic wages and gaps with living-wage benchmarks, 2016

| | | | | DIFFERENCE BETWEEN BASIC WAGE (PPP$) AND . . . | | |
| | | | | WAGEINDICATOR | | |
COUNTRY	AVERAGE BASIC WAGE IN NOMINAL USD	AVERAGE BASIC WAGE IN PPP$	WORLD BANK POVERTY LINE (2 PEOPLE)	LOWER BOUND	HIGHER BOUND	ASIA FLOOR WAGE
Bangladesh	81.2	214.6	99.0	−169.6	−301.0	−806.4
Cambodia	130.9	380.3	264.8	N/A	N/A	−640.7
China	296.5	560.5	444.9	N/A	N/A	−460.5
India	103.9	408.7	293.2	−357.8	−701	−612.3
Indonesia	152.9	497.7	382.1	−15.1	−211.1	−523.3
Pakistan	121.5	443.5	327.9	−215.1	−629.8	−577.5
Philippines	193.1	495.6	380.0	N/A	N/A	−525.4
Sri Lanka	104.2	329.1	213.6	N/A	N/A	−691.9
Vietnam	155.5	458.5	343	−307.1	−600.9	−562.5

TABLE 5.17. Take-home pay and gaps with living-wage benchmarks, 2016

| | | | DIFFERENCE BETWEEN AVERAGE TAKE-HOME PAY (PPP$) AND . . . | | |
| | | | WAGEINDICATOR | | ASIA FLOOR WAGE |
COUNTRY	AVERAGE TAKE-HOME PAY IN NOMINAL USD	TAKE-HOME PAY IN PPP$	LOWER ESTIMATE	HIGHER ESTIMATE	
Bangladesh	127.4	336.8	−47.4	−178.9	−684.2
Cambodia	232.2	674.5	N/A	N/A	−346.5
China	485.1	917.0	N/A	N/A	−104.0
India	154.0	605.4	−161.2	−504.4	−415.6
Indonesia	239.0	778.5	265.8	69.7	−242.5
Pakistan	203.5	742.8	84.2	−330.5	−278.2
Philippines	255.0	654.2	N/A	N/A	−366.8
Sri Lanka	170.0	537.4	N/A	N/A	−483.6
Vietnam	233.6	688.7	−76.9	−370.8	−332.3

focus, appropriately, on basic wages—it is worth drawing a comparison with the AUDCO analysis (table 5.17), especially because the ApparelCo data serve to triangulate those results. When we compare take-home pay and living wages, the gap between the lower-bound WIF and take-home pay is reduced significantly.

TABLE 5.18. Percentage increase in basic wage to reach living wage estimates, 2016

COUNTRY	AVERAGE MONTHLY BASIC WAGE FOR 2016 (PPP$)	PERCENTAGE INCREASE FROM BASIC WAGE TO MEET:		
		WAGEINDICATOR LOWER ESTIMATE	WAGEINDICATOR HIGHER ESTIMATE	ASIA FLOOR WAGE
Bangladesh	214.6	79.0	140.3	375.8
Cambodia	380.3	N/A	N/A	168.5
China	560.5	N/A	N/A	82.2
India	408.7	87.5	171.5	149.8
Indonesia	497.7	3.0	42.4	105.1
Pakistan	443.5	48.5	142.0	130.2
Philippines	495.6	N/A	N/A	106.0
Sri Lanka	329.1	N/A	N/A	210.2
Vietnam	458.5	67.0	131.1	122.7

What Wage Increase Is Needed to Reach Living Wage Estimates?

Again, similar to the AUDCO analysis, we calculated the percentage increase in basic wages needed for ApparelCo's supply chain factories to meet living wage benchmarks (table 5.18).

The differences among countries are significant. Wages would have to increase by only 3 percent in Indonesia, but by 88 percent in India, to reach the lower-bound WIF estimates, and wages would have to *at least* more than double in all countries to reach AFWA wage estimates.

Overall, the data from this triangulation analysis show a consistent picture. In ApparelCo's factories, the average basic monthly wage is higher than the applicable local minimum wage and also higher than the relevant international poverty line in monthly terms. That is good news, as it meets ApparelCo's code commitments that require wages to be above the minimum. However, there is a large gap between basic monthly wages and living wage estimates, which runs counter to ApparelCo's commitment to pay a wage that provides some amount of discretionary income to its workers.

Conclusion

What do the analyses in this chapter tell us? In most countries, average basic wages are higher than the local minimum (except in a very small number of factories).

There is a significant gap between average basic wages and take-home pay, hinting that overtime is a highly necessary component of take-home pay. Further, wages are by and large above the World Bank international poverty lines for two people for the respective years. Thus, to the extent that codes of conduct state that wages must be paid above the minimum, these data suggest that condition is largely met.

There are, however, large gaps between average basic monthly wages and various estimates of living wages—which should cover basic needs of workers and their families and provide a little left over for discretionary income (the two most common elements in the varying definitions). In almost all countries and industries studied, basic monthly wages earned from regular working hours without overtime fall below even the lower-bound WIF living wage estimates. In other words, the AUDCO and ApparelCo datasets suggest that wages in their factories generally fall far below the commitment in some codes to pay a living wage.

These analyses hint at the limited impact of private regulation in enabling a living wage for workers in global supply chains. Looking at results that consistently show average basic wages falling below even the lowest living wage estimate, one can only conclude that private regulation has a long way to go. Private regulation may have made progress in ensuring that workers are paid correctly and transparently (see chapter 4) but has yet to make progress in meeting living wage commitments.

Are these commitments even meaningful? These results raise that question for some companies and MSIs. To be sure, factory owners can be "forced" by codes of conduct to ensure they pay wages according to the law and that the factories' wage structures correspond to the law and industry practices. But to "force" factory owners to pay living wages that are considerably higher than the local labor market clearing wage (i.e., the wage at which the supply of labor is equal to the demand for labor), minimum wage, and poverty lines, companies that make living wage commitments must integrate their sourcing practices with their codes. That task may require a reexamination of purchasing practices that are perhaps contributing to lower wages and high overtime.[34] And it will definitely require higher purchasing prices to suppliers to enable them to pay above the local labor market clearing wages.

This conclusion is consistent with a 2019 report on living wages from ASN Bank, which has been monitoring the progress of fourteen leading firms in instituting a living wage in their global supply chains.[35] Its key findings are that there needs to be more transparency generally and specifically regarding wages (i.e., companies need to do more in terms of processes to collect wage data and to identify wage gaps), that companies must do more to mitigate the deleterious effects of their buying polices on worker wages, and most of all that companies must reexamine their internal systems and promote internal collaboration in ways that will allow a closer integration of compliance and sourcing practices. While the ASN report is not sanguine that all its fourteen companies will be able to institute a living wage in the next decade, progress on these dimensions will get them part of the way.

Fundamentally, though, companies must accept that a living wage is a basic human right of workers and must be prepared to pay the price to support that right. Further, companies must collaborate so that all of them sourcing from a given factory work together to pay the price for that living wage to be sustainable.

There is much left to be done.

FREEDOM OF ASSOCIATION AND COLLECTIVE BARGAINING IN GLOBAL SUPPLY CHAINS

with Matt Fischer-Daly and Christopher Raymond

What can we say about freedom of association (FOA) and collective bargaining (CB) in global supply chains?[1] FOA and CB are core labor rights, and anecdotal evidence suggests that they are the two core labor rights complied with the least. This chapter makes several arguments. First, leading apparel brands source primarily from countries in which the national institutional support for FOA and CB is weak.[2] Second, the quality of information regarding FOA and CB rights produced by private regulation, including by firms and multi-stakeholder initiatives (MSIs), is poor; typically, the number of violations of FOA and CB found is small, consisting only of a small proportion of overall code of conduct violations, despite substantial evidence that workers' efforts to organize are routinely violated. Third, the nature of FOA and CB violations highlights a range of obstacles for workers to exercise their rights in a meaningful way—and two large datasets show that global companies and MSIs are not ensuring that their suppliers and members, respectively, enforce compliance with FOA and CB standards. Finally, where FOA and CB *do* exist, compliance with *all* code provisions is significantly higher.

In this chapter, we use diverse datasets from brands, auditing firms, MSIs, and Better Work to assess FOA and CB in the global apparel industry and substantiate the arguments. The breadth of the data permits systematic and comprehensive analysis of the incidence and nature of FOA violations and the influence of FOA and CB on overall labor standards in the industry.[3]

Our analysis of the industry data suggests a puzzle. FOA and CB show great promise for improving compliance with codes of conduct overall—the expressed goal of private regulation—but FOA and CB are the least supported rights in current private regulation efforts. In other words, most companies with private regulation programs are eschewing the very rights that could potentially improve the functioning of their private regulation programs.

What are freedom of association and collective bargaining?

The year 2019 marked the hundredth anniversary of the formation of the International Labour Organization, established by the Treaty of Versailles (Part XIII) based on the view that social peace depends on fair treatment in the workplace and that freedom of association and collective bargaining are essential for progress toward those goals. At the end of World War II, the Philadelphia Declaration reaffirmed the ILO's fundamental principles and established them in an updated ILO Constitution. Further, the Universal Declaration of Human Rights, the International Covenant on Political and Economic Rights (Article 22), and the International Covenant on Economic, Social and Cultural Rights (Article 8) reiterate freedom of association as a universal human right.

In the ILO, each member country (represented by the national government, employers' associations, and workers' unions, referred to as the "social partners") has agreed that the ILO conventions regarding FOA and CB have constitutional status. This means that by virtue of becoming an ILO member, all 187 member states agree to comply with the ILO's Freedom of Association and Protection of the Right to Organise Convention (No. 87) and the Application of the Principles of the Right to Organise and to Bargain Collectively Convention (No. 98). ILO Convention 87 establishes the state duty to protect worker and employer rights to establish and join organizations in order to further and defend their respective interests, and ILO Convention 98 establishes the state duty to protect workers against antiunion discrimination and to protect workers' and employers' organizations against interference, particularly any actions that would subjugate workers' organizations to employers' control.

The ILO Workers' Representatives Convention (No. 135) clarifies the meaning of "workers' representatives" as follows:

> persons who are recognised as such under national law or practice, whether they are—
>
> (a) trade union representatives, namely representatives designated or elected by trade unions or by member of such unions;
>
> (b) or elected representatives, namely, representatives who are freely elected by the workers of the undertaking in accordance with provisions of national laws or regulations or of collective agreements and whose functions do not include activities which are recognised as the exclusive prerogative of trade unions in the countries concerned.

The ILO Promotion of Collective Bargaining Convention (No. 154) defines "collective bargaining" as follows:

> all negotiations which take place between an employer, a group of employers or one or more employers' organisation, on the one hand, and one or more workers' organizations, on the other, for—
>
> (a) determining working conditions and terms of employment; and/or
> (b) regulating relations between employers and workers; and/or
> (c) regulating relations between employers or their organisations and workers' organisations.

FOA and CB rights are internationally recognized as core and fundamental human rights of global citizens. They are often referred to as "enabling" or "process" rights, the protection of which make possible the fulfillment of additional universally recognized rights. FOA and CB rights are linked to "democracy [which] necessarily implies the right of association, including the right to form and join trade unions."[4] Thus, in 1998 when the ILO recast its objectives to promote "decent work," FOA and CB were among the "core labor rights," along with the freedom from child and forced labor and freedom from discrimination.

FOA remains incomplete and highly contested in the contemporary global economy. Substantial portions of the world's working population have been excluded from state protections of FOA by law, both historically and to this day; examples include African workers under colonialism,[5] US agricultural workers,[6] Chinese workers generally,[7] debt slaves in India and prison workers in the United States,[8] and so forth. Union density and collective bargaining coverage in more than three-quarters of the world's countries stands at less than 30 percent and is declining. Even in countries and economic sectors with apparently robust rule-based labor relations systems (e.g., the European Union and the automotive sector), the experiences of precarity, constant insecurity, and unpredictability have increased since the 1970s.[9] Clearly, FOA and CB have not been realized as *universal rights* for a majority of the world's population.

While the erosion in FOA rights and the incidence and practice of CB in advanced nations can be linked to multiple causes (e.g., structural change causing declines in union density and the unwillingness or incapacity of governments to enforce labor laws), this erosion also reflects employer strategies under the logic of contemporary capitalism. While industrial relations (IR) systems were introduced to regulate conflict and preserve industrial peace, the logic of industrial peace underlying the design of most IR systems has been replaced by competition that tilts the balance of power more firmly toward employers.[10] Accelerated globalization has reinforced the shift in balance by allowing employers to "whipsaw" workers by playing one national workforce against another, thus weakening labor power at home and abroad. Competition has increasingly become the dominant logic driving behavior of private and public actors, with businesses and governments fixated on profit and income growth, respectively.[11] Facilitated by state policies and technology, capital has expanded globally; lacking similar support, labor has not globalized, labor law enforcement has not kept pace, and respect for workers' rights has eroded.

In developing countries with generally smaller industrial sectors, fractured unions, poor enforcement of the law, and large informal sectors, union density and collective bargaining coverage have been lower. Limited support and even adversarial policies toward FOA and CB occur even in states that have ratified the ILO conventions (which have the status of treaties under international law). The lack of institutional support for FOA and CB is particularly important when we examine FOA in global supply chains where capital locates production wherever labor costs are lower, pitting workers from different locations against one another and putting downward pressure on wages and working conditions.[12] Globalized production networks thus reduce workers' bargaining power.

What Does Prior Research on FOA and CB in Global Supply Chains Show?

The theory of change in private regulation (the adoption of which has expanded dramatically over the past twenty-five years) is that global brands can ensure compliance with standards set in their codes by regularly conducting social audits of supplier factories' labor practices and incentivizing factory management to comply by linking purchasing decisions to factories' performance on audits.[13] However, the accumulated evidence to date indicates that the model has not assured FOA.[14] To review what is known about FOA and CB in global supply chains, we begin with ambiguity in codes of conduct, with an emphasis on the global apparel industry.

Ambiguity Continues in Codes of Conduct

A review of codes at the end of their first prominent decade found that less than 30 percent mentioned FOA.[15] While a few early adopters included freedom of association and collective bargaining rights in their codes, the majority of companies and business associations did not.[16] While many codes today refer to ILO core conventions, the ambiguity of commitments to FOA continues to draw critiques of symbolic adoption of codes as "window dressing" to protect brand reputations.[17]

The approaches of prominent MSIs to FOA and CB indicate the variation in code language. The Fair Labor Association (FLA) code, for instance, states: "Employers shall recognize and respect the right of employees to freedom of association and collective bargaining."[18] The Ethical Trading Initiative (ETI), an MSI with company members drawn mostly from the United Kingdom, has a more specific code on FOA and CB that states:

2.1 Workers, without distinction, have the right to form trade unions of their own choosing and to bargain collectively,

2.2 The employer adopts an open attitude towards the activities of trade unions and their organizational activities.

2.3 Worker representatives are not to be discriminated against, and have access to carry out their representative functions in the workplace.

2.4 Where the right of FOA and CB is restricted by law, the employer facilitates, and does not hinder, the development of parallel means for independent and free association and bargaining.[19]

Similar to the ETI, the code of the Fair Wear Foundation (FWF), the members of which are mostly European buyers, states:

> The right of all workers to form and join trade unions and bargain collectively shall be recognised (ILO Conventions 87 and 98). The company shall, in those situations in which the right to freedom of association and collective bargaining are restricted under law, facilitate parallel means of independent and free association and bargaining for all workers. Workers' representatives shall not be the subject of discrimination and shall have access to all workplaces necessary to carry out their representation functions (ILO Convention 135 and Recommendation 143).[20]

While similarly recognizing workers FOA and CB rights, the three codes differ in approach. The FLA is the least specific, while the FWF and ETI clarify the duty of employers in jurisdictions that do not protect FOA and CB. The ETI further identifies positive ("adopt an Bopen attitude") and negative ("not discriminate") boundaries for employer behavior. SA8000 (Social Accountability International), which certifies factories, also requires that factory management directly inform workers about their FOA and CB rights, apart from provisions similar to those of ETI. The point here is that there is variation (policy multiplicity), leading to ambiguity.

Private Regulation Has Not Overcome Institutional Antagonism to FOA and CB

The locations brands select for production affect assurance of FOA and CB and code compliance more generally. Suppliers are more likely to comply with private codes when operating in national states with more effective enforcement of labor laws supporting freedom of association and collective bargaining rights.[21] Laws and normalized practices antithetical to labor rights impede compliance with labor rights standards.[22] A 2018 study of several thousand firms in the apparel industry found the vast majority of sourcing is from countries rated in the bottom quartile for FOA by the World Justice Project.[23]

These findings reflect, to some degree, the current structure of the apparel industry. Changes in international trade and investment public policies, telecommunications, and transportation have facilitated the globalization of production networks since the 1970s. Key policy changes with respect to global apparel include the admission of China into the World Trade Organization, the phaseout of the Multilateral Fiber Agreement (MFA), and the development of multilateral and bilateral trade agreements that not only facilitated the proliferation of production facilities in diverse locations but also reinforced competition based on low labor costs.[24]

Neoliberal reforms at the national level, most concentrated in structural adjustment programs (SAPs), have also been a key driver of the geographic distribution of garment production and the paucity of FOA and CB protections. Since the 1980s, the International Monetary Fund has conditioned national states' access to finance on the liberalization of capital accounts, privatization of industries, government spending austerity, flexible labor policy, and export orientation—based on the premise that such measures will attract foreign investment and thus provide governments with foreign exchange to repay debts and increase national income. SAPs typically decentralize collective bargaining, allow negotiators to deviate from legal minimums, impose tighter restrictions on strikes, exempt small- and medium-size enterprises from labor laws, introduce temporary and other contracts with fewer social protections, set longer standard working hours, and expand the use of labor contractors.[25] Countries such as Vietnam, Bangladesh, Indonesia, and Cambodia all underwent structural adjustment programs prior to their emergence as key sources of garment manufacturing.

Many states have followed the logic of competition, maximizing employer discretion to control labor costs in order to achieve capital accumulation and competitiveness in the global industry.[26] Unionization, collective bargaining, and collective action generally are curtailed by states using laws and extralegal practices (e.g., by authoritarian governments such as those in China and Vietnam);

by labor market conditions unfavorable to workers (e.g., low incomes and high unemployment, as in Bangladesh and Indonesia); and by employer repression against workers (e.g., impunity for violence against trade unionists in Honduras, El Salvador, Guatemala and Colombia).[27] These methods of curtailment are not mutually exclusive, as states and employers utilize various overlapping and complementary strategies.

Recognizing this policy environment, some researchers have hypothesized that multinational companies themselves might serve a diplomatic function with respect to FOA and CB. The "boomerang" model explains actors in transnational advocacy campaigns pursuing leverage globally to affect concerns locally.[28] Looking at whether that model might be a strategy to address the conflict between code commitments to FOA and CB and production locations hostile to FOA and CB, a researcher found that brands have remained generally silent to worker appeals for pressure on their domestic governments for greater FOA and CB protection, even though the companies have responded to instances of blatant violence and, to a lesser degree, minimum wage debates.[29]

The Monitoring Industry Pays Little Attention to FOA and CB

Given the contradiction between code commitments to FOA and CB and the political-economic contexts of sourcing, it is perhaps unsurprising that the evidence to date indicates almost no improvement on enabling and distributive rights.[30] The few instances of codes increasing respect for FOA have appeared when organized workers pressure companies,[31] particularly in supply chains with long-term buyer-supplier relations or in cases where suppliers produce for few firms in markets with high consumer demand for decent working conditions.[32] Absent such pressure, private regulation tends to ignore FOA and CB.

Although the $80 billion social auditing industry entails hundreds of thousands of audits of workplaces each year, the code-audit paradigm does not consider workers in the supply chain as the omnipresent monitors of workplaces.[33] Rather, the view is that workers are subordinate objects to be regulated by their employers and their employers' buyers.[34] Auditors often do not even record whether workers are unionized or covered by a collective bargaining agreement (CBA).

Inconsistent reporting on FOA and CB means many studies of labor standards have avoided FOA altogether.[35] For example, a study of FLA-conducted audits from 2002–2008 found minimal detection and remediation of FOA and CB violations.[36] The study contrasted the lack of findings of FOA violations with widespread reporting of such violations in the same context by various governments and the tripartite ILO supervisory system. The study also compared the FLA's record to the Worker Rights Consortium (WRC) and found the WRC was six times more likely to detect FOA and CB violations than FLA. Further examining a specific FOA complaint by a worker to the FLA, the study found that the FLA placed the burden of proof on the complainant, accepted the position of its member company despite authoritative determination of FOA violations, and acted to remediate the violation only when the company came under boycott pressure.

Underlying the distinction in how the FLA and WRC address FOA are differences in governance. Whereas the FLA has brands and no unions on its governing board, the WRC has unions and no brands. Furthermore, the WRC can mobilize consumer boycotts of noncompliant brands led by United Students Against Sweatshops, a sanction absent from the FLA and most MSI models. The difference points to a broader tension in private regulation between the public legitimacy gained by including FOA and CB in codes of conduct and the importance of control over production to competing global brands. Decoupling policy and outcomes is one way in which global companies or brands can manage this tension.

Workers and Labor Standards: A Question of Agency

A consensus has developed over the past quarter-century that worker agency is essential to achieving good labor standards in supply chains. The lack of FOA and CB in global apparel supply chains, uncovered in multiple studies, both denies workers a fundamental right and hinders compliance generally.[37] The findings of these studies motivated a range of initiatives along two different paths, both aimed at improved working conditions: first, increased worker participation (in the absence of formal worker representation through trade unions) on committees established by companies or governments; and, second, collective negotiation by workers with companies.

In the early 2000s, multiple initiatives aimed to create means for workers to participate collectively in their workplaces, particularly where sourcing was increasingly concentrated and institutional support for FOA and CB was lacking. A prominent Reebok initiative directly supported worker elections of representatives at one of its supplier factories in Shenzhen, China. This initiative eventually collapsed after the brand ended its support and factory management changed.[38] A decade later, workers committees were found *not* to empower workers with voice and risked being used by managers to avoid unions, in violation of ILO Convention No. 135 on Workers' Representatives.[39] In Bangladesh, the law requiring "worker participation committees" explained that the committees intend to "inculcate and develop a sense of belonging and worker commitment."[40] In a project by H&M in Bangladesh, workers did not receive information about the committee to which they were to elect representatives, understood the committee as dominated by management, and did not trust that the committee represented them.[41]

Better Work, the joint program of the ILO and the IFC (the World Bank Group's private-lending branch) in operation since 2007, has required worker-management committees called Performance Improvement Consultative Committees (PICCs) at all participating factories.[42] With the PICCs, Better Work sought to establish a mechanism through which workers could address standards violations[43] by linking trade incentives to labor standards, leveraging the ILO's expertise, and replacing company-led monitoring with "internationally credible workplace inspection and information" based on the ILO's tripartite structure.[44]

PICCs showed promise as a starting point to institute social dialogue at the factory level by establishing norms of communication and joint problem-solving between management and workers. To be successful, there were important preconditions, such as freely elected worker members and representation of women. The evidence is mixed. In factories with well-functioning PICCs, workers are healthier, supervisors are less stressed, and there are fewer instances of abuse and sexual harassment.[45] PICCs in Vietnam, though, were unable to address substantive issues; workers did not feel protected from retaliation; and noncompliance on minimum wages, social security payments, overtime wages, overtime hours, health and safety, and FOA and CB standards remained the norm after four years of the program.[46] In Lesotho, PICCs, which had played an important role in improving compliance, disintegrated after the Better Work program concluded, and gains that had been made evaporated.[47]

These experiences corroborated research that has found that nonunion worker committees do not result in effective worker voice.[48] Nonunion committees lack enforcement sanctions to ensure that noncompliance with workplace standards is remedied; such committees often do not offer genuine representation of workers and do not provide workers with the sources of power that make unions effective.[49]

In contrasting environments where FOA and CB are less restricted, worker agency has yielded improved compliance. In Indonesia, unions and workers adopted multiple ways to leverage corporate social responsibility (CSR) commitments to improve working conditions, including "whistleblowing" to convince brands to negotiate, "warnings" to publicize noncompliant conditions, and preparation—particularly building local capacity. These tactics "spurred improvements in working conditions," suggesting potential for labor to leverage CSR commitments into what Bartley and Egels-Zandén call "contingent coupling" of CSR commitments and actual working conditions.[50]

Effects on Employment Relations

During the first half of the twentieth century, the model of triangular negotiations between workers, employers, and brands was widely applied when price points, turnaround time, and other purchasing practices of buying companies reduced profits of manufacturers, which then relieved financial pressure by lengthening, intensifying, and devaluing workers' labor. Recognizing that terms of employment hinged on buyers' purchasing practices, the US-based International Ladies' Garment Workers' Union (ILGWU) negotiated "jobbers agreements" in which buyers committed to regular contracting from only unionized manufacturers, while manufacturers committed to improved wages, hours, safety and health, and other terms and conditions typical of CBAs.[51] Public policies supported enforcement of these triangular bargaining agreements.

Several initiatives in the twenty-first century have adapted the triangular model to the contemporary global apparel industry. For example, the Accord on Fire and Building Safety in Bangladesh is a legally binding agreement between brands and trade unions to improve health and safety in that country's apparel industry. A committee chaired by the ILO and comprising company and union representatives governs the Accord. It requires buyers to pay for some factory safety improvements, commit to multiyear purchasing from suppliers, and end business with noncompliant suppliers; requires suppliers to include worker and union representatives on health and safety committees; and establishes legally binding contractual commitments and a grievance system to resolve disputes.[52] During its first five years, the Accord made unprecedented progress in coupling policy, practice, and outcomes. The Accord remediated worker complaints, required brands to cease purchases from suppliers that refused to improve labor practices, and held brands accountable for their share of the duty to respect labor rights by using a dispute-resolution mechanism with arbitration as its final step.[53]

In 2019 in Lesotho, local trade unions and women' rights NGOs supported by global unions and NGOs signed an agreement with the apparel production company Nien Hsing Textile and three global brands that seeks to eliminate gender-based violence and harassment by applying the triangular governance model.[54] Additional efforts at adapting the triangular negotiation model to the present apparel industry include the Alta Gracia apparel line in the Dominican Republic, the General Workers Central–Russell agreement in Honduras, and the Indonesian Freedom of Association Protocol (FoAP).[55]

A pattern emerges from this review. While the international community—including governments, workers, and employers—has established FOA and CB as fundamental workers' rights, respect for these rights has largely been absent in the contemporary apparel industry. This reality stands in sharp contrast to the theory and empirical evidence that indicate these rights are key to improving labor standards. In addition, among the many initiatives that set FOA and CB as standards, those designed to establish triangular collective bargaining with workers, employers, and apparel brands stand out for achieving labor standard improvements.

Several new datasets allow for exploring further FOA and CB in global supply chains and the relationship between them and labor standards—and substantiating the four arguments raised at the beginning of this chapter.

Substantiating the Arguments about FOA and CB

Primary Sourcing from Countries with Low Institutional Support for FOA and CB

To demonstrate that global apparel companies typically source from countries with weak institutional support for FOA and CB, we combine export data, union density data, and measures of institutional support for FOA and CB from the World Justice Project (WJP) and Labour Rights Indicators (LRI) to provide an overview of the institutional support for FOA and CB in the top garment-exporting countries. We use the sourcing locations of three leading global retailers—Gap Inc., H&M, and Primark, all with robust private regulation programs—to show that a large majority of their garments are sourced from countries with low institutional support for FOA and CB.

Table 6.1 shows institutional support for FOA and CB in the ten top countries for apparel (ready-made garments) exporting, using six indicators. The ILO rankings are self-explanatory. The WJP index measures perception of rule of law based on surveys of households and thematic experts (120,000 households and 3,800 experts surveyed in 2019). One of the WJP index's eight factors is fundamental rights, within which the subfactor "fundamental labor rights are effectively guaranteed" measures "the effective enforcement of fundamental labor rights, including freedom of association and the right to collective bargaining, the absence of discrimination with respect to employment, and freedom from forced labor and child labor."[56] The Labour Rights Indicators (LRI) indexes reported violations of FOA and CB rights from nine sources.[57] The country profiles provide detailed and verifiable information over time that can be traced back easily to the original textual source.[58] To address whether institutional support for FOA and CB relates to rule of law generally, we also analyze the WJP overall rule-of-law index and factor in regulatory enforcement, which measures the degree to which

TABLE 6.1.   FOA and CB institutional support in the top clothing exporting countries

COUNTRY (WORLD TRADE ORGANIZATION 2019)[1]	RATIFICATION OF ILO FOA/CB CONVENTIONS	FUNDAMENTAL LABOR RIGHTS ENFORCEMENT (0–1)[2]	FOA AND CB VIOLATIONS (0–10)	UNION DENSITY[3] (IN %)	RANK ON RULE OF LAW INDEX/TOTAL COUNTRIES	REGULATORY ENFORCEMENT SCORE (0–1)
TOP 10 EXPORTERS						
China		0.32	10.0	44.9 (2015)	82/126,	0.50
Bangladesh	C87,98	0.40	7.30	5[4] (2016)	112/126	0.45
Vietnam		0.63	10.0	14.6 (2011)	81/126	0.63
India		0.50	6.23	12.8 (2011)	68/126	0.41
Turkey	C87,C98	0.38	5.74	8.2 (2016)	109/126	0.41
Hong Kong (China)	C87,C98	0.76	N/A	26.1 (2016)	16/126	0.76
Indonesia	C87,C98	0.60	5.19	7 (2012)	62/126	0.52
Cambodia	C87,C98	0.50	6.36	9.6 (2012)	125/126	0.27
USA		0.56	3.45	10.3 (2016)	20/126	0.70
RISING EXPORTERS						
Ethiopia	C87,C98	0.31	2.94	9.6 (2013)	118/126	0.33
Bulgaria	C87,C98	0.67	3.09	13.7 (2016)	91/126	0.67
Myanmar	C87	0.54	4.16	1 (2015)	110/126	0.49

[1] The European Union is the second-largest exporter, after China, but density figures for the whole of the EU are not available, and not all EU member states export garments. Bulgaria is included as one of the largest clothing exporters in the EU. Ethiopia—which has had double-digit growth in clothing exports since 2010—is added to the top ten clothing exporters. Myanmar and Vietnam are added as top-ranked locations where U.S.- and EU-based brands plan to increase sourcing.
[2] World Justice Project (2019) Rule of Law Index.
[3] International Labour Organization 2019.
[4] The ILO does not include a union density statistic for Bangladesh. This estimate is from Danish Trade Union Development Agency (2020).

all government regulations are effectively enforced, applied without improper influence, in a timely fashion, respecting due process, and specifically without unlawful and uncompensated state expropriation.[59]

As table 6.1 suggests, the top apparel-exporting countries have weak institutional support for FOA and CB. Most score low on enforcement of fundamental labor conventions, and most have high scores for FOA and CB violations. The largest exporting country, China, and the third-ranked exporter, Vietnam, prohibit FOA by law and thus receive the highest scores for FOA and CB violations. The union density in most of these countries is low (note that China and Vietnam have state-controlled unions).

The correlation matrix shown in table 6.2 indicates that institutional support for FOA and CB is not necessarily related to ratifications of ILO conventions or the general rule of law but is associated with stronger regulatory enforcement. While simply indicating associations, not causal relationships, the correlations suggest countries that have ratified ILO FOA and CB conventions are characterized

TABLE 6.2.   Correlations between indicators of regulatory institutions

	RATIFICATIONS 87/98	CORE LABOR STANDARDS ENFORCEMENT	FOA/CB VIOLATIONS	UNION DENSITY	OVERALL RULE OF LAW	OVERALL REGULATORY ENFORCEMENT
Ratifications 87/98	1					
Fundamental labor standards enforcement	−0.1100	1				
FOA/CB violations	0.4407	0.1762	1			
Union density	−0.4289	−0.3303	−0.5771	1		
Overall rule of law	0.6202	−0.4093	−0.0484	−0.1794	1	
Overall regulatory enforcement	−0.4250	0.6320	0.0366	0.1235	−0.7015	1

Sources: ILO NormLex; Center for Global Workers' Rights (2016); World Justice Project (2019).

by weaker enforcement of fundamental labor standards and higher numbers of reported FOA and CB violations. Stronger ranking on the WJP rule-of-law index overall is related counterintuitively to weaker regulatory and core labor standards enforcement, while stronger general regulatory enforcement apparently indicates stronger labor standards enforcement. It is not surprising that reporting of FOA and CB violations is apparently higher in countries scoring higher on general and labor standards enforcement.

Tables 6.3, 6.4, and 6.5 show the sourcing decisions of three global brands—H&M, GAP Inc, and Primark—and corroborate earlier findings that apparel brands tend to source from countries where institutional support for FOA and CB is low.[60]

These findings from the three companies concerning institutional support for FOA and CB and the location decisions of the global apparel industry are consistent with prior research and support our argument. They indicate a pattern in the apparel industry of organizational policy-practice decoupling: brands decouple the policy of respect for FOA and CB that is expressed in codes from sourcing practice by selecting locations for production where support for FOA and CB is low.

Low Levels of Detection of FOA and CB Violations

Since institutional support for FOA and CB is weak, and workers, their advocates, governments, the tripartite ILO, and researchers report regular violations of these

TABLE 6.3.   Gap Inc. supplier factories, April 2019

COUNTRY	NUMBER OF FACTORIES	PERCENTAGE
China	197	25.8
Vietnam	152	19.9
India	106	13.9
Indonesia	68	8.9
Cambodia	50	6.5
Bangladesh	46	6.0
Sri Lanka	41	5.4
Guatemala	18	2.3
S. Korea	17	2.2
Pakistan	13	1.7
Jordan	9	1.1
Egypt	7	0.9
Philippines	6	0.7
Portugal	6	0.7
Haiti	5	0.6
Turkey	4	0.5
USA	3	0.3
El Salvador	3	0.3
Dominican Republic	2	0.2
Colombia	1	0.1
Honduras	1	0.1
Italy	1	0.1
Myanmar	1	0.1
Taiwan	1	0.1
Total	763	100

Source: Gap Inc. Factory List (April 2019a).

core labor rights, one would expect to find that private regulation audit reports include a large number of violations of FOA and CB. However, that is not the case. Here we use two new data sources to substantiate our argument that the incidence of FOA violations reported by auditing codes of conduct is relatively low compared with other violations of labor standards in corporate codes. The data here are the same data from the global auditing company AUDCO that were used in earlier chapters, along with the data ApparelCo used in chapter 5's triangulation analysis. These complementary data add new evidence that private regulation reports relatively few FOA and CB violations relative to violations of other standards: when we examine the absolute numbers of FOA and CB violations recorded in the AUDCO data (21,041 audits), we find very low reporting levels (figures 6.1

TABLE 6.4. H&M's supplier factories (first-tier manufacturing factories only), August 2019

COUNTRY	NUMBER OF FACTORIES	PERCENTAGE
China	463	29.13
Bangladesh	265	16.67
Turkey	219	13.78
India	168	10.57
Italy	101	6.35
Indonesia	69	4.34
Vietnam	43	2.70
Myanmar	41	2.60
Cambodia	33	2.07
Pakistan	29	1.85
Romania	26	1.63
France	15	0.94
Sweden	14	0.88
Bulgaria	13	0.81
Sri Lanka	13	0.81
Germany	11	0.69
Ethiopia	9	0.56
Poland	9	0.56
Czech Republic	4	0.25
Morocco	4	0.25
Finland	4	0.25
Netherlands	4	0.25
USA	4	0.25
Finland	4	0.25
Lithuania	3	0.18
Taiwan	3	0.18
Spain	3	0.18
Hungary	3	0.18
Denmark	2	0.12
Thailand	2	0.12
Greece	2	0.12
Kenya	2	0.12
United Kingdom	2	0.12
Estonia	1	0.06
Croatia	1	0.06
Luxembourg	1	0.06
Macedonia	1	0.06
Rwanda	1	0.06
South Korea	1	0.06
Total	1,596	100

Source: H&M Supplier List (accessed August 6, 2019).

TABLE 6.5.   Primark's supplier factories, July 2018

COUNTRY	NUMBER OF FACTORIES	PERCENTAGE
China	517	51.55
India	148	14.76
Bangladesh	94	9.37
Turkey	78	7.78
Cambodia	23	2.29
Pakistan	21	2.09
Romania	21	2.09
Vietnam	20	1.99
United Kingdom	17	1.69
Myanmar	11	1.10
Sri Lanka	11	1.10
Italy	7	0.70
Portugal	6	0.60
Republic of Moldova	5	0.50
Morocco	4	0.4
Germany	3	0.3
Ireland	3	0.3
France	2	0.2
Honduras	2	0.2
Republic of North Macedonia	2	0.2
Georgia	1	0.1
Greece	1	0.1
Indonesia	1	0.1
Netherlands	1	0.1
Slovakia	1	0.1
South Korea	1	0.1
Tunisia	1	0.1
USA	1	0.1
Total	1,003	100

Source: Our global sourcing map (Primark 2019).

and 6.2). Only a tiny percentage of overall violations reported via audits concerned FOA and CB, whether by country or industry.

These low numbers reinforce the oft-repeated argument that the private regulation audit regime does not reliably detect and report FOA violations. If FOA and CB violations are low in absolute terms, they also constitute a relatively small fraction of the total violations found in all 21,041 of AUDCO's reliable audits between 2011 and 2016, as tables 6.6 and 6.7 show for countries and industries.

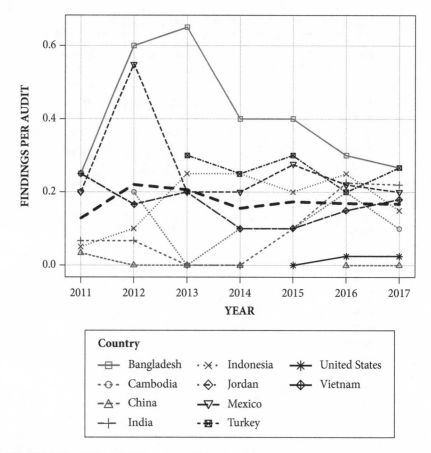

FIGURE 6.1. FOA violations per audit by country

Chart by author.

The ApparelCo data offer a way to triangulate the AUDCO data. Table 6.8 shows that despite evidence of substantial FOA and CB violations in many of the countries in which ApparelCo sources, its audit records barely include FOA violations.

Finding a low level of violations on FOA and CB in places antagonistic to these standards is consistent with earlier research,[61] and aligns with the notion of means-ends decoupling—namely, that brands and auditors decouple the practice of auditing from the outcomes aimed at in codes of conduct by not assessing, or inadequately assessing, compliance with FOA and CB standards.[62]

There are several possible *interrelated* explanations for why organizations hired to audit labor standards report such a small number of FOA and CB violations. It may be that the typical one- or two-day audit does not allow enough time to uncover FOA findings. AUDCO's audit duration for small factories of less than two hundred

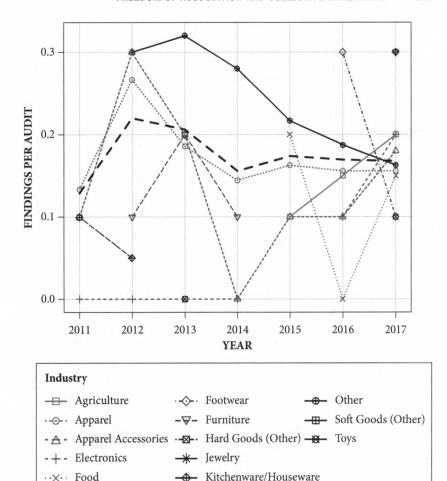

FIGURE 6.2.   FOA violations per audit by industry

Chart by author.

workers is a single day, or two days for larger factories; ApparelCo audits average two person-days. Uncovering FOA and CB violations requires more intensive conversations with workers, which auditors may not have to time to do—ApparelCo audits include more than seven hundred items, leaving very little time for a meaningful conversation about FOA with workers. The lack of sufficient time to address a core labor standard clearly raises questions about the purpose of the audits and whether they may be disconnected from the labor standards expressed in codes.

Another possibility concerns auditor training, which has a significant effect on compliance and compliance improvement.[63] It may be that auditors are simply not well trained to uncover FOA and CB violations. Well-trained auditors

TABLE 6.6. Proportion of FOA violations per audit by country, 2011–2017 (n = 21041 AUDCO audits)

COUNTRY	2011	2012	2013	2014	2015	2016	2017
Bangladesh	3.07	6.78	6.22	3.57	3.67	3.30	2.68
Cambodia	N/A	1.39	0.00	0.81	0.81	1.53	0.93
China	0.34	0.00	0.00	0.00	N/A	0.00	0.00
India	0.96	1.12	0.00	0.00	1.09	2.89	2.12
Indonesia	0.60	1.47	3.45	2.46	2.44	2.86	1.49
Jordan	2.50	N/A	N/A	1.69	N/A	N/A	N/A
Mexico	2.33	4.01	1.45	1.72	1.84	1.75	2.00
Turkey	N/A	N/A	2.27	2.38	3.30	1.95	4.00
United States	N/A	N/A	N/A	N/A	0.00	0.43	0.50
Vietnam	1.92	1.55	1.97	1.04	1.02	1.40	1.37

TABLE 6.7. Proportion of FOA violations per audit by industry, 2011–2017 (n = 21041 AUDCO audits)

INDUSTRY	2011	2012	2013	2014	2015	2016	2017
Agriculture	N/A	N/A	N/A	N/A	0.56	1.27	2.70
Apparel	1.77	3.2	2.09	1.55	1.69	1.70	1.71
Apparel accessories	1.48	3.69	2.59	0.00	1.13	1.24	2.20
Electronics	0.00	0.00	0.00	0.00	N/A	1.38	2.36
Food	N/A	N/A	N/A	N/A	1.89	0.00	1.68
Footwear	N/A	N/A	N/A	N/A	N/A	2.16	0.68
Furniture	N/A	0.82	1.54	0.71	N/A	N/A	1.92
Hard goods (other)	0.95	N/A	0.00	N/A	N/A	N/A	1.05
Kitchenware/housewares	1.41	0.78	N/A	N/A	N/A	N/A	2.91
Other	N/A	3.15	3.18	2.79	2.22	1.92	1.70

Note: Excludes soft goods (other), toys, and jewelry industries because they do not report on FOA findings. Also excludes the cases where industries are "unknown."

know that it is important to contact and interview workers outside of the factory to obtain relevant information regarding FOA and CB, as well as other core labor standards such as freedom from discrimination.

Audit fraud is another factor. Even were auditors able to talk to the workers in the factory, those workers may have been coercively coached to provide "desirable" responses—something that is all too common.[64] Chapter 1 highlights the prevalence of "audit consultants" that coach workers.

Finally, it may be that brands and supplier factories hire auditors and instruct them not to report FOA and CB violations—the equivalent of telling a housing

TABLE 6.8.   Proportion of audit violations per issue, 2010–2017

ISSUE	PERCENTAGE OF TOTAL VIOLATIONS FOUND
Occupational health and safety	47.9
Wages, benefits and terms of employment	10.7
Working hours	5.8
Chemical storage	5.7
Chemical disposal	5.1
FOA	0.4
Other	24.4
Total	100.0

Note: Our own elaboration based on ApparelCo's data.

inspector not to check the foundation or a doctor not to check the patient's pulse. Research into the mechanics of regulation has repeatedly found that auditors are not always required to assess FOA and CB standards and are influenced by the firms that hire them.[65]

The Nature of FOA and CB Violations

Even though the audits by brands and audit firms report few incidences of FOA and CB violations, it is still instructive to examine what industry data indicate about the *nature* of typical FOA violations, since it provides an idea of the typical obstacles workers face in successfully unionizing or implementing a CBA.

So, then, what are "typical" FOA and CB violations? While the ILO has rich data on these issues,[66] we explore the information offered by the private regulation industry. Neither of the AUDCO and ApparelCo datasets provide any indication of the nature of FOA violations, so to answer this question we use data from two multi-stakeholder organizations: the Fair Labor Association (FLA) and the Fair Wear Foundation (FWF). The FLA typically audits 5 percent of a member company's supplier factories, and over the 2002–2019 (January) period published 1,620 such workplace monitoring reports, each with the number and nature of violations found regarding the FLA's Code of Conduct. FWF also audits a percentage of its more than ninety member company factories. We analyze 1,421 FWF audit reports from the period 2008–2018 from factories in twelve countries. Both MSIs use their own trained auditors.

We begin with the FLA, which focuses on uncovering violations of its code of conduct provisions. Its monitoring reports do not indicate whether workers at a factory have union representation. We set aside audits in China and Vietnam (because FOA is legally restricted in the two countries) from the 1,546 FLA audits, which reduced the total to 981 records—in which we found 775 FOA violations, with wide variation across countries (table 6.9).

Not surprisingly, there are substantial violations in Bangladesh and the United States, two countries with strong traditions of union avoidance or suppression. The large number of incidences found in Indian factories likely reflects practice more than policy, given more protective legislation but relatively poor enforcement of core labor standards

We prioritized clarity and consistency in categorizing the violations of FOA or CB standards reported in FLA reports (table 6.10).

Given that the FLA requires its members have a policy regarding FOA and CB consistent with the FLA code of conduct, the large number of reported violations regarding the absence of a policy is remarkable. The FLA reports also indicate weak implementation of FOA and CBA provisions and active union suppression, consistent with other research.[67]

To triangulate the FLA data, we examined the nature of FOA violations using data from the FWF, which like the FLA uses its own trained auditors to assess compliance by a sample of members with the FLA code of conduct. Table 6.11 shows FWF audits by country during the period 2008–2018.

The FWF audit procedures require auditors first to interview workers outside the factory and then audit against the code at the factory. To assess compliance with the code standards on FOA and CB, auditors record responses to the following questions:

TABLE 6.9. FLA reports of FOA violations (excluding China and Vietnam), 2002–2019

COUNTRY	FOA FINDING	COUNTRY	FOA FINDINGS	COUNTRY	FOA FINDINGS
Albania	1	Guatemala	10	Peru	4
Argentina	1	Haiti	2	Philippines	7
Bangladesh	91	Honduras	31	Portugal	1
Brazil	3	India	104	Singapore	2
Bulgaria	4	Indonesia	43	Slovenia	6
Cambodia	13	Jordan	11	South Korea	3
Dominican Republic	1	Macau	3	Sri Lanka	10
Ecuador	1	Malaysia	21	Taiwan	3
Egypt	10	Mexico	102	Thailand	30
El Salvador	36	Myanmar	11	Tunisia	7
Georgia	2	Pakistan	50	Turkey	61
				USA	88
Total					775

TABLE 6.10. Types and frequencies of FOA and CB violations (excluding China and Vietnam), 2002–2019 (per FLA)

CATEGORY OF FOA VIOLATIONS	FREQUENCY
1. Inadequate FOA/CB policy	231

Examples
The factory does not have a written policy on FOA or CB
The factory FOA or CB policy is incomplete or not updated
Factory does not have a policy on grievances

2. Inadequate FOA administration and implementation	145

Examples
CBA is not posted or communicated to workers
No staff responsible for managing industrial relations
No written record of union activities
No office space or facilities provided to union
Poor implementation of CBA provisions
Copy of CBA not provided to workers

3. Undemocratic union elections	79

Examples
Workers' representatives are not elected by workers
The election for union representation has not been conducted
The election of union leaders has not been conducted properly

4. Union suppression tactics by employers	65

Examples
Workers are not free to join a union
Union activists are dismissed
Union activists are discriminated against
Workers are discouraged from joining unions
Foreign and temporary workers are not allowed to join union
Physical and verbal violence against union activists and members

5. Inadequate worker awareness of FOA and CB	57

Examples
Workers are not aware of their FOA or CB rights
Workers are not aware that a union exists in the factory
Workers are not aware that a CBA exists in the factory
Workers lack knowledge of how the union functions
Union representatives are not aware of their rights and responsibilities
Workers are not aware of committees that ostensibly represent them

6. Management interference in union affairs	44

Examples
Worker representatives are not independent from management
Union affiliation to existing union is required as a condition of hiring
No genuine representative structures exist
Existing representation structures are controlled by management
Supervisor functions as worker representative

7. Lack of worker-management social dialogue	44

Examples
Committee meetings are held, but no records are kept
No meetings have been held
Meetings are not conducted regularly
No regular meetings of welfare committee are held as per policy
No system is in place to follow up on issues discussed at meetings
No system exists for regular communications between management and union

TABLE 6.10. (continued)

CATEGORY OF FOA VIOLATIONS	FREQUENCY
8. Lack of training	42
Examples	
Workers are not provided training with regard to FOA/CB rights	
Training is not effective	
There is no training on FOA/CB for supervisors	
Orientation for new workers does not include FOA/CB policy	
9. Inappropriate fee practices	15
Examples	
Union fees are not deducted	
Union fees are deducted without consent from workers	
10. Observations related to FOA and CB (not all are violations)	53
Examples	
Union does not exist in factory	
Required worker committees are nonexistent.	
Laws are not followed on committees	
Union is not effectively representing workers	
Worker committee(s) not effectively representing workers	
Total	775

Note: By themselves, these observations do not constitute a violation of FOA and the FLA code of conduct.

- Does the factory infringe on the rights of workers to unionize?
- Does the factory have a CBA?
- Does the factory allow workers to approach unions for assistance?
- Does the factory allow trade unions to approach workers?
- Is there an independent workers committee or union free from management involvement?

The FWF audit records show the proportion of all code violations that concerned FOA and CB. Table 6.12 presents the responses by FWF auditors to the MSI's required questions concerning FOA and CB by country and type of observation. (We excluded Belarus, Hong Kong, Mongolia, Nepal, Laos, and Sri Lanka because of their low proportions.) The FWF reports substantially more violations of FOA or CB than the FLA reports, and the FWF records indicate more consistently the nature of the violation.

The vast majority of factories audited by the FWF were not compliant with its code provisions concerning FOA and CB. The most common observation is that workers lack independent representation.

Beyond the required questions, FWF auditors also include details in their audit reports that provide further data for assessing the nature of reported FOA and CB violations. Table 6.13 includes the written comments from the audits (349 of

TABLE 6.11.   Number of FWF audits with FOA
information, 2008–2019

COUNTRY	NUMBER OF AUDITS
Bangladesh	118
Belarus	1
Bulgaria	38
China	502
Hong Kong	1
India	149
Indonesia	19
Lao People's Democratic Republic	1
Macedonia, Republic of	54
Moldova, Republic of	13
Mongolia	1
Morocco	7
Myanmar	29
Nepal	1
Philippines	1
Romania	51
Sri Lanka	3
Thailand	17
Tunisia	75
Turkey	191
Ukraine	5
Vietnam	144
Total	1,421

1,421) that included them, which we categorized. The lack of awareness among workers noted as the most common concern suggests that the presence of a union and CBA are insufficient to ensure workers' voice in their terms and conditions of employment.

These data from the FLA and FWF regarding the nature of FOA violations are remarkably similar. In general, many factories lack FOA and CB policies, workers lack information regarding their rights under the law and CBAs, and factory managers regularly suppress unionization and intimidate workers against exercising their FOA and CB rights. Furthermore, management interference in union elections and worker committees is common, and workers receive inadequate training concerning their rights. Thus, the evidence indicates a chasm between policies supporting FOA and CB rights—expressed in company and MSI codes of conduct—and the exercise of these enabling rights.

TABLE 6.12. Proportion of FOA and CB violations in FWF audits, 2008–2018

COUNTRY	NO. OF AUDITS	% OF TOTAL	FOA AND CB VIOLATIONS (%)					FULLY COMPLIANT WITH FWF CODE (%)
			THE FACTORY INFRINGES ON WORKERS' RIGHTS TO ORGANIZE	THE FACTORY DOES NOT HAVE A CBA	THE FACTORY DOES NOT ALLOW TRADE UNIONS TO APPROACH WORKERS	THE FACTORY DOES NOT PERMIT WORKERS TO ACCESS TRADE UNIONS	THERE IS NO INDEPENDENT UNION OR WORKERS COMMITTEE THAT IS RUN BY WORKERS WITHOUT MANAGEMENT INVOLVEMENT	
Bangladesh	118	8.3	0.85	81.36	3.39		93.22	1.69
Bulgaria	38	2.7		50.00			36.84	28.95
China	502	35.3	0.20	0.20	0.20	0.20	89.64	6.57
India	149	10.5	6.71	32.89	3.36		43.62	18.79
Indonesia	19	1.3		21.05				63.16
Macedonia, Republic of	54	3.8	7.41	75.93	3.70	3.70	9.26	11.11
Moldova, Republic of	13	0.9		61.54			23.08	
Morocco	7	0.5					28.57	57.14
Myanmar	29	2.0	6.90	86.21	3.45		34.48	3.45
Romania	51	3.6	1.96	21.57			17.65	11.76
Thailand	17	1.2	5.88	58.82			29.41	11.76
Tunisia	75	5.3		1.33			4.00	76.00
Turkey	191	13.4	9.42	3.14	2.62	1.57	30.89	48.69
Ukraine	5	0.4					40.00	20.00
Vietnam	144	10.1		4.17			45.14	20.14
Total	1,421		2.67	19.70	1.27	0.42	56.58	20.34

TABLE 6.13. FWF auditors' notes on the FOA and CB status of member factories, 2008–2018

FOA AND CB ISSUES	NUMBER
AWARENESS	140
"Workers are not aware of CBA."	74
"Workers are not aware of their labor rights of FoA or CB."	34
"Workers lack knowledge of how union functions."	13
"Workers or representatives lack awareness of representatives' rights and responsibilities."	11
"Workers committee is considered a substitute representation for trade union."	5
"There is no trade union at the factory, but the workers do not feel they need one."	3
SOCIAL DIALOGUE	78
"No dialogue mechanism, dialogue meetings are not conducted regularly as required."	41
"The labor conference is not organized every year as required."	17
"Dialogue meeting has been held, however there is no complete written dialogue meeting polices or procedures (e.g., meeting result has not been communicated to workers)."	9
"The employee grand meeting has not been organized once a year as required by law."	9
"No regular meeting of welfare committee."	2
IMPLEMENTATION AND ADMINISTRATION	69
"CBA is not posted or communicated to workers."	29
"Union fee is deducted from workers' monthly salary without their written consent."	15
"Poor implementation of CBA."	9
"No written record for union's activities."	7
"There is no collective bargaining agent active in the facility."	7
"Office space or facilities are not provided."	2
POLICY	46
"The factory does not have a written FOA policy or procedure."	34
"The CBA policy is incomplete, not in detail, or not updated in time."	12
UNION ELECTIONS	11
"The election of union members and leaders has not been conducted properly."	11
TRAINING	5
"Training on FOA is not provided."	5
Total	349

The Role of Unions and CBAs in Compliance

Theory and prior evidence suggests that freedom of association, as an enabling right, should result in improvements in all labor conditions and, hence, compliance with codes of conduct provisions. To examine whether FOA and CB, where they are upheld, *do* significantly improve compliance, we used the same FWF dataset to examine the difference in compliance between factories with and without CBAs, regardless of unionization (since many unionized workers are covered by a CBA).[68]

Notably, there are CBAs that reflect little worker participation, perhaps most notoriously collective contracts signed by state-controlled unions (e.g., many in China and Vietnam) and by company-controlled unions (e.g., many in Mexico).

The FWF data show there were fewer overall code violations at factories with CBA than those without, and, on average, across all of MSI's factories in thirteen countries, compliance is generally higher in factories with a CBA and in most countries with a CBA, except Tunisia and Bulgaria (table 6.14).

While these findings would be more robust with details from qualitative surveying and interviews of the workers and managers at the factories, the findings nevertheless provide systematic evidence that the presence of a CBA significantly enhances compliance, corroborating prior research.[69]

To triangulate our results, we used a second dataset from the ILO-IFC Better Work program. Better Work shared its data from 1,970 assessments conducted in 2017–2018 at 1,244 participating factories in Cambodia, Haiti, Indonesia, Jordan, Nicaragua and Vietnam.[70]

Most of the factories participating in Better Work are in Cambodia (41 percent), Vietnam (29 percent), and Indonesia (18 percent), reflecting the length of the program in Cambodia (eight years longer than any other country) and the larger size of the textile and apparel sectors in all three countries compared with the

TABLE 6.14. Compliance in factories with and without CBAs, 2008–2018

COUNTRY	NUMBER OF AUDITS	NUMBER OF AUDITS IN FACTORIES WITH CBA	NUMBER OF AUDITS IN FACTORIES WITHOUT CBA	NONCOMPLIANCE RATE IN FACTORIES WITH CBA (%)	NONCOMPLIANCE RATE IN FACTORIES WITHOUT CBA (%)
Bangladesh	98	18	80	29	37
Bulgaria	32	62	17	39	13
China	448	448	1	23	45
India	137	93	44	27	35
Indonesia	13	11	2	23	26
Macedonia	49	13	36	16	21
Moldova	11	3	8	20	30
Myanmar	24	5	20	40	41
Romania	49	40	9	29	36
Thailand	17	7	10	24	29
Tunisia	61	60	1	23	14
Turkey	177	171	6	27	34
Vietnam	127	121	6	20	27
Total	1,244				

others. (Note that in Haiti, Jordan, and Cambodia, factory participation in BW is compulsory; in the other countries, it is voluntary—and where participation is voluntary, it is likely that the better factories might be the ones to volunteer.)

We assessed the relationships between FOA and CB with both characteristics of the factory and other labor standards, focusing on the Better Work program's assessment of the "clusters"—its term for categories of labor standards that indicate compliance or noncompliance with national laws and international norms—detailed in chapter 4: child labor, compensation, contracting, discrimination, forced labor, freedom of association, occupational safety and health, and work time. Better Work gauges compliance with standards on each point by asking a series of questions to management and workers during each assessment, when the program also gathers descriptive data about the factory. These robust data permit analysis of how the context may affect FOA and CB, and how FOA and CB may affect compliance with other labor standards.

Table 6.15, which reports factory performance across the Better Work dataset, shows that compliance rates were high across all categories. The percentage of unionized factories ranged from 55 to 82 percent across the six countries, although the average union density in those factories varied significantly. The number of factories with formal collective bargaining was lower than the number of factories with unions, except in the case of Haiti.

But were compliance rates higher in unionized factories than in nonunion factories and in factories with collective bargaining? Table 6.16 aggregates the data across factories in all Better Work countries and shows that compliance was highest when there was both a union and a CBA—clear evidence that FOA and CB together enhance compliance significantly.

TABLE 6.15. Compliance rates in Better Work countries, 2017–2018

	CAMBODIA	VIETNAM	INDONESIA	JORDAN	HAITI	NICARAGUA
Number of assessments	814	560	351	149	47	47
Unionized factories (%)	66.58	99.82	56.32	82.55	74.47	73.91
Overall compliance	84.50	91.57	87.60	89.17	87.09	94.86
Compliance forced labor	99.79	99.95	99.96	99.63	100.00	100.00
Compliance discrimination	99.65	99.71	96.26	96.48	99.91	100.00
Compliance child labor	98.87	96.55	99.57	98.99	99.39	100.00
Compliance FOA	97.97	95.51	98.21	86.85	99.26	99.52
Compliance compensation	84.54	93.52	85.72	91.50	83.71	97.79
Compliance contracts and HR	80.24	89.10	81.64	89.83	93.35	94.56
Compliance working time	81.21	82.27	83.86	98.32	91.75	94.83
Compliance OSH	65.60	85.14	79.37	82.60	71.67	85.46

TABLE 6.16. Unions, collective bargaining, and overall compliance, Better Work

UNION AND CBA INTERACTION	NUMBER OF FACTORIES	OVERALL COMPLIANCE %	T-TESTS
Union with CBA (A)	903	90.61	A vs. B -17.67***
Union but no CBA (B)	586	83.97	B vs. D -4.31***
CBA, but no union (C)	34	86.48	A vs. C -3.48***
No union, no CBA (D)	441	81.63	C vs. D -3.89***

*p<0.1, **p<0.05, ***p<0.01.

Table 6.17 shows the effect of FOA and CB on other specific labor standards. There were differences between union and nonunion factories and those with and without CBAs. Union factories do slightly better on compliance with forced labor provisions but are not significantly different from nonunion factories with respect to discrimination or child labor. Factories with CBAs show no significant differences on forced labor and discrimination. Those without CBAs, surprisingly, did significantly better than factories without CBAs did on child labor standards. Unionized factories performed significantly better in terms of compliance with wages, human resources and contracts, hours of work, and occupational safety and health. Those with CBAs significantly outperform factories without CBAs on these outcome variables. These findings are consistent with decades of research that shows that FOA and CB enable improvement of working conditions.

One curious result is that nonunion and non-CBA factories report higher compliance on FOA and CB than factories with unions and CBAs.[71] This result is entirely consistent with industrial relations research findings that unionized workers covered by a CBA communicate grievances much more than nonunionized workers.[72] The argument is that unionized workers with a CBA have (through a contractual dispute-resolution process) far more protections against retaliation for communicating negative (or any) information to management and are thus more likely to report violations of standards than those other workers. Similarly, where conditions of work are spelled out in CBAs, workers are more likely to know their rights to communicate violations. In effect, the workers are defending the process rights, FOA and CB, that enable higher standards with respect to compensation and other employment terms and conditions.

In sum, the analysis of Better Work data reiterates the central principle of FOA and CB as enabling rights. Compliance with outcome standards such as wages, hours of work, contracts, and occupational safety and health is significantly enhanced by union representation and collective bargaining. This principle held even in this sample of highly compliant factories that chose to participate in the Better Work program.

TABLE 6.17. Compliance rate difference per unionization and CBA status in factories participating in Better Work, 2017–2018

CLUSTER	NO. OF ITEMS PER CLUSTER	OVERALL MEAN COMP. RATE	COMP. RATE FOR UNION FACTORIES	COMP. RATE FOR NONUNION FACTORIES	T-TEST FOR DIFFERENCE	COMP. RATE FOR CBA FACTORIES	COMP. RATE FOR NO CBA FACTORIES	T-TEST FOR DIFFERENCE
Forced labor	12	99.86	99.91	99.71	-2.31*	99.91	99.82	-1.79
Discrimination	37	98.84	99.00	98.38	-5.16	98.84	98.84	0.05
Child labor	6	98.38	98.36	98.46	0.24	97.70	99.02	3.61***
FOA/CB	24	96.54	95.84	98.75	12.22***	94.42	98.48	18.77***
Wages	29	88.13	89.72	83.18	10.76***	92.59	84.05	19.29***
Human resources & contract	23	84.39	86.08	79.14	11.1.05, 2***	88.97	80.21	18.23***
Hours of work	14	83.86	84.89	80.70	5.27*	86.57	81.38	-8.88***
Occupational safety and health	59	75.52	78.25	66.96	12.24***	83.59	68.14	24.34***

Note: "Comp." = compliance.
*p < 0.1, **p < 0.05, ***p < 0.01.

Conclusion

These analyses support the four arguments that opened this chapter. Apparel brands clearly tend to source their garments primarily from countries where institutional support for FOA and CB is weak. Private regulation audits by brands and MSIs report a low incidence of FOA and CB violations despite higher levels of FOA violations reported by workers in those countries, their advocates, and the ILO. Brands do not actively hold their suppliers accountable or support them to comply with FOA and CB standards, and MSIs do not hold their members, primarily brands, accountable to their codes of conduct. Workers face a number of obstacles to organize successfully and bargain collectively, ranging from a lack of policies to active union suppression and a lack of awareness and training. Nevertheless, our data provide emphatic support for the argument that FOA and CB significantly enhance compliance, in both average and highly compliant factories.

If sourcing from locations with weak institutional support for FOA and CB indicates *policy-practice decoupling*, and auditing with little regard to FOA and CB indicates *means-ends decoupling*, the strong positive relationship between unionization and collective bargaining with compliance points to the solution. Many have argued that the lack of these enabling rights hinders upgrading of all standards,[73] and we have a hundred years' worth of industrial relations evidence that unionization and collective bargaining improve labor conditions in factories. More recent research in the global supply chains domain shows clearly how unionization and collective bargaining help *couple* private regulation goals with positive worker outcomes.[74]

The evidence suggests that it makes sense for companies serious about their codes of conduct to support unionization and collective bargaining *actively*. FOA and CB help private regulation achieve its stated goals. And more than 70 percent of ETI's member companies agreed that promoting FOA and CB was the most sustainable means to promoting positive change in working conditions within supply chains. Why most companies do not remains a puzzle.

If private regulation is to achieve higher labor standards, it should focus on enabling rights, such as FOA and CB. How can all the actors in the private regulation ecosystem alter their current approaches to prioritize FOA and CB?

First, global buyers must align sourcing with labor standards. Buyers should institute policies that require them to drop suppliers that have been resistant to workers exercising their FOA rights. Buyers must include respect for FOA as a key condition in future orders. Additionally, buyers should coordinate with other buyers to enter into triangular agreements with suppliers and unionized workers, and develop and implement plans to transition the supply chain to be completely covered by agreements between the brand, suppliers, and unionized workers. Where independent unionization or collective bargaining are prohibited by law, buyers should consult with local labor advocates, home-country labor federations, and the ILO and together facilitate education for workers on FOA, election of worker members to a committee, access for all workers to a complaint mechanism that covers labor standards and the functioning of the committee, and a clear set of employment practices over which the committee has influence. There is a lot more global buyers must do to overcome the nature of FOA violations reported in tables 6.10 and 6.13.

Second, buyers must expand on the FOA policies in their codes of conduct, adding four conditions necessary for the sustainable compliance with FOA and CB standards: the "elect, represent, protect and empower framework."[75] The conditions are as follows:

- Workers must elect their union representatives or representatives on committees (if no union is present), because such elections allow workers democratic control over their representatives and afford the elected representatives the legitimacy they need to carry out their activities effectively.
- Representatives must be allowed to carry out their representative functions, which means codes should emphasize that supplier factories provide time and facilities for representatives to arrange training and meet with workers, especially before and after key negotiations and other important meetings with management.
- Worker representatives and all workers must be protected from employer reprisal for representative activities and must be protected from dismissal for these activities.
- Workers must have some leverage (apart from strikes); workers must know that global buyers will incentivize and sanction supplier management to ensure that workers' rights are protected.

In terms of monitoring compliance with labor standards, buyers should commit to and use supply-chain labor standards monitoring by organizations independent of all companies in the supply chain. Many buyers have begun to use the ILO in countries where Better Work operates. Monitoring must include off-site worker interviews, union participation, a robust complaint system, adequate time to assess labor conditions at all facilities, and distribution of audit reports to workers in the factories. Global buyers can support more effective monitoring by increasing transparency, particularly by publishing audit reports on their websites.

Global apparel brands have in recent years taken steps to influence government labor policies and practices, such as supporting minimum-wage increases and urging cessation of worker repression. Acting together as an industry, buyers must lobby governments to ratify and implement laws aligned with ILO conventions covering FOA and CB and publicly communicate concern to governments when workers are retaliated against for exercising FOA, as well as expressing this concern to suppliers in the company's supply chain. The European Union's announcement on February 12, 2020, that the preferential trade access of Cambodia to EU markets would be partly suspended for some products given the restrictions on FOA (among other civil rights) is an example of buyers working together with the EU to enhance FOA and CB. Buyers must reinforce the message with action by selecting suppliers in jurisdictions that protect FOA. As an industry, buyers can collectively call on governments in home countries and supplier countries to improve labor rights enforcement under national action plans (NAPs) of the United Nations Principles for Business and Human Rights. In addition, buyers should support FOA and CB rights in international bodies such as the ILO, including recognition of workers' right to strike. Furthermore, companies must support inclusion of ILO core conventions in labor chapters of agreements regulating trade and investment, as well as robust mechanisms of dispute resolution for labor complaints. Such efforts would establish the accountability infrastructure for companies to comply with labor standards with less risk of being undercut in the marketplace by companies that do not comply.

Institutional theory with respect to organizational decoupling suggests a particular role for niche institutions in enhancing coupling of policies, practices, and outcomes (discussed in greater length in chapter 9). Focused initiatives are showing promise of meaningful shifts in the apparel industry. The Freedom of Association Protocol (FoAP) in Indonesia is one example. The FoAP is a multiparty agreement created by Indonesian unions, suppliers, and global brands (Nike, Adidas, Puma, and New Balance) to improve FOA and CB by establishing specific standards for participating factories and introducing a grievance procedure for violations. By the end of 2016, the FoAP applied to approximately thirty thousand workers in Java and was demonstrating progress. Many workers participated in the FoAP's design and implementation, were effectively represented by unions in using the grievance system, and were enjoying workplace improvements. But inconsistent implementation of the FoAP exposed a key limitation: that the brands had not established incentives and sanctions to support suppliers' participation.[76]

The evidence is compelling that freedom of association and collective bargaining constitute the best pathway for achieving the coupling of private regulation programs and concrete improvements for workers in global supply chains. Adopters of private regulation need to do more to achieve that coupling.

Part 3
OVERVIEW
Prospects

How might private regulation be improved? While the institutional perspectives adopted in this book indicate pathways for progress, consideration of the future requires attention to a variety of current changes taking place in the context in which private regulation operates. These contextual changes impose further challenges for private regulation if it is to improve workers' lives and wages in the global supply chain.

Much of the production of garments, textiles, athletic shoes, toys, and electronics occurs in countries that are "weak" with respect to enforcing labor legislation, even if their laws conform to ILO standards. This weakness occurs because "these states are either one-party regimes, highly decentralized or simply lack the administrative capacity to enforce a uniform set of standards."[1] In some cases, this inability to enforce standards may be because the elite has captured the state—best exemplified by the Bangladesh government, which has had an uncertain relationship with the Accord on Fire and Building Safety in Bangladesh—the one example of brands having come together to improve factory safety conditions.[2] Even in one-party states such as China or Vietnam, local and regional authorities are often reluctant to enforce legislation given their interest in attracting investment for local or regional economic development.[3]

Compliance with codes that set labor standards is weaker where the rule of law is weaker.[4] Clearly, then, private regulation cannot be seen in isolation but must be examined in connection with state capacity and willingness to enforce standards. Researchers have begun to examine a mix of approaches in which state efforts complement private approaches.[5]

Highly mobile global industry players also threaten improvements in labor standards. Relentless price pressure drives global firms to search for the cheapest costs, even as their corporate codes of conduct espouse improving labor standards.[6] Apparel-sourcing destinations have changed a lot over time, moving from Taiwan and Hong Kong in the 1980s to China; then from coastal China to inland China; and thereafter to Vietnam, Laos, Cambodia, and Bangladesh.[7] Cheap labor costs in Bangladesh have made it the second-largest producer of garments after China, despite its many disadvantages such as corruption, low productivity, low safety, and terrible infrastructure.[8] H&M, for example, is the biggest buyer of clothes made in Bangladesh. And, as I write, garment production is moving into newer low-cost destinations such as Myanmar and Ethiopia.

Steadily declining prices for apparel (relative to other consumer goods) also results in the "sourcing squeeze" in garment-producing countries. The "hyper-competitive structure of apparel global supply chains," writes one researcher, "has contributed to a buyer-driven sourcing squeeze that has pushed down wages, shortened lead times, and contributed to low wages, health and safety concerns and violations of freedom of association rights."[9] In fact, since the Rana Plaza factory fire in Bangladesh in 2013, the price paid by lead firms to suppliers has actually declined by 13 percent (a decline that cannot be explained by fluctuations in cotton prices) and has resulted in supplier profits being reduced by 13.3 percent between 2011 and 2016 and real wages being reduced by 6.47 percent. Clearly this squeeze puts pressure on wages and working conditions.

The rise of *fast fashion* has added to the pressure on factory working conditions; it requires that suppliers make products more quickly (lead times in Bangladesh declined by 8 percent between 2011 and 2015), compelling factory owners to use more overtime and subcontract production to other factories (often without knowledge of the buyers). The rise of online retailers (exemplified by Amazon and Alibaba) and other discount retailers has two very distinct effects: it has reduced barriers to entry for small producers, who can leverage the online retailers' marketing ability to sell the producers' wares, and, even more important, it has reduced the size of orders to suppliers. These effects have resulted in a trend toward smaller and smaller factories with more contingent workforces. In fact, in many of these smaller factories in China, the permanent workforce comprises less than 20 percent of the total workforce. And, as our interviews with auditors from a major auditing company suggest, many of these factories are run from a home or in a village environment, creating downward pressure on living standards and making "auditing" even more difficult.

Fast fashion and *mass customization* have increased pressure on global brands and global suppliers to automate. Low-cost, labor-intensive traditional garment production, sustained by slow production cycles and consumer acceptance of indifferent quality, has given way to fast fashion's requirement of shortened production cycles, for which automation is likely required. As demand for both quality and speed have increased, a number of new technologies have been incorporated into different stages of the manufacturing process in global garment supply chains. Prior to the sewing process, automation has been introduced to produce rolls of fabric and to spread and cut them. Now automation is being introduced into the sewing process, with new fabric-gripping technology to cut, spread, and feed fabric into automatic sewing machines (sewbots), the use of pattern sewing machines, button machines, cuff machines. and so forth. In 2018, a Georgia entrepreneur patented a sewbot that can completely machine-stitch a pair of jeans, for example.

Automation poses significant challenges for today's global garment industry. As automation becomes cheaper, it will potentially hasten the movement towards nearshoring, particularly in the context of rising freight prices, the need for quicker delivery times, and increasing consumer aversion to sweatshop manufacturing. Further, increased protectionism is appearing to drive the United States under President Trump to retreat from its earlier stance as a champion of free trade and free markets—increasing the possibility of nearshoring or "onshoring." Mass customization has the potential to exacerbate this movement even further, as evidenced by the opening by Adidas of a highly automated "Speedfactory" first in Germany in 2016 and then another the next year in the United States to meet demand for faster delivery of new styles to the company's major markets.

Automation and nearshoring potentially pose threats for displacement and loss of livelihoods of millions of workers in the world's garment-producing centers. They could result in the development of a two-tier industry: highly automated factories with fewer workers, and a continuing "tail" of extremely low-cost producers to service markets in the developing countries, where cost pressures would seriously threaten labor standards. As it is, there is considerable "home work" in the garment industry, where working conditions are often worse than those in the usual sweatshop.[10]

Evidence of these drivers can be seen in a McKinsey survey of global garment firms, which showed that 51 percent expect that production of simple garments such as T-shirts and jeans will become fully automated and 30 percent expect complex garments will be automated—leading overall to a 40-percent reduction in the workforce.[11] This reduction will be complemented by a significant and radical supplier consolidation (a potential positive for labor standards as firms and suppliers engage in longer-term relationships). However, 66 percent believe customization and nearshoring will push relocation from developing to developed countries, with significant movement by 2025.

If nearshoring occurs as predicted, customers will become less concerned about sweatshops, since nearshore locations for Western markets typically have better labor standards than current garment producers. With the loss of that pressure, the low tier in the developing world will likely descend into intensive sweatshop conditions. Fully 36 percent of respondents also believe the political turmoil in Western nations, the rise in protectionism, and a withdrawal from free trade will change the economic equation between offshore and nearshore production.

It is not at all clear, however, that we are close to a nearshoring revolution in athletic shoes and garments. In November 2019, Adidas announced its two Speed-factories would both close within a few months, raising the question of whether automation and nearshoring is cost effective today. News reports indicate that the factories were not flexible enough to reconfigure production systems quickly to meet rapid changes in demand, and that flexibility was more likely to be found in Asia. In addition, nearshoring is never going to be cost-effective for the least-expensive garments, such as socks.

These changes have both positive and negative implications for the future of labor standards in global supply chains. An overall reduction in developing world employment will mean that many poor countries will lose out on an important escalator for economic development and remain trapped in a low-cost cycle to service domestic markets, while the more advanced suppliers and manufacturers will graduate to automated production, also resulting in fewer workers. The emergence of a two-tier manufacturing system will create downward pressure on wages and labor conditions in global supply chains.

At the same time, it is clear that customer preferences in advanced countries have been changing, especially as we transitioned from Generation X to millennials and now to Generation Z. There is increasing evidence that the current generation of consumers in advanced countries is becoming more conscious and demanding ethically sourced production. These changing preferences have been well documented.

Most relevant to this book is the demand that global companies be more transparent about their supply chains. As demand for consumer-facing radical transparency increases, global companies will be under pressure to improve the effectiveness of their private regulation efforts, given that those efforts may have a more direct connection with sales. Already, customer demands for "traceability" have prompted many firms such as H&M and Gap Inc. to disclose where their garments are produced and even reveal the locations of their second-tier suppliers. Therefore, even if some forces are driving a movement toward automation and nearshoring, changing consumer preferences will drive a move toward transparency and, consequently, shine a spotlight on private regulation efforts. It is in this context that this part of the book examines future prospects of private regulation.

Finally, a major challenge for private regulation is how to extend these programs to other tiers in the supply chain. For the past twenty-five years, private regulation efforts have focused solely on the first-tier suppliers, usually the factories that produce the apparel or shoes. However, there are many other tiers below that first tier. In apparel, for example, the tier immediately below the factories consists of the manufacturers that weave the fabric; below that there are the spinning and ginning mills that make the thread to weave the fabric; below that tier are the cotton fields. And a number of tiers exist in the production of accessories that are also supplied to the factory, such as buttons, beadwork, and so forth. Many of those accessories are made by smaller factories that farm out work to "home workers."[12] Private regulation, in general, has not yet "touched" the tiers below the first tier.

As this book goes to press, the world is reeling from the Covid-19 pandemic, which has raised questions about the viability and sustainability of the private regulation model as global firms cut orders, resulting in suppliers unable to pay workers their wages or make severance payments. It is clear that many global buyers are in deep financial trouble; several have entered bankruptcy proceedings.

What are the implications of Covid-19 for private regulation? Some contend that global firms will diversify their supply chains further, reducing their dependence on some countries such as China. It is possible that for U.S. firms, diversification could include more sourcing from nearer locations, such as countries in Central and South America. That would present an opportunity for improvement in private regulation, as U.S. buyers could choose locations where laws are better enforced.

Another possibility is that global buyers will rationalize their supply chains, keeping only the most compliant suppliers and investing in longer-term relationships with them. That will create the conditions for improvement in private regulation programs. However, in their efforts to diversify their supply chains, some global buyers could begin to source from a new tranche of low-cost countries, led by Ethiopia and Myanmar, where labor costs and labor standards are lower.

Whichever options are chosen, it is clear that the need to improve private regulation will still exist.

Part 3 of this book focuses on ways in which private regulation can be improved. The key implication of institutional theory is that for better coupling of private regulation practices with outcomes for workers, we must transform the current opaque institutional field into a more transparent one. In general, this would require actors in the field to solve the barriers to coupling caused by practice multiplicity, behavioral invisibility, and causal complexity. The perspective offers a number of different ways to achieve this.

Chapter 7 examines the potential for changes in corporate governance to overcome the decoupling problem in private regulation, through a detailed examination of the case of benefit corporations. It argues that the B-Corp movement is a false promise because of the legal limitations of actors to seek remedy if a benefit corporation does not meet its "benefit goals" and because of a variety of issues in the certification process for such a corporation. This argument is supported through the analysis of the private regulation program of a leading benefit corporation, which shows that its status has in no way improved coupling between private regulation practices and outcomes. It would seem that the benefit corporation certification is simply another modern ritual of due diligence, although we need additional research on benefit corporations to confirm this conclusion.

Chapter 8 focuses on a detailed investigation of a global retailer's attempt to integrate sourcing and compliance as a way to increase the coupling of private regulation and worker outcomes. The chapter offers a fascinating inside view of the seven-year effort to change the global retailer's sourcing model and rationalize its supply chain in ways that set the stage for increasing compliance. The case study shows how this global retailer successfully aligned its sourcing and compliance activities (achieved internal organizational "coupling") and offers lessons for the rest of the industry. The aim is to lay bare the challenges that companies face in attempting this kind of alignment, but also to argue that such alignment of sourcing and compliance inside the global corporation is a vital and necessary step toward the coupling of private regulation practices and worker outcomes.

Chapter 9 focuses on specific ways in which opacity can be reduced—through the use of niche institutions, by stimulating the internalization goals of private regulation, and through fostering a critical mindset. The chapter draws attention to the varieties of transparency required and specifically to the integration and inclusion of workers in private regulation programs to stimulate internalization of goals, especially through worker participation in compliance auditing and through methods such as surveys by which workers' perspectives are heard. The chapter highlights the need for more data sharing, data analysis, and predictive modeling and concludes with specific recommendations for the variety of actors in private regulation to move the institutional field from opacity to transparency.

Only through data analysis can we generate the predictive models that allow for evidence-based decision making and identification of other means by which the coupling of private regulation programs with worker outcomes can be increased. The presence of unions in global supply chains significantly enhances coupling, alongside a number of different variables related to auditing.[13] Workers and trade unions, in what has been called contingent coupling, can help "shrink the gap between practices and outcomes" for workers by leveraging the private regulation policies of brands.[14] This possibility suggests there is an appropriate role for workers and unions in helping to overcome means-ends decoupling.

It is important to point out that my analysis of the problems, progress, and prospects of private regulation relates primarily to first-tier suppliers. The challenge facing private regulation is how labor practices can be improved throughout the supply chain—that is, incorporating multiple tiers of suppliers. It has taken twenty-five years of effort to get the private regulation industry to where it is today. Progress over that period has not been significant. Improving private regulation today is crucial if it is to address labor standards in the entire global supply chain effectively, with multiple tiers of suppliers. There are, in other words, mountains to climb.

ARE CHANGES IN CORPORATE GOVERNANCE AN ANSWER?

with Matt Fischer-Daly

The private regulation model has shown limited progress in improving labor conditions in global supply chains, and there has been significant decoupling between private regulation policies and outcomes for workers. A common explanation is that global companies adopt private regulation policies "symbolically," as an exercise to mitigate risks to brand value and profitability. Companies communicate publicly their expectation that their suppliers will meet the standards in the companies' codes of conduct but are not willing to pay to enable suppliers to do so. Rather, these global companies have been "squeezing" suppliers with a significant reduction in the price they are paid.[1]

Companies behave this way to increase profits; after all, isn't the sole purpose of the corporation to maximize shareholder return?[2] Since the 1980s, however, the argument that corporations have duties to society or at least to their "stakeholders" (workers, consumers, and communities affected by their operations) has grown stronger.[3] More recently, the notion of "shared value" has gained currency—the key argument being that "corporations must create economic value in a way that also created value for society by addressing its needs and challenges."[4]

The "benefit corporation" is practical manifestation of this notion. In the United States, a benefit corporation is a type of for-profit corporate entity that includes among its goals—in addition to profits—a positive impact on society, workers, the community, and the environment. The management of a benefit corporation operates the business with the same authority and behavior as in a traditional corporation (C-Corp) but is required to consider the impact of its decisions not only on shareholders but also on stakeholders. Benefit corporation status thus frees managers from liability risks when pursuing nonprofit goals and, in principle, functions as a defense so social and environmental goals are not pushed aside in favor of profit maximization.

The first law permitting benefit incorporation dates to 2010; as of February 2020, thirty-six US states allow a company to incorporate as a Benefit Corporation—and at that date there were approximately 5,500 such companies. Some 92 percent of all benefit corporations are registered in just ten states, with a quarter of them registered in Oregon. At this writing, another five states are considering such laws.

Since 2007, companies have also been able to obtain private certification as a "B-Corp" from the nonprofit B Lab, regardless of their public incorporation status. By 2019, 2,786 organizations in seventy industries and sixty-five countries had obtained the B-Corp certification.[5]

In this chapter, we use "benefit corporation" to refer to the concept, "Benefit Corporation" to refer to a legally incorporated benefit corporation, and "B-Corp" for companies certified by B Lab, an organization founded to encourage business to be "a force for social good." B Lab developed and maintains the B-Corp certification program for companies that have social objectives. B Lab also offers management programs and B-impact software to certified companies, and otherwise advocates for the introduction of benefit corporation statutes in US states.

Benefit corporations can prioritize whatever benefits to society they choose. For example, a benefit corporation could select environmental preservation as its public benefit, in which case it would be expected to align decisions with this goal along with profits for shareholders. Alternatively, a benefit corporation could prioritize workers' rights in its supply chain as its public benefit. This managerial freedom to prioritize stakeholder interests without risk of shareholder retaliation distinguishes the benefit corporation from traditional business corporations. It is reasonable to expect, therefore, that benefit corporations, particularly those prioritizing supply-chain workers' rights, would evince better performance in improving labor practices in global supply chains relative to C-Corps.

Despite the explosive growth in benefit corporations, and significant explorations of the model, there seem to be no rigorous scholarly examinations of whether actual Benefit Corporations or certified B-Corps have met their chosen goals. The research question in this chapter is whether benefit corporation status facilitates a better implementation of the private regulation model in ways that improves labor practices in global supply chains. The case examined is a company both incorporated as a Benefit Corporation *and* certified as a B-Corp. The company has clearly defined workers' rights throughout its supply chain as one of its "public benefit" goals, alongside profitability.

The company, hereinafter called Brand-Y, is a global retailer selling higher-end apparel to a stable consumer base. In addition to its early adoption of the benefit-corporation model, Brand-Y is also a privately held corporation, further reducing pressure from shareholders to maximize profits. In addition to its early adoption of the benefit-corporation model, the company lists leadership in promoting business according to the B-Corp mantra of "business as a force for good" as one of its four prioritized benefits. Its first prioritized benefit is a commitment to the human rights of workers in its supply chain. The research question is important because the foundational incorporation status permits, in principle, a closer coupling between organizational policies (the company's code of conduct), practices, and outcomes for workers in its global supply chain. Thus, Brand-Y constitutes an ideal case for examining whether this form of stakeholder capitalism works for improving labor conditions in the global supply chain. This appears to be the first empirical examination of the private regulation of supplier labor standards of a benefit corporation.

Some General Legal Background on Corporations

Since the establishment of the corporation as a concept, scholars have debated whether corporations must be accountable only to shareholders or to all stakeholders. Corporate purpose is a state-level policy in the United States. Into the nineteenth century, states granted corporate status and limited liability "only in order to perform a stated public function" and only later made "any and all legal purposes" permissible.[6]

Maximizing returns to shareholders gained traction as a doctrine with the 1919 *Dodge v. Chrysler* ruling that "the business firm is organized and carries on primarily for the profit of stockholders. The powers of the directors are to be employed for that end."[7] Subsequent court cases reiterated that the fiduciary duty of a corporation's board of directors is shareholder wealth maximization, including a 2010 ruling that a decision that "'seeks not to maximize the economic value of a for-profit Delaware corporation for the benefit of its stockholders' is an invalid corporate purpose and inconsistent with directors' fiduciary duties."[8] However, as courts have also held, "it is in the limited context of a change of control that the interests of shareholders appear to take precedence over all other constituencies."[9]

Proper corporate purpose remains debatable. Most legal scholars recognize that there is no legal prohibition of corporate consideration of nonprofit interests.[10]

The American Law Institute Principles of Corporate Governance can be interpreted to mean that directors may consider nonshareholder interests to comply with laws, abide by ethical norms of business conduct, or to contribute reasonably to charity, but "these three conditions do not appear to alter the precedential value of traditional fiduciary duty cases."[11] Recalling the early statutory requirement of "public function," some argue that corporations have a duty to stakeholders, including any groups or individuals who can affect or are affected by the pursuit of a business organization's objectives,[12] and that restricting corporate purpose to shareholder returns is not only a "myth" but in fact harmful.[13]

Beginning in the 2010s, business scholars have popularized the concept of creating shared value for the company and society.[14] The benefit-corporation model aims to free managers from liability risks when pursuing nonprofit goals.[15] The model aims to function as a defense against social and environmental goals being "pushed aside if they are not embedded in a company's foundational documents."[16] The model also responds to a perceived demand for ethically produced products. Often cited are a 2010 study by consulting firm Cone Communications that found 80 percent of respondents would likely choose a brand that supports a cause over one that does not, price and quality being similar, and a 2015 Neilsen survey in which 66 percent of respondents reported a willingness to pay more for socially responsible products, an increase from 50 percent in 2013.[17]

Incorporated Benefit Corporations

The incorporation statutes for Benefit Corporations have three requirements concerning purpose, governance, and reporting. First, a Benefit Corporation must establish a purpose to pursue a public benefit. In most states, the purpose must be a "general public benefit," defined as a "material, positive impact on society and the environment, taken as a whole, as assessed against a third-party standard, from the business and operations of a benefit corporation."[18] Delaware defines the general benefit as "the best interests of those materially affected by the corporation's conduct."[19] California and Minnesota require the company to define one or more specific benefits instead of a general benefit.[20]

There are many public benefits a company could select as its *purpose*, including these:

Providing low-income or underserved individuals or communities with
    beneficial products or services;
Promoting economic opportunity for individuals or communities beyond
    the creation of jobs in the ordinary course of business;

Preserving the environment;

Improving human health;

Promoting the arts, sciences, or advancement of knowledge;

Increasing the flow of capital to entities with a public benefit purpose; or

The accomplishment of any other particular benefit for society or the environment.[21]

With respect to *governance*, the directors and officers of a Benefit Corporation have a duty to consider many stakeholders, including workers in the corporation's supply chain.

> The directors of a benefit corporation, in considering the best interests of the corporation: shall consider the effects of any action or inaction upon:
>
> (i) the shareholders of the benefit corporation,
>
> (ii) the employees and workforce of the benefit corporation, its subsidiaries and its suppliers,
>
> (iii) the interests of customers as beneficiaries of the general public benefit or specific public benefit purposes of the benefit corporation,
>
> (iv) community and societal factors, including those of each community in which offices or facilities of the benefit corporation, its subsidiaries and its suppliers are located,
>
> (v) the local and global environment,
>
> (vi) the short-term and long-term interests of the benefit corporation, including any benefits that may accrue to the benefit corporation from its long-term plans and the possibility that these interests may be best served by the continued independence of the benefit corporation and
>
> (vii) the ability of the benefit corporation to accomplish its general benefit purpose and any specific public benefit purpose.[22]

As for *reporting*, most states require Benefit Corporations to publish a biennial report on their pursuit of the public benefit that is verified by a third party that meets "a recognized standard for defining, reporting and assessing overall corporate social and environmental performance."[23] Specifically, that standard is

> (1) Comprehensive in that it assesses the effect of the business and its operations upon the interests listed in section 301(a)(1)(ii), (iii), (iv) and (v).
>
> (2) Developed by an organization that is independent of the benefit corporation and satisfies the following requirements:

(i) Not more than one-third of the members of the governing body of the organization are representatives of any of the following:

(A) An association of businesses operating in a specific industry the performance of whose members is measured by the standard.

(B) Businesses from a specific industry or an association of businesses.

(C) Businesses whose performance is assessed against the standard.

(ii) The organization is not materially financed by an association or business described in subparagraph (i).

(3) Credible because the standard is developed by a person that both:

(i) Has access to necessary expertise to assess overall corporate social and environmental performance.

(ii) Uses a balanced multi-stakeholder approach, including a public comment period of at least 30 days to develop the standard.

(4) Transparent because the following information is publicly available:

(i) About the standard:

(A) The criteria considered when measuring the overall social and environmental performance of a business.

(B) The relative weightings, if any, of those criteria.

(ii) About the development and revision of the standard:

(A) The identity of the directors, officers, material owners and the governing body of the organization that developed and controls revisions to the standard.

(B) The process by which revisions to the standard and changes to the membership of the governing body are made.

(C) An accounting of the sources of financial support for the organization, with sufficient detail to disclose any relationships that could reasonably be considered to present a potential conflict of interest.[24]

The model legislation also provides a mechanism—the benefit enforcement proceeding—by which parties can challenge Benefit Corporations' claims to pursue public benefits. This dispute settlement mechanism is restricted to Benefit Corporation shareholders and unlikely to result in sanctions for decisions that do not benefit the public. Whether the Benefit Corporation is a publicly or privately held company, the *only parties* with standing to sue it are the corporation itself, one of its directors, or a shareholder with more than 2 percent of shares in a class or series—although, like C corporations, Benefit Corporations could grant standing to others in their bylaws.[25] Even with standing, the benefit enforcement proceedings are generally limited to injunctive remedies, although further remedies might be available if corporate managers failed to consider stakeholders.[26]

Certified B-Corps

A second way corporations implement the benefit corporation model of business is by acquiring B-Corp certification from B Lab. Bart Houlahan and Jay Coen Gilbert, previously executives of the basketball apparel and footwear company And 1, and Andrew Kassoy, previously a partner at the private equity firm MSD Real Estate Capital, L.P., established B Lab as a 501(c)(3) organization in 2006, with a board of members whose membership included people with experience in business, finance, and economic development. B Lab helped write the Model Act on which most states based their benefit corporation statutes and lobbied for the statutes.[27]

The first B-Corps were certified in 2007. B Lab certifies companies as B-Corps if they follow certain procedures. If an organization seeking certification is in a state with Benefit Corporation legislation, the company must reincorporate under that legislation; if not, the company must reincorporate if such legislation is passed—in either case, within four years of the legislation going into effect.[28] However, B Lab does not require an organization to incorporate as a Benefit Corporation to obtain B-Corp certification in states (or countries) where there is no relevant legislation. Certified B-Corps pay fees to B Lab and sign the B-Corp Declaration of Interdependence, a commitment to considering business impacts on stakeholders.[29] The fees range from $500 to $25,000 annually, depending on the size and complexity of a company and its stated "benefit goals." B Lab has a three-year certification cycle and apparently visits 10 percent of B-Corps every year.[30]

To obtain certification, an organization must complete an online self-assessment, the benefit impact assessment (BIA), and complete a disclosure questionnaire "to identify potentially sensitive issues related to the company (e.g., historical fines, sanctions, material litigation, or sensitive industry practices)."[31] The questionnaire addresses internal governance and impacts on employees, communities, customers, and the environment. The BIA was developed and is revised triennially by B Lab's Standards Advisory Council, comprising B Lab staff and independent organization representatives, in a process that includes a public comment period.[32] B Lab publishes B-Corps' BIA scores via data.world.[33] The BIA is divided into five sections, each worth 40 points; to achieve certification, a company must score at least 16 points in each of them. That bar—80 points of a possible 200—is a very low one.

The section of the BIA that addresses labor standards in a company's supply chain is called "community impacts" and can be found in Appendix B. It shows that B Lab's assessment asks only about lead-firm methods of monitoring and whether and how the company sets and monitors labor standards—*not about actual supplier labor practices*. This approach has an important implication: it means that the B-Corp certification *assumes that the private regulation efforts of companies are effective*, despite all the evidence to the contrary presented in the earlier chapters of this book. In other words, B Lab evaluates *policy*, but not *practice* or *effectiveness*.

Obtaining B-Corp certification also requires completion of the disclosure questionnaire, which "does not affect the company's score on the B Impact Assessment" but through which B Lab can require an organization to "describe how the company has addressed" any issues disclosed that "B Lab deems . . . to be material" and "demonstrate that management systems are in place to avoid similar issues from arising."[34] The questionnaire asks about a variety of sensitive and controversial issues (e.g., whether there are legal complaints about the company, or whether it has a problem with child labor) that need to be remedied before certification. How B Lab verifies the true-or-false responses to statements such as "Company allows workers to freely associate and to bargain collectively for the terms of one's employment" is obscured by its policy that companies may "oppose efforts to unionize" and obtain certification if the company determines such efforts are in workers' interests.[35]

After a company submits a BIA and disclosure questionnaire, B Lab requests supporting documentation (but does not specify what that documentation must entail) and conducts a conference call to review the self-assessment. B Lab then uses the BIA and the disclosure questionnaire to makes its certification decisions. A company could be eligible for certification on the basis of its BIA score but may still not receive certification because of what the company states in the disclosure documents, because B Lab "reserves the right to refuse certification if the company is ultimately deemed not to uphold the spirit of the community."[36]

Under B Lab's internally controlled complaint procedure, anyone can submit a complaint online. B Lab investigates those it deems "material, credible, and specific" regarding a B-Corp's "intentional misrepresentation of practices, policies or outcomes claimed within the B Impact Assessment, including the B Impact Assessment Disclosure Questionnaire" or "breaches of the B Corp Community's

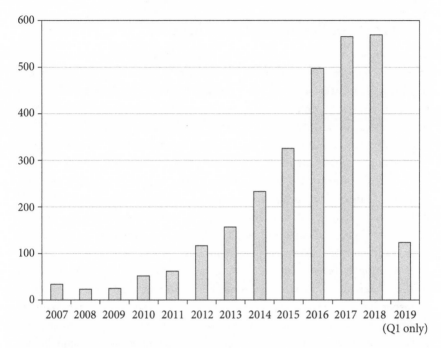

FIGURE 7.1. Annual B-Corp certifications

Chart by author.

core values as expressed in the B Corporation Declaration of Interdependence." The final step is a resolution by the B Lab Board of Directors.

Certified B-Corps, like incorporated Benefit Corporations, have been increasing dramatically in number. Figure 7.1 show the increase over time; of April 2019, there were 2,784 certified B-Corps.

B Lab has certified corporations around the world.[37] Of the total 2,784 certified B-Corps in October 2019, 43 percent are in the United States, and 66 percent of all certified B-Corps are in English-speaking countries with liberal market economies, such as the United States, Canada, Australia, and the United Kingdom. The remaining certified B-Corps are distributed widely across the rest of the world.

B-Corps are spread across 130 different industries, mostly in service sectors, with the largest numbers of certified B-Corp in food and beverage (313 firms), marketing and communications services (189 firms), IT software and web services (184 firms), management and financial consulting (160 firms), sustainability consulting (137 firms), home and personal care (137 firms), education and training services (120 firms).[38] The largest manufacturing sector is apparel, footwear, and accessories, accounting for 93 firms and 3 percent of the total of certified B-Corps.

The Limits of Benefit Corporations

While there are advantages to the increasingly popular benefit corporation concept, it is important to highlight the model's limitations. Corporate governance scholars and practitioners are critical of benefit corporations. Some argue that the vague definition of "public benefit" raises the risk of whitewashing nonbeneficial behavior because the duty to nonshareholder stakeholders is not enforced.[39] Even if one makes the assumption that the public-reporting requirement means stakeholders know about a Benefit Corporation's duty to consider their interests,[40] conflicting interests among stakeholders are likely to lead Benefit Corporations to default to prioritizing profit maximization.[41] After all, incorporation or certification only expands the fiduciary role of directors in considering the impacts of their decisions on all stakeholders; ultimately, only shareholders have the power to hold company managers accountable to their goals.

Restricting the benefit enforcement proceeding to *shareholders* (and only those holding 2 percent of the shares) means "benefit corporation legislation denies [nonshareholder] constituencies standing to enforce" the public benefit requirement.[42] The predominant limit to injunctive remedies means proceedings can result only in an order that the benefit corporation actually consider nonshareholder stakeholder interests.[43] Furthermore, the "business judgment rule" and clauses that exculpate corporate directors and officers render "liability of care cases almost impossible" for C corporations, "and the increases under any of the benefit corporation statutes are all extremely modest."[44] Lack of accounting for corporate commitments risks rendering benefit corporation status meaningless, as an author of the Benefit Corporation Model Act cautioned.[45] And as a chief justice of the Delaware Supreme Court wrote, "When corporate fiduciaries [are] allowed to consider all interests *without legally binding constraints*, they [are] freed of accountability to any."[46]

The verification mechanism is another weakness of the benefit corporation model. There is no accreditation of B Lab or other third-party verifiers,[47] so they "can be as stringent, or not, in their conceptualization of what it means to actually 'create' a public benefit as would best serve their needs and the needs of the benefit corporation that procures their services."[48] Far from providing clarity on business impacts on society and the environment, the third-party verifiers currently used are inconsistent and imperfect, and they rely on self-reporting by the company seeking verification of its benefits.[49] For example, Brand-Y's B-Corp private certification claims legal compliance and additional social benefits despite requiring no evidence of standards in supply chains where the norm is noncompliance for the large number of stakeholders that produce brands' products. Lack of transparency on the documentation reviewed raises questions about the basis for responses to questions on the BIA self-assessment such as "What percent of your employees are 'Satisfied' or 'Engaged'?"

Furthermore, reporting requirements are not rigorous. In practice, most Benefit Corporations do not issue the report required by statute. The only estimate to date found only eight of one hundred Benefit Corporations had issued a report.[50] While reporting may improve over time, "there is no requirement to disclose that portion of the corporate assets committed to the beneficial purpose."[51]

Some have critiqued benefit corporations as just another profit-oriented business strategy. An empirical study of Benefit Corporation enactment proceedings found initial attention on the public interest has shifted to the business benefits of the status.[52] Company advantages include access to capital, particularly from philanthropists and socially responsible investors; liability protection for nonprofit decisions; and the "warm glow" that comes from believing one has made a difference.[53] Others identify B-Corp certification as a marketing tactic, emphasizing that while it is used interchangeably in the marketplace (despite the clear differences between the two), certifications "have no legal status whatsoever; it is merely a brand."[54] The certified B-Corp can be but does not have to be a legally incorporated Benefit Corporation.

Like other unaccredited third-parties, B-Corp certification has been critiqued for a lack of due diligence about human rights, gaps in standards, reliance on corporate self-reporting, and a scoring system that allows certification despite low performance on rights issues.[55] B Lab's own reporting indicates that complaints raised are addressed but not necessarily resolved; for example, certified B-Corps can conduct antiunion campaigns.[56] Most important, a critical weakness of B Lab certification is that it evaluates *policy* but does not examine the effects of that policy in practice. In the private regulation space, where policy-practice decoupling is endemic, how can B Lab certification possibly improve labor standards in global supply chains?

The hope of reducing negative impacts on stakeholders by elevating their interests to those of shareholders remains compelling despite these limitations and has motivated proposals for changes: increased transparency, disclosure of financial information, third-party oversight, and guidance on balancing stakeholder interests.[57] An improved benefit corporation status that permits stakeholders to hold corporations accountable for their impacts in a meaningful way offers significant opportunity to address the gaps in labor standards across global supply chains.

Analyzing Benefit Corporation Status: The Brand-Y Case

Brand-Y (a pseudonym) was established in the 1980s and is privately held. Its founder and CEO holds majority ownership, and its 150 nonretail employees own significant shares. Brand-Y generates more than $300 million in annual revenue selling bridge-line apparel—fine clothing priced below high-end designers, in its own stores, in department stores, and through its website. Brand-Y's pitch to consumers is not price, and its higher-end market position provides relative price inelasticity of demand for its products compared to low-cost and fast-fashion apparel brands. Brand-Y also has a relatively small supply chain.

The company is both legally incorporated as a Benefit Corporation and, since 2015, certified as a B-Corp. Having adopted the industry-preferred practices for aligning profit and nonprofit goals, Brand-Y offers a critical case for assessing the relationships between policies, practices, and outcomes concerning supply-chain labor standards. The company defines four "benefits" in its incorporation documents, prioritizing its commitment to labor standards in the supply chain:

- *Benefit 1* is to minimize the company's negative impacts on society and the environment. This includes "improving the livelihoods of workers in our supply chain" as well as using organic cotton, recycled fiber, nontoxic dyes; and reducing its carbon footprint and waste. In fact, Brand-Y commits to working with suppliers that comply with SA8000 standards, including payment of a living wage.[58]
- *Benefit 2* is the creation of an inclusive workplace where employees are included in the financial success of the company through profit sharing, and in which women make up a majority of the workforce.
- *Benefit 3* is supporting women and society through the provision of grants to a variety of social and environmental organizations.
- *Benefit 4* is to lead the apparel industry to adopt more ethical practices through collaboration with other organizations involved in private regulation and through the use of the brand as a platform for public advocacy.

Brand-Y's communications echo these priorities and the stakeholder-oriented business scholarship emphasis on a long-run value rather than short-term profitability. Throughout its history, the company has cultivated a brand associated with human rights and environmental sustainability. Consistent with such a vision, it was an early adopter of the benefit corporation model, having obtained certification from B Lab and reincorporated as a Benefit Corporation once that status was established under US state law. Brand-Y's messaging, including its benefit reports, state that the company prioritizes people over profit, identifies the tensions between costs and nonprofit goals, and uses social auditing to ensure compliance with labor standards throughout its global supply chain.

Adopting the private regulation model with regard to labor standards was a voluntary choice by Brand-Y for its global supply chain. The company faced no public pressure from labor activists. No laws regulate apparel brands' purchasing, marketing, and sale of apparel based on labor standards in production, apart from anti–forced labor laws.[59] According to Brand-Y, its customers have not asked about labor standards, consistent with evidence of weak consumer pressure.[60]

Participation in multi-stakeholder initiatives (MSIs) has shaped Brand-Y's use of the model. The brand has participated in the US-based MSI Social Accountability International (SAI) and used SA8000, the standard developed by SAI, as the brand's supplier code of conduct since the late 1990s.[61] The SAI standard differs from other codes in that it explicitly commits the company to pay living wages. Brand-Y has also participated in other MSIs that encourage use of the private regulation model, including the Ethical Trading Initiative, Sustainable Apparel Coalition, Responsible Sourcing Network, American Sustainable Business Coalition, and Social and Labor Convergence Project.

Brand-Y's pitch to consumers is not price, and its higher-end market position provides relative price inelasticity of demand for its products, compared with low-cost and fast-fashion apparel brands. Brand-Y also has a relatively small supply chain.

Brand-Y generously provided the data for our study, including its records of audits of its suppliers. The analysis comes from 213 audits. Box 7.1 details the data.

We complemented analysis of audit records with data from the brand's purchase order database and semistructured interviews with Brand-Y compliance staff prior and throughout the analysis of the data. Interviews particularly informed our analysis of Brand-Y's responses to its audit information.

Brand-Y completed one BIA during the period for which its audit records were available and another in 2017, when the brand also issued its first statutorily required benefit report. The audit records were the basis for Brand-Y's benefit corporation reporting. Neither the benefit report nor the BIA included more details about labor standards at the brand's suppliers than the company's audit records did; the benefit report and BIA communicated only that the company conducted such assessments.

Table 7.1 reports Brand-Y's BIA scores for the two years in which the company completed the assessment and compares these scores with average scores for other firms in the apparel, footwear, and accessories category, as well as with the 5,800 assessments of all certified B Corps spread over five years. Brand-Y scored higher than the global average on its environmental policies, governance

Box 7.1. Brand-Y Data

Brand-Y provided 245 compliance assessment records from 1999–2016 from thirty-eight garment manufacturing suppliers located in China, the United States, India, Peru, South Korea, Turkey, Ethiopia, Portugal, and Uruguay. Of these, 24 were self-assessments by factory management and did not provide sufficient information to infer their assessment of compliance with Brand-Y's labor standards. The remaining records included direct assessments by Brand-Y, but were mostly third-party assessments by audit firms with which the company had contracted. Deleting 8 records with extensive missing information left 213 usable records available for analysis.

These records showed that approximately 70 percent of Brand-Y's garments were manufactured in China and 25 percent in the United States, and suppliers in these two countries accounted for 80 percent of factory workers in the brand's supply chain. There were sufficient longitudinal data only to study compliance over time in the China, India, and US factories. Overall, these factories employed an average of 242 workers, 60 percent female; 37 percent of the factories used subcontracted labor. Only one factory had a collective bargaining agreement. The average relationship with suppliers was eleven years, and Brand-Y purchased 57 percent of the total production from each of the suppliers, indicating a higher degree of leverage than is usual in the apparel industry.

The audit records provide ratings of compliance with SA8000's nine standards concerning freedom of association and collective bargaining rights, forced labor, child labor, discrimination, remuneration, working hours, occupational health and safety, disciplinary practices, and management systems. In Brand-Y's archives, the audit records were classified into three groups, to which we assigned a three-point scale: critical noncompliance (1), noncompliance requiring corrective action (2), or compliance (3). For broader comparisons, we averaged the ratings on the individual items to produce an overall compliance rating (OCR).

TABLE 7.1. Brand-Y and average benefit impact assessment (BIA) scores

	BRAND-Y 2015	BRAND-Y 2017	AVERAGE SCORE FOR ALL APPAREL AND FOOTWEAR B-CORPS 2012–2017	AVERAGE SCORE FOR ALL B-CORP ASSESSMENTS 2012–2017 (RANGE)
Overall score	81.6	92.2	95.8	97.19 (80–184)
Community	16.8	22.0	42.2	31.00
Customers	0.0	0.0	4.0	15.03
Environment	27.3	32.1	23.6	17.96
Governance	5.6	14.4	11.8	12.40
Employees	31.7	27.5	17.5	22.70

policies, and policies for its employees and lower than the global average for community and overall score.

Brand-Y emphasizes supplier compliance with SA8000 labor standards as its community benefit goal. The company does not have a specific consumer benefit goal. B Lab has also recognized Brand-Y as one of its top performers for multiple years.

Brand-Y's Audits

For Brand-Y's suppliers, the mean overall compliance rating (aggregated across all issues, factories and years) was 2.54 on the 3-point scale, not fully compliant but relatively close. Yet Brand-Y's data, even on the most concrete, measurable standards, paint a different picture. Mean compliance on health and safety was 1.87. Working hours regularly exceeded national laws and the code standard, and there was no evidence that workers ever received a living wage. Table 7.2 details these findings.

Flagging reliability concerns (addressed later), only 57 percent of audit records provided consistent data for only five control variables: country location, years supplying Brand-Y, factory size measured by the number of workers, time, and the audit firm used. Multivariate regression of overall compliance on these variables indicated significant effects of country location and audit firm, and a faint time effect, all shown in table 7.3.

When the country effect is looked at more closely, taking China and the United States as the countries that accounted for most production and workers in Brand-Y's supply chain, the audit records indicated that US-based factories were more likely to approach compliance with wage and working hours standards than China-based factories. This country effect is consistent with prior research emphasizing institutional contexts.[62] Compliance ratings also appear to be influenced by which

TABLE 7.2. Descriptive statistics of dependent and independent variables

VARIABLES	LEVEL OF ANALYSIS	OBSERVATIONS	REPORTING FREQUENCY	MEAN	STANDARD DEVIATION
DEPENDENT VARIABLES					
Overall compliance rating		190	0.89	2.54	0.42
Freedom of association and collective bargaining rights		184	0.86	2.70	0.62
Forced labor		189	0.89	2.87	0.38
Child labor		194	0.91	2.75	0.56
Discrimination		189	0.89	2.82	0.48
Remuneration		199	0.93	2.39	0.81
Working hours		198	0.93	2.38	0.88
Occupational health and safety		203	0.95	1.87	0.70
Disciplinary practices		186	0.87	2.81	0.48
Management systems		121	0.57	1.89	0.72
INDEPENDENT VARIABLES					
Years supplying brand	Brand-supplier relationship	213	1.00	11.61	4.53
Percentage production for brand	Brand-supplier relationship	87	0.41	0.57	0.39
Order volume	Brand-supplier relationship	24	0.11	161.33	60.59
Turnaround time	Brand-supplier relationship	24	0.11	95.50	32.73
Number of workers	Supplier-worker relationship	121	0.57	242.33	273.31
Subcontracted labor	Supplier-worker relationship	54	0.25	0.37	0.49
Percentage workers female	Supplier-worker relationship	50	0.23	0.61	0.20
Assessment firm	Auditing practices	175	0.82	6.49	4.95
Percent workers interviewed	Auditing practices	45	0.21	0.12	0.22
Announced or unannounced audit	Auditing practices	61	0.29	0.90	0.30

firm audited the factory. Given the significant relationship indicated by regression analysis, we examined audit-firm variation more closely. Over the seventeen years studied, Brand-Y used twenty-two audit firms. Although all were auditing against the same standard, SA8000, there were systematic differences in compliance ratings across audit firms (table 7.4).

TABLE 7.3. Potential determinants of overall compliance ratings

VARIABLE	COEFFICIENT	STANDARD ERROR	SIGNIFICANCE
Time	0.001	0.002	
Country location (Reference-China)			
India	−0.11	0.17	
USA	0.66	0.12	***
Factory size	−0.003	0.001	
Years supplying Brand-Y	−0.01	0.03	
Audit firm (Reference Firm 1)			
Audit Firm 3	0.23	0.28	
Audit Firm 4	−0.47	0.22	*
Audit Firm 6	−0.32	0.19	
Audit Firm 7	0.37	0.15	*
Audit Firm 8	−0.15	0.22	
Audit Firm 10	−0.12	0.15	
Audit Firm 11	−0.03	0.20	
Audit Firm 12	−0.35	0.17	*
Constant	8.66		
N	92.0		
R-Square	0.27		

*p < 0.1, **p < 0.05, ***p < 0.01.

Given differences across audit firms, we compared results of two firms (audit firms 12 and 7) that conducted announced audits of the same factories (Suppliers A and B) against the same standards (SA8000). As table 7.5 shows, auditors' ratings varied, particularly their evaluations of freedom of association and collective bargaining, wages, occupational health and safety, and management systems. These findings are consistent with weaknesses of auditing identified in prior research and also indicative of the causal indeterminacy and difficulty measuring results that characterize institutional decoupling.[63]

Further clouding any causality, time had an ambiguous effect. The faint positive effect of time on compliance indicated by the limited multivariate regression analysis (table 7.3) was contradicted by plotting overall compliance ratings from each audit over the seventeen-year period by country location, shown in figure 7.2. The plotted ratings indicate that compliance *declined* rather than *increased* over time, especially after 2012 in the two largest countries (China and the United States).

Figure 7.2 also indicates an ambiguous longitudinal effect, which is consistent with prior results finding instability of audit data, with firms cycling in and out

TABLE 7.4. Overall compliance rating (OCR) means by audit firm and audit type

AUDIT FIRM	N	OCR MEAN	STANDARD DEVIATION	STANDARD ERROR
1	50	2.79	0.18	0.02
3	4	2.46	0.37	0.18
4	8	2.13	0.47	0.16
6	10	2.26	0.38	0.12
7	29	2.47	0.56	0.10
8	6	1.90	0.16	0.06
9	2	2.88	0.15	0.11
10	13	2.45	0.30	0.08
11	8	2.32	0.30	0.10
12	15	2.32	0.54	0.14
17	1	3.00	.	.
18	1	2.33	.	.
19	1	2.22	.	.
20	1	2.00	.	.
21	1	2.55	.	.
22	2	2.94	0.078	0.05
Total	152	2.511	0.44	0.03
F	4.60***			
Audit type				
Announced	6	2.45	0.45	0.18
Unannounced	50	2.69	0.31	0.04
Total	56	2.67	0.33	0.04
F	2.92*			

TABLE 7.5. Compliance rating variation by audit firms at the same supplier in China, 2015 (all of these audits were announced)

COMPANY	SUPPLIER A		SUPPLIER B	
Audit firm	Audit firm 12	Audit firm 7	Audit firm 12	Audit firm 7
Month	February	May	March	August
Overall compliance rating	2.11	2.78	1.78	2.50
Freedom of association and collective bargaining rights	2	3	1	3
Forced labor	3	3	3	3
Child labor	3	3	3	3
Discrimination	3	3	2	3
Remuneration	2	1	2	1
Working hours	3	3	2	3
Occupational health and safety	1	3	1	1
Disciplinary practices	1	3	1	3
Management systems	1	3	1	Unreported

TABLE 7.6. Apparel brand scores on B Lab's benefit impact assessment (BIA), 2007–2018

	BRANDS	COMPLETED SUPPLIER CODE QUESTIONS	AVERAGE SCORE	MINIMUM	MAXIMUM
Certified	93	18 (19%)	8.17	8.17	8.17
Decertified	42	22 (51%)	8.22	8.21	8.23
All BIA respondents	135	40 (30%)	8.20	8.19	8.20

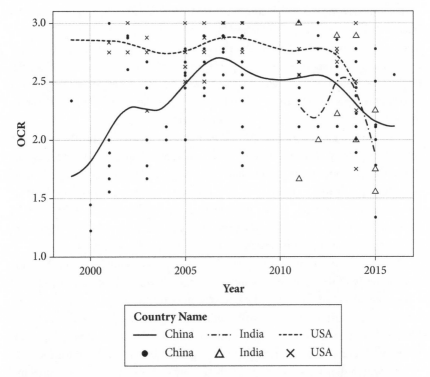

FIGURE 7.2. Overall compliance ratings over time by country, 1999–2016

Chart by author.

of compliance.[64] The data suggest that the faint positive effect of time was driven by the steady increase in compliance ratings in China between 2000 and 2008, a period when US-based factories' compliance was stable. But at least some of the data underlying that increase was "fabricated" (as discussed later).

Brand-Y's audit records provided inconsistent data. Although the records included data for 190 overall compliance ratings (89 percent of all records), a lot of data were missing. Important variables, such as order volume and turnaround times, were hardly ever recorded. More than 60 percent of audit records lacked data on important variables such as the percentage of production bought by the brand, and data on many supplier characteristics, such as whether they used subcontracted workers, the gender of workers, the percentage of workers interviewed for the audit, and whether the audit was announced in advance. Some records lacked ratings for one or another code standard, and many did not report corrective actions—that is, the steps factory managers were expected to take to become compliant.

The credibility of audit ratings was undermined by additional details recorded in audit reports. Auditors misreported on code standards. For example, while most audit records stated full compliance with Brand-Y's code requirements on freedom of association and collective bargaining rights, 96 percent of the audits did not report whether workers were represented by a union or whether there had been unionization efforts. Of the 4 percent of audits reporting such basic data, all but one were audits of factories in China, where, in violation of freedom of association conventions, the only union allowed is the All-China Federation of Trade Unions, controlled by the governing party.

On discrimination, most auditors included no information other than the compliance rating. Those who did seemed to ignore what they found; for example, auditors reported that male managers pressured female workers to "go out with them for drinks and more" and then rated the factory as fully compliant on the nondiscrimination standard. In another case, auditors reported different wages for male and female workers of the same status doing the same job and yet rated the factory as fully compliant with the nondiscrimination standard.

On wages, auditors arbitrarily used their own, lower standard. Brand-Y's code of conduct requires payment of a living wage. Only three audit reports included a living-wage calculation, and the auditors in two of those excluded the actual wage rates paid. In multiple reports, auditors wrote a variation of this opinion: "All workers are paid at least the legal minimum wage, so by definition, this meets their basic needs." This approach demonstrates auditors' disregard for the code against which they were auditing and the widely documented gap between a living wage and the legal minimum.[65]

Brand-Y's Business Decisions

Brand-Y's decisions were also notable, beginning with its choices of business partners. The company chose to source 70 percent of its products in China, where compliance with the brand's code was effectively impossible because the national government does not permit freedom of association and collective bargaining rights. For sourcing in China, the company relied on a vendor that stated that it did not agree with the brand's code, specifically the living-wage standard, and refused access to auditors hired by Brand-Y to review a major supplier's accounting system after the brand discovered prior audit falsification. For monitoring, Brand-Y hired third-party audit firms that underreported essential information and regularly misrepresented and disregarded the company's standards. Brand-Y's suppliers in China falsified audit records with the apparent support of auditors and the vendor.

Brand-Y adjusted its approach slightly in response. A tip concerning audit falsification from a factory worker led Brand-Y staff to convene a meeting with its suppliers in China. The factory managers reported that noncompliance was their strategy to deliver product orders at the set price, and falsification was their strategy to retain Brand-Y's business. In response to these falsified records, Brand-Y hired a new audit firm, which conducted more in-depth baseline assessments. These included interviews of workers in their communities, who provided a more realistic picture of factory conditions, primarily reporting longer hours and lower pay than prior audit records showed.

Brand-Y also hired a labor-compliance consultant to deliver capacity-building workshops to managers and workers at the brand's suppliers in China, as it did two additional times during the seventeen years studied. The training covered labor laws, codes of conduct, occupational health and safety, conflict management, noncompliance root-cause analysis, pay and working hours accounting, noncompliance remediation, human resource practices, and compliance self-assessments. Although the consultant reported increased learning by workshop participants, Brand-Y's compliance data do not indicate an increase in compliance.

There is no indication that Brand-Y used purchasing practices to drive compliance with its labor standards, behavior consistent with prior research.[66] Over seventeen years, the brand received audit reports of noncompliance, with indications of misreporting by auditors, vendor, and suppliers, and yet continued to provide its business to these suppliers.

Despite the persistent unreliability of its audits and the gaps in compliance with labor standards, Brand-Y was still able to obtain benefit corporation status. The company issued its first report to fulfill the benefit corporation requirement and completed another BIA in 2017. In its two BIAs, the company left blank the questions concerning "supplier monitoring and evaluation, certifications and tenure, labeling standards, and supplier Code of Conduct." Not responding to these questions did not affect its B-Corp certification. According to B Lab's publicly available dataset, only 19 percent of certified B-Corp apparel companies completed the BIA questions concerning supplier codes of conduct, and responders averaged 8 out of 40 points in the category.

In its public benefit report, Brand-Y stated that B-Corp certification was the third-party standard and B Lab the third party that verified its report. In the report, the company noted that obtaining data from workers and about living wages was a challenge and otherwise stated nothing about the labor standards at its suppliers. Evident failure towards the prioritized benefit of labor standards throughout the supply chain proved no obstacle to benefit corporation status; B Lab obliged the company in disregarding the data.

The findings suggest Brand-Y implemented a private regulation program decoupled from outcomes for workers, and that Benefit Corporation incorporation and B-Corp certification supported the decoupling. The brand's audit records indicated continuous noncompliance with its minimum standards and no clear improvement over time. The audit data are essential under the private regulation model; they are supposed to guide brand sourcing decisions to incentivize supplier compliance. Yet Brand-Y's auditing did not provide reliable data. With reports of noncompliance and indications from the fabricated audits that conditions were worse than reported, Brand-Y did not align purchasing and compliance. This failure to implement the third pillar of the model is consistent with prior findings. It also raises questions about why Brand-Y continued to use the model even as evidence of its ineffectiveness mounted over seventeen years.[67] And it raises the question of why B-Lab would not require such data to be reported.

The considerable gaps between Brand-Y's private regulation policy, practice, and outcomes indicate the company engaged in symbolic adoption.[68] It did not implement the model fully, ignoring the third pillar of the model that requires integration of sourcing with compliance. Brand-Y's extensive implementation of the model's formal processes and persistent lack of labor standards compliance suggest practice-outcomes decoupling.

Purchasing practices are precisely the type of decisions that benefit corporations, particularly those prioritizing supply-chain labor standards, should and could address. Relieved of pressure to maximize profits, benefit corporation directors should face fewer constraints on decisions to source only from factories respecting workers' rights. Instead, Brand-Y managed a supply chain with suppliers located in countries with labor laws and enforcement practices antagonistic toward international labor standards; contracted with vendors and suppliers not fully supportive of the brand's code; and relied on audit firms with divergent approaches, including some that communicated indifference to the brand's code.

Benefit corporation status should also facilitate management decisions to use models with aligned practices and outcomes and to adjust the company's approach when evidence indicates practice-outcome decoupling. Having established respect of workers' rights as a corporate goal alongside profitability, the benefit corporation management should respond to evidence of decoupling by altering the company's method of achieving the goal. Brand-Y continued audits that yielded unreliable audit data throughout the seventeen years studied. The brand's compliance team could only infer but not empirically verify suppliers' compliance status in order to convince the sourcing department to select certain suppliers. In this sense, decoupled audits and labor standards reinforced decoupled compliance from decision making about sourcing, exemplifying the interrelationship between policy-practice decoupling and means-ends decoupling highlighted in earlier research.[69]

The case of Brand-Y indicates that benefit corporation status risks functioning as a decoupling mechanism. Legal Benefit Corporation status requires verified reporting by a third party, which in turn assumes the effectiveness of the code audit model. The most commonly used third party, B Lab, does not require minimum labor standards; it asks only about processes of monitoring suppliers. Even if there were minimum standards or if the processes interrogated were robust, demonstrating compliance with them is unnecessary for B-Corp certification. In addition, ambiguity regarding benefit reporting made it possible for Brand-Y's to provide no information about actual labor standards in its benefit reporting.

Brand-Y's case shows that B-Corp certification and legal Benefit Corporation status may be achieved without providing any information about actual supply-chain labor standards. The Benefit Corporation and B-Corp reporting require no such information. Disregarding outcomes facilitates both decoupling of the policy of considering stakeholders from company practices and of practices from impacts on stakeholders.

The lack of access to remedy for stakeholders negatively affected by Benefit Corporations or B-Corps reinforces the practice-outcome decoupling effect of benefit corporation status. Given the ambivalence of Brand-Y's vendor and auditors towards the brand's code of conduct, it is implausible that workers at Brand-Y's suppliers understood the standards in the code, much less the associated benefit corporation status and dispute-resolution mechanisms. In the unlikely scenario that a worker producing apparel for any benefit corporation brand knew the company's status, access to remedial justice for violations of labor standards is effectively impossible. To sue, the worker in the far-flung supply chain would need to own shares of the Benefit Corporation, even more difficult with a private company such as Brand-Y. To file a complaint with B-Corp, the worker would depend on the response of the certifier B Lab, which would have to weigh whether pressuring the brand would negatively affect relationships with its clients, the brands. The brand could simply switch to another third party and retain legal Benefit Corporation status. Thus, workers in the supply chain of any Benefit Corporation or B-Corp have no meaningful say in the judgment that the corporation is benefiting them.

In sum, while it is reasonable to expect that a benefit corporation, given its goals, would do a better job in the implementation of private regulation relative to

C-Corps, the results here do not suggest that is the case. Clearly, it seems possible to obtain and retain benefit corporation status even if one of the key benefit goals—in this case, assurance of minimum labor conditions in the supply chain—is not met.

What explains the curious result of Brand-Y's private regulation program? Why did the brand continue with the program despite the evidence of its ineffectiveness? When the link between practices and outcomes is unclear, technical procedures such as auditing become ends in themselves, as they serve to confer legitimacy in the face of normative external pressures.[70] Brand-Y has long maintained a reputation as a more "responsible" brand by virtue of its claims, which are highlighted by its benefit corporation status. In addition, while not facing government regulation or pressure from labor or the public, Brand-Y operated in an environment in which brands increasingly adopted standardized approaches. Brand-Y's participation in multi-stakeholder initiatives exposed it to mimetic pressure to benchmark against competitors, indicated by its use of SA8000 standards. As both models spread, Brand-Y adopted them, avoiding the risk of eroding its reputation as an ethical company. In this sense, legitimacy appeared to motivate Brand-Y's adoption and continued use of the private regulation and benefit corporation models.[71]

Most important, this case points to the limits of benefit corporation status as currently granted under law or private certification. The legal Benefit Corporation status does not offer a mechanism to hold companies accountable for their benefit claims and relies on noncredible third-party verifiers. As the most common verifier, B Lab creates confusion instead of clarity around corporate impacts on society. In particular, BIA assessments ask about corporate policies and practices but not about their effects on worker outcomes. Furthermore, B Lab raises questions about the reliability of its assessment process by permitting even companies that define labor standards in the supply chain as a prioritized benefit to avoid answering questions about them. Neither benefit-corporation statutes nor B-Corp certification provide stakeholders with meaningful access to mechanisms for remedy of negative impacts by benefit corporations. The result is a benefit-corporation status based on selective self-reporting of policies and practices without any verification of actual social impacts.

Despite the promise of facilitating alignment, benefit corporation status is creating the incentive for symbolic adoption and decoupling of policy from practice.

Conclusion

Critics have argued that corporations have not been achieving improvements in labor conditions because they have engaged in symbolic adoption of the private regulation model or decoupling practices from outcomes, under pressure to maximize profit for shareholders. Benefit corporations are significantly relieved of this pressure and expressly establish positive impacts on stakeholders as a goal alongside profitability. As a privately held company and early adopter of the private regulation and benefit corporation models, Brand-Y is a perfect case to investigate the utility of benefit corporation incorporation and certification for stakeholder interests. If benefit corporation status were to result in a strong consideration of stakeholder interests (here, the interests of workers in the supply chain), we should expect to see this in Brand-Y's case.

The investigation, though, provides no evidence that Benefit Corporation legal status or B-Corp certification increase the likelihood of compliance with internationally recognized labor standards in supply chains. The company's benefit report clearly indicates that one of its selected "benefits" is labor standards in the supply chain. Brand-Y set adherence to SA-8000 standards, including payment of living wages, as its code for suppliers. Whether workers experienced such standards—and Brand-Y's audit records indicated they did not—had no bearing on the company's obtaining and maintaining Benefit Corporation incorporation and B-Corp certification. The study suggests benefit corporation status has more to do with writing policies to score adequately on assessments and evaluations than with any serious consideration of whether those policies result in practices and outcomes benefiting stakeholders.

The implications for the reform and improvement of benefit corporation status are compelling and clear. The benefit corporation concept of organizing corporations around the interests of all stakeholders—including shareholders, workers, impacted communities, and consumers alike—could in principle support alignment of corporate behavior with social needs and norms. As evidenced in the Brand-Y case, Benefit Corporation statutes and B-Corp certification fail to achieve such alignment.

To improve, evaluation of delivery of the public benefits claimed by benefit corporations needs to be more stringent. Evaluators need to assess practices and outcomes of policies rather than simply whether these policies exists. There must also be a mechanism that permits stakeholders to hold corporations accountable for their impacts in a meaningful way. Establishing stakeholder access to remedy negative impacts offers significant opportunity to address the gaps in labor standards across global supply chains. Without these changes, B-Corp certification and Benefit-Corporation incorporation will remain a false promise.

ALIGNING SOURCING AND COMPLIANCE INSIDE A GLOBAL CORPORATION

As noted in earlier chapters, the private regulation model consists of three pillars: setting standards that govern labor practices in global supply chains; auditing; and incentivizing compliance by linking brands' future sourcing decisions to that compliance by "punishing" factories that do not show improvement and "rewarding" those that do.[1] Purchasing practices have received less research attention than the other two pillars.[2] This chapter presents a detailed case study of one global retailer's effort to link sourcing strategies with compliance efforts.

Some research suggests purchasing practices of buyers actually contribute to lower compliance. Through low prices and short turnaround times, brands "squeeze" suppliers,[3] who react by violating labor standards.[4] Short turnaround times between order placement and delivery and unpredictable order changes often lead to excessive overtime, as supplier managers drive workers to fulfill orders out of fear of losing the customer's business.[5]

Other research argues that consumer and activist campaigns have had success in influencing companies to reward factories that comply well.[6] Multi-stakeholder initiatives such as the Fair Labor Association (FLA), Ethical Trading Initiative (ETI), and Fair Wear Foundation (FWF) increasingly require their members to adopt "responsible" sourcing practices and tie their purchasing orders to compliance. And newer initiatives such as Better Buying have created a unique system for suppliers to communicate with their buyers about purchasing practices that are working well and those that need improvement, without risking their business relationship. The initiative's buyer rating system examines seven key buyer purchasing practices that affect a supplier's ability to adhere to the terms of any contract and operate efficiently, while providing a safe work environment and maximizing profitability.

We actually know very little about whether global companies align purchasing practices with compliance. Using audit results to persuade suppliers to improve is what the private regulation model requires. How widespread, for instance, is the practice of incentivizing suppliers by rewarding more compliant ones with more orders—the "carrot" encouraged by many MSIs? We do not know.

Then there's the "stick"—eliminating factories from the supply chains that fail to meet a certain improvement threshold. The thresholds vary from company to company and are not publicly reported. Most companies do not publicly report the number of factories they have dropped from their supply chain. How many companies use that stick? We do not know.

We do know that dropping factories is not always easy, as suppliers are not instantly substitutable. Consider, for example, the symbiotic relationship between Apple and Foxconn—one cannot live without the other. Besides, dropping factories has negative social consequences as well, because the workers in those dropped factories are in danger of losing their livelihoods. And once dropped, companies will no longer have leverage over the factory to improve labor conditions, which is the ultimate goal of private regulation. For all these reasons, companies may not be motivated to use the stick approach.

Some companies help suppliers improve by providing guidance on how to eliminate root causes of noncompliance, and through a variety of formal and informal "capability-building" efforts.[7] Some research has documented the limited and contingent effects of persuasion and capability programs.[8] There is some limited evidence supporting the carrot approach, although the increase in orders was minor.[9] An increase in compliance with certain labor standards, such as health and safety, enabled factories in Cambodia to secure long-term sourcing relationships with some companies.[10] And Vietnamese exporters reported a higher willingness to comply when incentivized by higher prices from global firms.[11]

Missing from prior research are investigations of what goes on *inside* global firms, which can incentivize suppliers to comply with more orders *only* if there is some degree of integration between global firms' compliance and sourcing departments. There is considerable skepticism that such integration or alignment exists; instead the evidence in the well-studied apparel supply chain is that there is a decoupling between sourcing practices and compliance within most global companies.[12] Even in a benefit corporation, where one would expect a more serious effort to improve compliance through such linkages, the study in chapter 7 found no evidence of links between purchasing practices and compliance. And in a case study of a global supplier to seventy global brands, interviews with the supplier's marketing managers suggest no connection at all between sourcing practices and compliance of those brands.[13]

The common assumption that sourcing decisions are based on the compliance records of suppliers is largely unwarranted. Why do we see this decoupling? Sourcing managers and compliance managers respond to different sets of incentives. Sourcing managers are rewarded on the basis of price, quality, and timely delivery of the product, while compliance managers are generally rewarded for increasing compliance.[14] But organizational processes do not integrate these disparate reward structures. In institutional theory terms, externally induced legitimacy structures (such as codes of conduct) are buffered from the organizational core (sourcing departments).

Global firms have not typically been willing to share sourcing information with researchers, but my own conversations with various managers suggest that most sourcing departments do not formally include compliance in their models for assessing suppliers. In most firms, sourcing and compliance departments exist in silos. Compliance groups are unable to influence sourcing departments, which tend to have greater power given their contributions to the bottom line. Compliance department personnel, who have relatively little organizational power to fulfill the commitments their companies make, are the ones representing those companies in MSIs, and there are almost no sourcing people involved—further evidence that there is little integration. A regional compliance manager of a very large leading global firm in the fast fashion space told me compliance personnel didn't even have access to sourcing data *from their own company*. Integration won't happen until the compliance or corporate social responsibility (CSR) departments have sufficient organizational power in the corporate hierarchy, or if there is a top-down *diktat* to better integrate the two functions.

Two case studies attempted to document company efforts to align sourcing and compliance, even though the results of those efforts are as yet unknown. The first occurred at New Balance, a global athletic shoemaker.[15] New Balance created a scorecard to evaluate supplier performance on a range of dimensions, such as quality, reliability, productivity (PPH, or pairs of shoes per person per hour), development efficiency (on time, sample preparation), a survey of New Balance leadership regarding the supplier factory, and the CSR score. CSR compliance accounted for only 15 percent of the total scorecard. The compliance team "approved" factories based on the CSR scores in tests of the scorecard. However, sourcing personnel would push back when "certain factories were not approved" and accused compliance personnel of "looking only at compliance and not seeing the risk to the other dimensions to the scorecard."[16] The story indicates the difficulties of aligning compliance and sourcing.

A study of Nike also looks at efforts to align sourcing and compliance.[17] In 2009, the company launched an initiative, Rewire, to create a new department called "sustainable manufacturing and sourcing" to replace the previously independent departments. It would oversee compliance as well as capacity building among suppliers. The department would use a scorecard approach, with a metric called the "manufacturing index" to rate supplier performance in four equally weighted areas: cost, quality, delivery, and sustainability. Nike would prioritize suppliers with the highest ratings. At the same time, the company's "categories and product" department, which developed plans for product lines, was also rating factories' gross product margins, units, style counts, productivity, and revenue. "There is always a dynamic productive tension between the two departments with their differential metrics," a Nike manager explained.[18]

There is, however, one landmark study (so-called because it was the first to marry compliance and sourcing data) that shows the results of the efforts of a global brand to achieve integration between compliance and sourcing.[19] A North American maker of active apparel, a relatively small company with a reputation as a leader in environmental and social standards, had a supply chain of only seventy factories. The researchers obtained compliance information from audits and data on sourcing, including order dates, prices, and order volumes. The researchers were able to match compliance records (including all communication between the compliance department and the factory) with purchasing records.

The analysis revealed a highly engaged compliance department that communicated regularly with the factories and made a variety of suggestions to improve compliance but that had no connection whatsoever with sourcing practices. In many instances, the value of orders increased despite higher numbers of violations being found and decreased even as a factory improved on compliance.

"The signals sent by the purchase orders appeared to undercut the efforts of the compliance team," the researchers wrote.[20] Compliance managers were effective in terms of both persuading and problem-solving, often with positive results in the factories, and had some success in terminating the most egregiously violating suppliers, but the right mix of incentives for sourcing and compliance staff did not exist for the bulk of the factories in the middle range.

What is particularly interesting about this case is that the relationship (or lack thereof) between sourcing and compliance had *nothing* to do with either price or delivery times. In fact, more orders were given to a factory with higher violations even though it charged a higher price for the product.

There were many difficulties in flexibly adjusting order volumes in the context of compliance information. First, the researchers note that placing an order involved coordination among staff members from multiple departments: "Each team signed off on specific attributes of a purchase order, such as product specifications, projected sales, and the availability and price of inputs. This coordination took place under extreme time pressure to issue orders early enough to allow factories time to source inputs needed for manufacturing." Second, as a relatively smaller brand, this company needed to meet minimum order quantities specified by each factory to ensure production capacity was reserved, which injected "rigidity into the relationship."[21] And third, finding replacement factories that could produce this company's highly specialized products would have been difficult. Thus, there were significant transaction costs to altering orders based on compliance data.

Most important, especially for this chapter, is that "many staff involved in the purchase order process did not view monitoring as central to their roles [and] key compliance managers were not involved in meetings in which orders were allocated to factories."[22] The lessons from this study are that there is need for much greater coordination between compliance and sourcing in order to "flexibly adjust order volumes in response to compliance information" and that the "intensity of this challenge may be different for differing supply chain structures."[23]

Of course, it is possible that other firms might have instituted systems that resulted in coupling purchasing practices with compliance more tightly than the firm in that study did. But given the general unwillingness of brands to share their sourcing information with anyone, we know nothing about the success of any such efforts.

The Pangia Case

The case study of Pangia (not the company's real name) that follows reports on one global retailer's efforts to align sourcing and compliance. Pangia, located in the United States, is among the larger global retailers of apparel and accessories. Its apparel lines comprise several different brands (which have changed over time) in different market segments. Pangia's supply chain extended to more than 2,000 factories (before 2010) in twenty countries. Most of its products are sourced from Asia.

The case presents the variety of challenges Pangia faced in restructuring the traditional sourcing function to be more strategic and enhance the integration of compliance with sourcing decisions. This was by no means a simple process—it took roughly seven years from strategy formulation to implementation. The lessons are important for other companies grappling with the difficult issue of aligning compliance with sourcing.

Building Compliance Capability

Pangia's organizational structure before 2010 reflected the different brands in its portfolio. As each new brand was introduced, new dedicated design, production planning, sourcing, and marketing teams were created. In the late 1990s, when consumer activism forced global brands to enact private regulation, Pangia established a compliance team at the corporate level, in the corporate responsibility department, that was charged with enacting and monitoring the company's newly developed code of conduct for suppliers.

As the compliance team developed policies and procedures for evaluating the compliance performance of factories in the supply chain, the team began to notice connections between the quality of factory procedures, management systems, and compliance. But because Pangia typically had only a small percentage of a factory's production, the company's compliance strategy was difficult to enforce. Still, the company continued to build its compliance capability.

A key change in compliance strategy came when Pangia recognized it could not effectively implement such a strategy on its own but needed to collaborate with, and learn from, the experiences of external stakeholders. The company began to dialogue with various multi-stakeholder institutions and NGOs, even those critical of Pangia's responsibility efforts. For example, Pangia was among several apparel brands in a multi-stakeholder coalition[24] that worked with the US government to pressure the Uzbekistan government to prohibit child labor in that country's cotton fields. These activities not only increased organizational capacity, but also increased Pangia's knowledge about the extended elements of its supply chain (particularly about fabric mills, embroidery, accessories, and cotton), and enhanced its external credibility among stakeholders.

The compliance team within the corporate responsibility department, however, realized its activities that were recognized outside the company were not as widely known within the Pangia organization beyond corporate headquarters. The team's efforts had not quite percolated into the different brands organized in their divisional structures. As a compliance department officer noted, there were "relatively few conversations regarding whether the garments were being designed for good labor practices in the first place," and "the social responsibility organization was managing the consequences of sourcing decisions, but not the choices themselves."[25]

The remit of the corporate responsibility department was increased to direct greater collaboration efforts within the company. The vice president leading the department gradually began elevating its visibility within the company. The department was reorganized to consolidate social (labor) issues, environmental issues, and stakeholder engagement, and labor compliance, further embedding corporate responsibility in the larger organization.

Thus, the compliance activity had been evolving during the 1996–2008 period. The team had introduced a compliance monitoring system early on, increased the group's capacity to collaborate with external organizations, successfully developed the skills and capabilities of people within the corporate responsibility group, and created the organizational architecture to provide the labor compliance team with greater visibility inside and outside the company. The team had also improved its factory measurement capacity through a system of factory ratings that enabled the compliance team to communicate its results better to other parts of the company (discussed further later). Its approach to compliance was quite sophisticated, not only assessing factories using its own internal auditors, but also having those auditors help build factory capability to improve compliance through consultation and engagement. Further, the team introduced a series of programs to help the mostly female factory workers enhance their skills to function better in the workplace but also to improve their lives when they left the workplace.

These efforts motivated the members of the group to pose important questions about the future of Pangia's social responsibility and compliance organization. They wondered whether the function could move beyond simply "mitigating risk" to "creating value." An internal report from that time asked: What are the impacts? Do suppliers have the capability to improve? Who all needs to be involved in the decision? Pangia had been successful at creating internal visibility and external credibility about its social responsibility efforts, but whether the company could leverage those assets in the marketplace to create value remained an unanswered question.

Despite the evolution of the compliance team within the corporate responsibility group, there was relatively little direct interaction between it and the sourcing teams at the various brands; while the compliance team had the "tools" (structures, measurement, and vision) to engage the enterprise more broadly, such conversations were not taking place. There had been some brief encounters between compliance and sourcing, but they were sporadic, not systematic. As a sourcing representative told me, "There was a time that the two people in our respective roles [compliance and sourcing] . . . I don't know if they disliked each other; they just did not even acknowledge each other." Each was responding to different incentives and functioning in a silo.[26]

Pressures for Change in Sourcing

A series of developments in the decade of the 2000s motivated Pangia to reexamine its organizational structure as it related to sourcing. The environment was becoming more competitive; there were more competitors in the customer segments Pangia operated in and pressures on margins. Sourcing managers "had the ability to be less strategic and just do," as the then supply chain leader said, "because the business was there, and the profits were there. As the business became more and more complex and competitive, there is a need for companies like ours to be even more strategic in our operations."

One significant competitive issue Pangia confronted, the supply chain leader noted, was the difference in margins between the company and its significant competitors in Europe:

> When you compared with other global brands, especially in Europe, their margins are almost double American ones given the tax structure in the United States. European countries, when sourcing from Bangladesh, Cambodia, or Vietnam, enjoy about between 10 and 20 points of advantage over a US retailer, due to preferential trading arrangements. On top of that, there is a 7 to 12 percent tax haven versus we are paying 36 percent and then probably another 20 percent duty . . . That is almost a 50-point spread.[27]

Another issue in the decade of the 2000s was the "structural shift" in the economics of the industry: downward pressure on prices as a result of the growth of e-commerce, typified by the rise of Amazon, whose platform implicitly permitted the integration of customer demand with sourcing, making it possible for Amazon to place orders in much smaller lots than before and at a lower price, noted the supply chain leader. For Pangia, that pressure posed the need to optimize costs, which became even more apparent when the company began to benchmark with other firms in the industry. That benchmarking, in turn, led Pangia to question whether it was "optimizing macro and micro economics" in a way consistent with its size as a garment producer. A key question was whether Pangia could leverage it size to increase buying power at lower costs—which the company could do but was not doing. Although one of the larger players in the apparel industry, Pangia was run like a group of small companies, with each individual brand making its own purchasing decisions.

The increasing level of transparency regarding social responsibility demanded by customers and NGOs, powered mostly by social media, also prompted Pangia to question its approach. As the supply chain leader put it, "Our approach on labor had been very compliance driven, but was not what we would call a 'sustainable economics or sustainable development.'"

The demands for more transparency raised questions about Pangia's sourcing strategy. For instance, the company found that tracing the supply chain for the organization as a whole was a significant challenge given the independent sourcing relationships of different Pangia brands. And another question arose: In an era of more pressure on margins, could more responsible sourcing provide a competitive advantage?

By 2012, Pangia's supply chain strategists felt that more competitive, sustainable supply chain management could become a key source of strategic advantage in an increasingly competitive marketplace, especially from an economics point of view. Rationalizing the supply chain to deal only with better-quality vendors might maximize the economic benefits. And after rationalizing, they thought, the vendors the company dealt with could be urged to follow more socially responsible practices in their factories. The key concept became to combine "sustainable economics with sustainable development." A small "reform team" was created in the company.

In the view of the supply chain leader, optimizing costs required consolidating the supply chain and reducing the number of vendors and factories while, at the same time, investing in sustainable long-term relationships with vendors (in a partnership model) that would realize a series of mutual gains on the cost side. Improving compliance, if it were to be the source of a differentiated competitive advantage for Pangia, would be impossible if the company continued to have a large number of vendors and thousands of factories producing its clothes. As a compliance representative suggested, "As long as we've got thousands of factories, we are not going to be able to solve this."

A smaller supply chain, involving deeper relationships based on a partnership model, would enable both cost optimization and improved compliance. A smaller supply chain would mean fewer vendors and factories to assess and would increase the ability of Pangia's compliance teams to engage in continuing dialogue with factory managers, and most important, to engage in capability development programs. Improved compliance would also result from the long-term relationships with vendors and factories, as they would have incentives to address the root causes of noncompliance, rather than just undertake short-term fixes. Overall, longer-term relationships with vendors and factories would promote honesty, transparency, and cooperation between Pangia and its vendors/factories in ways that would help improve long-term sustainable compliance. The need to optimize costs was the binding constraint, however, and would require a complete change in sourcing strategy and methodology.

Toward "Category-based Sourcing"—a New Model of Sourcing Strategy

The goals of reorganization were encapsulated in the language of "sustainable economics" that focused on optimizing costs and "sustainable development" that involved building longer-term partnership-based relationships with suppliers to realize mutual gains, including improvement in sustainability. The key element in sustainable economics was to realize the economies of large-scale buying for the company, which at the time was impossible given the brand-based sourcing model.

The first step was to begin a detailed analysis of the existing system and promote conversations across the company's sourcing networks on the need for change. The supply chain leader's "reform team" was helped in this endeavor by a demonstration project with products on the "nonmerchandising" side of the business, such as paper, bags, and so forth. For these products, the team invested in indexing prices for a variety of commodities, such as oil, and provided the information to all product and design teams for these ancillary products. The team published commodity price movements monthly so everyone in the company understood the effects on their products. And the group evaluated suppliers based on these data. Once gains from a more data-driven approach to evaluating suppliers on the nonmerchandising side of the company were apparent, the reform team was able to obtain top management support, including from the CEO, for expanding this approach to the merchandising side of the business.

With that buy-in, the first step was to translate the demonstration project to the merchandising side, beginning with an analysis of one specific category of product that examined the different categories of materials sourced across all the brands. Denim was chosen as a place to start. It was a reasonably large category for the company, but it was relatively simple in terms of the range of products.

Conversations and data collection with different brands' sourcing departments quickly uncovered the key problem created by each brand having its own independent sourcing organization.[28] As the supply chain leader noted, "We had cases where for the same yard, we were paying three or four different prices to the same vendor because we negotiated with that vendor on an individual brand basis." In many cases, different brand sourcing teams had independent relationships with the same vendors and were competing for the same vendors' capacity.

The reform team also analyzed fabric producers, the second tier of the supply chain, and found that different brands within Pangia were sourcing from the same producer at different prices. In effect, the brands were *competing against themselves* for vendor capacity.

As a regional sourcing manager for one of the brands said,

> I was the sourcing manager for one of the brands, and for one product line for that brand [sweaters]. I and several other sourcing managers for different brands each had developed relationships with vendors and, often, the same vendor. The net result was the same vendor would receive

an order from Brand A, another one from Brand B, and a third one from Brand C, for the same product, and might suddenly become overloaded, so that one of the brands would suffer in terms of quality, delivery, or open the risk to subcontracting.

Each of the different regional sourcing offices could place orders with vendors anywhere. If the office wanted to source from an Indian vendor, it had to go through the India country office where regional sourcing managers for different brands were located. This created some degree of internal competition among Pangia's regional offices as well. As a senior sourcing manager told us,

> The way we used to work was that my brand would send out a program of what we wanted to source. We would send it to all the geographic offices. Each of the offices would deal with their vendors and do the sample style and sample costing. Generally, India was good for wovens, but Korea and Singapore much better for knits. I needed to "protect my territory" so my Hong Kong office could place the order.

More important, she recalled that Pangia's "net capacity with each vendor was diminished as a result of the competition for orders across brands, and the competition across our offices, and we did not have a close relationship with the vendors as a company." In short, because the company was being run as a series of small organizations, it was unable to leverage its large size to optimize buying power.

The competitive process also affected relationships with vendors. As another sourcing director explained,

> I was dealing with 50 to 70 vendors. We were very cost focused. As long as you give me the right costs, we are okay—but no long-term relationship, no long-term business planning, and so on. And the vendor will never know whether they would get the same order for the next season. But at the same time, we have been dealing with these vendors for many years. They know our patterns, how we work, so they will generally reserve some of their capacity for us. We have often had instances where they reserve capacity for us, but at the last minute we had to change the order and drop units, due to changes in the market.

The focus of the reform team's efforts would clearly need to be to rationalize sourcing to make it more efficient from a cost optimization point of view (sustainable sourcing) but also to develop better relationships with vendors to realize mutual gains, including compliance (sustainable development). In sum, each brand, with its own design people, product development people, and dedicated sourcing people, organized according to geographies, each dealing with their vendors in a very transactional way, competed not only for vendor capacity across brands but also across the regional offices. The demonstration project for the non-merchandising side had yielded the key insight that it was possible to achieve significant savings to be realized through more centralized buying for different categories of products. Hence, the potential for savings on the merchandising side seemed huge.

From Independent Brand Sourcing to "Category-based Sourcing"

The second step was to change the sourcing organizational structure completely. The key concept was to extend what had been learned from the analysis of denim to all other categories—hence the name "category-based sourcing." Sourcing would be done by categories of products across the different brands. The essential design change was a shift from brand- and geography-based sourcing to category-based sourcing, through which Pangia could capitalize on its size and buying power. Ideally, sourcing for a single category would be centralized, perhaps in one or two geographical regions. This effort was completed by 2013.

Organizational Resistance

Simply to articulate a new strategy required change at the sourcing leadership level. As the supply chain leader noted, "Any potential change in sourcing strategies had to reckon with resistance to the change in the established ways of doing business. Since sustainable economics and sustainable development involved developing different relationships with existing vendors, the solution required change in leadership and talent."

While the company's top management had bought into the concept, the reform team quickly encountered resistance from multiple other constituencies—first from the product development leaders within sourcing, responsible for allocating orders to different vendors. For them, the relationship with the vendor—developed over a long period—was paramount. They felt their work ended once they nominated the fabric and provided the order to the vendor. As one sourcing product development manager put it, "Well, I've always worked with that vendor in my five previous jobs, and so that vendor is the best vendor."

An example illustrates the primacy of these vendor relationships. When the reform team showed three pairs of jeans to the product development people for one brand and told them which of their vendors produced them, the product development people would immediately say that the pair made by a particular vendor was of "lower quality." When the same pair of jeans was shown without the vendor identified, the product development people said it was "high quality." Clearly what mattered was prior history and experience with vendors rather than an objective assessment of the quality of the product. Further, as the reform team dug into the mill-level data for the denim category, it became clear that the product development people did not know much about the mill level, a critical gap given how crucial fabric costs were to the final product.

Another problem was that although the product development teams had dealt with the same vendors for many years, the relationship was highly transactional, not a partnership. "We can't do long-term relationships with vendors," a product development manager explained. "We can't lock in pricing for the long term. And we can't index our pricing, because that is not the way the industry works."

The product development managers' reliance on their long (even if transactional) relationships with vendors complemented the siloed way in which the company operated. Competition between Pangia's brands and offices resulted in attitudes exemplified by what one sourcing manager said: "I can't possibly make my jeans at the same factory as [another Pangia brand]."

It was clear to the reform team that, as the supply chain leader put it, "Product development people within sourcing were very internally focused."

It also became clear to the reform team that any change to a more strategic sourcing model unified across all brands for different categories would require a fundamental change of talent from people who had always executed in a transactional way, over and over. The only way to change this was to "divorce the people from product development," said the supply chain leader.

Previously, developing the product and placing it with the vendor was done by product development people. Divorcing those two roles enabled the reform team to hire people from within who truly understood both strategic sourcing and product development. The reformers found there was talent in the company with natural tendencies toward those two different "buckets," but the team also found significant talent gaps in the same buckets.

The reform team focused on trying to inculcate in the product development organization an appreciation for examining and using data to drive sourcing decisions, rather than the transactional model that the organization had used for so many years. As the supply chain leader noted, "It really brought up the question of talent, because clearly the existing talent was not necessarily wired to follow a more data-driven approach."

It was the reform team's effort at mining the data regarding purchasing that brought about a change in thinking, although it took many cycles of product development to get people to appreciate what was wrong with the prior approach. The reformers also faced resistance from design teams, which were not directly involved in sourcing but felt the reform effort's focus on data and costs was "squishing their creativity." The reform team tried to convince design teams that the product quality they were getting was not really "fact-based" in technical terms but mediated by historic relationships with vendors stewarded by product development teams. A member of the reform team told us, "Design people argued that 'you guys don't care about the product.' And the production and sourcing teams kept saying that divorcing product management and sourcing and creating a new model based on categories will not work." Resistance to these changes precipitated a fair number of departures.

The reform effort also involved detailed conversations with the vendors, some of which had been supplying the company for decades. They showed resistance as well. They were not accustomed to think in terms of the long-term relationships the strategic sourcing model demanded. As a member of the reform team explained,

> We created what was called a "proposal," which vendors were asked to fill out. There was much confusion about this process. We built out a grid asking them to cost long term. They were resistant to doing that. The vendors who were closest to our product development and production folks had the biggest "allergic" reaction, but many of our vendors were also "old school." They had built the business on the basis of relationships with sourcing or product people, and did not understand that category management would improve their relationships with the company rather than hurt them.

The reform team spent much time educating vendors, trying to get them to think about costs and to view the process objectively. It took many conversations before vendors became converts. "But some of our larger vendors got it right away," a member of the reform team told us. "With our largest vendor—they moved from us teaching them to them teaching us. With our promise of orders over multiple years, we gave them the economic security to make their business more sustainable."

These conversations with vendors, and the focus on data rather than relationships, were particularly important in convincing vendors of the value of a data-driven approach. For instance, the reform team examined the wovens category and found that one country dominated (Country I). However, that country was performing the worst in terms of delivery times. Looking outside that country revealed that certain factories invariably performed better on delivery times. So, a member of the reform team called a meeting of the Country I–based vendors, provided them with the data, and asked them to improve. This data-driven approach not only revealed that Pangia had problems in the different elements of its sourcing scorecards across the categories and regions but also provided the reform team with the basis for productive conversations with vendors.

Enacting the Change

Despite resistance, the reform team proceeded with the reorganization. Sourcing was reorganized with each category headed by a "category lead," centralized in one or two regions. For example, sourcing for knits would be centralized in Hong Kong, since most vendors were located there or in nearby Vietnam and China. People within the sourcing organization were reassigned to different countries based on their expertise in different categories. Each category team was divided into three subgroups: product development, vendor development, and technical operations. To seed the reorganization further, there was a big investment in cultural training, as many category leads had limited business exposure outside the country of their offices and needed to get out and meet vendors.

Some category leads were more supportive of the new concept than others. As the category lead for sweaters said,

> Each category can have a closer relationship with their vendors, and we can now develop a more strategic relationship with them, and in the next three years, we can use it to consolidate the vendor base. We can potentially work with the vendors to push them to open plants in other countries for mutual business benefits. In the past, we would never have been able to do anything like this. And since we will have a closer relationship with the vendors, we will be better able to discuss sustainability issues with them.

Another sourcing lead for a different category noted,

> For product development staff, it was a huge change. Earlier, they had only one boss and that was within the brand. Now they have two bosses— one a boss in the brand and me. And for me, my product development boss sits in New York, while I am based in Hong Kong. That takes time for them to get used to long-distance reporting relationships. But at the same time, it creates complexity, as you have to deal with different bosses who have very different styles. But the good thing about the category-based management structure is that it represents the creation of one team for each category, whereas before you had several multiple and siloed teams. And now, each person now has a new family, and there is space to grow.

Others were less positive about the introduction of category-based sourcing, even if they agreed with the concept. As a product development manager working for a category lead said,

> It takes a lot of time for this new model to sink in. Right now, I don't see efficiencies within this model. It would be good to have nice tools to support the system. Now these systems do not work well. We have many different tools, and my people are working all night sometimes to figure things out. What we need is one tool to capture everything. And many times, we get inaccurate information on orders and specifications.

The introduction of the reforms appeared to be faster in some places than others. As a product development manager stated, "USA is okay with the system, and maybe Japan, but China, they have a different system and the systems are not aligned for us to use it effectively." Others criticized the process for being "too top-down."

As the reform team reorganized with category leads at the apex of sourcing strategy, they encountered talent problems at the middle level as well. The departure of those who could not "leap across cultures" was no surprise, but the shortage of the right kind of talent was a big surprise. Given the new reporting structure, many were uncomfortable managing teams remotely. And it was difficult to find champions for the new model within the company. As the reform team went to meetings and pushed the advantages of category-based sourcing, they realized increasingly that the talent they needed to introduce the sourcing model effectively and work with the new systems was not quite available in the United States. The skill base for that kind of work existed more in Asia, so they built on that skill base, aggressively hiring sourcing people from diverse companies such as telecommunications and energy, "since," as one team member said, "the concepts underlying our model are not that different from industry to industry."

The transformation to category-based sourcing was a large-scale organizational change process that began in 2012 and took almost seven years to complete. "The patience we had to do it over time, and to do it slowly to accomplish the behavioral shift, was a key element of success," the supply chain leader said. "The category leaders were empowered to rationalize the supply chain and consolidate towards preferred vendors, but it was crucial that we did not ask the category management teams to rationalize their supplier base right away."

Vendor Tiers

Developing criteria for tiering vendors was important and was given a lot of thought. The process first involved collecting data from a vendor. One sourcing manager described it as resembling a request for proposals process with a vendor. The process looked at whether the vendor had the right kinds of machines, whether it was forward-looking in its management attitude, whether there were long-term investment plans, and the vendor's cost structure (to see how competitive it was). Pangia's own product development people would be asked about the vendor to get a sense of the vendor's flexibility, follow-up norms, and communication.

"We started to put the vendors into different 'buckets,'" another sourcing manager explained, "using criteria such as in-house design, price, delivery, clarity of information, transparency, management mindset, market intelligence capacity, and the possibility of co-creation. Some vendors have design capabilities as well, and when they do, we just buy from their line of products."

Explaining other reasons for why Pangia buys from a particular vendor, another sourcing manager said, "We think he's great because he invests more in his people, he is progressive, and he is not only looking for profit but also does some work on the environment. Also, he has more courage to debate with our top management. He has his own perspective."

Thus, the new category leads worked with their teams to do these vendor assessments and create the different buckets into which they would classify vendors. The team collectively decided the weights they assigned to different vendor attributes, but there were no hard-and-fast rules. Senior leadership was open to some groups having different weights. Since the guideline from the top was that Tier 1 vendors could constitute 10 percent of the total vendor base (although this guideline was not always followed), in some categories that 10 percent ended up with 60 percent of Pangia's sourcing.

Category leaders initially categorized all vendors as "Tier 1" even though the grading system allowed for only about 10 percent of all vendors to be so categorized. Tier 2 was expected to have the bulk of the vendors, who would understand they could potentially move to replace Tier 1 vendors. Those in Tier 1 would understand they could be replaced. Tier 3 included specialized vendors for smaller products such as beading. This process of trying to tier vendors took most of the time.

As the category leads began their focus on developing more sustainable long-term relationships with the top-tier vendors, they began to promise commitments beyond one year. In fact, Tier 1 vendors today may get guaranteed order commitments for two to three years—a significant departure from the old transactional model.

A long-term partnership-based relationship is now part of the conversations between Pangia and its vendors, and today fully 50 percent of the company's fabrics platform deals involves those kinds of relationships. This orientation increases the likelihood of vendors investing in their relationship with Pangia. After all, as the supply chain leader noted, "If you think your business is going away next year, why would you invest in it?"

The change is solidified through shared tools that constitute the infrastructure necessary to sustain long-term strategic relationships, such as a customer management software tool that allows for shared planning and a fabric library shared with fabric mills. Vendor dashboards are included in the shared software platform, as are scorecards on price, delivery, and quality, used by both sourcing managers and vendors alike. This platform has led to better management control information, such as underlying commodity prices, and real-time reporting about fabric. As a leader in the sustainability department (the former corporate responsibility department) recounted, "It was interesting that for a large, established company, much of our costing was done in Excel."

The shift to "category-based sourcing" did reduce the head count—savings that were a key part of the business case for rationalizing. But even more important is that category-based sourcing has reduced product costs significantly—an entire quarter's worth of costs saved in one year alone.

Vendor scorecards, initially used primarily to determine whether a vendor should be Tier 1 and receive a long-term order commitment, gradually came to be used to have a data-driven conversation with the vendors and help solidify the shift away from the old transaction-based relationships.

An important consequence of this reform effort, particularly the development of long-term collaborative relationships with vendors and factories, was the possibility of engaging them on compliance issues. The results of the transformation of the company's sourcing model are examined in the next section.

Measuring the Results of the Transformation

To measure the results of Pangia's transformation, we look first at *rationalizing vendors*—the objective of classifying vendors into three categories and using that categorization to develop longer-term relationships. Table 8.1 shows the number of units shipped and the volume of business accounted for by different vendor tiers. Unfortunately, we have data only for three years, because the process of tiering vendors was not completed until 2014. The table suggests the strategy is beginning to work, as Tier 1 vendors have gradually increased their share in both cases—something that should be expected to continue—while Tier 3 vendors accounted for progressively less of the company's orders.[29]

The process of vendor consolidation implies factory consolidation as well, as Pangia deals with factories mostly through its vendors. From 2003 to 2017, the number of factories decreased by 59.5 percent. More important than the steady

TABLE 8.1.   Business volume by vendor tier (in percentages)

YEAR	TIER 1	TIER 2	TIER 3	OTHER
2015	60.5	26.0	10.3	1.4
2016	67.9	17.1	8.5	4.6
2017	67.4	19.7	7.4	3.1

decline in the number of factories with which Pangia was dealing, at least in terms of representing progress toward consolidation and the partnership model, is that a larger percentage of Pangia's products are now being sourced from factories associated with Tier 1 vendors.

Has the consolidation of vendors improved compliance overall? We next look at *compliance performance after consolidation.*

Pangia's auditors typically audit each factory once a year over one or two days, assessing the factory on about seven hundred different items. Audits result in a compliance score and action plan for remediation that are communicated to the factories. Over time, the scoring has become more stringent. Before 2015, the top score of 100 would be reduced by deductions for violations that differed depending on their severity and whether they had occurred more than once. The overall rating would lead to classification as A, B, C, or D (a failing grade) based on different total point thresholds. The scoring system was further altered in 2015 to be even more stringent, and was collapsed into three classes: A (good factories); B (factories that need improvement); and C (failing factories requiring immediate action).

With a smaller number of factories, a more stringent scoring system, and deeper relationships, we would expect to see improvements in compliance scores. Table 8.2 reports the distribution of factories based on their compliance scores. The data from 2016 onward are relevant here given the tweak in the scoring system in 2015.

As table 8.2 indicates, the percentage of A-grade factories has changed over time, showing increases after 2016. There are three things to note about the data in table 8.2. First, there has been an increase in the percentage of A-grade factories in Asia and, particularly, in the Europe/Middle East region, but not in the Americas. To some extent, the decline in the Americas is explained by the change in sourcing strategy and consolidation. Second, the percentage of B-grade factories has also increased over time, particularly in the Americas and Asia. Finally, and most important, the percentage of factories classified as C-grade reduced dramatically in all regions. This reduction is the best indicator that the strategy was beginning to work.

TABLE 8.2.   Share of factories in regions by compliance rating (in percentages)

FACTORY RATINGS	2015	2016	2017	2018
ASIA				
A grade	40.4	31	27.5	31.5
B grade	37.1	47.1	58	61.9
C grade	22.5	22	14.5	6.5
EUROPE AND MIDDLE EAST				
A grade	29.6	56.4	52.3	61.3
B grade	37	23.1	43.2	35.5
C grade	33.3	20.5	4.5	3.2
AMERICAS				
A grade	59.1	75	59	57.8
B grade	30.3	15.6	25.6	37.8
C grade	10.6	9.4	15.4	4.4

PROGRESS ON SPECIFIC COMPLIANCE ISSUES

While factory scores have improved, it is instructive to look at improvement across the different compliance categories. Table 8.3 reports progress on selected specific categories of provisions of the company's code of vendor conduct.

Table 8.3 presents longitudinal data on the number of violations *per audit* for each of four categories: labor, working conditions, compliance with laws, and environmental effects. Note the varying numbers for each until 2016. Note as well the very steady decline after 2016 in the violations per audit in all four categories. Thus, after the more stringent tweak to the compliance scoring system in 2015–2016, there is significant progress.

THE ALIGNMENT OF SOURCING AND COMPLIANCE

The company had, through its reform efforts, created the organizational climate to align sourcing and compliance more effectively. As noted earlier, the scorecards were a starting point for real conversations with vendors. To examine whether these efforts resulted in a more formal linkage between sourcing and compliance, we looked at orders given to suppliers, measured by supplier shipments to Pangia. If there was a formal integration between sourcing and compliance, we would expect to see A-grade factories getting more orders and C-grade factories getting fewer orders.

This process of aligning sourcing with compliance is ongoing. Table 8.4 shows some of the results. As the system has "settled," A-grade factories have accounted for an increasing proportion of units shipped, while C-grade factories' share has steadily declined. This is the picture we would expect to see if compliance and sourcing were becoming more closely linked.

TABLE 8.3. Progress on compliance for specific categories: number of violations per audit

CATEGORY	2010	2011	2012	2013	2014	2015	2016	2017	2018
Labor	5.95	7.29	8.05	8.99	9.16	9.16	10.17	9.55	8.65
Working conditions	4.74	5.80	6.74	7.01	6.43	6.07	6.48	5.78	5.90
Compliance with laws	2.37	2.94	3.06	3.25	2.85	2.85	2.98	2.58	1.84
Environment	1.53	1.77	1.74	1.60	1.44	1.49	1.88	1.71	1.50

Clearly, Pangia's efforts in creating the climate for integration of sourcing and compliance had not borne fruit during the 2013–2016 period. C-grade factories still shipped more orders than A-grade factories in 2015, for example. The primary explanation for data from the earlier period is that while category management had been institutionalized, the linkage between compliance and sourcing had not. The data-driven approach and the use of scorecards promoted conversations with vendors, but decisions were still being taken by category teams were still taking decisions without adequate attention to compliance information. There was still some ambivalence among category leads about taking compliance into account, as the following comments capture.

On the positive side, a category lead told us,

> We know that compliance is part of the dashboard and we use it. I tell my vendors that if they make a mistake with sustainability issues, we will move the business. I recently did that with one of our Hong Kong vendors. He did not make improvements for ten years, and in the past we protected him; we were from the Hong Kong office and we wanted to protect the vendor. But under category management, our sourcing is more global as we have gotten rid of geographies.

Also on the positive side is this view from the then VP of sustainability, who noted:

> The long-term business relationships will make the vendor make improvements, too, in terms of compliance. It is like a journey for them to go along with us. In the past, we spent more time on auditing these vendors, but now we will spend less time on auditing and bring in other elements such as capacity building. As we hive off some of the auditing to Better Work, it will leave our compliance team to invest more in assessments and capacity building.

A senior director of sustainability noted further that the shift to category-based sourcing was not as big a change for sustainability personnel as it was for the

TABLE 8.4. Toward alignment: proportion of average units shipped by factories

GRADE	2014	2015	2016	2017	2018
A grade factories	24.04	29.95	33.29	38.80	43.31
B grade factories	21.51	31.07	28.95	25.10	26.20
C grade factories	35.41	34.31	29.24	30.73	23.09

sourcing people, as compliance always functioned as a category of its own. "But we are equal to them in many ways," he added. "If we find egregious issues with a factory, we can revoke approval status, and sourcing cannot question that decision. But we don't want to use that power or overuse it, so we work with sourcing folks. What the shift in category management has accomplished for the compliance organization is that it is much easier for our voice to be heard."

Earlier on in the process, it was clear that the dashboards were not being used systematically, and that some factories were being dropped primarily because of price issues. While that is changing, there is still some ambivalence, as can be seen in a comment from a compliance team member: "But the most compliant member is not necessarily the best vendor. For example, we have a Korean vendor who is very high on compliance, but our Indian vendor [in the same category] is a better vendor when looked at more holistically."

A sustainability leader told me during our 2017 interview in 2017 that he felt more confident that the linkage between sourcing and compliance would manifest itself more clearly as time went on, and the data for 2017 and 2018 in table 8.4 appear to confirm his prediction. This sense of confidence had much to do with what had been accomplished during the 2013–2016 period. The basic architecture supporting category-based sourcing had been institutionalized. Pangia had made progress in concentrating its business with preferred vendors and factories. The software infrastructure created in support of category-based sourcing had enabled the company to create internal systems to develop a closer partnership between supplier sustainability, global supply chain, and data insights teams. Dedicated compliance teams had been created to assist factories to remedy code of conduct violations. These teams met monthly to evaluate progress toward compliance goals and figure out how to help "lagging" facilities, through training and education as well as implementing proactive measures to prevent violations. Since the sustainability teams now were tracking data by category as well as by country, the sustainability teams could better engage category leads and sourcing personnel within category teams. And those people began to be trained on labor standards and human rights issues.

Another indicator of the vice president of sustainability's confidence is the goal set by Pangia that it would *no longer* work with any C-grade factories by 2020.

Not only would the company remediate or cut C-grade factories from the existing chain; Pangia would no longer allow C-grade factories to be approved for production. Previously, the company would have allowed C-grade factories if they agreed to address the issues in question within a certain time frame. Now, after an initial assessment of a new factory, the supplier sustainability team would work with factory management to develop a time-bound corrective action plan and evaluate the factory again at the end of the agreed-upon time frame to determine whether the required remediation had been achieved, *before* the factory was approved as a supplier.

At the overall company level, Pangia had achieved a linkage between its sourcing and compliance, as indicated in table 8.4. Although we do not have newer data, it is clear that the trend is in the right direction, and more compliant factories are getting more orders, indicative of an increasingly tight coupling between sourcing and compliance.

COUNTRY DIFFERENCES

Although these results indicate that Pangia is moving in the right direction, we thought it instructive to look underneath the global data and assess trends in the different sourcing countries, given the history of country- or region-based sourcing teams under the old sourcing system. In other words, is there any evidence of differential progress across countries that could be related to vestigial relationships in the past? Hence, we look at the alignment of sourcing and compliance in terms of units shipped by different factories. Table 8.5 reports these results.

The data in table 8.5 present a mixed picture. Good progress in alignment would require a picture of steadily increasing sourcing volumes from A- and B-grade factories and steadily declining sourcing from C-grade factories. In terms of the proportion of total units (for that country) shipped by different classes of factories, the data for Bangladesh, Indonesia, and Sri Lanka conform to that picture. China shows an increase in sourcing from B-grade factories, and a decline from C-grade factories, but also a decline in sourcing from A-grade factories. India is an outlier in that sourcing from C-grade factories appear to have increased. What this country-level analysis indicates is that Pangia still has some way to go before achieving a full and sustained link between sourcing and compliance. It has achieved that link overall, but there is variation across specific countries.

Conclusion

A key component of private regulation is the requirement to link compliance with sourcing. The case study of Pangia, a global retailer that attempted to

TABLE 8.5. Proportion of factory's average units shipped by grade rating (in percentages)

	2014	2015	2016	2017	2018
INDONESIA					
A grade	25.7	42.7	32.4	35.4	32.5
B grade	13.9	35.6	28.0	20.9	44.9
C grade	60.4	21.7	39.6	43.6	22.6
SRI LANKA	2014	2015	2016	2017	2018
A grade	21.6	30.4	20.7	57.8	39.9
B grade	34.0	60.2	13.4	42.2	60.1
C grade	44.4	9.3	65.9	N/A	N/A
VIETNAM	2014	2015	2016	2017	2018
A grade	40.1	44.3	39.2	59.0	67.1
B grade	19.2	21.9	29.3	30.2	16.5
C grade	40.7	33.9	31.4	10.8	16.4
BANGLADESH	2014	2015	2016	2017	2018
A grade	11.4	12.7	18.3	16.1	19.7
B grade	42.1	53.3	28.0	19.1	47.2
C grade	46.5	34.0	53.7	64.8	33.1
CHINA	2014	2015	2016	2017	2018
A grade	37.4	33.1	35.8	40.7	33.3
B grade	42.2	41.5	35.8	34.9	44.1
C grade	20.4	25.4	28.4	24.5	22.7
INDIA	2014	2015	2016	2017	2018
A grade	11.5	23.6	10.9	7.0	20.4
B grade	62.2	22.4	32.7	46.5	26.8
C grade	26.3	54.0	56.4	46.5	52.8

align sourcing and compliance, offers some lessons that may be useful to other firms.

First, the case implies that it is highly unlikely large companies' compliance departments can establish the linkage between compliance and sourcing on their own. It is rare to find compliance departments with the power to compel sourcing departments to do so. In Pangia's case, the linkage was made possible because the company was under pressure to reform *sourcing* for business reasons (cost optimization, building better relationships with suppliers), and such reforms permitted the possibility of aligning compliance with sourcing. Thus, linking compliance with sourcing was a key benefit of reforming sourcing. A key ingredient that helped such alignment was Pangia's new strategy of developing long-term relationships with its suppliers as the company consolidated the supply chain.

Second, it is worth noting that the linkage would not have been possible had it not been for a well-developed compliance system already operating for many years with a high profile in the corporate organization. The implication is that well-developed compliance systems are a necessary, even if insufficient, condition for the linkage between sourcing and compliance.

Third, developing a software architecture that included comprehensive supplier scorecards facilitated linking compliance with sourcing. Those scorecards—which resulted from collaborative decision making by category teams that included sourcing, product development, and sustainability—made it possible to take factory ratings (compliance) into account. While our data in table 8.5 show that it was not always taken into account in sourcing decisions in different regions, including compliance in the scorecards meant it nonetheless needed to be discussed within the category team. The inclusion of compliance was reinforced by the belief within senior management that compliance could also be a source of sustainable competitive advantage.

Fourth, the Pangia case highlights the transactional mentality that permeates sourcing operations in the apparel industry. Pangia was able to get compliance into the equation only when the company succeeded in changing that mentality to a mindset based on building long-term "developmental" relationships with suppliers.

Fifth, the Pangia case makes clear that changing the transactional mentality may well require a change of talent. It may be necessary to recruit the necessary talent to make the new model of sourcing effective. Pangia's senior managers continually highlighted the difficulty of finding appropriate talent, especially people who could develop and use data-driven analytics that would feed into sourcing decisions and who wanted to work in the apparel industry. After all, as the supply chain leader noted, "Why would young graduates trained in data analytics join apparel firms when they can work at Google?"

Sixth, benchmarking with firms outside the industry was crucial for learning new lessons. As the supply chain leader who masterminded this organizational transformation told us, "Apparel only talks to apparel." In reforming its sourcing model, Pangia drew inspiration from other industries in which such relationships are common, such as electronics and automobiles. It is unlikely Pangia would have changed on its own had it not benchmarked with firms in other sectors.

The final lesson is that vendors *will* respond to incentives to change their behavior. There is a tendency in the industry for brand representatives to castigate vendors and factories as the source of the problems and resistant to new ways of working. The academic literature also tends to view suppliers as part of the problem. The Pangia case shows that vendors are able to appreciate and respond to the right incentives to develop long-term relationships that promote mutual gain. In fact, it was Pangia's sourcing model that was the source of the problem, driven by its sourcing practices that induced internal competition between its offices and external competition among vendors. Once the company changed that system, establishing long-term developmental relationships with vendors became possible.

Instituting organizational change efforts creates real challenges for companies. It can take a lot of time before there is success. But as the Pangia case shows, aligning sourcing and compliance is possible. The key is to get sourcing people to drive or be partners in the change effort.

FROM OPACITY TO TRANSPARENCY

Pathways to Improvement of Private Regulation

The first two chapters of this final section of the book have examined the potential of new developments in corporate governance in the form of so-called benefit corporations and the potential to integrate company purchasing practices with their private regulation efforts—both with the aim of enhancing compliance and workers' lives in the global supply chain. This final chapter of part 3 is about the ways in which the private regulation ecosystem can be transformed from opacity into transparency.

In general, the decoupling of the private regulation policies and practices adopted by companies from outcomes for workers can be traced to the *opaque* nature of the institutional field of private regulation.[1] The decoupling perspective can serve as a holistic theoretical lens through which to view private regulation, one that offers a more *systemic* explanation for the decoupling of private regulation policies and practices from outcomes. This explanation goes beyond simply blaming the lack of progress with private regulation on companies' symbolic adoption of policies as an image-building or risk-minimization strategy. While symbolic adoption may be the case with some companies, many others have clearly introduced and enacted practices to improve labor standards without achieving the expected outcomes.

The key implication of the *systemic* explanation is that it illuminates why companies continue to engage in the practice of auditing even if it does not lead to the desired outcomes: when the means and ends are unclear, technical procedures such as auditing become "ends in themselves."[2] To solve the problem of decoupling between practices and outcomes and thus make private regulation more effective, the opaque institutional field of private regulation must be made more transparent.

The coupling of policies, practices, and worker outcomes necessitates overcoming the barriers to compliance that exist in opaque institutional fields: the lack of knowledge, attention, and motivation caused by causal complexity, behavioral invisibility, and practice multiplicity.[3] Private regulation actors have always assumed that adopting and implementing a private regulation program would achieve improved working conditions. However, given that practice multiplicity, behavioral invisibility, and causal complexity "obscure the design and implementation" of private regulation programs, actors need to find ways to move the organizational field from opacity to transparency, which involves new ways of thinking and acting. For example, causal complexity requires a high degree of clarity with consistent and uniform rules, but implementation is made difficult by the substantial variation across the contexts in which private regulation operates and the fact that many issues are highly context specific (such as social insurance rules in China). Solutions to compliance problems need to vary according to institutional conditions in different locations.

The adoption of uniform rules essentially results in a trade-off: standardization may solve the problem of policy-practice decoupling but may not solve the problem of means-ends decoupling. These types of trade-offs are a key characteristic of fields with a high degree of opacity. Three interrelated ways to prevent such trade-offs have been suggested: create collaborative niche institutions, internalize private regulation goals, and foster a systematic mindset.[4] Together, they constitute the first steps toward creating a more transparent institutional field or ecosystem.

Create Collaborative Niche Institutions

The current tendency in private regulation is to shift to "universal" rules, exemplified by efforts by the Social and Labor Convergence Project to create a uniform audit protocol, or by the new "mandatory due diligence" legislation currently being considered by the European Union. Rules and solutions, however, must be "place conscious," tailored to specific contexts—countries, provinces, and other geographic entities.[5] There must be a way to transfer broad principles to unique approaches and practices that work in specific contexts. *Niche institutions* provide a way to strike a balance between universality and context specificity, but they will work only if there is significant collaboration among the actors.

What is a context-specific niche institution? The Accord on Fire and Building Safety in Bangladesh (the "Accord") and its sibling organization the Alliance for

Bangladesh Worker Safety (the "Alliance") are two examples. Both involve collaboration between global brands to improve safety in Bangladesh factories.

The coalition to create the Accord was led by different actors in the private regulation ecosystem: union federations (e.g., IndustriALL Global Union), critical NGOs (e.g., Oxfam), monitoring organizations (e.g., Workers Rights Consortium), and of course global brands sourcing from Bangladesh. Signed in 2013 by 222 global firms covering 1,600 factories in Bangladesh, the original Accord ended in 2018. A new, transitional Accord was signed in 2018 by 190 corporate signatories, encompassing 1,672 factories.[6]

Does this niche institution work? There is no question the Accord is making progress toward eliminating risks to workers in terms of building safety and fire hazards. By the time the first Accord ended in 2018, 85 percent of the safety hazards identified in initial inspections had been fixed, 150 factories had completed the safety remediation, and another 857 had completed more than 90 percent of the remediation required. Approximately 1.4 million workers had been trained on workplace safety, safe evacuation, and their rights under the Accord, while 891 joint labor-management committees had undergone safety training, with 239 committees completing the program.

Similarly, the Alliance (comprising twenty-nine companies) reported successes by the time it ceased operations in December 2018. Covering 1.3 million workers, 93 percent of the 714 Alliance factories had completed remediation, and 428 factories achieved completion of their corrective action plans; 1.6 million workers were trained on fire safety, a confidential 24-hour hotline was established and continues to operate, and worker safety committees are operating in 181 factories.

Admittedly, there is debate regarding the pace of progress, efficiency, and the number of Bangladeshi factories that are actually covered under the Accord.[7] Particularly now that the new one has commenced, there is a need for more critical evaluation of the Accord. But it must be acknowledged that this niche institution has reported some clear improvements in safety—and it is a strong example of what is being advocated here.

Niche institutions can work when there is a *supportive infrastructure*; for the Accord, that was the Bangladesh Accord Foundation. It supported the signatories in implementing the agreement by actually carrying out the inspections, monitoring remediation progress, reporting on progress in a transparent manner, providing training for safety committees, and operating a safety complaints mechanism. These collaborative arrangements also need to set *clear rules and expectations*. In this case, brands were required to disclose their factory lists, ensure their factories participated, and negotiate commercial terms to ensure it was financially feasible for factories to comply with safety and remediation requirements. Brands were expected to fulfill their Accord funding commitments while also making a commitment to preserve their supplier relationships for the duration of the Accord. That commitment struck at the tendency of firms to "cut and run" and provided the necessary longer-term horizon within which improvements could be made.

The key *catalyst* for the Accord was the Rana Plaza factory fire, which galvanized collaboration among the brands and resulted in the binding agreement with the unions. All niche institutions need catalysts in addition to supportive infrastructure. Of course, we should not be waiting for the next disaster that kills workers; we need other catalysts. Global brands, national governments, and critical NGOs can perform the necessary catalyzing function.

The Indonesian Freedom of Association protocol is another example of a niche institution. Its catalyst was the release of a critical report prior to the 2008 Beijing Olympic Games that denounced the violations of freedom of association and collective bargaining rights in global supply chains. This report spurred the June 2008 meeting between the Playfair Alliance[8] and major sportswear brands in Hong Kong.[9] At the meeting, Adidas representative Bill Anderson proposed a pilot national-level dialogue in Indonesia. After eighteen months of negotiations, a multiparty agreement was signed in June 2011 between six global brands (Adidas, Puma, Nike, New Balance, Asics and Pentland), 73 Indonesia-based suppliers to those brands (mostly Korean and Taiwanese owned), two global union federations (IndustriALL and ITUC), and five Indonesian union federations (SPN, KASBI, Garteks-SBSI, GSBI, and FSPTSK).[10] After another eight months, final "rules" were agreed upon.

Like the Accord, the Freedom of Association Protocol also sets clear rules and expectations. Suppliers are required to implement the protocol as a minimum workplace standard, and brands must ensure adoption of provisions by all first-tier suppliers and encourage adoption by second-tier suppliers. The protocol also outlines clear rules regarding unfair employer practices and union representatives' rights for time off to carry out their union duties. There is a supportive infrastructure of factory-level committees, as well as a national-level committee with representatives from each union, each brand and designated supplier, and NGOs.[11]

However, a more critical evaluation of the progress made by the Freedom of Association Protocol highlights several issues that create barriers to the long-term sustainability of the effort.[12] These issues include considerable tension between employers and unions during the protocol's implementation, modest institutional funding that is in jeopardy, and a lack of sustained engagement from all parties. The program comes under criticism for the relatively few global companies participating. The report emphasizes the need for "sustained, strategic collaboration among all actors and strategic monitoring and campaigning to extend the protocol" for it to build on its initial (fragile) success.

The Action, Collaboration, Transformation (ACT) initiative, a third example of a collaborative niche institution that is under development, aims to secure living wages for workers in garment supply chains through industry-wide collective bargaining integrated with reformed purchasing practices by participating global brands. Specifically, ACT requires that its member companies commit to (1) their purchasing prices including wages as an itemized cost that is consistent with the ACT labor costing protocol (which is detailed on ACT's website); (2) fair terms of payment; (3) better planning and forecasting regarding purchasing, to enable suppliers to plan capacity better; (4) providing their own employees with better training in planning and forecasting; and (5) responsible exit strategies when member companies decide to stop sourcing from factories. ACT applies to Cambodia, Bangladesh, Turkey, and Myanmar, where there is some form of collective bargaining at the industry level. ACT requires that member companies commit to source from these countries for a defined period of time and develop long-term partnerships with suppliers there.[13]

ACT was cofounded in 2015 by fifteen global apparel companies and the IndustriALL Global Union. The fifteen global apparel companies were members of the Accord (discussed earlier); the Ethical Trading Initiative, a multi-stakeholder institution based in the United Kingdom that includes unions on its governing board; or both. The key catalyst to ACT's formation was the experience of face-to-face relationships that built trust among apparel brands and between them and the IndustriaALL labor union under the Accord, coupled with the fact that apparel companies' inability to deliver on their promise to pay living wages was tarnishing their reputations.[14] Although ACT has yet to realize its objectives, it may yet become an effective niche institution.

The case study of practice multiplicity in chapter 2 serves to highlight further where collaborative niche institutions are necessary. The case study involved a large supplier serving more than seventy brands, each of which took a different approach to private regulation and used a vastly different set of rating scales, meaning that the supplier *simultaneously* received ratings of "good" and "poor" from different brands. The case illustrates the role a niche institution could play in ensuring that all the brands sourcing from that large supplier follow a uniform approach. Where there is at present no coordination among the brands sourcing from this factory, those brands could reap numerous benefits from collaborating and coordinating with one another, such as a common approach to auditing, acceptance of each other's audits, and perhaps even an agreement on paying wages consistent with their codes of conduct. Such collaboration and coordination would resolve the problem of practice multiplicity, allowing the brands sourcing from that factory to share best practices. Coordination would mitigate the problem caused by excessive heterogeneity among the buyers' private regulation programs.

In the particular case described in chapter 2, the supplier did make efforts to encourage its global buyers to work together. The different brands' corporate policies, however, did not appear to permit formal or informal coordination.

Niche institutions at a regional level are also recommended. In most countries, garment manufacturing is clustered around certain regions. Take the large garment clusters in Tiruppur and Ludhiana in India. Both have cluster-level institutions, but there are no formal institutional vehicles through which the global brands can coordinate and collaborate. Cluster offices, staffed by a cluster manager, could play a "midwife" function to bring together the different brands sourcing from Ludhiana or Tiruppur to create a niche institution.

China presents difficulties with auditing wages, hours, and benefits. Global buyers—apparel and home retailing companies—could establish niche institutions in the form of regional or provincial consortia *with* their suppliers to devise effective auditing.[15]

Niche institutions promote *collaboration in a competitive environment*, and in this way overcome the lack of collaboration between global brands that has been consistently identified as an obstacle to realizing sustainable improvements in labor practices in global supply chains. We need more such institutions at the supplier level, at local and regional levels, and at national levels. A geographic and institutional boundary to such institutions is crucial to ensure "place-conscious" solutions. The key, of course, is to identify potential *catalysts* for these efforts.

Stimulate Internalization of Private Regulation Goals

A second way to move the field from opacity to transparency requires that the institutional entrepreneurs (actors who were instrumental in developing private regulation initiatives) not only internalize the goals of private regulation programs themselves but also stimulate such internalization among other actors in the ecosystem. This is a key recommendation, stemming from the institutionalist perspective used here, to decrease opacity and the trade-offs between the two forms of decoupling.[16] Niche institutions may also contribute to such internalization, of course, but all the actors in the ecosystem need to find ways to stimulate internalization of the goals of private regulation among their constituents.

Global Companies

Most global companies do not exhibit the internalization of private regulation program goals within the boundaries of their organization. This is most commonly observed through the lack of integration, or even connection, between sourcing departments and compliance departments in global companies with private regulation programs (as shown in chapter 8). All too commonly, compliance staff do not even have access to their company's sourcing information.

Integrating sourcing and compliance efforts within corporations is crucial to the success of private regulation because sourcing practices are often a key reason, if not *the* reason, for compliance violations, particularly when it comes to working hours, overtime, and subcontracting. The Pangia case in chapter 8 shows how unlikely it is that integrating of sourcing and compliance functions could be brought about by compliance staff alone. That company needed the leadership of the sourcing department to achieve integration. But the effort does not end there: related corporate departments have also failed to internalize the goals. In my conversations with compliance staff in several companies, I have heard many accounts of how finance departments have failed to provide sufficient budgets for compliance departments' efforts to expand or improve their current private regulation programs.

Early efforts to promote the internalization of private regulation goals by all employees in global corporations have relied on the CEO communicating the importance of corporate social responsibility efforts to all employees and ensuring that the head of CSR or compliance held a sufficiently senior position in the corporation, perhaps reporting directly to the CEO. At both Nike and New Balance, it was important that the chief CSR officer report directly to the CEO to ensure that the function had the access and influence necessary to accomplish its goals.[17] Organizational structure, though, is typically insufficient for overcoming internal opposition and ensuring everyone will internalize the goals of private regulation. As New Balance's vice president of responsible leadership and global compliance said, "Marrying sourcing and compliance data could be seen as intrusive oversight—restricting sourcing decisions and operational flexibility, or adding unnecessary work, or even as a power grab."[18] Therefore, more attention must be paid to systems such as performance management. As long as sourcing managers are rewarded for obtaining products at the highest quality and cheapest price, and compliance managers are rewarded for compliance improvements, there can never be internalization.

Another case study of a company that tried to integrate sourcing and compliance found no connection at all between orders and the compliance record of suppliers.[19] The researchers attributed that disconnection to difficulties in flexibly adjusting order volumes and obtaining compliance information. Many of the supplier factories were producing a single product for the company, which made it difficult to drop factories because of poor compliance and replace them. The company also typically accounted for only a small portion of the production volume of each supplier factory; the company had to place a minimum order just to ensure the factory would reserve capacity for the company's orders in the following season, even if the compliance record of that factory was not adequate. Finally, placing an order required considerable coordination across a number of different departments, often under extreme time pressure, so that the transaction costs of an integrated approach were seen by many to outweigh the benefits—especially by sourcing staff who did not see compliance as central to their roles. Clearly, organizational systems and processes are necessary to support internalization.

Embedding compliance and sourcing within the same function shows promise. Pangia's strategic shift to category-based sourcing created new structures that integrated sourcing and compliance at the category level; over time, albeit with a few hiccups, that approach began to show results.

Multi-stakeholder Institutions

Multi-stakeholder institutions can better stimulate internalization of private regulation goals by increasing the stringency of their selection processes for new members and having more rigorous socialization processes for them.[20] MSIs such as the Fair Labor Association (FLA), Fair Wear Foundation (FWF), and the Ethical Trading Initiative (ETI) all have selection and socialization procedures for their members, while SA8000 has a process for suppliers that it certifies.

For example, ETI requires its members to meet standards that demonstrate a commitment to ethical trade, integrate ethical trade into their core business practices, drive year-to-year improvements in working conditions, support suppliers to make improvements through training and capacity building, and report openly and accurately about their activities. Member companies must submit an annual report to ETI.

ETI, however, does not require its members to disclose publicly how they are meeting these requirements. Hence, the extent to which ETI member companies have integrated sourcing and compliance practices is unknown, as is whether member companies are able to institute year-to-year improvements in factory working conditions, as well as the extent to which ETI members have internalized ETI's goals for private regulation. But if working conditions in their supply chains were significantly improved as a result of following ETI's requirements, it is safe to assume that member companies would be trumpeting these successes publicly, with comprehensive supporting data, to the private regulation ecosystem. ETI members do not do this on their own websites, and neither does ETI disclose the extent to which its members' private regulation programs are actually improving workers' lives.

The FLA requires its members to commit to the FLA principles of "fair labor and responsible sourcing" and adopt the FLA Code of Conduct. FWF has requirements similar to those of ETI. But we have no information about how these MSI's actually select members, and relatively little information regarding how they evaluate members' progress on their private regulation goals, or the process by which members are held accountable for progress (or lack thereof). Certainly, these MSI's all have evaluation procedures, some carried out by MSI officials and others by a committee of peer members, but the contents of these evaluations are, in the best tradition of private regulation, "confidential" and shrouded in secrecy. FLA does publish the results of audits for a percentage of its members' supplier factories on its website, and this is a good example of reporting on outcomes, but as noted they only do so for a small percentage of member factories. FWF publishes on its website annual "brand performance checks" regarding how well its member brands are doing in terms of policies and systems in their private regulation programs. This is useful, as it provides some indication of whether members' policies and practices are improving over time, but it does not report the outcomes for workers' data that are needed. Thus, although FWF and FLA provide a little more information compared to ETI, it is still not enough to understand whether their members have internalized the goals of private regulation.

There are, of course, ways in which MSIs could make their selection criteria more stringent. For instance, similar to what was described in our Pangia case, an MSI could require its members to completely integrate sourcing and compliance *as a condition of membership*, perhaps within three years of joining. Evidence that a member has integrated sourcing and compliance would constitute evidence of internalization. For instance, the ETI code requires paying living wages in the supply chain. It is important that ETI holds members accountable for progress toward that goal. As of this writing, there is absolutely no evidence that any ETI member is paying living wages in its global supply chain in the apparel industry.

It is not clear how ETI addresses its members' failure to do so or what the consequences of that failure might be for their continued membership in ETI. H&M, a member of ETI, made an explicit commitment to pay living wages in its supply chain by 2018, but it is far from being realized (see chapter 5). In theory, ETI could require that companies pay living wages within a certain number of years of joining, which would add a level of stringency to its selection procedures and stimulate internalization of the living wage goal among its members.

What might discourage MSIs from making their selection criteria more stringent? MSIs must strike a delicate balance between their financial survival and their efforts to improve working conditions in their member companies' supply chains. Since MSIs depend on the fees paid by their members to sustain their activities, adopting more stringent standards threatens their financial viability. Having overly stringent entry requirements and progress requirements, and very strict evaluation standards, could deter companies from joining or might even encourage them to leave. Similarly, expelling members for not showing sufficient progress might result in a steady outflow of members. This might explain why the aggregate data presented in chapter 4 indicates "middling" progress on code of conduct items generally.

There is a direct correlation between the stringency of MSI standards and the size of membership; the Business Social Compliance Initiative (BSCI), widely perceived to have the "least stringent" standards, has four times the membership of the FLA and eight times the membership of ETI, both of whose standards are relatively more stringent.[21] Hence, there are pragmatic limits to stricter selection and evaluation procedures for members of MSIs. But there is some leeway for more stringent *accountability* of member performance among MSIs.

Suppliers

To reduce overall opacity and the trade-off between the two types of decoupling, it is also important that suppliers internalize the private regulation goals of the global companies they supply. Without that commitment, improvements in the working conditions in supplier factories are unlikely.

Given the generally adversarial relationship between buyers and suppliers in the global apparel industry, however, it is difficult to see how this might happen. Buyers and suppliers often have different interests that provoke "mixed, often contradictory behaviors"; buyers want suppliers to invest to improve labor standards but also consistently "squeeze" suppliers for lower prices for their products, prompting suppliers to perhaps hide or falsify compliance data.[22] For this reason, the process of auditing has often been referred to as a "cat and mouse game" in which auditors chase elusive data, managers often offer nontransparent records, and workers are coached to give answers.[23] The empirical evidence in chapter 1 substantiates this characterization: data in roughly 45.11 percent of more than forty thousand audits conducted in 2011–2017 across twelve countries and thirteen different industries had been falsified or were of questionable accuracy.

The only way suppliers will internalize their buyers' private regulation program goals is through incentives. Global companies will have to reward suppliers for complying—and not necessarily in the form of paying a higher price for products. Incentives can take the form of long-term collaborative and partnership-based relationships that provide suppliers with longer-term orders. As the global supplier of seventy brands discussed in chapter 2 lamented, even relationships with buyers of more than fifteen years lacked coupling between auditing and sourcing practices, and long-standing customers would often defect after placing orders. The lack of stability makes it difficult to continuously improve compliance and outcomes for workers. The case study of HomeRetailer in chapter 4 shows that compliance improvement among suppliers can occur. In this case, the retailer adopted a strict requirement with respect to supplier compliance, but guaranteed it would source from the supplier until it met the compliance targets over a five-year period.

Pangia's efforts (chapter 8) show it is indeed possible to develop stable, long-term collaborative relations with suppliers. Not only were Pangia's suppliers guaranteed long-term orders with firm commitments for three years, but the company shared software with suppliers so they could jointly plan production. In effect, Pangia rationalized its supply chain to deal with a smaller number of vendors but deepened its relationship with those vendors to create a partnership model that positively affected compliance. This example demonstrates the utility of partnership-based buyer-supplier relationships in encouraging suppliers to internalize the goals of buyers' private regulation practices. Nike and New Balance are among the companies that have been moving in a direction similar to Pangia's approach.

Workers in the Supply Chain

One way for adopters of private regulation such as global companies to stimulate the internalization of private regulation goals among their supplier factories is to involve factory workers in the achievement of those goals. The private regulation model as currently practiced does not incorporate a clear role for workers in supplier factories. But workers in supplier factories are the *most* knowledgeable about the very working conditions codes of conduct are designed to improve. Workers' knowledge and experience needs to be harnessed.

Why does this design flaw exist? It is likely that initial adopters of the private regulation model in the early 1990s (e.g., Nike, Adidas, Gap Inc.) assumed workers would have a voice in improving working conditions through labor unions or workplace-level committees, since most codes required respect for freedom of association and introduced such committees in one form or another. This assumption, though, was unwarranted: unionization and other representative structures are few and far between in most garment-exporting countries (see chapter 6), and where they do exist, worker committees and other forms of parallel representation have not really equipped workers with a voice in global supply chains.[24]

Another explanation is that early adopters felt workers would be rendered incapable of providing input, partly because of employer intimidation. There is

considerable evidence that workers who must be interviewed at the factory by auditors are intimidated or coached by employers to provide "desirable" answers
to auditors. One study of Vietnam suggests workers are quite willing to cooper-
ate with management to provide desirable answers and hide compliance violations, as long as management negotiates with them on more important issues such
as pay and working hours.[25]

How, then, can workers provide input for improving compliance? There have
long been calls for auditors to interview workers off-site. These offsite interviews
would allow the auditors more freedom to probe in certain areas, although it is
not always easy to obtain worker addresses. But few audit guidance documents
require these offsite interviews. The online audit guidance document for Social
Compliance Auditors developed by the ISEAL Alliance, for instance, includes no
such provision, nor does Amfori BSCI's auditing. By contrast, the Supplier Ethical Data Exchange (Sedex) has extensive guidelines for its Sedex Members Ethical Trade Audit (SMETA) and highlights the need to interview workers without
management representatives present and where management cannot even watch
the interview. But while the guidance document suggests off-site interviews may
be appropriate in certain cases, they are not required.

The Fair Wear Foundation implemented a requirement for its auditors to conduct off-site worker interviews in communities where they live and, where possible, for these interviews to take place in advance of the factory audit. FWF also
requires its auditors to interview other stakeholders such as local trade union leaders, municipal officials with knowledge of the factory, and others.

I analyzed FWF's offsite worker interviews and found them to be a valuable
complement to audit reports (which include on-site interviews). The interviews
did vary, though. Off-site interviews with Bulgarians were very detailed, giving a
vicarious sense of what it meant to work in the factory to a greater degree than
the audit report. These interviews provided a holistic, qualitative picture of the
climate in the workplace that helped make sense of the audit report. Off-site interviews with workers in an Indian factory, in contrast, simply mirrored the results in the audit report.

Beyond audit interviews, *hotlines* can inform and improve private regulation
with workers' views. Workers call a hotline with a complaint about a code violation, and a mobile monitoring platform such as LaborLink allows global brands
to see the information in real time on their dashboards, gradually building up a
full picture of workers' perspectives on key issues. In Bangladesh, for example a
hotline first established by the Alliance for Bangladesh Worker Safety is available
to any ready-made garment factory in the country; since its inception in 2013,
what is now known as the Amader Kotha Helpline has received more than 223,000
calls from workers in more than a thousand factories. In January 2020, its

website reported receiving an average of 2,800 calls per month about four hundred issues, on average, and involving an average of 250 factories. In 92 percent of the cases, the workers were motivated to disclose their names.

There is also evidence indicating that hotlines can help couple private regulation practices with worker outcomes directly. Doug Cahn, the Helpline's global project manager, reports on the website that "factory managers learn about and fix problems quickly before they escalate." There are, though, problems with hotlines: only a small percentage of workers use them, and Amader Kotha data suggest women are less likely than men to do so.

Despite these problems, the data provide some indication of what is important to workers at any given time, as table 9.1 shows. Amader Kotha classifies the issues in these calls as "urgent," which require immediate intervention by the factory management and global brands, and "nonurgent," which can be dealt with over a longer period of time. Most issues in both categories are covered in codes of conduct.

In addition to hotlines, *worker surveys* are becoming more commonplace in the private regulation ecosystem, as more companies try to adopt a more worker-centric approach to supplier performance management. For example, Gap Inc.'s supplier sustainability team was interested in greater insights into the issues that matter most to workers in its supplier factories in China, India, Vietnam, Cambodia, and Guatemala, beyond what was in the company's code of conduct. The survey (conducted by Verité) was aimed at helping supplier management by assessing workers' sense of value, engagement, knowledge, and overall well-being.

TABLE 9.1.   Amader Kotha helpline calls on urgent and nonurgent issues, December 2014–November 2019

URGENT ISSUES	CALLS	NONURGENT ISSUES	CALLS
Fire safety	476	Fire (outside factory)	2,802
Structural issues (cracks in walls/beams)	352	Health: inadequate facilities	816
Blocked egress routes, locked factory exits	235	Fire danger outside factory	397
Structural: shaking walls/windows	163	Lack of adequate drinking water	258
Fire danger	65	Occupational safety hazards	257
Physical abuse	349	Wages and bonuses	5,577
Freedom of association	330	Benefits	3,908
Bribery or corruption	76	Termination	3,177
Physical harassment	73	Verbal abuse	2,668
Sexual harassment	59	Leave	1,202

Notably, the survey found "fair treatment," "immediate supervisors," communication and feedback, and training and development were the most influential factors in survey scores—some issues not included in Gap Inc.'s code. Remediation plans were established based on the survey results, and later reassessments carried out in several factories showed improvement in a variety of code of conduct items. This experience illustrated the potential for worker input to help mitigate the decoupling problem between the company's private regulation practices and worker outcomes in the supply chain.

Nike introduced a similar worker engagement and well-being survey that the company describes on its website as "a tool for factory management to get a holistic understanding of worker experiences in their factories." The confidential survey, administered through vetted third-party vendors, comprises twenty-one questions about safety, stress, financial security, and well-being—including many aspects of workers' experiences that are not specifically in Nike's code of conduct, such as how often workers get sick or feel job stress, whether supervisors care about workers, whether workers are treated with respect and fairness, social relationships at work, the prevalence of sexual harassment, the ability to meet family needs on workers' pay, and so on. Results are provided to management immediately through the tech platform and must be shared with workers immediately in order to "catalyze factory management to further engage employees."

The Worker Sentiment Survey (WSS), developed by LaborLink and owned by ELEVATE, a global auditing firm that provides a number of services to the private regulation ecosystem, can be integrated with the audit assessment by being administered at the same time. The focus of this survey, however, is not compliance but rather worker perceptions, preferences, and insights that provide an overall sense of the work climate in factories, which can then be used to help factory management systems in ways that would improve coupling between code of conduct provisions and actual worker outcomes. ELEVATE's client firms are provided with survey results, which the firms can then share with supplier factory management. Workers respond through anonymous digital channels. The survey's seventeen questions are grouped into five categories—work atmosphere, grievance mechanisms, wages and hours, production efficiency, and workforce stability—that are combined (with differential weights) to provide an overall "sentiment score" for the factory.

As of September 2019, the WSS had been deployed in 1,594 factories, with valid surveys from more than seventy-five thousand workers. Client interest in the WSS has been growing, and by December 2019 WSS surveys were being conducted in more than 150 factories each month in ten countries. Table 9.2 presents selected aggregated results of all completed surveys as of June 2019 for selected questions, to give a sense of what these surveys reveal.

TABLE 9.2. Worker sentiment survey insights (1,274 factories)

SURVEY QUESTION	AGGREGATED RESPONSE RESULTS
If you had a suggestion or complaint about your work, are you willing to speak up?	Yes: 81% Maybe: 12% No: 7%
Which channel do you trust the most to raise a suggestion or complaint?	Directly with management: 68% Union or worker committee: 7% External helpline: 1% Factory hotline: 1% Use suggestion box: 20% No trusted channels exist: 3%
In the past six months, have you raised a suggestion or complaint?	More than once: 11% Once: 9% No: 81%
If you raised a suggestion or complaint, do you think it will be treated seriously by management?	Yes: 82% Maybe: 13% No: 5%
Has a coworker or supervisor made unwelcome sexual remarks or physical contact to you or others in the last twelve months?	No: 93% Experienced physical contact: 1% Experienced sexual remarks: 3% Experienced both: 3%
Are there protective measures for pregnant workers in your factory?	Yes: 58% I don't know: 26% No: 16%

While the aggregate results are overwhelmingly positive, it should be noted that the results for *individual* factories would be different. ELEVATE managers told me in interviews that there is significant variation across factories, countries, and male and female respondents. For example, managers said 30 percent of workers in Indian and Bangladeshi factories have witnessed or experienced sexual harassment, but that information almost never comes through in audit findings. And although audit results indicate grievance systems work, survey results suggest workers do not trust management in some factories and countries.

The bottom line is that it is extremely important to include workers as key actors in private regulation because their input and insights will enable supplier management to more closely internalize the goals of private regulation programs of global companies. While methods of gaining workers' input such as anonymous surveys may not yet be mainstream practice, they need to be if we are to reduce decoupling. Surveys are more likely to be scalable compared to the more difficult (but more necessary) task of promoting unionization and worker representation.

Of course, the gold standard would be for workers to be trained and empowered to monitor compliance, rather than to use auditors. This notion is at the heart of what is being called "worker-driven social responsibility," which highlights that worker organizations must be the driving force in creating, monitoring, and enforcing programs designed to improve their wages and working conditions. To accomplish that goal, "monitoring and enforcement mechanisms must be designed in ways that to provide workers an effective voice in the protection of their rights."[26] As chapter 6 suggests, unionization and collective bargaining are key to any such effort.

Foster a Systemic Mindset

A systemic mindset is "instrumental in coming to grips with the lateral and multilevel complexity that reigns in relatively opaque fields, such as socioenvironmental governance," suggest institutional theorists.[27] Fostering a systemic mindset among actors in the private regulation field, such as global companies and suppliers, requires active consideration of how specific actions or programs will affect other actors, institutions, and other programs in the space, both directly and indirectly.[28]

One way to do so would be for actors in the ecosystem to study the interconnections between actors and factors in relation to a specific issue in codes of conduct, perhaps studying or simulating the effects of specific actions. For example, sustainability standards that limit both working hours and overtime (a provision found in most codes of conduct) often have the unintended consequence of encouraging supplier factories to subcontract production to less compliant factories, a fairly routine occurrence in the apparel industry. It is also important to distinguish between major and minor causes and to consider the uncertain effects of important variables. Reducing casual complexity requires a careful consideration of the variables that matter in enhancing compliance and whether the effects of these variables are consistent across different institutional contexts, regions, and factory types.

For this to happen, two conditions must be met. The first is increased transparency at all levels. Causal complexity could be reduced if global companies, multi-stakeholder initiatives, and auditing firms publicly disclosed data regarding the *effects* of their private regulation practices. This level of transparency does not currently exist in the private regulation field; most brands and MSIs do not publicly disclose *any* data. The second condition concerns the need for extensive analysis of the data already accumulated. These data could be used to better understand cause and effect—to ask what works where and whether best practices exist. Such analyses would lead to more evidence-based decisions and the creation of predictive models.

The Varieties of Transparency

There are many varieties of transparency. While transparency with global companies' external stakeholders is a hot topic right now, it is actually transparency *within the private regulation ecosystem itself* that is more important to better coupling of private regulation practices with outcomes.

Transparency with Companies' External Stakeholders

Transparency is seen as a foundation of supply-chain management because companies manage what they can measure.[29] But when actors in the private regulation ecosystem speak of "supply-chain transparency," they are using the term loosely. Typically, their primary focus is on the *external stakeholders of global companies.*

John Ruggie, the architect of the United Nations Guiding Principles on Business and Human Rights, sees transparency as businesses' ability not only to "know internally" that they are exercising due diligence but also to "show externally" that this is the case.[30] "Knowing internally" is crucial for companies to manage risks in their supply chain effectively and to identify whether and where progress is being made. This aspect of transparency is vital to the credibility of corporate responsibility strategies. "Showing externally" is important to satisfy key stakeholders, such as investors concerned about different dimensions of company performance; civil society groups who are critical of corporate CSR initiatives but who can also help companies in identifying and avoiding potential adverse human rights impacts; and, importantly, the consumers who buy products.[31] The lack of transparency has confounded efforts to assess the effectiveness of global firms' sustainability commitments.[32]

Considerable attention has been paid to the importance of transparency to consumers. The fashion industry is reportedly facing a rising trust deficit, especially from millennial consumers who demand more background information on the products that they buy.[33] Consumers are becoming more concerned about the labor conditions under which their clothes are made and the environmental impacts of their production. Increasingly, consumers want to support brands that follow ethical and sustainable practices.

As the Fairtrade Foundation puts it, "Transparency is really an expansion of the idea of quality, as markets and consumers have evolved. So while quality may have meant more specific things regarding physical products earlier, we now include many other dimensions such as responsibility and sustainability."[34] In other words, transparency can be an important source of competitive advantage in the future.

The apparel industry's current focus is on *traceability*—that is, making the supply chain more visible. In 2016, a coalition of nine labor and human rights organizations endorsed the "transparency pledge" as a "minimum standard" for supply chain disclosure.[35] The pledge requires each signatory company to publish on its website, in searchable format, the full names and addresses of all its authorized production units and processing facilities, their parent companies, the types of products made, and the numbers of workers at each site. This information must be published within three months of signing the pledge and updated twice a year. At this writing, several leading brands had already done so, and several that have signed the pledge are making progress on posting the information.[36]

Traceability, however, is not easily achieved, particularly when trying to make suppliers other than those at the Tier 1 level visible. Consider brand Nudie Jean's efforts:

> In 2012, Nudie's CEO officially initiated the transparency project with the vision "of becoming the most transparent company in the world." Ideally, Nudie wanted to present the names of all suppliers involved in producing all Nudie products [for complete traceability] and disclose the sustainability conditions at all suppliers [the sustainability dimension of supply-chain transparency]. When the project was launched on Nudie's website in mid 2013, Nudie disclosed nearly all the names of its suppliers and presented summaries of factory audit results for those suppliers that had been audited. . . . Nudie was unable to be fully transparent as of the project launch in 2013 for several reasons, such as suppliers' refusing disclosure of their names, Nudie managers' unwillingness to disclose particularly sensitive information, and technical limitations [in terms of tracing products though the supply chain].[37]

Transparency, however, goes beyond simply gaining visibility into the extended supply chain. Transparency also involves the process by which a company takes action to manage risks more efficiently based on insights gained through greater visibility. For example, the NGO Fashion Revolution would like global companies not only to disclose their supplier lists but also to reveal on their websites their supply-chain policies, how those policies are put into practice, the governance mechanisms, how the brand assesses the policies' implementation, and how remediation is handled if problems are found. In addition, the NGO has called for disclosure of brand action on key "spotlight" issues such as gender equality, female empowerment, freedom of association, reduction of waste, and introduction of recycling. Assessing two hundred fashion companies on these dimensions, Fashion Revolution found an average score of 21 out of a maximum of 250.

The highest scores were achieved by Patagonia, Adidas, and Puma, which each scored 160.[38]

The demands made by Fashion Revolution align with the "radical transparency" concept, which goes even further to state that companies should be open about almost everything. Radical transparency would remove all barriers to free and easy access to corporate information in ways that would help hold corporations accountable for everyone's benefit.[39] Radical transparency calls for information on how items are made, the provenance of their materials, the environmental impacts of the manufacturing process, and the labor conditions under which the products were made. Patagonia, which details "how the products are made, where the materials are sourced, and the conditions for the workers who create these materials" is one of the stronger examples of radical transparency; these practices help explain Patagonia's prices.[40]

"Hypertransparency" requires more annual detail than radical transparency by requiring corporations to set clear annual targets for social responsibility and report extensively on how they are meeting these targets, so stakeholders can hold corporations accountable.

Box 9.1 provides a comprehensive conception of transparency, incorporating radical notions and identifying six dimensions that serve as an important framework for what might be called the "transparency journey" of companies.

In general, transparency about where products are made and the challenges encountered in those areas is important both so that buyers can make informed choices regarding sustainable sourcing strategies and so that consumers can make informed choices about the products they buy. Transparency also helps employers improve and encourages them to demonstrate that they are raising their standards for working conditions in these locations.

Transparency within the Industry and Private Regulation Ecosystem

To reduce opacity in private regulation, there is a need for transparency to overcome the problems caused by behavioral invisibility, practice multiplicity, and causal complexity. This transparency needs to be focused toward what could be called the "back end" rather than the "front end"—that is, transparency *within* the supply chain ecosystem rather than *for* global corporations' consumers and external stakeholders. Without this transparency, we will not be able to answer four key questions: Which practices work? Where do they work? Why do they work? What are the emerging *best* practices? All actors in the private regulation space need to engage in this "back-end" transparency for private regulation efforts to be improved.

Box 9.1. A Transparency Framework Focused
on External Stakeholders

1. *Traceability information* that reports on the different actors involved in a supply chain (including production, transport, and processing systems), their role, and the nature and rigidity of connections between actors (including contractual and supplier relationships and the power implications thereof) and to production localities. Traceability information provides transparency around associations among actors and between actors and places.

2. *Transaction information* that reports on the purchasing practices and investment decisions of different supply-chain actors. This includes commodity purchases, sales of inputs to the commodity production process, and patterns of economic investment and ownership—including by actors outside the primary supply chain. Transaction information helps identify which actors are the main beneficiaries of a given supply chain—and hence who may share responsibility for any sustainability concerns.

3. *Impact information* that reports on social and environmental impacts, as well as other risks associated with specific stages in a supply chain as related to different production, transport, processing, and consumption processes. Impact information provides transparency around the sustainability of individual supply-chain stages, and thus sets a baseline for assessing the performance of the actors involved.

4. *Policy and commitment information* that refers to the supply-chain actors' policies and commitments to increase the sustainability of their operations, and the processes by which changes in performance will be assessed (e.g., against current practices or agreed benchmarks). Policy information provides transparency on any differences in the levels and strengths of policies adopted by different actors, including sustainability commitments.

Box 9.1. (continued)

5. *Activity information* that reports on actions taken by supply-chain actors—for example, in terms of production, sales, purchasing, processing, and investment decisions—in order to deliver on the targets that are set out by the actors' policies and commitments. Activity information provides transparency on the type and extent of new actions that actors are taking to change their behavior.

6. *Effectiveness information* that reports on the effectiveness of a given intervention to reduce negative environmental and social impacts and thus improve the performance of a given supply-chain actor, or production or processing location, as set against a specific target, baseline, or set of comparators. Effectiveness information provides transparency around how much (or little) progress is made by a given actor or place.

Note: Adapted from Gardner et al. 2019.

Identifying emerging best practices is particularly important for private regulation. Institutional theorists suggest the importance of institutional isomorphism, a process that forces "one unit in a population to increasingly imitate other units that face the same set of environmental conditions."[41] Three forces are important in enacting this need to imitate others:

- *Coercive forces* refer to those formal and informal pressures exerted on actors by other organizations. These could be laws but also, and more relevant to our context, they can involve pressures on MSI member companies to adopt certain private regulation goals such as a living wage.
- *Mimetic processes* explain the replication of practices in an organizational field. Organizations faced with uncertainty, such as when goals and practices are ambiguous and poorly understood (as in opaque institutional fields), "tend to model themselves after similar organizations in their field that they perceive to be more legitimate or successful."[42] An example is the remarkable similarity in the efforts of Nike, New Balance, and Pangia to integrate sourcing and compliance.

- *Normative pressures* from the profession (of sustainability executives) and professional networks (such as those fostered by MSIs) create institutional isomorphism by developing norms for what sustainability executives are supposed to achieve.

While together these three powerful forces encourage the diffusion of practices generally, the successful diffusion of *best* practices requires transparency among all, not just global companies.

TRANSPARENCY BY GLOBAL COMPANIES

To support the diffusion of best practices, global companies need to share their supply-chain data and their private regulation program experiences with the private regulation ecosystem. This sharing should include their capability-building programs and audit results at different suppliers, so other firms sourcing from the same suppliers can understand what does and does not work. It would also be useful if companies shared supplier factory audit results with workers in the factory, as a way to encourage workers to internalize the goals of the program and promote problem-solving discussions between workers and management. Since companies are increasingly willing to be more transparent to satisfy external stakeholders, it is plausible they could do the same for the private regulation ecosystem.

TRANSPARENCY BY MULTI-STAKEHOLDER INSTITUTIONS

Most MSIs require their members to report on their progress. MSIs could play a key role in identifying and diffusing best practices if they would analyze and circulate the lessons learned from the data and these reports.

For example, FWF has a process called "Brand Performance Checks" through which it assesses how each of its members is doing on improving labor conditions in the supply chain. These assessments, available on FWF's website, result in a benchmarking score that rates its member brands: "leader," "good," or "needs improvement." Little has been done, however, to analyze these performance evaluations in the aggregate to extract lessons and best practices. These analyses are published online for all member brands, although outcomes data do not accompany these brand performance checks. The key for FWF is to integrate brand performance checks with outcomes data and analyze those data to provide its members with a better sense of what practices work. Doing so, even if suitably anonymized, would help reduce opacity in the field.

ETI requires its brand members to submit annual reports on their ethical trading activities that are constructed around benchmarks and key performance indicators. These reports are supposed to be shared with other ETI members. That would be one way of promoting shared learning across the member companies regarding what works and what does not in private regulation programs. However, this information is shared with members only if they sign a confidentiality agreement. Because we do not know how many have signed such an agreement, we also do not know whether this is an effective method of disseminating best practice.

An ETI external review highlighted the importance of enabling change among its member companies by sharing lessons learned and disseminating knowledge and experience gained among members, policymakers, and other key stakeholders in a bid to enhance the impact of their ethical trading activities to support member companies to endeavor to roll out innovative solutions."[43] For such sharing to be effective, the reports from members must have sufficient detail and be credible. As the external review reported, however, "it is challenging to assess the veracity of the information disclosed within the annual report, which is confidential," and "the annual reporting process does not really amount to more than a self assessment." Thus, there are problems with the quality, depth, and integrity of the information.

While ETI makes an effort to disseminate learnings to members at its various conferences and breakfast meetings, it is unclear whether members make use of the lessons to improve their own programs—because ETI offers no evidence. Most important, to my knowledge ETI itself has not begun to analyze the voluminous data contained in member reports to produce key lessons and identify best practices. As the external report noted, "at the very least, these reports provide a vast reservoir of data which could, in theory, be scrutinized as a means of assessing results in terms of the impact of member organizations on the life of workers in their supply chains."[44]

The FLA conducts detailed assessments when reaccrediting its member companies, looking for "continued implementation of the workplace standards" and focusing on "key components that innovatively support the FLA's mission to 'improve workers' lives worldwide.'"[45] These assessments look at implementation of responsible purchasing practices, civil society engagement, remediation efforts, and program innovations. The assessments also involve testing selected data points or information sources to verify actions taken by a company. FLA staff members draw on multiple sources of evidence, including factory-level assessments, observation, annual reports, and so forth. These FLA reaccreditation reports are evidently quite detailed.

Thus, the FLA has data regarding programs that work or do not work. It is possible companies share case studies with other FLA members at conferences from time to time, but is not clear that the FLA itself culls and analyzes data to draw lessons for its members.

Sedex claims its services "enable members to bring together many different kinds of data, standards and certifications . . . and to drive continuous improvement across their value chains."[46] Sedex's proprietary audit methodology, SMETA, includes a guide to conducting audits, a common audit format, and a common corrective action plan format. Nearly twenty thousand SMETA audits are uploaded to the Sedex platform each year.[47] Members can also upload their own audits to the Sedex platform, and buyers, auditors, and suppliers that are Sedex members can store, share, and report on supply-chain information on the platform. Sedex also offers its members the "Sedex Data Monitor," which allows them to analyze their performance and benchmark against industry peers.

With more than fifty thousand members from thirty-five industrial sectors around the world, and with nearly twenty thousand audits uploaded every year, Sedex has amassed a huge quantity of data on how private regulation works.[48] But it is not clear that Sedex analyzes the mass of data at its disposal to reveal patterns, uncover lessons, and shed light on the relationships among variables that are needed to reduce the causal complexity that drives opacity.

Social Accountability International (SAI), which has certified more than four thousand factories worldwide, also sits on a mountain of data drawn from its audit reports. These reports, though, are not in the public domain, and there is no evidence whatsoever that SAI has analyzed the data to find evidence of what does and does not work.[49]

Finally, there is the Fair Factories Clearinghouse (FFC), which in theory is the ideal type of organization to facilitate industry-facing transparency—not least because FFC also emphasizes collaboration among its members. According to its website,

> FFC facilitates sharing of information relating to workplace conditions among FFC members to promote transparency in accordance with antitrust and anti-competition guidelines. This results in a global clearinghouse of factory information, allowing members to identify common needs for workplace improvement, prioritize them and attack them together. Collaboration lowers costs, reduces labor load, increases learning, improves leverage and enhances factory performance.[50]

Thus, FFC is a niche institution that facilitates collaboration among brands to improve compliance and workers' lives. Its audit management system allows members to manage audit data and analyze supply-chain information, and its platform facilitates sharing information that can help identify common needs for workplace improvement so members can attack them together. But little is known regarding the extent to which members use the data, there is little evidence of collaboration, and examples of collaboration have not been widely shared. What *is* known is that FFC has a massive amount of data that could be usefully employed to reduce opacity.

TRANSPARENCY BY SUPPLIERS

As part of the private regulation ecosystem, suppliers also have a key role to play in fostering industry-facing transparency. First and foremost, suppliers need to be more transparent about the data they present to auditors. As this book's opening chapter highlighted, more than a third of audits present falsified data.

The lack of transparency among suppliers is partly a result of the lack of transparency among global buyers, as well as the nature of supplier relationships with buyers. If the buyer-supplier relationships were partnership-based rather than adversarial, suppliers would have less of an incentive to falsify data.

Many suppliers are members of multi-stakeholder institutions such as FLA and Sedex. Since these suppliers experience the private regulation programs of a variety of global buyers, the suppliers could be analyzing their experiences and providing feedback to the ecosystem on how private regulation programs work. Supplier AAA provided the data for research reported in chapter 2 that offers valuable insights into how private regulation programs work when seen from the other side. Other suppliers, many of which have well-functioning human resource departments, could provide a variety of metrics on their websites regarding buyer behavior. In fact, the US-based Better Buying (BB) initiative has created a platform through which suppliers can anonymously rate the purchasing practices of the companies that buy their products. These ratings, which are collated and provided to global companies by BB, inform them of how their purchasing practices can be improved so as to better couple buyers' private regulation programs with working condition improvements in supplier factories.[51]

To repeat, the current emphasis for transparency is geared more toward global companies' external stakeholders. It emphasizes descriptive information. But the greater need is for transparency *within* the private regulation ecosystem itself. That will allow the analytical focus that will yield better results in increasing the effectiveness of private regulation.

Toward Evidence-Based Decisions through Data Analysis and Predictive Models

Moving from opacity to transparency in the private regulation ecosystem requires not only the availability of data regarding the effects of private regulation programs but also the analysis and diffusion of that data through transparency. These data must also form the basis for improving private regulation in ways that affect worker outcomes.

There are several barriers to realizing this objective. First, not all global buyers or retailers collect adequate data on their private regulation programs. In some companies, compliance departments may possess the results of audits conducted in their supplier factories, but these data may not have been compiled in an analyzable form. Many companies still store audit results on paper. Several firms my research colleagues and I are working with gave us audit data in piles of paper files, which we then had to encode into a database before beginning our analysis.

Second, the data are often incomplete, in a variety of ways. There may not be consistent records for all factories or all regions. A lot of information may be missing. There may be audit results but relatively information about factory characteristics that could help explain why there are violations. And, as I have argued earlier, audit information is not complemented with data on sourcing practices. Sourcing data and factory characteristics data are both necessary to analyze comprehensively the drivers of code of conduct violations.

Third, even if companies have data in an analyzable form, the data are often not analyzed—for a variety of reasons. In some cases, small compliance departments have insufficient time to do data analysis while also fulfilling their day-to-day duties. The benefit corporation discussed in chapter 7 had only three managers in its sustainability office to deal with labor compliance in its entire global supply chain. Even in much larger global firms with larger compliance departments, time constraints are still a problem, because such firms have larger supply chains. A global apparel firm with which we worked had done a remarkable job assembling a comprehensive range of compliance, sourcing, and pricing data but had not made much progress in actually analyzing the data precisely because of these sorts of time constraints.

Fourth, there is a shortage of data analysis talent. Most compliance and sustainability departments lack the necessary skills to manipulate and draw useful inferences from data. Why would people with statistics and other qualifications choose to work for an apparel company's compliance department when they could work for, say, Google? Furthermore, the salaries in these departments tend to be lower than those paid in departments with a more operational focus, such as finance, marketing, sourcing, engineering, product development, and so forth. This talent shortage is endemic—and even more acute for sustainability departments in small- and medium-size companies.

Time constraints and talent shortages may also explain why the various MSIs do not, for the most part, publish analyses of the huge amount of data at their disposal. There are some exceptions. In recent years, FWF has made a massive effort to input, clean, and systemize its data from audits and brand performance checks; some of these data are sources in this book. The ILO's Better Work program has fewer constraints in terms of time and talent and has assembled high-quality data from different countries, some of which have also been used in this volume.

The academic research community, which has the interest and capabilities to analyze and draw lessons from such data, could offset these time constraints, budget problems, and talent shortages if both companies and MSIs were more willing to share their data. But a deeply held sense of secrecy interferes. Companies are often unwilling to share data on labor on their private regulation programs, perhaps because they know they are not doing an effective job and they fear their reputations will be damaged if details were made public. MSIs are unwilling to share data for the same reasons, not only because of confidentiality provisions in their membership agreements. There is an easy solution: anonymize the data so researchers can still analyze the information without disclosing company names, and have researchers sign nondisclosure agreements.[52]

Data analysis by the research community can lead to insights for more *evidence-based decision making*, which is largely absent in private regulation programs and helps explain why there are so few significant annual, measurable improvements with regard to many labor rights and standards. There are examples of academic analyses helping in this way. One of the companies discussed briefly in chapter 8, a maker of active apparel with a good reputation for its private regulation efforts, had attempted to integrate its sourcing practices with its supplier factories' compliance strategies, rewarding factories that showed improvement in compliance with more orders and longer-term relationships.[53] An analysis of the company's sourcing, pricing, and supplier compliance data indicated the strategy worked well for factories at the extreme ends of the compliance scale—that is, very good factories were rewarded with more orders, and very poor factories were terminated—but factories in the middle of the compliance scale, even if they made compliance improvements, were not similarly rewarded. An analysis of Nike's supply chain led to similar actionable insights, as did a study of auditing practices and auditor training on compliance improvement.[54] Our own data analysis in chapter 8 showed large compliance gaps in the case of a B-Corp that had been under the impression its private regulation program was working well. Other studies of the toy industry, FWF, and Nudie Jeans have yielded valuable insights for evidence-based decision making.[55]

Beyond data analysis, the vast amount of data on labor practices available within global companies and various MSIs could also be employed to create predictive models to develop private regulation further. It would be interesting, for example, to develop a predictive model of the factors that make a factory highly compliant. Such a tool would be particularly useful for global brands making factory selections, since factories are continually dropping out of the supply chain and new factories are added. It would be also useful to develop predictive models that could show which factories are likely to pay higher wages. And it would be extremely useful to develop predictive models related to subcontracting, which is a key problem in the apparel industry.

Most supply-chain data on labor practices offer little information on the factory features crucial for compliance, such as the nature of factory management and the soundness of general management systems. David Hayer, former Gap Inc. vice president for sustainability, famously said that the only variable that mattered for compliance was the attitude of the factory management toward private regulation. With adequate data, his argument could be tested and modeled. It will also be important to develop predictive models on compliance with respect to specific items such as health and safety. Controlling for the national institutional environment and other macro variables, as well as customer and product types, do factories that perform better on health and safety compliance differ systematically from other factories? Do factories producing more complex, high-value-added products tend to have better compliance records? Similarly, what distinguishes factories that pay a "decent" wage? In light of the fact that one-third of suppliers across multiple industries seem to falsify data, can we model the determinants of transparent suppliers?

Box 9.2 examines how some other researchers have used predictive modeling with respect to compliance.

As for our own predictive modeling, the data in the different datasets used in this book do not offer sufficient information on supplier variables to develop such models. We were unable to create and test a predictive model for which suppliers are less likely to falsify data, for instance. While we found country, industry, supplier size, and supplier wage levels to be important, the absence of other supplier information was too significant a barrier to overcome.

To illustrate the possibilities further, though, here we extend the excellent work in building predictive models described in box 9.2.[56] We use Better Work data from seven countries (described in several earlier chapters). What we are attempting to explain here (i.e., the dependent variable) is the compliance level, with the goal of identifying the characteristics that account for higher levels of compliance. We measure several potential determinants of compliance.

In our initial model, we examine the impact of the assessment cycle. Better Work factories have gone through multiple assessments; the argument here is that factories in later cycles should evidence higher levels of compliance than

Box 9.2. Predictive Modeling Efforts

There have been limited efforts to predict compliance.[1] Much of the research has only scratched the surface: it suggests that highly compliant factories are generally situated in countries with better institutional environments and higher per capita GDP and that larger factories supplying reputation-conscious buyers tend to be more compliant. But there is very little evidence with respect to other correlates of high compliance across industries and countries.

One key contribution to the development of predictive models used data from a global auditing company to examine the *determinants of compliance improvement* in 3,276 suppliers across fifty-five countries.[2] These data included a number of interesting variables not found in other datasets, including audit sequence, auditor training, who pays for the audit, and composition of the audit team. There were data on supplier size, supplier age, the nature of the supplier workforce, supplier wage practices, and unionization levels, as well as industry and country control variables that have been analyzed exhaustively by others.

The analysis indicates greater compliance improvement when there is a union at the supplier factory, when the audit is paid for the buyer, when the audit team is mixed gender, when the audit team members are more experienced, and when the factories are larger and dominated by female workers. In addition, suppliers with high-powered incentive structures such as piece rates improve less than suppliers without such structures. Despite so many more variables than in many previous efforts, the researchers lament the absence of more critical supplier-level variables such as profitability and supplier management characteristics, which could matter significantly.

This research points to the potential benefits likely if the research community were able to do more predictive modeling.

1. Short, Toffel, and Hugill 2018.
2. Bird, Short, and Toffel 2019.

factories in earlier cycles, largely because Better Work includes postaudit training on how to improve. We add a measure for supplier size, using the actual number of workers (hypothesizing that larger factories will be more compliant), and supplier age (assuming factories that have been operating for many years will show higher compliance). We look at the duration of the assessment (i.e., number of days), expecting that longer durations will result in higher compliance rates. We have measures of the suppliers' workforce, including female and migrant worker ratios, the share of contingent workers, and use of subcontractors. We added a novel composite measure of the suppliers' human resource management capacity, which evaluates the extent to which the supplier employs formal, modern HR practices—important in helping test David Hayer's hypothesis that quality of management matters.

We also include a measure for unionization in the supplier factory, given the important finding that unions and collective bargaining improve coupling through improved compliance levels. Our data identify each supplier's biggest buyer, so we examine the impact of the brand's reputation—measured by whether the buyer is on *Fortune*'s list of "Most Desirable Brands." We added a measure to ascertain whether these buyers were partners with Better Work. Table 9.3 presents the results of our tentative model.

The results in table 9.3 indicate that we are able to account for 53 percent of the variance in compliance, which is a reasonably good result compared with our previous knowledge in this area—even though it suggests we are missing several important variables. The results also confirm many of the assumptions stated earlier. Supplier size did not seem to matter to such a degree, perhaps because there was not much variation in factory size in this sample. Contrary to prior research, our results indicate that newer suppliers evidence better compliance than older ones, but this may reflect that these are factories that have joined Better Work. While the ratio of female workers was not important, compliance was significantly reduced with increases in the percentage of foreign migrant workers, the use of contingent workers, and the use of subcontractors. The presence of unions and collective bargaining significantly enhanced compliance. Compliance was higher if the top three buyers were also Better Work partners, a very robust result that is testament to why Better Work factories are, in general, so much better than the average. This result emphasizes the potential importance of expanding the program to other countries and shows that country context matters. And it sounds as if David Hayer was right—the quality of supplier HR practices strongly predicts compliance.

Data and analyses like these can provide the basis for developing far more refined predictive models that can help the industry move forward. The key lesson is that there is a need for actors within the private regulation ecosystem,

TABLE 9.3.   Predictors of compliance

VARIABLE	COEFFICIENT	STANDARD ERROR	SIGNIFICANCE
Assessment cycle	0.360	0.061	***
Assessment person days	−0.788	0.128	***
Supplier size	.202	0.158	
Supplier age	−0.057	0.018	***
Female worker ratio	−0.005	0.023	
Percentage of foreign migrant workers	−0.035	0.012	***
Formal HR policies of supplier	1.770	0.080	***
Percentage of contingent workers	−0.035	0.007	***
Supplier's use of subcontracting	−0.518	0.279	*
Union at supplier	0.776	0.404	*
CBA agreement at supplier	0.886	0.515	*
Top three buyers are BW partners	0.864	0.179	***
Customer 1 brand reputation (*Fortune*)	0.701	0.430	
2018 assessment year	0.321	0.251	
Cambodia	−2.086	0.610	***
Indonesia	−.1680	0.552	***
Jordan	1.676	.907	*
Haiti	−1.185	0.916	
Nicaragua	3.763	0.733	***
Constant	80.825	1.067	***
Number of observations	1302		
R-square	0.530		

Source: Better Work data.
Note: The dependent variable overall compliance was calculated for each of the eight clusters by adding up the total number of violations found for each cluster, divided by the total number of questions on which the factories were assessed, multiplied by 100. For the five countries in the table, Vietnam is the reference category. *Fortune* magazine compiles annually a list of the most admired companies by reputation. This variable reflects the ranking of the supplier's largest customer.
*p < 0.1, ** p < 0.05, *** p < 0.001.

such as brands, auditing firms, and multi-stakeholder institutions, to collect more systematic data about suppliers. This is necessary to create useful models to understand the practices that do and do not work so best practices can be derived. This is the path to promoting the coupling of private regulation initiatives and improvements in compliance in ways that improve workers' lives in global supply chains.

In sum, the institutional perspective adopted in this book highlights the importance of collaborating niche institutions, stimulating the adoption of private regulations goals, and fostering a systemic mindset in order to move the private regulation ecosystem from its current opacity to more transparency. These constitute some methods by which private regulation programs can be improved by reducing decoupling between practices and outcomes for workers in global supply chains.

CONCLUSION

What plausibly explains why we have not seen sufficient progress in private regulation, despite more than twenty-five years of effort by global corporations? What do analyses of the data show? What do these analyses suggest to improve private regulation in ways that would increase coupling between practices and outcomes—namely, better lives for workers? Those are the three questions that have been at the heart of this book.

The key findings and arguments are worth repeating here, in conclusion. The lack of progress in labor conditions in global supply chains is the result of the high degree of field opacity, which is caused by the problems of behavioral invisibility, practice multiplicity, and causal complexity (as detailed in part 1, "Problems").

Progress (part 2) has been quite limited. Barring clear reductions in the hours of work and improvements in how wages are paid, the effects of private regulation are uncertain for many labor rights and outcomes. Further, global companies are failing to ensure that suppliers in their far-flung supply chains adhere to companies' codes of conduct requiring suppliers to pay a reasonable living wage and to support and enhance workers' freedom of association rights. Given the incontrovertible evidence that unionization and collective bargaining are a surefire method of significantly increasing compliance and the coupling of code provisions with outcomes for workers, it is especially surprising that companies fail to ensure support for workers' freedom of association.

To evaluate prospects (part 3) requires a critical look at popular corporate governance initiatives such as benefit corporations. But the analysis here suggests that such changes in corporate governance are not the way to improve workers' lives in global supply chains. Rather, what's needed is to integrate compliance programs with sourcing practices—even if the process of doing so successfully is a tortuous one (as in the example of Pangia in chapter 8). Beyond such integration, private regulation can also be improved through the use of niche institutions, by stimulating all the actors in the ecosystem to internalize private regulation goals, and by fostering a systemic mindset. That mindset requires greater transparency *within* the ecosystem, rather than simply with external stakeholders. That approach also necessitates more and better-quality data, along with concerted efforts to analyze the huge amounts of data that are currently available, so we can draw lessons, identify causes and effects, derive what works in different contexts, and assist in creating predictive models that will enable actors within the private regulation ecosystem to make more evidence-based decisions. Together, these steps would do much to move the organizational field of private labor regulation from its current level of opacity to greater transparency. In turn, that would lead to a greater degree of coupling between companies' private regulation programs and actual improvement in workers' lives in global supply chains.

These suggestions, of course, stand on the shoulders of researcher giants who came before.

Many other suggestions have been made to reform and improve private regulation that are not canvassed extensively in this book. An important one is to reform the buyer-supplier contract to make the contract "work both ways"—that is, level the playing field so suppliers and workers can sue for buyer compliance. A second concerns institutionalizing unemployment insurance for supply chain workers. After the large numbers of layoffs in supplier factories due to the cancellation of orders by global buyers in the wake of Covid-19, the New Conversations Project at Cornell University has suggested that buyers sourcing from a supplier factory pay a contributory premium towards unemployment insurance for workers. This would be a particularly effective (and low-cost) way to provide relief for workers in global supply chains in countries where there is no social security or unemployment insurance, which is the case in the majority of garment exporting nations.

A third suggestion is that global buyers reform their sourcing to source only from countries with good labor standards, or at a minimum, clearly indicate to those country's governments that they will stop sourcing if labor laws are not enforced. Along similar lines, buyers could source only from factories with a viable collective bargaining agreement and a representative union. Fourth, there needs to be more effective interaction between private regulation programs and public programs (although we need further research into the various ways in which such complementarity occurs and is effective).

Private regulation is not a panacea. Researchers have pointed to other steps that could improve working conditions in supply chains. For one thing, national governments need to do a better job enforcing existing labor laws; indeed, it was governments' failure to do so that gave rise to private regulation. Another step is regionalization—harmonizing national labor standards within regional trade blocs through arrangements similar to those employed by the European Union (EU). Furthermore, labor standards could be improved if the International Labour Organization (ILO) could be more forceful with its members with respect to adhering to ILO conventions. Linking labor standards with trade agreements presents yet another potential solution to the issue of sweatshop practices in global supply chains.

Other steps, too, could help.

We should not be overly optimistic about prospects for improvement, however. Governments in garment-exporting countries have an abysmal record of labor law enforcement. The EU is the only regional initiative that harmonizes labor standards. The ILO remains limited in its ability to force member countries to improve labor standards. And even though the United States formally links trade and labor standards, it is the only country that does so—and it does so *poorly*. Finally, collective bargaining is generally rare in global supply chains.

All this leaves private regulation as one of the few tools we have at our disposal. We must do what we can to improve this tool, even if ultimately it may not be the best possible one to use. My views are consistent with Stephen Stills song lyric: "If you can't be with the one you love, love the one you're with."

Appendix A

PRIOR RESEARCH ON THE DETERMINANTS OF COMPLIANCE

The tables in this appendix summarize the determinants of compliance found in earlier studies. In each of tables A.1 through A.5, these determinants are listed as *causal variables* in the left-hand column. The tables then indicate each study's focus, type, data source, and illustrative examples of relevant publications. The lists in the right-hand columns of these tables are not comprehensive.

The dependent variable *compliance* should be understood overall to include both measures of overall compliance and compliance with specific standards such as wages or hours; some studies focus more on specific standards than overall code compliance. Most studies focus on compliance, but some focus on compliance improvement across time, arguably the more relevant dependent variable. It should be noted that the direction of the relationship is not specified—that is, all results found to be significant correlates of the dependent variable are included, whether the direction was positive or negative.

It is difficult to make comparisons across the studies listed in all these tables. The variations across studies, the lack of systematic data collection, and the fact that data are not typically made available in ways that allow comparisons inhibit drawing generalization about the determinants of compliance that benefit or inform actors' decisions. A cause identified in one study might not be found in others. "Given the vast array of work on this topic," as one group of researchers wrote, "we know surprisingly little about how various insights and findings fit together, and we still face significant gaps in data and research."[1] This is one reason we have causal complexity.

While the tables primarily indicate one or both of two dependent variables—compliance and compliance improvement—in reality, there is a lot more variation. Some studies focus on specific compliance variables, such as process rights, while others focus on hours, wages, overtime, and other outcomes. Findings based on different dependent variables are not directly comparable with one another.[2] Further contributing to causal complexity, specific data are used quite differently, and in some cases data are used inappropriately to measure the concept of interest to the researchers—thus often assuming a causal relationship that is not justified.

Another problem lies in what, specifically, is captured by the determinants. This is an overall problem with these studies, as the specifics of the tables show. Table A.1 begins with the context of *country* and *institutions*.

TABLE A.1. Putative determinants of compliance found in prior research: supplier country and institutional context causal variables

CAUSAL VARIABLE	DEPENDENT VARIABLE (FOCUS)	STUDY TYPE	DATA TYPE	EXAMPLE STUDIES
Country (where country is a dummy variable)	Compliance	Quantitative analysis	Auditing firm	Toffel, Short, and Ouellet (2015); Short, Toffel, and Hugill (2018)
Press freedom	Compliance	Quantitative analysis	Multi-stakeholder organization (FLA)	Stroehle (2017)
Supplier country per capita GDP, rich vs. poor	Compliance; compliance improvement	Quantitative analysis	Auditing firm, multi-stakeholder organization (FLA), global buyer	Stroehle (2017); Toffel, Short, and Ouellet (2015); Distelhorst, Hainmueller, and Locke (2017)
Labor laws and other variables supporting freedom of association	Compliance; compliance improvement	Quantitative analysis, qualitative case studies	Auditing firm, global buyer, multi-stakeholder organization	Toffel, Short, and Ouellet (2015); Locke, Qin, and Brause (2007); Koçer and Fransen (2009)
Rule of Law Index from World Justice Project	Compliance	Quantitative analysis	Multi-stakeholder organization (FLA), global buyer	Stroehle (2017); Locke (2013)
Lack of labor law enforcement	Compliance	Qualitative case study	Global buyer	Egels-Zandén (2007)
Labor market features of supplier country or province	Compliance	Qualitative case study	Global buyer	Egels-Zandén (2014)

The country context can be decisive. One reason is that causal variables such as *rule of law*, *press freedom*, and *labor law* are based on written documents and not on actual implementation. The assumption that something de jure leads to de facto better practice is often unwarranted in a given country.[3] India offers an instructive illustration: the country has highly protective labor legislation, but there are numerous issues with how that legislation is implemented; and while union formation in India is easy, winning recognition as a *bargaining agent* is complicated and varies across states. In the countries where apparel production is sourced—China, Bangladesh, India, Cambodia, Vietnam, Myanmar, Ethiopia, Indonesia, Turkey, Honduras, and El Salvador, for example—legislation, enforcement, and collective bargaining all vary Most of these countries have been generally characterized as repressive labor regimes, with very low union density.[4]

Consideration of regional (state and province) and local variation in institutions and practices is a serious omission in most studies of compliance. Across China's provinces and cities, for instance, there is considerable variation in rules regarding payment of wages, social security contributions, calculation of overtime hours, and so forth—making even these easy-to-audit items quite difficult to track.[5] Supplier factories' locations in different parts of the country could affect compliance in numerous ways.

Table A.2 focuses on buyer variables. There is some consistency in the research regarding the importance of long-term *buyer-supplier relationships* or collaborative relationships in improving compliance. There is also some support for the tendency of reputation-sensitive buyers (who have faced criticism in the press for labor violations in their supply chains) to have more robust private regulation programs, leading to better compliance in their factories. But the number of such buyers is relatively small. And while *leverage* is widely assumed to be an important predictor, it turns out that empirical support for this proposition is found primarily in the analysis of company supply chain data by one set of researchers.[6]

One difficulty with these buyer variables is that they are based on studies of global buyers that are perhaps leading practitioners of private regulation, such as Nike, HP, IKEA and so forth. It would be hard to generalize from these leading buyers to the industry as a whole.

Table A.3 focuses on supplier variables. There are two very consistent results with respect to *supplier characteristics*: the *type of industry* matters (although it is not clear why), and supplier *factory size* matters (there is in research support for the notion that larger suppliers may be more compliant than smaller ones). These results are generally true in cross-sectional analyses of multi-stakeholder data. Although foreign-owned suppliers have been found to be more compliant than domestically owned ones in more than one study, it is important to point out that foreign-owned suppliers may be a tiny fraction of the overall supplier population,

TABLE A.2. Putative determinants of compliance found in prior research: buyer variables

CAUSAL VARIABLE	DEPENDENT VARIABLE (FOCUS)	STUDY TYPE	DATA TYPE	EXAMPLE STUDIES
Per capita GDP in buyer country	Compliance improvement	Quantitative analysis	Auditing firm	Short, Toffel, and Hugill (2018)
Size (buyer employment)	Compliance improvement	Quantitative analysis	Auditing firm	Short, Toffel, and Hugill (2018)
Buyer exposure, sensitivity/reputation, branding	Compliance; compliance improvement	Quantitative analysis, qualitative case studies	Auditing firm, multi-stakeholder organization (Better Work), global buyer	Short, Toffel, and Hugill (2018); Oka (2010a); Ang et al. (2012); Lund-Thomsen and Nadvi (2010); Frundt (2000); Armbruster-Sandoval (2005)
Collaborative and long-term buyer-supplier relationships	Compliance	Qualitative case studies	Global buyers, company, multi-stakeholder organization (Better Work)	Locke, Qin, and Brause (2007); Oka (2010b); Knudsen (2013); Frenkel and Scott (2002); Lim and Phillips (2008); Locke (2013)
Leverage (percentage of supplier production accounted for by buyer)	Compliance	Qualitative case study	Global buyer	Locke (2013)
Purchasing practices	Compliance	Qualitative case studies and reviews	Global buyers, suppliers	Anner (2018); Oxfam (2010); Barrientos (2013); Ngai (2005); Sum and Ngai (2005); Jiang (2009); Locke, Qin, and Brause (2007); Amengual, Distelhorst, and Tobin (2019)
Weak private regulation programs of buyer	Compliance	Qualitative case studies	Global buyer	Egels-Zandén (2007); Yu (2008)
Capacity-building programs for suppliers by buyers	Compliance; compliance improvement	Qualitative case study	Global buyer	Locke (2013)
Benefit corporation status	Compliance	Qualitative case study	Global buyer	Chapter 7 of this book
Privately owned firm	Compliance	Qualitative case study	Global buyer	Kuruvilla and Fischer-Daly (2020)

TABLE A.3. Putative determinants of compliance found in prior research: supplier and factory characteristics causal variables

CAUSAL VARIABLE	DEPENDENT VARIABLE (FOCUS)	STUDY TYPE	DATA TYPE	EXAMPLE STUDIES
Industry type	Compliance	Quantitative analysis	Auditing firm	Toffel, Short, and Ouellet (2015); Locke (2013)
Supplier ownership (foreign or domestic)	Compliance	Qualitative case studies	Global buyer	Locke, Qin, and Brause (2007); Koçer and Fransen (2009)
Factory age	Compliance	Quantitative analysis	Multi-stakeholder organization (Better Work)	Brown, Dehejia, and Robertson (2018)
Size (number of workers)	Compliance (Hours)	Quantitative analysis and qualitative case study	Multi-stakeholder organization (FLA)	Smyth et al. (2013); Locke, Qin, and Brause (2007)
Proportion of female workers	Compliance (Hours)	Quantitative analysis	Multi-stakeholder organization (FLA)	Smyth et al. (2013)
Proportion of migrant workers	Compliance (Hours)	Quantitative analysis	Multi-stakeholder organization (FLA)	Smyth et al. (2013)
Communication and workplace systems at supplier	Compliance improvement	Quantitative analysis	Multi-stakeholder organization (Better Work)	Ang et al. (2012)
Modern wage practices at supplier	Compliance improvement	Quantitative analysis	Multi-stakeholder organization (Better Work)	Ang et al. (2012)
Labor unions at supplier	Compliance improvement	Quantitative analysis	Multi-stakeholder organization (Better Work)	Ang et al. (2012); Bartley and Egels-Zandén (2015)
Size of union	Compliance improvement	Quantitative analysis	Multi-stakeholder organization (Better Work)	Ang et al. (2012)
Physically irreversible compliance point (factory having achieved compliance)	Compliance improvement	Quantitative analysis	Multi-stakeholder organization (Better Work)	Ang et al. (2012)
Integration of labor practices into company systems	Compliance	Qualitative case study	Global buyer	Frenkel and Scott (2002)
Supplier participates in social labeling	Compliance	Qualitative case study	Global buyer	Chakrabarty and Grote (2009)

and thus ownership may not be as important a variable in explaining compliance as these studies highlight.

A big problem here is that only one study (of Better Work) has examined the effects of *supplier management* quality in affecting compliance.[7] This is a huge omission, given that decades of industrial relations research highlights that improvements in working conditions are largely the result of what managers and workers do on a regular basis. A key explanation for this omission is that both multi-stakeholder databases as well as data provided by brands contain relatively little in terms of factory management characteristics or worker characteristics. David Hayer, former vice president of sustainability at Gap Inc., suggested that there was really only one variable that was central to compliance: the quality of supplier factory management.[8] Unfortunately, this variable is rarely measured by buyers or auditors.

Similarly, worker characteristics are also important determinants of compliance. Industrial relations research suggests that skilled workers are more capable of making improvements in their workplace conditions than unskilled workers. Regular workers tend to have more voice with regard to their work conditions than temporary or contract workers. Local workers with "hukou" in China tend to exercise greater voice to improve conditions than migrant workers, as do male workers relative to female workers. The proportion of female and migrant workers is quite key in many countries; research finds compliance is generally lower when these proportions are high. Thus far, however, only the Better Work study has examined the importance of those variables.

As would have been predicted by decades of industrial relations research, the presence of a union at the workplace substantially improves compliance—although the presence of unions in most global supply chains in other countries is quite minimal. This variable has been included only in investigations by Better Work.

Not surprisingly, researchers who study private regulation have paid considerable attention to *private regulation process variables* (table A.4). There is substantial agreement among researchers regarding the weaknesses of auditing in detecting compliance, although only one or two studies have examined the specific impact of a variety of auditing variables in improving compliance.[9] Results suggesting that better trained and more experienced auditors improve compliance are intuitive but also constitute a robust finding across auditing company datasets.[10] Some researchers find that factories that have undergone repeated audits and inspections tend to show better compliance.[11] Others suggest factories often cycle in and out of compliance.[12] The studies of Better Work factories also suggest that, when measured over multiple years, the positive impact of repeated audits on compliance decays over time.[13]

TABLE A.4.   Putative determinants of compliance found in prior research: private regulation process causal variables

CAUSAL VARIABLE	DEPENDENT VARIABLE (FOCUS)	STUDY TYPE	DATA TYPE	EXAMPLE STUDIES
Audit scores (indicator of compliance)	Compliance	Qualitative case study	Global buyer	Locke (2013)
General weaknesses of social auditing	Compliance	Qualitative case studies	Global buyers	Esbenshade (2004); Lebaron and Lister (2015); Locke, Amengual, and Mangla (2009); Pruett (2005); Locke (2013); Frundt (2004); Chan (2010); Barrientos and Smith (2007); Armbruster-Sandoval (2005); Egels-Zandén (2007)
Whether audit is announced	Compliance improvement	Quantitative analysis	Auditing firm	Short, Toffel, and Hugill (2018)
Auditor training	Compliance improvement	Quantitative analysis	Auditing firm	Short, Toffel, and Hugill (2018)
Auditor paid by supplier	Compliance improvement	Quantitative analysis	Auditing firm	Short, Toffel, and Hugill (2018)
Type of prior audit (re-audits)	Compliance; compliance improvement	Quantitative analysis	Auditing firm	Short, Toffel, and Hugill (2018); Toffel, Short, and Ouellet (2015)
Audit duration	Compliance improvement	Quantitative analysis	Auditing firm	Short, Toffel, and Hugill (2018)
Audit team gender	Compliance improvement	Quantitative analysis	Auditing firm	Short, Toffel, and Hugill (2018)
Auditor tenure	Compliance improvement	Quantitative analysis	Auditing firm	Short, Toffel, and Hugill (2018)
Number of auditors	Compliance	Quantitative analysis	Auditing firm	Toffel, Short, and Ouellet (2015)
Multiple inspections of factory	Compliance	Quantitative analysis	Auditing firm	Toffel, Short, and Ouellet (2015)
Year	Compliance	Quantitative analysis	Auditing firm	Toffel, Short, and Ouellet (2015)
Total number of audits and auditing frequency	Compliance	Quantitative analysis	Global buyer	Distelhorst, Hainmueller, and Locke (2017); Esbenshade (2004)

Table A.5 presents some additional general factors that serve as causal variables, and table A.6 lists a number of hypothesized determinants of compliance (also listed as causal variables) advanced by different researchers but not supported by their empirical data. In some cases, the same variable was found to be supported in some studies and not in others.

TABLE A.5. Putative determinants of compliance found in prior research: general factors causal variables

CAUSAL VARIABLE	DEPENDENT VARIABLE (FOCUS)	STUDY TYPE	DATA TYPE	EXAMPLE STUDIES
Public disclosure of audit report or results	Compliance improvement	Quantitative analysis	Multi-stakeholder organization (Better Work)	Ang et al. (2012)
Complementarity between private regulation and public regulation	Compliance; compliance improvement	Qualitative case studies	Global buyer, auditing firm	Locke (2013); Amengual (2010); Levine, Toffel, and Johnson (2012)

TABLE A.6. Hypothesized determinants of compliance not supported in prior research

CAUSAL VARIABLE	DEPENDENT VARIABLE (FOCUS)	STUDY TYPE	DATA TYPE	EXAMPLE STUDIES
SUPPLIER COUNTRY				
Foreign Direct Investment (FDI) inflows	Compliance improvement	Quantitative analysis	Auditing firm	Short, Toffel, and Hugill (2018)
Labor laws and other institutional support for FOA	Compliance improvement	Quantitative analysis	Auditing firm	Short, Toffel, and Hugill (2018)
BUYER/COUNTRY				
Per capita GDP in buyer country	Compliance improvement	Quantitative analysis	Multi-stakeholder organization (FLA)	Stroehle (2017)
Buyer size	Compliance	Quantitative analysis	Multi-stakeholder organization (FLA)	Stroehle (2017)
Buyer stock market listing	Compliance	Quantitative analysis	Multi-stakeholder organization (FLA)	Stroehle (2017)
PRIVATE REGULATION PROCESS				
Previous auditor (participated in factory audit before)	Compliance improvement	Quantitative analysis	Auditing firm	Short, Toffel, and Hugill (2018)
Female audit team (prior audit)	Compliance improvement	Quantitative analysis	Auditing firm	Short, Toffel, and Hugill (2018)
Mixed-gender audit team	Compliance improvement	Quantitative analysis	Auditing firm	Short, Toffel, and Hugill (2018)
Auditor tenure prior audit	Compliance improvement	Quantitative analysis	Auditing firm	Short, Toffel, and Hugill (2018)

TABLE A.6. (continued)

CAUSAL VARIABLE	DEPENDENT VARIABLE (FOCUS)	STUDY TYPE	DATA TYPE	EXAMPLE STUDIES
SUPPLIER CHARACTERISTICS				
Absence of collective bargaining	Compliance	Qualitative case studies	Global buyers	Sabel, O'Rourke, and Fung (2000); Locke, Qin, and Brause (2007); Barrientos (2013)
Whether supplier is a high-value-added supplier	Compliance	Quantitative analysis	Global buyer	Distelhorst, Hainmueller, and Locke (2017)
Whether supplier participates in capacity-building programs of buyer	Compliance	Quantitative analysis	Global buyer	Distelhorst, Hainmueller, and Locke (2017)
High-volume supplier of buyer	Compliance	Quantitative analysis	Global buyer	Distelhorst, Hainmueller, and Locke (2017)
Whether supplier has CSR commitments	Compliance	Quantitative analysis	Global buyer	Distelhorst, Hainmueller, and Locke (2017)

B LAB BENEFIT IMPACT ASSESSMENT QUESTIONS ABOUT SUPPLIER LABOR STANDARDS

TABLE B.1.

QUESTION	ANSWER OPTIONS
What are your company's policies regarding independent contractors that do not work for the company more than 20 hours per week for longer than a six-month period?	We have independent contractors, but have not engaged in any of these practices
	We have a formal routine process for independent contractors to receive post-project or -contract performance feedback
	We have a formal routine process for independent contractors to communicate post-project or post-contract feedback to the company
	Our independent contractors are verified to either work on a time-bound basis, split their time with work for other clients, or have been offered employment
	N/A—we haven't used independent contractors in the last year
	Independent contractors are paid a living wage (calculated as hourly wage when living wage data is available)
If you purchase product from farms or cooperative members, does your company utilize any of the following product collection mechanisms?	The product is weighed and checked for quality standards with the farmer or grower present
	Quality standards and pricing for different products that meet the different standards are clearly defined in all purchase agreements with farmers
	None of the above
	N/A

TABLE B.1. (continued)

QUESTION	ANSWER OPTIONS
How do you collect a majority of the product from the farms or cooperative members you source from?	N/A
	Farmer brings product to our location
	Collect for a location within five miles (or 8 km) of a majority of farms
	Collect for a location greater than five miles (or 8 km) from most farms
	Collect and transport directly from the farm
What is the average length of contract your company has with the farms you source from?	Six to twelve months
	No forward contracts signed
	N/A—no crop purchases
	Less than six months
	Greater than twelve months
What is the average tenure of your company's relationships with suppliers?	Our company has had a relationship with a majority of our suppliers (on a currency basis) since our first year of operations.
	Don't know
	Average tenure of supplier relationships is less than 12 months
	Average tenure of supplier relationships is greater than 60 months
	Average tenure of supplier relationships is greater than 36 months
	Average tenure of supplier relationships is greater than 12 months
Do you comply with third-party traceability and labeling standards to ensure that the origination and supply chain of all products is tracked?	Yes
	No
	N/A—no relevant industry traceability standard
During the last fiscal year, what percentage of products or crops grown (on currency basis) had an environmental certification?	Don't know
	100%
	75–99%
	25–74%
	10–24%
	1–9%
	0%
Does your company screen or evaluate Significant Suppliers for social and environmental impact?	Yes
	No
Does your company subcontract support services (staffing) essential to the delivery of your services to other individuals or organizations?	Yes
	No

TABLE B.1. (continued)

QUESTION	ANSWER OPTIONS
Does your company review or set requirements regarding the labor practices of its subcontracted service providers that includes the following topics?	Professional development opportunities
	Payment of a living wage (for employees and contractors)
	Payment at or above industry benchmarks
	Other labor practices
	None of the above
	N/A
	Employee benefits provided
	Compliance with international human rights and labor standards (for employees and contractors)
	Compliance with all local laws and regulations
What percentage of your subcontracted services (on a currency basis) is accountable to the formalized code of conduct or requirements described in the previous question?	N/A
	100%
	75–99%
	50–74%
	21–49%
	1–20%
	0%
Which of the following methods are used to evaluate the social or environmental impact of your subcontracted services?	Other
	None of the above
	Company utilizes third party risk or impact assessment tools (BIA)
	Company shares policies or rules with subcontractors but does not have a verification process in place
	Company requires subcontractors complete self-designed assessment
	Company has third parties conduct routine audits/reviews of subcontractors at least every two year
	Company conducts routine audits/reviews of subcontractors at least every two years
What percentage of your subcontracted services (on a currency basis) is evaluated based on the methods selected in the previous question?	N/A
	100%
	75–99%
	50–74%
	21–49%
	1–20%
	0%

TABLE B.1. (continued)

QUESTION	ANSWER OPTIONS
What does your company formally screen for regarding the social or environmental practices and performance of your suppliers?	We have no formal screening process in place
	Third-party certifications related to positive social and/or environmental performance
	Positive practices beyond what is required by regulations (e.g., environmentally-friendly manufacturing process, excellent labor practices)
	Other—please describe
	Good governance, including policies related to ethics and corruption
	Compliance with all local laws and regula-tions, including those related to social and environmental performance
What methods does your company use to evaluate the social or environmental impact of your suppliers?	We use third-party risk or impact assessment tools (Sedex, BIA)
	We share policies or rules with suppliers but we don't have a verification process in place
	We require suppliers to complete an assessment we designed
	We have third parties conduct routine audits or reviews of suppliers at least every two years
	We conduct routine audits or reviews of suppliers at least every two years
	Other—please describe
	None of the above
Please select the types of companies that represent your Significant Suppliers:	Technology
	Raw materials
	Professional service firms (consulting, legal, accounting)
	Product manufacturers
	Other—please describe
	Office supplies
	Marketing and advertising
	Independent contractors
	Farms
	Benefits providers

Source: B Lab analytics: https://b-analytics.net/ (variable in dataset: ia_comunity_it_suppliers_distributors).

Notes

PREFACE

1. "New Conversations Project," Cornell University School of Industrial and Labor Relations, https://www.ilr.cornell.edu/new-conversations-project-sustainable-labor-practices -global-supply-chains.

INTRODUCTION

1. Blanchard 2018.
2. Agnew 2018.
3. Anner 2020.
4. Bartley 2007; Fligstein 2005.
5. Bartley 2007.
6. This model has also been referred to as the private governance model, or "private politics."
7. Fung, O'Rourke, and Sabel 2001.
8. Riisgaard 2009; Bartley 2007.
9. Thorlakson, de Zegher, and Lambin 2018.
10. Short, Toffel, and Hugill 2018.
11. Short, Toffel, and Hugill 2018, 2.
12. I am indebted to Darell Doran for this calculation.
13. Undertaken by Richard Locke, Tim Bartley, Niklas Egels-Zanden, and Jodi Short, and their various colleagues.
14. Issued by NGOs such as the Clean Clothes Campaign and the Workers Rights Consortium.

PART 1

1. For example, Appelbaum and Lichtenstein 2016.
2. Bartley et al. 2015, 161.
3. Frenkel 2001; Mamic 2004; Barrientos and Smith 2007; Anner 2012; Locke 2013; Egels-Zandén and Lindholm 2015; Esbenshade 2004; Rodríguez-Garavito 2005; Locke, Qin, and Brause 2007; Koçer and Fransen 2009; Appelbaum and Lichtenstein 2016.
4. Locke 2013. Mean compliance rates of all Nike suppliers between the 2001–2004 period and the 2009–2012 period look remarkably similar.
5. Toffel, McNeely, and Preble 2019, 18.
6. Similarly critical views emerge in different types of studies: analysis of audit data from specialized auditing firms (e.g., Toffel, Short, and Ouellet 2015); analysis of audit data from multi-stakeholder initiatives such as the Fair Labor Association (Anner 2012; Stroehle 2017) and Fair Wear Foundation (Egels-Zandén and Lindholm 2015); and semipublic auditing reports by ILO's Better Factory Cambodia (BFC) project (Oka 2010b; Ang et al. 2012). A variety of NGO investigative reports reach a similar conclusion (e.g., Oxfam, Labour Behind the Label). And evidence from qualitative case studies complement this evidence from empirical studies (Egels-Zandén 2007; Ngai 2005;

Lund-Thomsen et al. 2012; Yu 2008), as does evidence from worker surveys (e.g., Chan and Siu 2010).

7. Nova and Wegemer 2016, 24.

8. Bartley et al 2015, 162.

9. Esbenshade 2004; Bartley 2007; Rodríguez-Garavito 2005; Frundt 2004.

10. Locke 2013.

11. For example, Li and Fung in the apparel industry, and Foxconn in electronics.

12. Locke 2013, 35.

13. A variety of problems have been uncovered; see Locke 2013; Bartley et al. 2015; Short, Toffel, and Hugill 2016.

14. Bartley et al. 2015.

15. A report published by the AFL-CIO titled "Responsibility Outsourced" (Finnegan 2013) contains more evidence regarding auditing, while articles by Short, Toffel, and Hugill (2018) and Short et al. (2019) evaluate the effect of auditing practices and auditor training on compliance, using data provided by a large auditing firm. For more comprehensive reviews of the auditing industry, see the recent Clean Clothes Campaign publication *Fig Leaf for Fashion: How Social Auditing Protects Brands and Fails Workers* (2019).

16. Kuruvilla et al. 2020.

17. As Bartley et al. (2015, 166) suggest, "some brands and retailers have well-staffed and well-meaning compliance departments, but these departments rarely have the power to shape decisions of the production/sourcing departments. This lack of connection between compliance and sourcing is a key failure in the design of private regulation."

18. Anner 2018.

19. Vaughan-Whitehead and Caro 2017.

20. Locke 2013.

21. This has been demonstrated in various studies by Locke and his colleagues in studies of Nike (e.g., Locke et al. 2007; Locke and Romis 2010; Locke, Amengual, and Mangla 2009), which have been summarized in Locke (2013), as well as others, such as Oka 2010a; Knudsen 2013; Distelhorst et al. 2015; Toffel, Short, and Ouellet 2015; Hsieh, Toffel, and Hull 2019.

22. Koçer and Fransen 2009; Toffel, Short, and Ouellet 2015.

23. Oka 2010a, 2010b.

24. Moran 2002; Baumann-Pauly et al. 2013.

25. Mosley 2010.

26. Quinn 1997; Fülöp, Hisrich, and Szegedi 2000.

27. Esbenshade 2004; Nova and Wegemer 2016.

28. Kuruvilla and Fischer-Daly n.d.

29. Meyer and Rowan 1977.

30. Bromley and Powell 2012, 7 and 15.

31. Bromley and Powell 2012, 13–14.

32. Bromley and Powell 2012, 14.

33. Bromley and Powell 2012; Wijen 2014; Briscoe and Murphy 2012.

34. Wijen 2014, 302.

35. Bromley and Powell 2012, 6.

36. Wijen 2014.

37. Wijen 2014, 307.

38. Kuruvilla et al 2020.

39. Wijen 2014, 305.

40. Wijen 2014.

41. Wijen 2014, 306.

42. Wijen 2014, 303.

1. BEHAVIORAL INVISIBILITY

1. Wijen 2014, 307.

2. E.g., Locke 2013; Short, Toffel, and Hugill 2018.

3. Anner 2012; Egels-Zandén and Merk 2014.

4. Barrientos and Smith 2007; Distelhorst, Hainmueller, and Locke 2017; Short, Toffel, and Hugill 2018.

5. Kuruvilla et al. 2020.

6. Chatterji and Toffel 2010; Toffel, Short, and Ouellet 2015; Stroehle 2017.

7. These results are available from the author upon request.

8. Roberts and Engardino 2006; Egels-Zandén 2014.

9. "Third-level auditing consultant" 2016. Based on the information this consultant shared in blogs, he was born in 1984 in Guilin, Guangxi, and graduated from Guangxi University of Finance and Economics in 2006. He explained his initial motivation for publishing his work logs in their entirety: "I want to share details of my personal life while hiding my identity, revealing the interesting and meaningful aspects of my work." As of February 2019, his work logs had been accessed nearly seven thousand times.

10. Tianya 2019.

11. Strauss and Corbin 1994; Bryman 2016. Following the method, the research took a thematic coding approach, which involves generating initial or open codes and then aggregating codes that are linked by a common theme or idea to form categories, which are further aggregated into important theoretical variables or constructs. We used the text and images from the advertisements of the audit consulting companies to generate first-order codes for each of the fifteen companies studied. We then selected themes from this coding process that were common to all the companies. We followed a similar process when analyzing the auditing coach's work logs. We coded every incident reported in the work log and then compared across incidents to find similarities and differences. The resulting categories were labeled, compared, and grouped to generate a picture of the varieties of services provided by the auditing coach, using a time-based framework that lists the different activities of the audit consulting *before*, *during*, and *after* the audit.

12. June 19, 2017.

13. November 11, 2016.

14. August 31, 2016.

15. China's Protection for Underage Workers Act ([1994] No. 498) has specific provisions on the use of underage workers in terms of permissible job types, working hours, labor intensity, and protection measures. These workers may not be assigned to lift heavy weights, to do jobs that expose them to toxic conditions, or to do other work classified as harmful or dangerous. These provisions explain why the audit coach falsified the birth year of the worker, even though that worker was technically not engaged in "child labor."

16. June 30, 2017.

17. August 31, 2016.

18. June 22, 2016.

19. June 7, 2017.

20. November 25, 2016.

21. July 28, 2016.

22. July 29, 2016.

23. September 5, 2016.

24. December 29, 2016.

25. July 14, 2016.

26. July 16, 2016.

27. June 22, 2016.

28. October 5, 2016.

29. June 21, 2017.

30. Locke (2013) highlighted the differential interests of buyers and suppliers. All the suppliers I interviewed as part of my research for this book consistently complained about brands wanting suppliers to increase compliance (the costs of which suppliers must bear), while continually squeezing them on the price of products.

31. Schuler and Christmann 2011.

32. Anner 2018.

33. Distelhorst, 2020.

34. Graffin and Ward 2010.

35. As suggested by Meyer and Rowan 1977.

36. Meyer and Rowan 1977.

37. Meyer and Rowan 1977, 359.

38. Jiang and Bansal 2003.

39. Bromley and Powell 2012; Wijen 2014.

40. Bromley and Powell 2012.

2. PRACTICE MULTIPLICITY IN THE IMPLEMENTATION OF PRIVATE REGULATION PROGRAMS

1. Wijen 2014, 307.

2. O'Rourke 2006, 5–6.

3. OECD 1999.

4. Both WRAP and BSCI, which are more business controlled, are perceived by observers as "less stringent" (Fransen 2011; Fransen and Burgoon 2012) and tend therefore to attract membership from more global brands. In fact, BSCI has four times the membership of FLA and eight times that of ETI (see Fransen 2011, table 4). Clearly, these organizational differences between MSIs matter as they compete for business participation (Fransen 2011).

5. Center for the Study of Work, Labor, and Democracy 2014.

6. Fair Labor Association 2015, 1.

7. Fransen 2011. Fransen analyzed one major failed effort toward convergence, the Joint Initiative on Accountability and Workers Rights (JO-IN), which began in 2004. JO-IN participants—which included the FLA, WRC, SAI, ETI, FWF, and the Clean Clothes Campaign (a nongovernmental organization)—wanted to create a common labor standard for the apparel industry.

8. Reinecke, Manning, and Von Hagen 2012, 791.

9. Fransen 2011, 359.

10. O'Rourke 2006, 906.

11. Details available upon request from the author.

12. Interviews were conducted with two marketing managers; three officers of the supplier's own corporate social responsibility department, including the head of sustainability; and ten plant-level sustainability executives (five per factory) responsible for implementing sustainability initiatives but also for compliance with the codes of conduct of their global customers. I also interviewed the head and deputy head of manufacturing.

13. This experience is broadly consistent with the frequent complaint of "audit fatigue" by suppliers that service multiple brands.

14. Interview with AAA's sustainability officer.

15. The variation could also result, at least in part, from a lack of uniform training for auditors.

16. I acknowledge that the number of instances of noncompliance is less important than the severity of those issues, but it was impossible to judge severity by examining the

audit reports, given the absence of weighting information and the fact that particular auditors' conceptions of severity might differ.

17. Interview with AAA's chief sustainability officer.

18. Frenkel and Scott 2002.

19. Locke 2013.

20. Locke 2013.

21. SLCP website, https://slconvergence.org/.

22. Social & Labor Convergence Program 2018.

23. At the time of writing, SLCP is engaged in discussions about merging its data collection instrument with that of the ILO's Better Work program.

24. Wijen 2014.

25. Kuruvilla et al. 2020.

26. Wijen 2014.

3. CAUSAL COMPLEXITY

1. Locke 2013.

2. Locke (2013), for example, uses Nike's M-Audit scores to look at Nike's progress over time.

3. Although Locke's (2013) research provides evidence of the importance of this variable in several studies, recent research by Kuruvilla et al. (2020) shows that leverage does not matter at all in compliance in a study of one firm's global supply chain.

4. HomeRetailer also provided audit scores on two other outcome standards: that workers shall have one day off within every seven days and that they shall enjoy paid leave according to local laws and customs. Since we obtained payroll information for only one month, we were not able to calculate compliance on these standards. An earlier analysis (Kuruvilla et al. 2020) highlights the difficulties in measuring or auditing the four "outcome standards." The actual assessment of wages, hours, and other easy-to-assess items is far more complex than previously believed, given the variety of local, regional, and industry regulations and practices that must be taken into account while auditing. While I do not know exactly how HomeRetailer's auditors assessed the standards, it is unlikely that their efforts were as comprehensive as ours, given that they completed their work in only two days. It took three members of our team working over several days to assess these standards, including extensive research to account for local practices and local and regional variations in rules and regulations. Thus, differences between HomeRetailer's audit assessments and our efforts would be expected.

5. Since compliance outcomes for individual workers are nested within thirty suppliers, we used multilevel linear regression to analyze antecedents of compliance outcomes for workers. (Some suppliers may systematically comply better than others, and thus supplier-level variables may influence individual-level outcomes.) Essentially, the model we test is whether our compliance index could be predicted by the retailer's *audit scores*, its *leverage over the supplier* (measured by the percentage of that supplier's production accounted for by HomeRetailer), and the *length of relationships* (in years) between the supplier and HomeRetailer. We added controls for industry, region, and workforce characteristics. If these three variables associated with the private regulation model were found to be significant predictors of our compliance index, we would conclude that that these variables, found to be important determinants of compliance in prior research, would generalize to our sample as well. If not, we would conclude that there is evidence of causal complexity.

6. Note that this gap or underreporting constitutes a lower bound because we assessed only four measurable items and only for the month covered in the payroll data provided.

7. This analysis used Poisson regression. Since the dependent variable of audit scores is count data (i.e., how many items are compiled), Poisson modeling is more appropriate than the typically used ordinary least square (OLS) estimation, designed for continuous dependent variables such as wages.

8. For example, Wijen 2014.

PART 2

1. See, e.g., Barrientos and Smith 2007; Egels-Zandén 2014.

2. Walsh and Greenhouse 2012.

3. Most of these analyses are by Drusilla Brown and her colleagues at the Tufts University Labor Lab, https://sites.tufts.edu/laborlab.

4. Bartley et al. 2015.

5. Ahmed and Nathan 2014.

4. HAS PRIVATE REGULATION IMPROVED LABOR PRACTICES?

1. Appelbaum 2016, 48.

2. Bartley et al. 2015, 161. A significant majority of the research literature hews to this view; see Frenkel 2001; Mamic 2004; Esbenshade 2004; Rodríguez-Garavito 2005; Barrientos and Smith 2007; Locke, Qin, and Brause 2007; Koçer and Fransen 2009; Locke 2013; and Appelbaum and Lichtenstein 2016.

3. These data do not capture *slavery* specifically.

4. A more exhaustive analysis of the progress on freedom of association in chapter 6 uses multiple datasets.

5. The dramatic increase in Bangladesh is probably attributable to the activities of the Accord on Fire and Building Safety and the Alliance for Bangladesh Worker Safety, which were established after the Rana Plaza factory fire and have focused primarily on uncovering violations with respect to safety and health in Bangladesh factories.

6. Anner 2012.

7. Locke 2013.

8. Graphs for each category that show how these categories of violations play out across countries and industries for each category are available from the author upon request.

9. Locke 2013.

10. Whether this finding can be generalized to other samples is unclear without comparable data.

11. For a detailed description and analysis of Better Work, see Brown, Dehejia, and Robertson 2013.

12. Better Work data for Bangladesh, the seventh country, was not available.

13. Rossi 2015, 507–8.

14. Although we report only eight cycles here, the Better Work data did include twenty-eight factories that were on their ninth to fourteenth cycles. The pattern noted continues for these factories—that is, there is improvement on most clusters (with exceptions for wages and safety and health clusters, but only for a very small number of factories). More research may be necessary to understand these outliers.

15. Anner 2017b.

16. In his study of Nike, the most comprehensive study of a single supply chain, Locke (2013) found that improvement was not sustained. The distribution of audit scores (compliance ratings) in Nike supplier factories had not changed between the early and late 2000s.

17. HomeRetailer singled out these items in the early phase of its code of conduct implementation, believing compliance with them was difficult for suppliers. Compliance was compulsory for all the other items.

18. Egels-Zandén (2014), a study of toy manufacturers in Guangdong, China.

5. WAGES IN GLOBAL SUPPLY CHAINS

1. Joint Ethical Trading Initiative 2015, 6.

2. These approaches have been reviewed and described extensively elsewhere; see Bryher 2019; Anker and Anker 2017b; Vaughan-Whitehead 2011; Guzi and Kahanec 2018; Asia Floor Wage n.d.; Van Klaveren 2016. The different approaches to implementing these approaches have also been well described in prior literature (Hohenegger and Miller 2017; ASN Bank 2019). Hence the review here will be necessarily brief.

3. The AFWA wage of 1,181 PPP$ translates into 37,661 takas for Bangladesh; 1,939,606 real in Cambodia; 23,588 rupees in India; 5,886,112 rupiah in Indonesia; 37,886 rupees in Pakistan; 58,093 rupees in Sri Lanka; and 4,547 yuan in China. See https://asia.floorwage.org/.

4. GLWC includes Fairtrade International, GoodWeave International, the Rainforest Alliance, and Social Accountability International.

5. Global Living Wage Coalition 2018, based on the living wage calculations developed by Richard Anker and Martha Anker (2017b).

6. The GLWC estimates for India vary across regions. For the garment cluster in Tiruppur, Tamil Nadu, the benchmark is 14,670 rupees, whereas it is only 8,929 rupees for Bhadohi in Uttar Pradesh.

7. WageIndicator 2019a. This is consistent with Anker and Anker's (2017b) definition noted in the GLWC description.

8. Clothing is included as a part of the 10 percent margin kept aside for unanticipated expenses.

9. The brands include C&A, Debenhams, H&M, Inditex, Primark, Tchibo, PVH, and twelve others.

10. Fair Wage Network 2019.

11. FWN's website suggests it is active in several sectors. Illustrative case studies focus on companies such as Ikea, Adidas, Unilever, H&M, and Puma, among others, but do not present any data regarding wage progression in their supplier factories. See http://fair-wage.com/.

12. Hohenegger and Miller 2017.

13. Fair Wear Foundation 2017.

14. Fair Labor Association 2016, 2018, 2019.

15. Bartley (2018), for example, showed there was no wage *premium* linked to buyer-imposed labor standards when he compared wages in SA8000-certified factories and uncertified factories.

16. Adler-Milstein and Kline 2017.

17. A series of ILO reports attempt systematic cross-country analyses of trends and minimum wage payments in the global and Asian garment industries (Huynh 2017; Cowgill and Huynh 2016; Cowgill, Luebker, and Xia 2015; Luebker 2014).

18. McMullen and Majumdar 2016.

19. Musiolek et al. 2017.

20. Bryher (2019), which followed up on a CCC 2014 report with the same title. The brands included Adidas, Amazon, C&A, Decathlon, Fruit of the Loom, Gap, G-Star RAW, H&M, Hugo Boss, Inditex, Levi Strauss, Nike, Primark, Puma, PVH, Tchibo, Under Armour, Uniqlo, and Zalando—of which fourteen responded to the survey in full and six responded in part. Details on the survey and weights allocated to the different questions are available on CCC's website: https://cleanclothes.org/news/2019/major-brands-are-failing-on-living-wage-commitments.

21. Fair Labor Association 2016.

22. See https://www.fairlabor.org/global-issues/fair-compensation.

23. Egels-Zandén 2017.

24. Anner 2018.

25. Vaughan-Whitehead and Caro 2017. Better Buying's report (Dickson 2019) also touches on these issues.

26. In addition to the problem of exchange rate variation, one limitation in using nominal wages is that they do not account for inflation in consumer prices. Therefore, we converted these nominal wages into "real" wages. We first converted nominal wages in local currencies to real wages in reference year 2017, using consumer price indices (CPIs) available on the International Monetary Fund website (IMF 2019). "Wage in year z" $\times \dfrac{\text{CPI of 2017}}{\text{CPI of year z}} =$ The worth of "wage in year z" in 2017. We then converted these real wages to 2017 US dollars (USD), using corresponding USD currency rates.

27. We calculate average monthly basic wages by multiplying average basic hourly wages by the weekly working hours considered to be a standard work week according to national law in each country, and then by 4.33 (an average number of weeks in a month, obtained by dividing 52 weeks per year with 12 months). The legal standard work week was obtained from the WageIndicator foundation and the ILO (WageIndicator 2019b; International Labour Office and International Finance Corporation 2013). The standard work week is 48 hours for all countries in the sample except for China (44), Indonesia (40), and Turkey (45).

28. World Bank 2019.

29. WageIndicator 2019c.

30. Horne and de Andrade 2017.

31. AFW uses a different rupiah-to-PPP conversion factor (4985.7) than ours (4245.56).

32. World Bank 2015. The three-stage poverty lines used in the AUDCO analysis were only introduced only in 2017, so here we used the same figure across all countries for data from 2016.

33. Note that WIF living wage estimates are not available for all countries in the ApparelCo dataset and that the AFWA wage estimate is available only for Asian countries.

34. Anner 2018; Vaughan-Whitehead and Caro 2017.

35. ASN Bank 2019.

6. FREEDOM OF ASSOCIATION AND COLLECTIVE BARGAINING IN GLOBAL SUPPLY CHAINS

1. Case studies, in particular based on complaints concerning FOA and CB (e.g., Worker Rights Consortium reporting), have provided the basis for substantial prior research on FOA and CB, and some scholars have assessed sets of cases from specific initiatives, such as a multi-stakeholder initiative (Barrientos, Gereffi, and Rossi 2011) and the International Labour Organization–International Finance Corporation (ILO-IFC) Better Work program (Anner 2017b).

2. This argument is consistent with prior research (e.g., Distelhorst and Locke 2018).

3. That the four organizations whose data are used in this chapter *shared* those data signals what we hope is increasing transparency in the global apparel industry around freedom of association. The wide scope of analysis permitted by the large datasets provides nuanced insights into FOA in the apparel industry.

4. Leary 2003, 43.

5. Cooper 2004.

6. Perea 2011.

7. Friedman 2014.

8. Brass 2010.

9. Castel 2000.

10. Frenkel and Kuruvilla 2002.

11. Laval and Dardot 2017.

12. Anner et al. 2006.

13. Fung, O'Rourke, and Sabel 2001.

14. Mamic 2004.

15. Jenkins 2001, 22.

16. Compa and Hinchliffe-Darricarrère 1995. Earlier multilateral codes included the 1976 Organization for Economic Cooperation and Development (OECD) Guidelines for Multinational Enterprises and 1977 International Labor Organization (ILO) Tripartite Declaration of Principles Concerning Multinational Enterprises. Privately introduced codes included the 1977 Sullivan Principles, 1984 MacBride Principles, 1988 Slepak Principles, 1991 Miller Principles, and 1991 Maquiladora Standards of Conduct.

17. Esbenshade 2004; Bartley 2007; Appelbaum and Lichtenstein 2016.

18. Fair Labor Association 2011, 4.

19. Ethical Trading Initiative n.d.

20. Fair Wear Foundation n.d.

21. Rodríguez-Garavito 2005; Barrientos, Gereffi, and Rossi 2011; Anner 2012; Locke 2013; Toffel, Short, and Ouellet 2015.

22. Fransen 2011; Merk 2008.

23. Distelhorst and Locke 2018, 707.

24. Weisbrot et al. 2017.

25. Atleson et al. 2008.

26. Frenkel and Kuruvilla 2002.

27. Anner 2015.

28. Keck and Sikkink 1998; Den Hond and Bakker 2012.

29. Oka 2018.

30. Esbenshade 2004; Rodríguez-Garavito 2005; Barrientos and Smith 2007; Locke et al. 2007; Fransen 2013; Lund-Thomsen and Lindgreen 2014; International Labour Office 2016; Locke 2013; Appelbaum and Lichtenstein 2016.

31. Riisgaard 2009; Bartley and Egels-Zandén 2015.

32. Koçer and Fransen 2009.

33. Finnegan 2013.

34. Egels-Zandén and Merk 2014; Selwyn 2017.

35. Toffel, Short, and Ouellet 2015.

36. Anner 2012.

37. O'Rourke 1997; Bair and Gereffi 2001; Locke et al. 2007; Anner 2012; Fransen 2013.

38. Chan 2016.

39. Bartley and Lu 2012; Egels-Zandén and Merk 2014.

40. US Senate Foreign Relations Committee, quoted in Claeson 2014, 38.

41. Granath 2016.

42. The Better Work program has operated in Bangladesh, Cambodia, Haiti, Indonesia, Jordan, Lesotho, Nicaragua, Vietnam, and (more recently) Ethiopia.

43. Better Work 2013.

44. Polaski 2009.

45. Brown et al. 2016.

46. Anner 2017b.

47. Pike 2018.

48. Bartley and Lu 2012; Egels-Zandén and Merk 2014.

49. Kidger 1991; Bryson 2004, 230; Terry 1999.

50. As found by Bartley and Egels-Zandén (2016) in their study in Indonesia.

51. Anner, Bair, and Blasi 2013.

52. Anner, Bair, and Blasi 2013.

53. Arengo, Foxvog, and Newell 2019.

54. Worker Rights Consortium 2019.

55. Adler-Milstein and Kline 2017; Berliner et al. 2015, 119–124; Conner, Delaney, and Rennie 2016.

56. The eight factors are constraints on government powers, absence of corruption, open government, fundamental rights, order and security, regulatory enforcement, civil justice, and criminal justice (World Justice Project 2019, 10–13).

57. The nine sources are ILO Committee of Experts on the Application of Conventions and Recommendations reports; ILO Conference Committee on the Application of Standards reports; the ILO Declaration Annual Review Country Baselines; Representations under Article 24 of the ILO Constitution; Complaints under Article 26 of the ILO Constitution; ILO Committee on Freedom of Association reports; national legislation; the International Trade Union Confederation Annual Survey of Violations of Trade Union Rights; and the US Department of State's Country Reports on Human Rights Practices.

58. Center for Global Workers' Rights 2016. For a detailed explanation of the methodology see http://labour-rights-indicators.la.psu.edu/.

59. For further description of the WSJ overall rule-of-law index and regulatory enforcement factor, see https://worldjusticeproject.org/our-work/research-and-data/wjp-rule-law-index-2019.

60. A linear regression model of the relationship between the countries where H&M sourced its products and Labour Rights Indicators indicated a significant positive relationship between the brand's sourcing locations and violations of FOA and CB ($\beta = 1.20$; $p < 0.000$; R-squared $= 0.32$), while a separate regression model indicated a negative relationship between H&M's sourcing locations and the World Justice Project index of fundamental labor rights enforcement ($\beta = -20.75$; $p < 0.01$; R-squared $= 0.30$).

61. Anner 2012; Toffel, Short, and Ouellet 2015; Short, Toffel, and Hugill 2016; and Egels-Zandén and Lindholm 2015.

62. Bromley and Powell 2012.

63. Short, Toffel, and Hugill, 2016.

64. For example, Bartley et al. 2015.

65. Toffel, Short, and Ouellet 2015; Short, Toffel, and Hugill 2016.

66. International Labour Organization 2017.

67. Anner 2012; Li, Friedman, and Ren 2016; Orleck 2018.

68. It is important to note that missing data on the relationship between CBAs and overall code compliance reduced the number of factories for this analysis to 1,243.

69. For example, Barrientos, Gereffi, and Rossi 2011.

70. The dataset did not cover ILO Better Work Bangladesh, where Better Work has conducted assessments since 2015. For more information regarding Bangladesh, see https://idowedo.fr/wp-content/uploads/2018/10/Better-Work-Bangladesh-at-a-Glance_Web.pdf. And also see https://betterwork.org/blog/portfolio/better-work-bangladesh-annual-report-2019-an-industry-and-compliance-review/.

71. According to Better Work, this could be the result of a data coding issue. Noncompliance is coded as 1, while no evidence of noncompliance is coded as 0. If most questions in the FOA cluster are contingent on union or CBA presence, factories without unions, CBAs, or both will have a lot more zeros than factories with a union. For instance, if there is no union in the first place, there is no evidence that the factory is noncompliant with union operations.

72. Freeman and Medoff 1984; Doucouliagos, Freeman, and Laroche 2017.

73. See, e.g., Barrientos, Gereffi, and Rossi 2011.
74. Bird, Short, and Toffel 2019; Bartley and Egels-Zandén 2016.
75. Anner 2017b.
76. Conner, Delaney, and Rennie 2016.

PART 3

1. Lichtenstein 2016, 101.
2. The term of the Accord was extended for three transition years beginning January 1, 2019.
3. Lichtenstein 2016.
4. Toffel, Short, and Ouellet 2015; Short, Toffel, and Hugill 2016, 2018.
5. See, for example, Amengual and Chirot 2016; Tampe 2018.
6. See, for example, Nova and Wegemer 2016; Anner 2018.
7. Lichtenstein 2016.
8. Nova and Wegemer 2016.
9. Anner 2018, 2.
10. Mezzadri 2017.
11. Andersson et al. 2018.
12. Mezzadri 2017.
13. Bird, Short, and Toffel 2019.
14. Bartley and Egels-Zandén 2016.

7. ARE CHANGES IN CORPORATE GOVERNANCE AN ANSWER?

1. Anner 2019.
2. Friedman 1970.
3. Freeman and Evan 1990; Freeman and Phillips 2002.
4. Porter and Kramer 2011, 4.
5. B Lab 2019a.
6. Hiller 2013, 288.
7. Baudot, Dillard, and Pencle 2020, 2; Stecker 2016; Clark and Vranka 2013, 17; Hiller 2013.
8. *eBay Domestic Holdings v. Newmark*, 16 A.3d 1 (Del. Ch. 2010). Most publicly traded US companies are incorporated in Delaware (Clark and Vranka 2013, 10; Baudot, Dillard, and Pencle 2020, 5), although most private companies are incorporated in their home state (McDonnell 2014, 68).
9. Robson 2015, 510.
10. Clark and Vranka 2013, 11.
11. Weismann 2017, 6.
12. Freeman 1984.
13. Stout 2012.
14. Porter and Kramer 2011.
15. Clark and Vranka 2013; McDonnell 2014.
16. Honeyman 2014.
17. Cone LLC 2010; Nielsen 2015.
18. B Lab 2017.
19. Del. Code Ann. tit. 8, § 362(a).
20. Cal. Corp. Code § 2602(b)(2) and Minn. Stat. Ann. § 304A.104(2).
21. Model Legislation § 102(a). Cal. Corp. Code § 14601(e). See also, e.g., Md. Code Ann., Corps. & Ass'ns § 5-6C-01(d); N.J. Stat. Ann. § 14A:18-1; Vt. Stat. Ann. tit. 11A, § 21.03(6).

22. Model Legislation § 201(c).

23. Delaware permits but does not require third-party verification of the report. Del. Code Ann. tit. 8 §366(b), (c).

24. Model Legislation § 102(a). See also, e.g., Cal. Corp. Code § 14601(g).

25. McDonnell 2014; Loewenstein 2017; Lee 2018. Delaware restricts standing only to directors.

26. McDonnell 2014, 42.

27. McDonnell 2014, 30.

28. B Lab 2019d.

29. B Lab 2019c.

30. Stecker 2016, n. 11. As of May 25, 2019, the B Lab website did not mention visits to B-Corps.

31. B Lab n.d.a.

32. B Lab 2019e.

33. https://data.world/solutions/unite-and-discover-2/.

34. B Lab n.d.b.

35. B Lab 2018.

36. B Lab n.d.a.

37. Variations of the benefit corporation have been established in the United Kingdom and Italy and remain under consideration in Australia, Argentina, Chile, Colombia, and Canada.

38. B Lab 2019b.

39. Lee 2018; Hiller and Shackelford 2018; Murray 2012.

40. Hiller and Shackelford 2018, 46.

41. André 2012, 139; McDonnell 2014, 62; Lee 2018, 1100.

42. Hacker 2016, 1750, 1763.

43. McDonnell 2014.

44. McDonnell 2014, 60–61.

45. Weismann 2017, 2, 26.

46. Quoted in Hacker 2016, 1762; emphasis added.

47. Clark and Vranka 2013, 25.

48. Hacker 2016, 1767.

49. Robson 2015, 518.

50. Murray 2015.

51. Weismann 2017, 21.

52. Baudot, Dillard, and Pencle 2020.

53. Lee 2018, 1083–91.

54. Weismann 2017, 19–20; Boatright 2018; Keating 2009.

55. Bauer and Umlas 2017.

56. B Lab n.d.b.

57. Nass 2014; Weismann 2017, 29.

58. SA8000 defines a living wage as "the remuneration received for a standard work week by a worker in a particular place sufficient to afford a decent standard of living for the worker and her or his family. Elements of a decent standard of living include food, water, housing, education, health care, transport, clothing, and other essential needs including provision for unexpected events." SA8000 Guidance states: "Minimum wages are often set to compete with low cost suppliers in other countries and not to promote workers' welfare. Therefore many countries have minimum wage levels that do not meet the basic needs of workers and their families. These wages also frequently do not reflect inflation and other factors that affect actual standards of living. Lack of enforcement of even these minimal rates of pay is common, forcing workers to work excessive

overtime in order to earn enough to meet basic needs" (Social Accountability International 2016, 82).

59. For example, the US Tariff Act, California Transparency in Supply Chains Act, and United Kingdom Modern Day Slavery Act.

60. Elliott and Freeman 2003; Devinney, Auger, and Eckhardt 2010.

61. See SAI website, www.sa-intl.org.

62. Locke et al. 2007; Koçer and Fransen 2009; Toffel, Short, and Ouellet 2015.

63. Bromley and Powell 2012.

64. Locke 2013.

65. Glasmeier n.d.; Cooper 2014.

66. See, for example, Lund-Thomsen and Lindgreen 2014; Ruwanpura and Wrigley 2011.

67. Oxfam 2010; Barrientos, Gereffi, and Rossi 2011; Locke 2013; Bartley and Kincaid 2015; Appelbaum and Lichtenstein 2016; Anner 2017.

68. Bromley and Powell 2012.

69. Bartley and Egels-Zandén 2016.

70. Bromley and Powell 2012.

71. DiMaggio and Powell 1983.

8. ALIGNING SOURCING AND COMPLIANCE INSIDE A GLOBAL CORPORATION

1. Fung, O'Rourke, and Sabel 2001.

2. Barrientos and Smith 2007; Mosley 2010; Mayer and Gereffi 2010; Ruwanpura and Wrigley 2011; Oka 2012; Locke 2013; Anner, Bair, and Blasi 2013; Bartley et al. 2015; Bartley and Egels-Zandén 2015; Distelhorst et al. 2015.

3. Anner 2018; Anner, Bair, and Blasi 2013.

4. Oxfam 2010; Barrientos, Gereffi, and Rossi 2011.

5. Locke 2013; Anner 2018.

6. Greenhill, Mosley, and Prakash 2009.

7. Locke 2013.

8. Locke 2013.

9. Distelhorst and Locke 2018.

10. Oka 2012.

11. Malesky and Mosley 2018.

12. Ruwanpura and Wrigley 2011; Egels-Zandén 2007; Oxfam 2010; Barrientos, Gereffi, and Rossi 2011; Bartley and Kincaid 2014; Appelbaum and Lichtenstein 2016.

13. Kuruvilla et al. 2020; see also chapter 2 of this book.

14. Locke 2013.

15. Toffel, McNeely, and Preble 2019.

16. Toffel, McNeely, and Preble 2019, 7.

17. Hsieh, Toffel, and Hull 2019.

18. Hsieh, Toffel, and Hull 2019, 8.

19. Amengual, Distelhorst, and Tobin 2019.

20. Amengual, Distelhorst, and Tobin 2019, 17.

21. Amengual, Distelhorst, and Tobin 2019, 19.

22. Amengual, Distelhorst, and Tobin 2019, 27.

23. Amengual, Distelhorst, and Tobin 2019, 27.

24. The coalition included the International Labor Rights Forum, As You Sew, the Center for Reflection Education and Action, Calvert Investments, and the Environmental Justice Foundation.

25. This observation is from a research report about Pangia not cited here to maintain the company's anonymity. The report is included in this book's bibliography.

26. Locke 2013.

27. Interviews conducted by the author, March 2017, at the company's headquarters and at regional offices throughout Asia.

28. This is not "technically" correct. Sourcing teams for each brand reported into their geography heads, and ultimately to the corporate head of supply chain issues, de jure, but de facto each brand had dedicated sourcing people.

29. Our interviews suggest the percentage sourced from preferred vendors had increased to 75 percent in 2018.

9. FROM OPACITY TO TRANSPARENCY

1. Wijen 2014; Briscoe and Murphy 2012.

2. Bromley and Powell 2012, 36.

3. Wijen 2014.

4. Wijen 2014, 312.

5. Bartley 2018.

6. There is voluminous literature on the Accord; see Anner, Bair, and Blasi 2013; Ter Haar and Keune 2014; Greenhouse and Yardley 2013; Baumann-Pauly, Labowitz, and Banerjee 2015; and Baumann-Pauly, Labowitz, and Stein 2018.

7. See the lively exchange between Anner, Bair, and Blasi (2013) and Baumann-Pauly, Labowitz, and Banerjee (2015). A major criticism concerns the narrow scope of the Accord. For example, Anner, Bair, and Blasi (2013) note that the Accord covers only worker safety and fails to address various other labor issues in corporate codes of conduct.

8. The Playfair Alliance is an alliance of labor unions and NGOs, including Industri-ALL, Maquila Solidarity Network, and the Clean Clothes Campaign, that has been campaigning for years to persuade selected apparel and footwear companies to improve labor practices in supply chains.

9. Conner, Delaney, and Rennie 2016.

10. SPN (National Workers Union) KASBI (Indonesian Congress of Allied Unions), Garteks-SBSI (Footwear, Leather, Textile and Garment Federation), GSBI (Indonesian Workers' Federation), FSPTSK (Federation of Textile, Garment and Footwear Unions).

11. Connor, Delaney, and Rennie (2016) offer a more critical evaluation of the progress made by the FOA Protocol. Their report highlights several issues that create barriers to the program's long-term sustainability. These issues include considerable tensions between employers and unions in its implementation; modest institutional funding that is in jeopardy; and a lack of sustained engagement from all parties. While there is more nuance in their report, they suggest that the program can be criticized for the relatively few global companies participating. The authors emphasize the need for "sustained, strategic collaboration among all actors and strategic monitoring and campaigning to extend the protocol" for the FOA Protocol to build on its initial (fragile) success.

12. Connor, Delaney, and Rennie 2016.

13. Ashwin et al. 2020.

14. Ashwin et al. 2020.

15. Kuruvilla et al. 2020.

16. Wijen 2014.

17. Hsieh, Toffel, and Hull 2019; Yoffie 1998; Toffel, McNeely, and Preble 2019.

18. Toffel, McNeely, and Preble 2019, 2.

19. Amengual, Distelhorst, and Tobin 2019.

20. Wijen 2014.

21. Fransen and Burgoon 2012.

22. Locke 2013, 35.

23. Bartley et al. 2015, 165.

24. Bartley and Lu 2012; Anner 2017a; Pike 2018; Granath 2016; Egels-Zandén and Merk 2014; Bryson 2004; Terry 1999.

25. Hoang 2019.

26. Worker-Driven Social Responsibility Network 2019.

27. Wijen 2014, 313.

28. Espinosa and Walker 2011.

29. Mohin 2018.

30. Mol 2010.

31. The investment community requires companies to be transparent. Many frameworks, from Dow Jones, Bloomberg, and others, measure companies on their environmental, social, and governance (ESG) practices, and investors and the public increasingly look to these for guidance regarding a company's business practices.

32. Gardner et al. 2019.

33. Ahmed et al. 2019.

34. Labrecque 2014.

35. IndustriALL Global Union, International Trade Union Confederation, UNI Global Union, Human Rights Watch, Clean Clothes Campaign, Maquila Solidarity Network, Worker Rights Consortium, International Corporate Accountability Roundtable, and International Labor Rights Forum.

36. Companies that signed the pledge and have already posted the information include, among others, Adidas, C&A, H&M, Levi Strauss & Co., Patagonia, Gap Inc., and Primark.

37. Egels-Zandén and Hansson 2016, 385–86.

38. Fashion Revolution, "Transparency Is Trending," 2019, https://www.fashionrevolution.org/transparency-is-trending/.

39. Gardner et al. 2019.

40. Marzullo 2018.

41. DiMaggio and Powell, 1983, 149.

42. DiMaggio and Powell, 1983, 152.

43. IOD PARC 2015.

44. IOD PARC 2015, 14.

45. Fair Labor Association Board of Directors Meeting 2018, 3.

46. Sedex 2019c.

47. Sedex 2019b.

48. Sedex 2019a.

49. Kelly et al. 2019.

50. Fair Factories Clearinghouse 2019.

51. See https://betterbuying.org/.

52. Indeed, such arrangements have allowed publication of important analyses that further our understanding of what works in private regulation and what are the key barriers and best practices. These can be found in the various works of Locke, Toffel, Bartley, Egels-Zandén, Amengual, Distelhorst, and their colleagues, among others. Some of the data used in this book have been obtained using nondisclosure agreements. The "New Conversations" project at Cornell University offers a fee-based service for global companies and MSIs seeking analysis of their supply-chain data with respect to labor practices.

53. Amengual, Distelhorst, and Tobin 2019.

54. Locke 2013; Short, Toffel, and Hugill 2018.

55. Egels-Zandén 2007; Egels-Zandén 2014; Egels-Zandén 2015; Egels-Zandén 2017.

56. Bird, Short, and Toffel 2019.

APPENDIX A

1. Berliner et al. (2015, 194).
2. Berliner et al. (2015).
3. Berliner et al 2015.
4. Anner 2017.
5. Kuruvilla et al. 2020.
6. Locke 2013. Locke and a variety of co-authors have published several articles, which Locke draws on for his 2013 book.
7. Ang et al. 2012.
8. Interview with the author, November 2018.
9. Toffel, Short, and Ouellet 2015; Short, Toffel, and Hugill 2018.
10. Short, Toffel, and Hugill 2018.
11. Toffel, Short, and Ouellet 2015; Short, Toffel, and Hugill 2018.
12. Locke 2013.
13. Brown, Dehejia, and Robertson 2013.

Bibliography

ACT. n.d. "Questions and Answers." ACT (Action Collaboration Transformation). Accessed June 19, 2019. https://actonlivingwages.com/wp-content/uploads/2019/05/ACT_COMMS_Factsheet_05-2019-WEB-1.pdf.

Adler-Milstein, Sarah, and John M. Kline. 2017. *Sewing Hope: How One Factory Challenges the Apparel Industry's Sweatshops.* Oakland: University of California Press.

Agnew, Harriet. 2018. "Katharine Hamnett Starts Fundraising for Expansion Effort: Designer Wants to Open 'Ethical and Sustainable Sourcing Centre for Europe's Luxury Brands.'" *Financial Times,* May 21, 2018. https://www.ft.com/content/61df3d12-5ce7-11e8-ad91-e01af256df68.

Ahmed, Nazneen, and Dev Nathan. 2014. "Improving Wages and Working Conditions in the Bangladeshi Garment Sector: The Role of Horizontal and Vertical Relations." Capturing the Gains Working Paper 40. http://www.capturingthegains.org/publications/workingpapers/wp_201440.htm.

Ahmed, Waqar, and Mohammed Omar. 2019. "Drivers of Supply Chain Transparency and Its Effects on Performance Measures in the Automobile Industry: Case of a Developing Country." *International Journal of Services and Operations Management* 33 (2): 159–186.

Alexa. 2019. "Tianya.cn Competitive Analysis, Marketing Mix and Traffic." Alexa. Accessed October 28, 2019. https://www.alexa.com/siteinfo/tianya.cn.

Amengual, Matthew. 2010. "Complementary Labor Regulation: The Uncoordinated Combination of State and Private Regulators in the Dominican Republic." *World Development* 38 (3); 405–14.

Amengual, Matthew, and Laura Chirot. 2016. "Reinforcing the State: Transnational and State Labor Regulation in Indonesia." *Industrial and Labor Relations Review* 69 (5): 1056–80. https://doi.org/0019793916654927.

Amengual, Matthew, Greg Distelhorst, and Danny Tobin. 2019. "Global Purchasing as Labor Regulation: The Missing Middle." *Industrial and Labor Relations Review* (forthcoming).

Amfori. 2017. "Amfori BSCI Code of Conduct." Brussels: Amfori.

Andersson, Johanna, Achim Berg, Saskia Hedrich, Patricio Ibanez, Jonatan Janmark, and Karl-Hendrik Magnus. 2018. "Is Apparel Manufacturing Coming Home? Nearshoring, Automation and Sustainability—Establishing a Demand Focused Apparel Value Chain." McKinsey & Company Apparel, Fashion and Luxury Group. October. https://www.mckinsey.com/~/media/mckinsey/industries/retail/our%20insights/is%20apparel%20manufacturing%20coming%20home/is-apparel-manufacturing-coming-home_vf.ashx.

André, Rae. 2012. "Assessing the Accountability of the Benefit Corporation: Will This New Gray Sector Organization Enhance Corporate Social Responsibility." *Journal of Business Ethics* 110 (1): 133–50. https://doi.org/10.1007/s10551-012-1254-1.

Ang, Debra, Drusilla Brown, Rajeev Dehejia, and Raymond Robertson. 2012. "Public Disclosure, Reputation Sensitivity, and Labor Law Compliance: Evidence from Better Factories Cambodia." *Review of Development Economics* 16 (4): 594–607. https://doi.org/10.1111/rode.12006.

Anker, Richard, and Martha Anker. 2017a. "Living Wage in Context: Wage Ladder and Wage Trends." In *Living Wages Around the World*, 307–22. https://doi.org/10.4337 /9781786431462.00025.

Anker, Richard, and Martha Anker. 2017b. "Overview of the Anker Living Wage Methodology." *Living Wages Around the World*, 17–30. https://doi.org/10.4337 /9781786431462.00007.

Anner, Mark. 2012. "Corporate Social Responsibility and Freedom of Association Rights: The Precarious Quest for Legitimacy and Control in Global Supply Chains." *Politics and Society* 40 (4): 609–44. https://doi.org/10.1177/0032329212460983.

Anner, Mark. 2015. "Labor Control Regimes and Worker Resistance in Global Supply Chains." *Labor History* 56 (3): 292–307. https://doi.org/10.1080/0023656X.2015 .1042771.

Anner, Mark. 2017a. "Monitoring Workers' Rights: The Limits of Voluntary Social Compliance Initiatives in Labor Repressive Regimes." *Global Policy* 8 (May): 56–65. https://doi.org/10.1111/1758-5899.12385.

Anner, Mark. 2017b. "Wildcat Strikes and Better Work Bipartite Committees in Vietnam: Toward an Elect, Represent, Protect and Empower Framework." Better Work Discussion Paper 24.

Anner, Mark. 2018. "Binding Power: The Sourcing Squeeze, Workers' Rights, and Building Safety in Bangladesh since Rana Plaza." State College: Pennsylvania State University Center for Global Workers' Rights. https://ler.la.psu.edu/gwr/documents/C GWR2017ResearchReportBindingPower.pdf.

Anner, Mark. 2019. "Squeezing Workers ' Rights in Global Supply Chains: Purchasing Practices in the Bangladesh Garment Export Sector in Comparative Perspective." *Review of International Political Economy*, 27 (2): 320–47. https://doi.org/10.1080 /09692290.2019.1625426.

Anner, Mark, Jennifer Bair, and Jeremy Blasi. 2013. "Towards Joint Liability in Global Supply Chains: Addressing the Root Causes of Labor Violations in International Subcontracting Networks." *Comparative Labor Law & Policy Journal* 35 (1): 1–43. https:// heinonline.org/HOL/Page?handle=hein.journals/cllpj35&id=13&collection =journals&index=#.

Anner, Mark, Ian Greer, Marco Hauptmeier, Nathan Lillie, and Nik Winchester. 2006. "The Industrial Determinants of Transnational Solidarity: Global Interunion Politics in Three Sectors." *European Journal of Industrial Relations* 12 (1): 7–27. https://doi.org /10.1177/0959680106061368.

Appelbaum, Richard P. 2016. "From Public Regulation to Private Enforcement: How CSR Became Managerial Orthodoxy." In *Achieving Workers' Rights in the Global Economy*, edited by Richard P. Appelbaum and Nelson Lichtenstein, 32–50. Ithaca, NY: Cornell University Press.

Appelbaum, Richard P., and Nelson Lichtenstein, eds. 2016. *Achieving Workers' Rights in the Global Economy*. Ithaca, NY: Cornell University Press.

Arengo, Elena, Liana Foxvog, and Sarah Newell. 2019. "Calling for Remedy." *International Labor Rights Forum*. Washington DC. Accessed August 7, 2020. https://laborrights .org/sites/default/files/publications/Calling%20for%20Remedy%205-14.pdf.

Armstruster-Sandoval, Ralph. 2005. *Globalization and Cross-Border Labor Solidarity in the Americas: The Anti-Sweatshop Movement and the Struggle for Social Justice*. Hove, UK: Psychology Press.

Ashwin, Sarah, Chikako Oka, Elke Schuessler, Rachel Alexander, and Nora Lohmeyer. 2020. "Spillover Effects across Transnational Industrial Relations Agreements: The Potential and Limits of Collective Action in Global Supply Chains." *ILR Review* 73 (4): 995–1020.

Asia Floor Wage Alliance. n.d. "What Is an Asia Floor Wage?" *Asia Floor Wage.* Accessed August 7, 2020. https://asia.floorwage.org/what.

ASN Bank. 2019. "Living Wage in the Garment Sector: Results of the 2018 Reviews." The Hague: ASN Bank.

Atleson, James, Lance Compa, Kerry Rittich, Calvin William Sharpe, and Marley S. Weiss. 2008. *International Labor Law: Cases and Materials on Workers' Rights in the Global Economy.* St. Paul, MN: Thomson West.

B Lab. n.d.a. "B Lab Controversial Issues Statement—Unionization Efforts by Employees." B Lab. Accessed November 20, 2019. https://blab-mktg-bcorporation -production.s3.amazonaws.com/Union Controversial Issues.pdf.

B Lab. n.d.b. "Disclosure Questionnaire." B Lab. Accessed November 20, 2019. https://bcor poration.net/sites/default/files/documents/standards/B_Corp_DisclosureQuestion naire-blank.pdf?_ga=2.103922624.1753471217.1558118960-1215022196.1558 118960.

B Lab. 2017. "Model Benefit Corporation Legislation With Explanatory Comments." B Lab. Accessed November 20, 2019. https://benefitcorp.net/sites/default/files/Model benefit corp legislation _4_17_17.pdf.

B Lab. 2019a. "B Corp Impact Data." B Lab. Accessed May 22, 2019. https://data.world/blab /b-corp-impact-data.

B Lab. 2019b. "Certification." B Lab. Accessed November 20, 2019. https://bcorporation .net/certification.

B Lab. 2019c. "Legal Requirements." B Lab. Accessed November 20, 2019. https:// bcorporation.net/certification/legal-requirements.

B Lab. 2019d. "Standards and Governance." B Lab. Accessed November 20, 2019. https:// bcorporation.net/about-b-lab/standards-and-governance?_ga=2.259819727 .492332492.1558886134-529895334.1558637991.

B Lab. 2019e. "State by State Status of Legislation." B Lab. Accessed November 20, 2019. https://benefitcorp.net/policymakers/state-by-state-status.

Bair, Jennifer, and Gary Gereffi. 2001. "Local Clusters in Global Chains: The Causes and Consequences of Export Dynamism in Torreon's Blue Jeans Industry." *World Development* 29 (11): 1885–1903. https://doi.org/10.1016/S0305-750X(01)00075-4.

Barrientos, Stephanie. 2013. "Corporate Purchasing Practices in Global Production Networks: A Socially Contested Terrain." *Geoforum* 44: 44–51.

Barrientos, Stephanie, Gary Gereffi, and A. Rossi. 2011. "Economic and Social Upgrading in Global Production Networks: A New Paradigm for a Changing World." *International Labour Review* 150 (3): 319–40. https://doi.org/j.1564-913X.2011.00119.x.

Barrientos, Stephanie, and Sally Smith. 2007. "Do Workers Benefit from Ethical Trade? Assessing Codes of Labour Practice in Global Production Systems." *Third World Quarterly* 28 (4): 713–29. https://doi.org/10.1080/01436590701336580.

Bartley, Tim. 2007. "Institutional Emergence in an Era of Globalization: The Rise of Transnational Private Regulation of Labor and Environmental Conditions." *American Journal of Sociology* 113 (2): 297–351. https://doi.org/10.1086/518871.

Bartley, Tim. 2018. "Beneath Compliance: Corporate Social Responsibility and Labor Standards in China." In *Rules without Rights: Land, Labor, and Private Authority in the Global Economy,* edited by Tim Bartley, 163–213. Oxford: Oxford University Press.

Bartley, Tim, and Doug Kincaid. 2014. "The Mobility of Industries and the Limits of CSR: Labor Codes of Conduct in Indonesian Factories." In *Corporate Social Responsibility in a Globalizing World,* edited by Kiyoteru Tsutsui and Alwyn Lim, 393–429. Cambridge: Cambridge University Press.

Bartley, Tim, and Doug Kincaid. 2015. "The Mobility of Industries and the Limits of Corporate Social Responsibility: Labor Codes of Conduct in Indonesian Factories."

In *Corporate Social Responsibility in a Globalizing World*, edited by Kiyoteru Tsutsui and Alwyn Lim, 393–429. Cambridge: Cambridge University Press.

Bartley, Tim, and Niklas Egels-Zandén. 2015. "Responsibility and Neglect in Global Production Networks: The Uneven Significance of Codes of Conduct in Indonesian Factories." *Global Networks* 15 (s1): S21–44.

Bartley, Tim, and Niklas Egels-Zandén. 2016. "Beyond Decoupling: Unions and the Leveraging of Corporate Social Responsibility in Indonesia." *Socio-economic Review* 14 (2): 231–55. https://doi.org/10.1093/ser/mwv023.

Bartley, Tim, and Zhang Lu. 2012. "Opening the 'Black Box': Transnational Private Certification of Labor Standards in China." Research Center for Chinese Politics and Business Working Paper 18. Indiana University Research Center for Chinese Politics and Business, Bloomington. https://doi.org/10.2139/ssrn.2169350.

Bartley, Tim, Sebastian Koos, Hiram Samel, Gustavo Setrini, and Nik Summers. 2015. *Looking behind the Label: Global Industries and the Conscientious Consumer*. Bloomington: Indiana University Press. http://www.iupress.indiana.edu/product_info.php?products_id=807542.

Baudot, Lisa, Jesse Dillard, and Nadra Pencle. 2020. "The Emergence of Benefit Corporations: A Cautionary Tale." *Critical Perspectives on Accounting* 67–68 (March). https://doi.org/10.1016/j.cpa.2019.01.005.

Bauer, Joanne, and Elizabeth Umlas. 2017. "Do Benefit Corporations Respect Human Rights?" *Stanford Social Innovation Review* 15 (4): 26–33.

Baumann-Pauly, Dorothee, Sarah Labowitz, and Nayantara Banerjee. 2015. "Closing Governance Gaps in Bangladesh's Garment Industry: The Power and Limitations of Private Governance Schemes." *SSRN Electronic Journal*. https://doi.org/10.2139/ssrn.2577535.

Baumann-Pauly, Dorothée, Sarah Labowitz, and Nate Stein. 2018. "Transforming the Garment Industry in Bangladesh: Sharing Responsibility." In *Sustainable Fashion: Governance and New Management Approaches*, edited by Sarah Margaretha Jastram and Anna-Maria Schneider, 41–50. New York: Springer International. https://doi.org/10.1007/978-3-319-74367-7_4.

Baumann-Pauly, Dorothée, Christopher Wickert, Laura J. Spence, and Andreas Georg Scherer. 2013. "Organizing Corporate Social Responsibility in Small and Large Firms: Size Matters." *Journal of Business Ethics* 115 (4): 693–705. https://doi.org/10.1007/s10551-013-1827-7.

Berliner, Daniel, Anne Regan Greenleaf, Milli Lake, Margaret Levi, and Jennifer Noveck. 2015. "Governing Global Supply Chains: What We Know (and Don't) About Improving Labor Rights and Working Conditions." *Annual Review of Law and Social Science* 11: 193–209. https://doi.org/10.1146/annurev-lawsocsci-120814-121322.

Better Work. 2013. "Better Work Vietnam Shows Path for Labour Law Reform." Washington, DC: International Labour Organization and International Financial Corporation. https://betterwork.org/global/wp-content/uploads/ILO-Better-Work-Vietnam.LRWeb_.pdf.

Better Work. 2016. "Progress and Potential: How Better Work Is Improving Garment Workers' Lives and Boosting Factory Competitiveness." Geneva: International Labor Organization.

Bird, Yanhua, Jodi L. Short, and Michael W. Toffel. 2019. "Coupling Labor Codes of Conduct and Supplier Labor Practices: The Role of Internal Structural Conditions." *Organization Science* 30 (4): 847–67. https://doi.org/10.1287/orsc.2018.1261.

Blanchard, Tasmin. 2018. "Bright Future? Fashion's Watershed Year as It Moves from Waste to Work." *Guardian*, December 31, 2018. https://www.theguardian.com/fashion/2018/dec/31/fashion-watershed-year-moves-from-waste-woke-sustainable.

Boatright, John R. 2018. "Benefit Corporation." In *The SAGE Encyclopedia of Business Ethics and Society*, edited by Robert W. Kolb, 232–34. Thousand Oaks, CA: Sage Publications. https://doi.org/10.4135/9781483381503.n95.

Brass, Tom. 2010. "Unfree Labour as Primitive Accumulation?" *Capital & Class* 35 (1): 23–38. https://doi.org/10.1177/0309816810392969.

Briscoe, Forrest, and Chad Murphy. 2012. "Sleight of Hand? Practice Opacity, Third-Party Responses, and the Interorganizational Diffusion of Controversial Practices." *Administrative Science Quarterly* 57 (4): 553–84. https://doi.org/10.1177/0001839212465077.

Bromley, Patricia, and Walter W. Powell. 2012. "From Smoke and Mirrors to Walking the Talk: Decoupling in the Contemporary World." *Academy of Management Annals* 6 (1): 483–530. https://doi.org/10.1080/19416520.2012.684462.

Brown, Drusilla, Rajeev Dehejia, Ann Rappaport, Mary Davis, Raymond Robertson, Laura Babbit, Elyse Voegeli, et al. "The Impact of Better Work: A Joint Program of the International Labour Organization and the International Finance Corporation." Tufts Labor Lab Working Paper. September 2016. Accessed August 8, 2020. https://sites.tufts.edu/laborlab/files/2016/06/Better-Work-Report-Final-Version-26-R-September-2016.docx

Brown, Drusilla, Rajeev Dehejia, and Raymond Robertson. 2013. "Is There an Efficiency Case for International Labour Standards." Better Work Discussion Paper 12. Geneva.

Brown, Drusilla, Rajeev Dehejia, and Raymond Robertson. 2018. "The Impact of Better Work: 2018 Firm Performance in Vietnam, Indonesia, and Jordan. Tufts University Labor Lab. Working Paper.

Bryher, Anna. 2019. "Tailored Wages: The State of Pay in the Global Garment Industry." Bristol, UK: Labour Behind the Label.

Bryman, Alan. 2016. *Social Research Methods*. Oxford: Oxford University Press.

Bryson, Alex. 2004. "Managerial Responsiveness to Union and Nonunion Worker Voice in Britain." *Industrial Relations* 43 (1): 213–41. https://doi.org/10.1111/j.0019-8676.2004.00324.x.

Castel, Robert. 2000. "The Roads to Disaffiliation: Insecure Work and Vulnerable Relationships." *International Journal of Urban and Regional Research* 24 (3): 519–35. https://doi.org/10.1111/1468-2427.00262.

Center for Global Workers' Rights. 2016. "Labour Rights Indicators." Center for Global Workers' Rights. Accessed November 1, 2019. http://labour-rights-indicators.la.psu.edu.

Center for the Study of Work, Labor, and Democracy. 2014. "A Comparison of Key Oversight Organizations' Codes of Conduct." Santa Barbara: Department of History, University of California, Santa Barbara. http://www.history.ucsb.edu/labor/sites/secure.lsit.ucsb.edu.hist.d7_labor/files/sitefiles/CSR_Research_Files/Code of Conduct Comparison 7-8-14.pdf.

Chakrabarty, Sayan, and Ulrike Grote. 2009. "Child Labor in Carpet Weaving: Impact of Social Labeling in India and Nepal." *World Development* 37 (10): 1683–93.

Chan, Anita. 2010. "Corporate Accountability and the Potential for Workers' Representation in China." In *Fair Trade, Corporate Accountability, and Beyond: Experiments in Globalizing Justice*, edited by Kate Macdonald and Shelley Marshall, 211–21. Aldershot, UK: Ashgate.

Chan, Anita. 2016. "CSR and Trade Union Elections at Foreign-Owned Chinese Factories." In *Achieving Workers' Rights in the Global Economy*, edited by Richard Appelbaum and Nelson Lichtenstein, 209–26. Ithaca, NY: Cornell University Press.

Chan, Anita, and Kaxton Siu. 2010. "Analyzing Exploitation: The Mechanisms Underpinning Low Wages and Excessive Overtime in Chinese Export Factories." *Critical Asian Studies* 42 (2): 167–90. https://doi.org/10.1080/14672715.2010.486599.

Chatterji, Aaron K, and Michael W. Toffel. 2010. "How Firms Respond to Being Rated." *Strategic Management Journal* 31 (9): 914–45. https://doi.org/10.1002/smj.840.

Claeson, Björn. 2014. "Dangerous Silence: Why the U.S. Military Exchanges Need to Address Unsafe and Illegal Conditions in Their Supplier Factories." Washington, DC: International Labor Rights Forum. https://laborrights.org/publications/dangerous-silence-exchanges-turn-blind-eye-suppliers.

Clark, William H., and Larry Vranka. 2013. "White Paper: The Need and Rationale for the Benefit Corporation: Why It Is the Legal Form That Best Addresses the Needs of Social Entrepreneurs, Investors, and, Ultimately, the Public." Benefit Corporation. Accessed on December 10, 2019. https://benefitcorp.net/sites/default/files/Benefit_Corporation_White_Paper.pdf.

Compa, Lance, and Tashia Hinchliffe-Darricarrère. 1995. "Enforcing International Labor Rights through Corporate Codes of Conduct." *Columbia Journal of Transnational Law* 33: 663–89. http://digitalcommons.ilr.cornell.edu/articles/177/.

Cone LLC. 2010. "Cone Cause Evolution Study." Cone LLC. Boston: Cone LLC. https://www.conecomm.com/research-blog/2010-cause-evolution-study#download-research.

Conner, Tim, Annie Delaney, and Sarah Rennie. 2016. "The Freedom of Association Protocol: A Localized Non-Judicial Grievance Mechanism for Workers' Rights in Global Supply Chains." Non-judicial Redress Mechanisms Report Series 19. http://corporateaccountabilityresearch.net/njm-report-xvix-protocol.

Cooper, David. 2014. "Raising the Federal Minimum Wage to $10.10 Would Save Safety Net Programs Billions and Help Ensure Businesses Are Doing Their Fair Share." Washington, DC: Economic Policy Institute. https://www.epi.org/publication/safety-net-savings-from-raising-minimum-wage/.

Cooper, Frederick. 2004. "Development, Modernization, and the Social Sciences in the Era of Decolonization: The Examples of British and French Africa." *Revue d'Histoire Des Sciences Humaines* 10 (1): 9–38. https://doi.org/10.3917/rhsh.010.0009.

Cowgill, Matthew, and Phu Huynh. 2016. "Weak Minimum Wage Compliance in Asia's Garment Industry." Bangkok: ILO Regional Office for Asia and the Pacific. https://www.ilo.org/wcmsp5/groups/public/—ed_protect/—protrav/—travail/documents/publication/wcms_509532.pdf.

Cowgill, Matthew, Malte Luebker, and Cuntao Xia. 2015. "Minimum Wages in the Global Garment Industry: Update for 2015." Bangkok: ILO Regional Office for Asia and the Pacific. http://www.ilo.org/wcmsp5/groups/public/—asia/—ro-bangkok/documents/publication/wcms_436867.pdf.

Danish Trade Union Development Agency, Analytical Unit. 2020 "Labour Market Profile Bangladesh—2020." Accessed August 11, 2020. https://www.ulandssekretariatet.dk/wp-content/uploads/2020/06/LMP-Bangladesh-2020-Final-version-1.pdf

Devinney, Timothy M., Pat Auger, and Gianna M. Eckhardt. 2010. *The Myth of the Ethical Consumer*. Cambridge: Cambridge University Press.

Dickson, Marsha A.(Better Buying). 2019. "Better Buying Index Report 2019: Purchasing Practices Performance in Apparel, Footwear, and Household Textile Supply Chains." Newark. www.betterbuying.org.

DiMaggio, Paul J, and Walter W Powell. 1983. "The Iron Cage Revisited: Institutional Isomorphism and Collective Rationality in Organizational Fields." *American Sociological Review* 48 (2): 147–60. https://doi.org/10.2307/2095101.

Distelhorst, Greg, Jens Hainmueller, and Richard M Locke. 2017. "Does Lean Improve Labor Standards? Management and Social Performance in the Nike Supply Chain." *Management Science* 63 (3): 707–28. https://doi.org/mnsc.2015.2369.

Distelhorst, Greg, Richard M. Locke, Timea Pal, and Hiram Samel. 2015. "Production Goes Global, Compliance Stays Local: Private Regulation in the Global Electronics In-

dustry." *Regulation and Governance* 9 (3): 224–42. https://doi.org/10.1111/rego
.12096.

Distelhorst, Greg, and Richard M. Locke. 2018. "Does Compliance Pay? Social Standards
and Firm-Level Trade." *American Journal of Political Science* 62 (3): 695–711. https://
doi.org/10.1111/ajps.12372.

Doucouliagos, Hristos, Richard B. Freeman, and Patrice Laroche. 2017. *The Economics of
Trade Unions, A Study of a Research Field and Its Findings.* New York: Routledge.

Egels-Zandén, Niklas. 2007. "Suppliers' Compliance with MNCs' Codes of Conduct:
Behind the Scenes at Chinese Toy Suppliers." *Journal of Business Ethics* 75 (1):
45–62.

Egels-Zandén, Niklas. 2014. "Revisiting Supplier Compliance with MNC Codes of Conduct: Recoupling Policy and Practice at Chinese Toy Suppliers." *Journal of Business
Ethics* 119 (1): 59–75. https://doi.org/10.1007/s10551-013-1622-5.

Egels-Zandén, Niklas. 2017. "The Role of SMEs in Global Production Networks: A Swed-
ish SME's Payment of Living Wages at Its Indian Supplier." *Business and Society*
56 (1): 92–129. https://doi.org/10.1177/0007650315575107.

Egels-Zandén, Niklas, and Niklas Hansson. 2016. "Supply Chain Transparency as a Consumer or Corporate Tool: The Case of Nudie Jeans Co." *Journal of Consumer Policy*
39 (4): 377–395. https://doi.org/10.1007/s10603-015-9283-7.

Egels-Zandén, Niklas, and Henrik Lindholm. 2015. "Do Codes of Conduct Improve Worker
Rights in Supply Chains? A Study of Fair Wear Foundation." *Journal of Cleaner Production* 107: 31–40. https://doi.org/10.1016/j.jclepro.2014.08.096.

Egels-Zandén, Niklas, and Jeroen Merk. 2014. "Private Regulation and Trade Union Rights:
Why Codes of Conduct Have Limited Impact on Trade Union Rights." *Journal of
Business Ethics* 123 (3): 461–73. https://doi.org/10.1007/s10551-013-1840-x.

Elliott, Kimberly Anne, and Richard B. Freeman. 2003. "Can Labor Standards Improve
Under Globalization?" Washington DC: Institute of International Economics.

Esbenshade, Jill. 2004. *Monitoring Sweatshops: Workers, Consumers, and the Global Apparel
Industry.* Philadelphia: Temple University Press.

Espinosa, Angela, and Jon Walker. 2011. *A Complexity Approach to Sustainability: Theory
and Application.* London: Imperial College Press.

Ethical Trading Initiative. 2006. "The ETI Code of Labour Practice: Do Workers Really Benefit?" London: Ethical Trading Initiative. 2006. Accessed August 7, 2020. https://
www.ethicaltrade.org/sites/default/files/shared_resources/impact_assessment
_summary.pdf.

Ethical Trading Initiative. n.d. "Base Code Clause 2: Freedom of Association." Ethical Trading Initiative. Accessed November 1, 2019. https://www.ethicaltrade.org/eti-base
-code/2-freedom-association-and-right-to-collective-bargaining-are-respected.

Fair Factories Clearinghouse (FFC). 2019. "Sharing Platform." FFC. Accessed November 26, 2019. https://www.fairfactories.org/home/sharing-platform.

Fair Labor Association Board of Directors Meeting. 2018. "New Balance Athletics, Inc. Assessment for Reaccreditation." Washington, DC: Fair Labor Association. https://
www.fairlabor.org/sites/default/files/documents/reports/new_balance_reaccre
ditation_report_public_edits_final.docx_.pdf.

Fair Labor Association. 2011. "FLA Workplace Code of Conduct and Compliance Benchmarks." Washington, DC: Fair Labor Association.

Fair Labor Association. 2015. "Draft Fair Compensation Workplan." Washington, DC: Fair
Labor Association. https://www.fairlabor.org/sites/default/files/fair_compensation
_work_plan_feb_2015.pdf.

Fair Labor Association. 2016. "Toward Fair Compensation in Global Supply Chains: Factory Pay Assessments in 21 Countries." Washington, DC: Fair Labor Association.

Fair Labor Association. 2018. "Toward Fair Compensation in Bangladesh: Insights on Closing the Wage Gap." Washington, DC: Fair Labor Association.

Fair Labor Association. 2019. "Toward Fair Compensation in Vietnam: Insights on Reaching a Living Wage." Washington, DC: Fair Labor Association.

Fair Labor Association. n.d. "Workplace Code of Conduct." Washington, DC: Fair Labor Association. Accessed September 5, 2019. https://www.fairlabor.org/sites/default/files/fla_code_of_conduct.pdf.

Fair Wage Network. 2019. "12 Fair Wage Dimensions." Fair Wage Network. Accessed June 20, 2019. http://fair-wage.com/12-dimensions/.

Fair Wear Foundation. n.d. "Labour Standards." Fair Labor Association. Accessed February 9, 2019. https://www.fairwear.org/labour-standards/.

Fair Wear Foundation. 2017. "FWF Wage Ladder." Fair Wear Foundation. Accessed September 12, 2019. https://www.fairwear.org/wage-ladder/.

Ferreira, Francisco, and Carolina Sánchez-Páramo. 2017. "A Richer Array of International Poverty Lines." World Bank Blogs. 2017. https://blogs.worldbank.org/developmenttalk/richer-array-international-poverty-lines.

Finnegan, Brian. 2013. "Responsibility Outsourced: Social Audits, Workplace Certification and Twenty Years of Failure to Protect Worker Rights." Washington, DC: AFL-CIO.

Fligstein, Neil. 2005. "States, Markets, and Economic Growth." In *The Economic Sociology of Capitalism*, edited by Victor Nee and Richard Swedberg, 119–43. Princeton, NJ: Princeton University Press.

Fransen, Luc. 2011. "Why Do Private Governance Organizations Not Converge? A Political-Institutional Analysis of Transnational Labor Standards Regulation." *Governance* 24 (2): 359–87. https://doi.org/10.1111/j.1468-0491.2011.01519.x.

Fransen, Luc. 2013. "Global Companies and the Private Regulation of Global Labor Standards." In *The Handbook of Global Companies*, edited by John Mikler, 437–55. Oxford: Wiley-Blackwell. https://doi.org/10.1002/9781118326152.ch26.

Fransen, Luc, and Brian Burgoon. 2012. "A Market for Worker Rights: Explaining Business Support for International Private Labour Regulation." *Review of International Political Economy* 19 (2): 236–66. https://doi.org/10.1080/09692290.2011.552788.

Freeman, R. Edward. 1984. *Strategic Management: A Stakeholder Approach*. Boston: Pitman.

Freeman, Richard Barry, and James L. Medoff. 1984. *What Do Unions Do?* New York: Basic Books.

Frenkel, Stephen J. 2001. "Globalization, Athletic Footwear Commodity Chains and Employment Relations in China." *Organization Studies* 22 (4).

Frenkel, Stephen J., and Sarosh Kuruvilla. 2002. "Logics of Action, Globalization, and Changing Employment Relations in China, India, Malaysia, and the Philippines." *Industrial and Labor Relations Review* 55 (3): 387–412. https://doi.org/10.1177/001979390205500301.

Frenkel, Stephen J, and Duncan Scott. 2002. "Compliance, Collaboration, and Codes of Labor Practice: The ADIDAS Connection." *California Management Review* 45 (1): 29–49. https://doi.org/10.2307/41166152.

Friedman, Eli. 2014. *Insurgency Trap, Labor Politics in Postsocialist China*. Ithaca, NY: ILR Press.

Friedman, Milton. 1970. "The Social Responsibility of Business Is to Increase Its Profits." *New York Times Magazine*, September 13, 1970.

Frundt, Henry J. 2004. "Unions Wrestle with Corporate Codes of Conduct." *WorkingUSA* 7 (4): 36–53. https://search.proquest.com/docview/236515056?pq-origsite=gscholar.

Fülöp, Gyula, Robert D. Hisrich, and Krisztina Szegedi. 2000. "Business Ethics and Social Responsibility in Transition Economies." *Journal of Management Development* 19 (1): 5–31. https://doi.org/10.1108/02621710010308135.

Fung, Archon, Dara O'Rourke, and Charles Sabel. 2001. *Can We Put an End to Sweatshops?* Boston: Beacon Press.

Gap Inc. 2016. "Code of Vendor Conduct." San Francisco: Gap Inc. https://www.gapinc .com/content/dam/gapincsite/documents/CodeofVendorConduct_FINAL.pdf.

Gardner, T. A., M. Benzie, J. Börner, E. Dawkins, S. Fick, R. Garrett, J. Godar, et al. 2019. "Transparency and Sustainability in Global Commodity Supply Chains." *World Development* 121: 163–77. https://doi.org/10.1016/j.worlddev.2018.05.025.

Glasmeier, Amy K. n.d. "Living Wage Calculator." Living Wage Calculator. Accessed August 29, 2017. https://livingwage.mit.edu/.

Global Living Wage Coalition. 2018. "The Anker Methodology for Estimating a Living Wage." Global Living Wage Coalition. Accessed June 9, 2019. https://www.globalli vingwage.org/about/anker-methodology/.

Graffin, Scott D., and Andrew J. Ward. 2010. "Certifications and Reputation: Determining the Standard of Desirability Amidst Uncertainty." *Organization Science* 21 (2): 331–46. https://doi.org/10.1287/orsc.1080.0400.

Granath, Sandra. 2016. "The Practice of Social Dialogue in the Readymade Garment Factories in Bangladesh—H&M Case Study." Uppsala: Uppsala University.

Greenhill, Brian, Layna Mosley, and Aseem Prakash. 2009. "Trade-Based Diffusion of Labor Rights: A Panel Study, 1986–2002." *American Political Science Review* 103 (4): 669–690. https://doi.org/10.1017/S0003055409990116.

Greenhouse, Steven, and Jim Yardley. 2013. "Global Retailers Join Safety Plan for Bangladesh." *New York Times*, May 13, 2013.

Guzi, Martin, and Martin Kahanec. 2018. "Estimating Living Wage Globally." Amsterdam: WageIndicator Foundation.

H&M. 2010. "Code of Conduct." H&M. Accessed December 10, 2019. https://sustainability .hm.com/content/dam/hm/about/documents/en/CSR/codeofconduct/Code of Con duct_en.pdf.

H&M. 2014. "Commitment Two: Choose and Reward Responsible Partners, H&M Sustainability Report." Stockholm: H&M. https://sustainability.hm.com/content/dam /hm/about/documents/masterlanguage/CSR/reports/HM_SustainabilityReport _2014_FINAL_Commitment_2.pdf.

Hacker, Michael A. 2016. "'Profit, People, Planet' Perverted: Holding Benefit Corporations Accountable to Intended Beneficiaries." *Boston College Law Review* 57 (5): 1747–81. https://lawdigitalcommons.bc.edu/bclr/vol57/iss5/7.

Hiller, Janine S. 2013. "The Benefit Corporation and Corporate Social Responsibility." *Journal of Business Ethics* 118 (2): 287–301. https://doi.org/10.1007/s10551-012-1580-3.

Hiller, Janine S., and Scott J. Shackelford. 2018. "The Firm and Common Pool Resource Theory: Understanding the Rise of Benefit Corporations." *American Business Law Journal* 55 (1): 5–51. https://doi.org/10.1111/ablj.12116.

Hoang, Dong. 2019. "Labour Standards in the Global Supply Chain: Workers' Agency and Reciprocal Exchange Perspective." *Societies* 9 (2): 38. https://doi.org/10.3390/soc 9020038.

Hohenegger, Klaus, and Doug Miller. 2017. "Labour Minute Costing, A Tool for Establishing Living Wage Floors in Garment Factories." Amsterdam: Fair Wear Foundation.

Den Hond, Frank, and Frank de Bakker. 2012. "Boomerang Politics: How Transnational Stakeholders Impact Multinational Corporations in the Context of Globalization." In *A Stakeholder Approach to Corporate Social Responsibility: Pressures, Conflicts, Reconciliation*. Aldershot: Gower.

Honeyman, Ryan. 2014. *The B Corp Handbook: How You Can Use Business as a Force for Good*. San Francisco: Berrett-Koehler Publishers.

Hsieh, Nien-hê, Michael W. Toffel, and Olivia Hull. 2019. "Global Sourcing at Nike." Boston: Harvard Business School Case Collection. https://www.hbs.edu/faculty/Pages/item.aspx?num=55877.

Hughes, Alex, Martin Buttle, and Neil Wrigley. 2007. "Organisational Geographies of Corporate Responsibility: A UK-US Comparison of Retailers' Ethical Trading Initiatives." *Journal of Economic Geography* 7 (4): 491–513. https://doi.org/10.1093/jeg/lbm011.

Huynh, Phu. 2017. "Developing Asia's Garment and Footwear Industry: Recent Employment and Wage Trends." Bangkok: ILO Regional Office for Asia and the Pacific. https://www.ilo.org/wcmsp5/groups/public/—ed_protect/—protrav/—travail/documents/publication/wcms_581466.pdf.

International Labour Office and International Finance Corporation. 2013. "Better Work Jordan: Guide to Jordanian Labour Law for the Garment Industry." Geneva: International Labour Organization.

International Labour Organization. 2016. "Decent Work in Global Supply Chains (Report IV)." Geneva: International Labour Organization. Accessed August 7, 2020 https://www.ilo.org/ilc/ILCSessions/previous-sessions/105/reports/reports-to-the-conference/WCMS_468097/lang--de/index.htm.

International Labour Organization. 2017. "NORMLEX Information System on International Labour Standards." International Labour Organization. Accessed November 3, 2019. https://www.ilo.org/dyn/normlex/en/f?p=NORMLEXPUB:11000:0::NO:::.

International Labour Organization. 2019. "The Future of Work in Textiles, Clothing, Leather and Footwear." Working Paper 326. Accessed August 11, 2020. https://www.ilo.org/sector/Resources/publications/WCMS_669355/lang--en/index.htm

International Monetary Fund (IMF). 2019. "Consumer Price Index (CPI)." IMF. 2019.

IOD PARC. 2015. "The Ethical Trading Initiative External Evaluation Report," April 4. https://www.ethicaltrade.org/sites/default/files/shared_resources/eti_external_evaluation_report_-_iod-parc_2015.pdf.

Jenkins, Rhys. 2001. "Corporate Codes of Conduct: Self Regulation in a Global Economy." Geneva: United Nations Research Institute for Social Development. http://www.unrisd.org/80256B3C005BCCF9/(httpAuxPages)/E3B3E78BAB9A886F80256B5E00344278/$file/jenkins.pdf.

Jiang, Bin. 2009. "Implementing Supplier Codes of Conduct in Global Supply Chains: Process Explanations from Theoretic and Empirical Perspectives." *Journal of Business Ethics* 85 (1): 77–92.

Jiang, Ruihua Joy, and Pratima Bansal. 2003. "Seeing the Need for ISO 14001." *Journal of Management Studies* 40 (4): 1047–67. https://doi.org/10.1111/1467-6486.00370.

Joint Ethical Trading Initiative. 2015. "Living Wages in Global Supply Chains: A New Agenda for Business." https://www.dieh.dk/dyn/Normal/3/23/Normal_Content/file/950/1461571467/ieh_eti_dieh_report_web.pdf.

Kalleberg, Arne L. 2009. "Precarious Work, Insecure Workers: Employment Relations in Transition." *American Sociological Review* 74 (1): 1–22. https://doi.org/10.1177/000312240907400101.

Keating, Robert. 2009. "LLCs and Nonprofit Organizations: For-Profits, Nonprofits, and Hybrids." *Suffolk University Law Review* 42: 553–86.

Keck, Margaret E., and Kathryn Sikkink. 1998. *Activists Beyond Borders: Advocacy Networks in International Politics.* Ithaca, NY: Cornell University Press.

Kelly, Ilona M., Christie Miedema, Ben Vanpeperstraete, and Ilana Winterstein. 2019. "Fig Leaf for Fashion: How Social Auditing Protects Brands and Fails Workers." Amsterdam: Clean Clothes Campaign. https://cleanclothes.org/file-repository/figleaf-for-fashion.pdf.

Kidger, Peter. 1991. "Employee Participation in Occupational Health and Safety: Should Union-Appointed or Elected Representatives Be the Model for the UK?" *Human Resource Management Journal* 2 (4): 21–35. https://doi.org/10.1111/j.1748-8583.1992.tb00264.x.

Knudsen, Jette Steen. 2013. "The Growth of Private Regulation of Labor Standards in Global Supply Chains: Mission Impossible for Western Small- and Medium-Sized Firms?" *Journal of Business Ethics* 117 (2): 387–98. https://doi.org/10.1007/s10551-012-1527-8.

Koçer, Rüya Gökhan, and Luc Fransen. 2009. "Codes of Conduct and the Promise of a Change of Climate in Worker Organization." *European Journal of Industrial Relations* 15 (3): 237–56. https://doi.org/10.1177/0959680109339399.

Kuruvilla, Sarosh, and Matt Fischer-Daly. n.d. "Are Changes in Corporate Governance the Answer? An Empirical Study of the Promise and Limits of Benefit Corporations in Improving Labor Conditions in Global Supply Chains." In *Private Regulation of Labor Practices in Global Supply Chains: Problems, Progress and Prospects*. Ithaca, NY: Cornell University Press (forthcoming).

Kuruvilla, Sarosh, Chunyun Li, Mingwei Liu, and Wansi Chen. 2020. "Field Opacity and Practice Outcomes Decoupling: Private Regulation of Labor Standards in Global Supply Chains." *Industrial and Labor Relations Review* (forthcoming). http://eprints.lse.ac.uk/101169/.

Labrecque, Sarah. 2014. "How Much Do Consumers Really Care about Transparency?" *Guardian*, March 12, 2014. https://www.theguardian.com/sustainable-business/transparency-consumers-care-livechat-roundup.

Laval, Christian, and Pierre Dardot. 2017. *The New Way of the World: On Neoliberal Society*, translated by Gregory Elliott. London: Verso.

Leary, Virginia A. 2003. "The Paradox of Workers' Rights as Human Rights." In *Human Rights, Labor Rights, and International Trade*, edited by Lance A. Compa and Stephen F. Diamond, 22–47. Philadelphia: University of Pennsylvania Press.

LeBaron, Genevieve, and Jane Lister. 2015. "Benchmarking Global Supply Chains: The Power of the 'Ethical Audit' Regime." *Review of International Studies* 41 (5): 905–24.

Lee, Jamie. 2018. "Benefit Corporations: A Proposal for Assessing Liability in Benefit Enforcement Proceedings." *Cornell Law Review* 103 (4): 1075–1100.

Levine, David, Michael Toffel, and Matthew Johnson. 2012. "Randomized Government Safety Inspections Reduce Worker Injuries with No Detectible Job Loss." *Science*, May 18.

Li, Zhongjin, Eli Friedman, and Hao Ren, eds. 2016. *China on Strike: Narratives of Workers' Resistance*. Chicago: Haymarket Books.

Lichtenstein, Nelson. 2016. "The Demise of Tripartite Governance and the Rise of the CSR Regime." In *Achieving Workers' Rights in the Global Economy*, edited by Richard P. Appelbaum and Nelson Lichtenstein, 95.

Lim, Suk-Jun, and Joe Phillips. 2008. "Embedding CSR Values: The Global Footwear Industry's Evolving Governance Structure." *Journal of Business Ethics* 81 (1): 143–56.

Locke, Richard, Matthew Amengual, and Akshay Mangla. 2009. "Virtue Out of Necessity?" Compliance, Commitment, and the Improvement of Labor Conditions in Global Supply Chains." *Politics and Society* 27 (2): 319–51.

Locke, Richard, Thomas Kochan, Monica Romis, and Fei Qin. 2007. "Beyond Corporate Codes of Conduct: Work Organization and Labour Standards at Nike's Suppliers." *International Labour Review* 146 (1–2): 21–40. https://doi.org/10.1111/j.1564-913X.2007.00003.x.

Locke, Richard M. 2013. *The Promise and Limits of Private Power: Promoting Labor Standards in a Global Economy*. Cambridge: Cambridge University Press.

Locke, Richard M., Fei Qin, and Alberto Brause. 2007. "Does Monitoring Improve Labor Standards? Lessons from Nike." *Industrial and Labor Relations Review* 61 (1): 3–31. https://doi.org/10.1177/001979390706100101.

Locke, Richard M., and Monica Romis. 2010. "The Promise and Perils of Private Voluntary Regulation: Labor Standards and Work Organization in Two Mexican Garment Factories." *Review of International Political Economy* 17 (1): 45–74. https://doi.org/10.1080/09692290902893230.

Loewenstein, Mark J. 2017. "Benefit Corporation Law." *University of Cincinnati Law Review* 85: 381–394. https://scholar.law.colorado.edu/articles/873.

Luebker, Malte. 2014. "Minimum Wages in the Global Garment Industry." Bangkok: ILO Regional Office for Asia and the Pacific.

Lund-Thomsen, Peter, and Adam Lindgreen. 2014. "Corporate Social Responsibility in Global Value Chains: Where Are We Now and Where Are We Going?" *Journal of Business Ethics* 123 (1): 11–22. https://doi.org/10.1007/s10551-013-1796-x.

Lund-Thomsen, Peter, Khalid Nadvi, Anita Chan, Navjote Khara, and Hong Xue. 2012. "Labour in Global Value Chains: Work Conditions in Football Manufacturing in China, India and Pakistan." *Development and Change* 43 (6): 1211–37. https://doi.org/10.1111/j.1467-7660.2012.01798.x.

Malesky, Edmund J., and Layna Mosley. 2018. "Chains of Love? Global Production and the Firm-Level Diffusion of Labor Standards." *American Journal of Political Science* 62 (3): 712–28. https://doi.org/10.1111/ajps.12370.

Mamic, Ivanka. 2004. *Implementing Codes of Conduct, How Businesses Manage Social Performance in Global Supply Chains*. Sheffield and Geneva: Greenleaf Publishing and International Labour Office. https://www.ilo.org/public/libdoc/ilo/2004/104B09_385_engl.pdf.

Marks and Spencer. 2018. "Global Sourcing Principles." Marks and Spencer. Accessed December 10, 2019. https://corporate.marksandspencer.com/documents/plan-a-our-approach/global-sourcing-principles.pdf.

Marzullo, Dan. 2018. "Modern Companies That Are Winning at Radical Transparency." Workest. October 4. https://www.zenefits.com/workest/modern-companies-winning-radical-transparency/.

Mayer, Frederick, and Gary Gereffi. 2010. "Regulation and Economic Globalization: Prospects and Limits of Private Governance." *Business and Politics* 12 (3): 1–25. https://doi.org/10.2202/1469-3569.1325.

McDonnell, Brett. 2014. "Committing to Doing Good and Doing Well: Fiduciary Duty in Benefit Corporations." *Fordham Journal of Corporate & Financial Law* 20 (1): 19–72. http://scholarship.law.umn.edu/faculty_articles/163.

McMullen, Anna, and Sanjita Majumder. 2016. "Do We Buy It? A Supply Chain Investigation into Living Wage Commitments from M&S and H&M." Bristol: Labour Behind Label. https://cleanclothes.org/resources/national-cccs/do-we-buy-it/view.

Merk, Jeroen. 2008. "Full Package Approach to Labour Codes of Conduct: Four Major Steps Garment Companies Can Take to Ensure Their Products Are Made under Humane Conditions." Amsterdam: Clean Clothes Campaign.

Meyer, John W, and Brian Rowan. 1977. "Institutionalized Organizations: Formal Structure as Myth and Ceremony." *American Journal of Sociology* 83 (2): 340–63. http://www.jstor.org/stable/2778293.

Mezzadri, Alessandra. 2017. *The Sweatshop Regime: Labouring Bodies, Exploitation, and Garments Made in India*. Cambridge: Cambridge University Press. https://doi.org/10.1017/9781316337912.

Mohin, Tim. 2018. "The Role of Corporate Transparency in a Fractured World." Accessed November 26, 2019. https://timmohin.com/2018/02/737/.

Mol, Arthur. 2010. "The Future of Transparency: Power, Pitfalls and Promises." *Global Environmental Politics* 10 (3): 132–43. https://doi.org/10.1162/GLEP_a_00018.

Moran, Theodore H. 2002. *Beyond Sweatshops: Foreign Direct Investment and Globalization in Developing Countries*. Washington, DC: Brookings Institution Press. https://www.jstor.org/stable/10.7864/j.ctvb9382w.

Mosley, Layna. 2010. *Labor Rights and Multinational Production*. Cambridge: Cambridge University Press. https://doi.org/10.1017/CBO9780511780998.

Murray, J. Haskell. 2012. "Choose Your Own Master: Social Enterprise, Certifications, and Benefit Corporation Statutes." *American University Business Law Review* 2 (1): 1–54.

Murray, J. Haskell. 2015. "An Early Report on Benefit Reports." *West Virginia Law Review* 118 (25): 33–35.

Musiolek, Bettina, David Hachfeld, Bojana Tamindžija, Stefan Aleksić, Oksana Dutchak, Artem Chapeye, Olívia Béládi, and Emese Gulyás. 2017. "Europe's Sweatshops: The Results of CCC's Most Recent Researches in Central, East and South East Europe." Amsterdam: Clean Clothes Campaign.

Nass, Mitch. 2014. "The Viability of Benefit Corporations: An Argument for Greater Transparency and Accountability." *Journal of Corporation Law* 39 (4): 875–93.

Neilsen. 2015. "The Sustainability Imperative." Neilsen Markets and Finances. Accessed November 20, 2019. https://www.nielsen.com/us/en/insights/report/2015/the-sustainability-imperative-2/.

Ngai, Pun. 2005. "Global Production, Company Codes of Conduct, and Labor Conditions in China: A Case Study of Two Factories." *China Journal* 54: 101–13. https://doi.org/10.2307/20066068.

Nova, Scott, and Chris Wegemer. 2016. "Outsourcing Horror: Why Apparel Workers Are Still Dying, One Hundred Years after Triangle Shirtwaist." In *Achieving Workers' Rights in the Global Economy*, edited by Richard P. Appelbaum and Nelson Lichtenstein, 17–31. Ithaca: Cornell University Press. https://doi.org/10.7591/9781501703355-003.

O'Rourke, Dara. 1997. "Smoke from a Hired Gun: A Critique of Nike's Labor and Environmental Auditing in Vietnam as Performed by Ernst & Young." San Francisco: Transnational Resource and Action Center. http://web.mit.edu/dorourke/www/PDF/smoke.pdf.

O'Rourke, Dara. 2003. "Outsourcing Regulation: Analyzing Nongovernmental Systems of Labor Standards and Monitoring." *Policy Studies Journal* 31 (1): 1–29. https://doi.org/10.1111/1541-0072.00001.

O'Rourke, Dara. 2006. "Multi-stakeholder Regulation: Privatizing or Socializing Global Labor Standards?" *World Development* 34 (5): 899–918. https://doi.org/10.1016/j.worlddev.2005.04.020.

OECD. 1999. "OECD Principles of Corporate Governance." Paris: OECD. https://www.oecd.org/officialdocuments/publicdisplaydocumentpdf/?cote=C/MIN(99)6&docLanguage=En.

Oka, Chikako. 2010a. "Accounting for the Gaps in Labour Standard Compliance: The Role of Reputation-Conscious Buyers in the Cambodian Garment Industry." *European Journal of Development Research* 22 (1): 59–78. https://doi.org/10.1057/ejdr.2009.38.

Oka, Chikako. 2010b. "Channels of Buyer Influence and Labor Standard Compliance: The Case of Cambodia's Garment Sector." In *Advances in Industrial and Labor Relations*, edited by D. Lewin, B. Kaufman, and P. Gollan, 17:153–83. Bingley: Emerald Group Publishing. https://doi.org/10.1108/S0742-6186(2010)0000017008.

Oka, Chikako. 2012. "Does Better Labour Standard Compliance Pay? Linking Labour Standard Compliance and Supplier Competitiveness." Better Work Discussion Paper Series 5. Geneva.

Oka, Chikako. 2018. "Brands as Labour Rights Advocates? Potential and Limits of Brand Advocacy in Global Supply Chains." *Business Ethics: A European Review* 27: 95–107. https://doi.org/10.1111/beer.12172.

Orleck, Annelise. 2018. *"We Are All Fast-Food Workers Now": The Global Uprising Against Poverty Wages.* Boston: Beacon Press.

Oxfam. 2010. "Better Jobs in Better Supply Chains." Oxford: Oxfam. https://www-cdn .oxfam.org/s3fs-public/file_attachments/b4b-better-jobs-better-supply-chains_3 .pdf.

Perea, Juan F. 2011. "The Echoes of Slavery: Recognizing the Racist Origins of the Agricultural and Domestic Worker Exclusion from the National Labor Relations Act." *Ohio State Law Journal* 72 (1): 95–138.

Pike, Kelly. 2018. "A Look at the Better Work Gap Inc. Program on Workplace Cooperation: Challenges and Opportunities for 'Training of Trainers' to Strengthen Industrial Relations and Social Dialogue in Supply Chains." Conference Presentation at the CRIMT International Conference in Montreal, Canada.

Polaski, Sandra. 2009. "Harnessing Global Forces to Create Decent Work in Cambodia." Washington, DC: Carnegie Endowment for International Peace. https://betterwork .org/global/wp-content/uploads/Harnessing-Global-Forces-to-Create-Decent -Work-in-Cambodia-Sandra-Polaski.pdf.

Porter, Michael E., and Mark R. Kramer. 2011. "Creating Shared Value." *Harvard Business Review* (January–February).

Pruett, Duncan. 2005. "Looking for a Quick Fix: How Weak Social Auditing is Keeping Workers in Sweatshops." Clean Clothes Campaign. Accessed August 11, 2010. https://digitalcommons.ilr.cornell.edu/cgi/viewcontent.cgi?article=2077&context =globaldocs

Quinn, John J. 1997. "Personal Ethics and Business Ethics: The Ethical Attitudes of Owner/ Managers of Small Business." *Journal of Business Ethics* 16 (2): 119–27. https://doi .org/0.1023/A:1017901032728.

Reinecke, Juliane, Stephan Manning, and Oliver von Hagen. 2012. "The Emergence of a Standards Market: Multiplicity of Sustainability Standards in the Global Coffee Industry." *Organization Studies* 33 (5–6): 791–814. https://doi.org/10.1177/0170840612 443629.

Riisgaard, Lone. 2009. "Global Value Chains, Labor Organization and Private Social Standards: Lessons from East African Cut Flower Industries." *World Development* 37 (2): 326–40. https://doi.org/10.1016/j.worlddev.2008.03.003.

Roberts, Dexter, and Pete Engardino. 2006. "Secrets, Lies, And Sweatshops." *Bloomberg Businessweek*, November 27, 2006. https://www.bloomberg.com/news/articles/2006 -11-26/secrets-lies-and-sweatshops.

Robson, Regina. 2015. "A New Look at Benefit Corporations: Game Theory and Game Changer." *American Business Law Journal* 52 (3): 501–55. https://doi.org/10.1111 /ablj.12051.

Rodríguez-Garavito, César A. 2005. "Global Governance and Labor Rights: Codes of Conduct and Anti-sweatshop Struggles in Global Apparel Factories in Mexico and Guatemala." *Politics and Society* 33: 203–33. https://doi.org/10.1177/0032329205275191.

Rossi, Arianna. 2015. "Better Work: Harnessing Incentives and Influencing Policy to Strengthen Labour Standards Compliance in Global Production Networks." *Cambridge Journal of Regions, Economy and Society* 8 (3): 505–20. https://doi.org/10.1093 /cjres/rsv021.

Rueda, Ximena, Rachael D. Garrett, and Eric F. Lambin. 2016. "Corporate Investments in Supply Chain Sustainability: Selecting Instruments in the Agri-food Industry." *Jour-*

nal of Cleaner Production 142 (4): 2480–92. https://doi.org/10.1016/j.jclepro.2016 .11.026.

Ruwanpura, Kanchana N., and Neil Wrigley. 2011. "The Costs of Compliance? Views of Sri Lankan Apparel Manufacturers in Times of Global Economic Crisis." *Journal of Economic Geography* 11 (6): 1031–49.

Schuler, Douglas A., and Petra Christmann. 2011. "The Effectiveness of Market-Based Social Governance Schemes: The Case of Fair Trade Coffee." *Business Ethics Quarterly* 21 (1): 133–56. https://doi.org/10.5840/beq20112116.

Sedex. 2019a. "About Us." Sedex. Accessed November 25, 2019. https://www.sedexglobal .com/about-us/.

Sedex. 2019b. "SMETA Audit." Sedex. Accessed November 25, 2019. https://www.sedex global.com/smeta-audit/.

Sedex. 2019c. "Who Is Sedex?" Sedex. Accessed November 25, 2019. https://www.sedex global.com/about-us/who-is-sedex/.

Selwyn, Benjamin. 2017. *The Struggle for Development.* Cambridge: Polity. https://www .wiley.com/en-us/The+Struggle+for+Development-p-9781509512782.

Short, Jodi L., Michael W. Toffel, and Andrea Hugill. 2016. "Monitoring Global Supply Chains." *Strategic Management Journal* 37: 1878–97. https://doi.org/10.1002/smj .2417.

Short, Jodi L., Michael W. Toffel, and Andrea Hugill. 2018. "Beyond Symbolic Responses to Private Politics: Codes of Conduct and Improvement in Global Supply Chain Working Conditions." Harvard Business School Working Paper 17–001.

Smyth, Russell, Xiaolei Qian, Ingrid Nielsen, and Ines Kaempfer. 2013. "Working Hours in Supply Chain Chinese and Thai Factories: Evidence from the Fair Labor Association's 'Soccer Project'." *British Journal of Industrial Relations* 51 (2): 382–408.

Social Accountability International. 2016. "Guidance Document for Social Accountability 8000 (SA8000®:2014)." New York: Social Accountability International.

Social & Labor Convergence Program. 2018. 2018 Annual Report. https://slconvergence .org/wp-content/uploads/2019/06/2018-Annual-Report-FINAL-1.pdf.

Stecker, Michelle J. 2016. "Awash in a Sea of Confusion: Benefit Corporations, Social Enterprise, and the Fear of 'Greenwashing.'" *Journal of Economic Issues* 50 (2): 373–381. https://doi.org/10.1080/00213624.2016.1176481.

Stout, Lynn. 2012. *The Shareholder Value Myth: How Putting Shareholders First Harms Investors, Corporations, and the Public.* San Francisco: Berrett-Koehler Publishers.

Strauss, Anselm, and Juliet Corbin. 1994. "Grounded Theory Methodology: An Overview." In *Handbook of Qualitative Research*, 273–85. Thousand Oaks, CA: Sage Publications.

Stroehle, Judith Christina. 2017. "The Enforcement of Diverse Labour Standards through Private Governance: An Assessment." *Transfer: European Review of Labour and Research* 23 (4): 475–93. https://doi.org/10.1177/1024258917731016.

Sum, Ngai Ling, and Ngai Pun. 2005. "Globalization and Paradoxes of Ethical Transnational Production: Codes of Conduct in a Chines Workplace." *Competition and Change* 9 (2): 181–200.

Tampe, Maja. 2018. "Leveraging the Vertical: The Contested Dynamics of Sustainability Standards and Labour in Global Production Networks." *British Journal of Industrial Relations* 56 (1): 43–74.

Ter Haar, Beryl, and Maarten Keune. 2014. "One Step Forward or More Window-Dressing? A Legal Analysis of the Recent CSR Initiatives in the Garment Industry in Bangladesh." *International Journal of Comparative Labour Law and Industrial Relations* 30 (1): 5–25.

Terry, Michael. 1999. "Systems of Collective Employee Representation in Non-union Firms in the UK." *Industrial Relations Journal* 30 (1): 16–30. https://doi.org/10.1111/1468-2338.00106.

Third-level auditing consultant (username). 2019. "Kaitie Jilu Gongzuo He Shenghuo Diandi (Blogs Recording My Life and Work)." Tianya Forum. October 28. http://bbs.tianya.cn/post-free-5502275-1.shtml.

Thorlakson, Tannis, Joann F. de Zegher, and Eric F. Lambin. 2018. "Companies' Contribution to Sustainability through Global Supply Chains." Proceedings of the National Academy of Sciences of the United States of America 115 (9): 2072–77. https://doi.org/10.1073/pnas.1716695115.

Tianya. 2019. "Tianya Jianjie (Introduction)." Tianya Forum. October 28. http://help.tianya.cn/about/history/2011/06/02/166666.shtml.

Toffel, Michael W., Eileen McNeely, and Matthew Preble. 2019. "New Balance: Managing Orders and Working Conditions." Boston: Harvard Business School Case Collection. https://www.hbs.edu/faculty/Pages/item.aspx?num=55485.

Toffel, Michael W., Jodi L. Short, and Melissa Ouellet. 2015. "Codes in Context: How States, Markets, and Civil Society Shape Adherence to Global Labor Standards." *Regulation and Governance* 9 (3): 205–23. https://doi.org/10.1111/rego.12076.

Turn Around H&M. 2018. "Lost and Found: H&M's Living Wage Roadmap." Accessed December 10, 2018. https://turnaroundhm.org/static/background-hm-roadmap-0f39b2ebc3330eead84a71f1b5b8a8d4.pdf.

Van Klaveren, Maarten. 2016. "Wages in Context in the Garment Industry in Asia." Amsterdam: WageIndicator Foundation.

Vaughan-Whitehead, Daniel. 2011. "How 'Fair' Are Wage Practices along the Supply Chain? Global Assessment in 2010–11." Paper prepared for the Better Work conference, October 26–28, 2011, Washington, DC.

Vaughan-Whitehead, Daniel, and Luis Pinedo Caro. 2017. "Purchasing Practices and Working Conditions in Global Supply Chains: Global Survey Results." ILO INWORK Issue Brief. Geneva: International Labour Office. https://www.ilo.org/wcmsp5/groups/public/—ed_protect/—protrav/—travail/documents/publication/wcms_556336.pdf.

WageIndicator. 2019a. "FAQ Living Wage." WageIndicator. Accessed September 12, 2019. https://wageindicator.org/salary/living-wage/faq-living-wage.

WageIndicator. 2019b. "Living Wages in Context." WageIndicator. Accessed September 12, 2019. https://wageindicator.org/salary/living-wage.

WageIndicator. 2019c. "Minimum Wage: Indonesia." Minimum Wage Regulations. Accessed September 12, 2019. https://wageindicator.org/labour-laws/labour-law-around-the-world/minimum-wages-regulations/minimum-wages-regulations-indonesia.

Walsh, Declan, and Steven Greenhouse. 2012. "Certified Safe, a Factory in Karachi Still Quickly Burned." *New York Times*, December 7, 2012. https://www.nytimes.com/2012/12/08/world/asia/pakistan-factory-fire-shows-flaws-in-monitoring.html.

Weisbrot, Mark, Lara Merling, Vitor Mello, Stephan Lefebvre, and Joseph Sammut. 2017. "Did NAFTA Help Mexico? An Update After 23 Years." Washington, DC: Center for Economic and Policy Research. http://cepr.net/publications/reports/did-nafta-help-mexico-an-update-after-23-years.

Weismann, Miriam. 2017. "The Missing Metrics of Sustainability: Just How Beneficial Are Benefit Corporations?" *Delaware Journal of Corporate Law* 42 (1): 1–50.

Wijen, Frank. 2014. "Means Versus Ends in Opaque Institutional Fields: Trading Off Compliance and Achievement in Sustainability Standard Adoption." *Academy of Management Review* 39 (3): 302–23. https://doi.org/10.5465/amr.2012.0218.

Worker Rights Consortium. 2019. "Leading Apparel Brands, Trade Unions, and Women's Rights Organizations Sign Binding Agreements to Combat Gender-Based Violence and Harassment at Key Supplier's Factories in Lesotho." Worker Rights Consortium. Accessed August 27, 2019. https://www.workersrights.org/press-release/leading -apparel-brands-trade-unions-and-womens-rights-organizations-sign-binding -agreements-to-combat-gender-based-violence-and-harassment-at-key-suppliers -factories-in-lesotho.

Worker-Driven Social Responsibility (WSR) Network. 2019. "What Is WSR?" WSR Network. Accessed September 28, 2019. https://wsr-network.org/what-is-wsr.

World Bank. 2015. "FAQs: Global Poverty Line Update." World Bank. Accessed August 27, 2019. https://www.worldbank.org/en/topic/poverty/brief/global-poverty-line-faq.

World Bank. 2019. "World Bank Country and Lending Groups." World Bank Data. Accessed September 13, 2019. https://datahelpdesk.worldbank.org/knowledgebase /articles/906519-world-bank-country-and-lending-groups.

World Justice Project. 2019. "Rule of Law Index." Washington, DC: World Justice Project. https://worldjusticeproject.org/sites/default/files/documents/ROLI-2019 -Reduced.pdf.

Worldwide Accredited Responsible Production. 2019. "Principle 6 FAQs." Worldwide Accredited Responsible Production. Accessed February 6, 2019. http://www .wrapcompliance.org/en/principle-6-faqs.

Yoffie, David B. 1998. "NIKE (A) (Condensed)." Harvard Business School Case 391–238.

Yu, Xiaomin. 2008. "Impacts of Corporate Code of Conduct on Labor Standards: A Case Study of Reebok's Athletic Footwear Supplier Factory in China." *Journal of Business Ethics* 81 (3): 513–29. https://doi.org/10.1007/s10551-007-9521-2.

Index

Note: Page numbers in italics indicate figures; those with a *t* indicate tables; those with a *b* indicate boxes.